Blockchain and AI for Security and Privacy in Smart Agriculture

Editors:

Randhir Kumar
Department of Computer Science and Engineering
SRM University, Amaravati, Andhra Pradesh, India

Prabhat Kumar
Department of Software Engineering
LUT School of Engineering, Lappeenranta, South Karelia, Finland

Sobin C.C.
School of Computer Science (SoCS)
University of Petroleum and Energy Studies, Dehradun

CRC Press
Taylor & Francis Group
Boca Raton London New York

CRC Press is an imprint of the
Taylor & Francis Group, an **informa** business
A SCIENCE PUBLISHERS BOOK

First edition published 2026
by CRC Press
2385 NW Executive Center Drive, Suite 320, Boca Raton FL 33431

and by CRC Press
4 Park Square, Milton Park, Abingdon, Oxon, OX14 4RN

CRC Press is an imprint of Taylor & Francis Group, LLC

Library of Congress Cataloging-in-Publication Data (applied for)

ISBN: 978-1-041-08282-8 (hbk)
ISBN: 978-1-041-13594-4 (pbk)
ISBN: 978-1-003-67056-8 (ebk)

DOI: 10.1201/9781003670568

Typeset in Palatino Linotype
by Prime Publishing Services

Preface

Blockchain and AI for Security and Privacy in Smart Agriculture provides an innovative outlook on how advanced technologies are redefining the future of farming. As smart agriculture increasingly integrates IoT devices, sensors, drones, and data analytics to enhance efficiency and sustainability, it also faces critical issues surrounding data privacy, security, and stakeholder trust. This book explores how blockchain and artificial intelligence (AI) effectively address these challenges. Blockchain's decentralized and tamper-proof system ensures secure data storage, transparency in agricultural processes, and end-to-end traceability within the supply chain—from producers to consumers. AI further strengthens this ecosystem by offering intelligent threat detection, predictive analytics, and real-time decision-making to enhance crop management, optimize resources, and mitigate risks. Targeted toward researchers, academics, policymakers, agri-tech entrepreneurs, and industry experts, this book combines foundational theory with real-world applications, case studies, and practical implementation models. It equips readers with the knowledge to design secure, privacy-preserving, and trustworthy smart farming systems that enhance productivity, reduce fraud, and build a sustainable agricultural future.

Contents

Chapter 1

Blockchain and Smart Contracts for Secure Agricultural Transactions

*Anam Ahsan** and *Malahim Nadeem*

The agricultural industry is facing constant problems related to a lack of transparency and efficiency, the fragmentation of information, and unsecure transactions. The blockchain and smart contract technologies have become unique solutions to address these problems by offering secure, decentralized ways of managing transactions and data. In this light, this chapter focuses on the applications of blockchain and smart contracts to the agricultural sector and their role in enhancing traceability of supply chains and automating financial transactions, protecting the ownership of land records, and simplifying the process of trading in commodities and insurance. Moreover, it discusses the integration of the Internet of Things (IoT) and artificial intelligence (AI) with blockchain to create decentralized agriculture systems and reliable applications in real-world settings and for the implementation of Layer 2 scaling solutions. The chapter discusses the important advantages of the technology along with the regulatory, technical, and social hurdles that need to be resolved before a wider adoption becomes feasible. The chapter concludes that blockchain technology has the potential to fundamentally transform agricultural practices by establishing a more secure, transparent, and trustworthy operational environment.

University of Lahore, Pakistan.
* Corresponding author: anam.ahsan@cs.uol.edu.pk

DOI: 10.1201/9781003670568-1

1. Introduction

The agricultural industry is an essential economic pillar of the world economy, providing the security of food and sustaining the lives of those living in rural regions. However, the industry faces significant challenges that concern security, integrity, transparency, and trust. Problems like food theft, supply chain transparency, insecure financial transactions, and land ownership disputes undermine the reliability and efficiency of markets for agricultural products (Dhillon and Moncur, 2023; Liu et al., 2020). The Global food losses and food waste. FAO (2011) estimates that 14% (valued at $400 billion per year) of the world's supply is wasted in between the harvest phase and when it is sold. This is primarily because of inefficiencies and a lack of visibility in the supply chain. These weaknesses not only hinder economic results but also threaten the safety of food and undermine public confidence.

In a more connected and globalized marketplace, secure transactions are vital for the sustainable development of agriculture. Farmers, suppliers, retailers, distributors, and customers require proof about the authenticity and quality of the agricultural product. Additionally, financial processes like insurance, payment claims, and transfers of land should be protected against delays, fraud, and mismanagement. As per the World Bank, inefficiencies in agricultural financial transactions and finance result in losses of billions of dollars for the world economy each year, underscoring the need for more secure, reliable systems.

Smart contracts and blockchain technology are emerging as promising tools to solve these problems (Cong and He, 2017). Blockchain is a decentralized and immutable digital ledger that offers unprecedented transparency, traceability, and security of transactions. Smart contracts are self-executing agreements embedded within the blockchain which enable automation, enforce compliance, and eliminate the need for trusted third parties. Together, these tools can help create more robust, efficient, and secure agricultural systems by protecting transactions and enhancing the trust of stakeholders throughout the value chain (Wang et al., 2021).

The chapter discusses the use of blockchain and smart contracts to protect agricultural transactions. They are examined in relation to improving supply chains as well as financial services, insurance, management of land, and commodity markets, as well as looking at their strengths and weaknesses. The chapter also highlights the integration of the Internet of Things (IoT) and artificial intelligence (AI) technologies with blockchain to develop smart agriculture systems. It explores Layer 2 solutions such as rollups and sidechains along with Plasma chains to solve issues related to scalability, speed, and cost. Case studies from real-world situations and the future possibilities for blockchain-based innovation in agriculture are also covered.

2. Overview of Blockchain Technology

Technology that uses blockchain technology is revolutionizing the storage and transmission of data. The advancement of this technology is one of the major breakthroughs that we have seen in the twenty first century. It is a distributed, decentralized ledger that allows secure, transparent, unalterable transactions (Sharma et al., 2020). It works through a computer network that verifies and records every transaction as a series of blocks, which are encrypted and connected to make up chains. Due to the rise of cryptocurrency like Bitcoin and Ethereum, blockchain technology has grown in popularity over the past couple of years. Blockchain technology is not restricted to only digital currencies. Multiple-layer structures allow for the broad applications of blockchain technology in diverse industries.

2.1 *Evolution of the Blockchain*

Blockchain technology has experienced significant changes since its creation, every phase of development bringing about improvements to the capabilities of blockchain and its applications. The development of blockchain technology can be divided into four different phases (as shown in Table 1.1).

Table 1.1: Evolution of blockchain.

Blockchain Version	Time Frame	Focus	Key Feature
Blockchain 1.0	2009–2014	Currency (Bitcoin)	Decentralized Digital Currency
Blockchain 2.0	2015–Present	Smart Contracts (Ethereum)	Programmable Autonomous Contracts
Blockchain 3.0	2017–Present	DApps	Decentralized Application with Improved Scalability
Blockchain 4.0	2018–Present	Industry Integration	Integration with IoT, AI, and Real World Systems

2.1.1 Blockchain 1.0—Currency (2009–2014)

Blockchain 1.0 is the first use of blockchain technology. It is mostly focused on digital currencies. The initial and most prominent use of blockchain technology is Bitcoin, which was created at the end of 2009 by an unknown entity dubbed Satoshi Nakamoto. Bitcoin made use of blockchain as a ledger that was a decentralized system to keep track of money transactions without the need for a centralized authority like the bank (White et al., 2019). The focus of this phase was blockchain, which served as a safe, unalterable, transparent, and secure method of storing and transferring value.

2.1.2 Blockchain 2.0—Smart Contracts

Blockchain 2.0 signified the expansion of blockchain technology into smart contracts. It was first introduced through the Ethereum network in 2015. Blockchain 2.0 led to the development of decentralized applications (DApps) by means of programmable contracts that take predefined actions if certain conditions are fulfilled. Smart contracts are self-executing agreements that have the contract's terms directly encoded in code. This technology is an effective tool to automate agreements and transactions, thus eliminating intermediaries and decreasing the risk of fraud or errors.

2.1.3 Blockchain 3.0—DApps

Blockchain 3.0 increased the possibilities of the blockchain, allowing it to incorporate the use of DApps that further improve the capabilities and flexibility of blockchain technology. Contrary to traditional apps that rely on a central server, DApps operate on networks that are decentralized, which provide more security, privacy, and control to users (Aufiero et al., 2024). This stage was focused on solving interoperability and scaling, along with the energy-consumption issues encountered by the previous blockchain platforms like Bitcoin and Ethereum. Blockchain 3.0 platforms, like EOS, Cardano, and Polkadot, were designed to offer more efficient solutions for creating DApps that offer greater scalability and quicker processing speeds.

2.1.4 Blockchain 4.0—Industry

Blockchain 4.0 represents the integration of blockchain technology in industry-specific solutions, with a focus on scalability and enterprise adoption and real-world applications (Li, 2022). This is the phase that brings blockchain into a fusion with new technologies like the IoT, AI, and big data, which allows blockchain to offer more advanced and tailored solutions to industries like manufacturing, agriculture and logistics, healthcare, and even government.

2.2 Architecture of Blockchain

As Figure 1.1 demonstrates, blockchain architecture can be divided into five primary levels, each with a different use. Gaining an understanding of these levels helps one to appreciate how blockchain systems work from the bottom up.

2.2.1 Hardware Infrastructure Layer

The layer of hardware infrastructure consists of the physical devices forming the backbone of the blockchain network. It covers servers, storage devices, and network hardware including routers. Additionally,

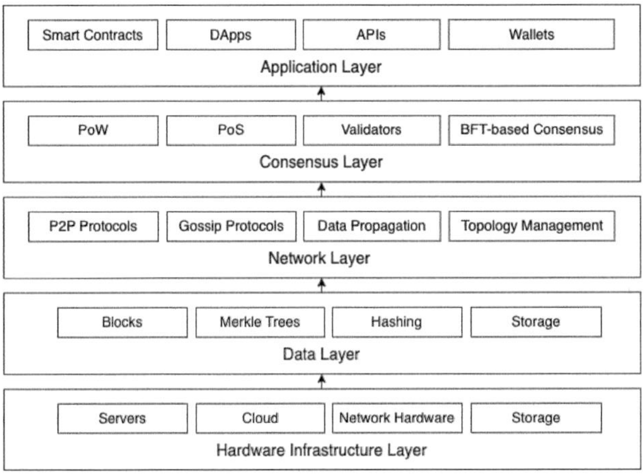

Figure 1.1: Blockchain architecture layers.

very important for growing blockchain infrastructure are cloud services (Dong et al., 2018). The hardware offers the computational capability and network required to enable distributed activities.

2.2.2 Data Layer (Ledger Layer)

All blockchain transactions are noted in a distributed ledger on the data layer, sometimes known as the ledger layer. Every block has transaction information and a cryptographic hash used to guarantee data integrity. The ledger is unchangeable; hence, no past information can be changed without network agreement. In the blockchain, this layer assures security and openness.

2.2.3 Network Layer (P2P Layer)

The network layer connects the nodes via peer-to-peer protocols which allow direct communication throughout the entire blockchain. In addition, these nodes discover each other as well as safely exchange blocks and transactions. This decentralized and distributed network ensures that no single entity has control over the flow of data. Additionally, it also supports the transmission of new information across the entire blockchain ecosystem.

2.2.4 Consensus Layer

This layer ensures that all nodes in the blockchain network fulfil a common agreement on the validity of transactions. The consensus algorithms like Proof of Work (PoW) or Proof of Stake (PoS) are used to validate and secure these transactions. In this process, Validators also known as the miners play a main role in proposing and validating new blocks. And this maintains trustlessness and decentralization in the system (Xiao et al., 2020).

2.2.5 Application Layer

The application layer is where users interact with blockchain networks through DApps and smart contracts. The interaction allows the execution of business logic, such as financial transactions or other automated processes. Moreover, this layer also includes wallets and Application Programming Interface that enable access to the blockchain's services.

2.3 Types of Blockchain

Blockchains are divided into four major types based on their degree of control over access and governance. Each type has its own purpose and has its own characteristics, which makes them appropriate for different usage situations.

2.3.1 Public Blockchain

Public blockchains are decentralized and accessible to all and allow anyone to join as a node. They can also view transactions and upload data without authorization. These blockchains are based on consensus mechanisms such as PoW or PoS to ensure the integrity of data and to stop manipulation. The public blockchains provide the highest levels of security and transparency because they are decentralized. Bitcoin as well as Ethereum are two of the most well-known examples of blockchains that are public (Krichen et al., 2022).

2.3.2 Private Blockchain

Private blockchains are permissioned systems where access is limited to authorized users. They are managed by a single company or an organization of trusted entities that oversee the regulations of governance as well as the validation of transactions. Private blockchains provide greater privacy and scalability when compared to public blockchains because they do not require complex consensus protocols and can handle transactions faster. They are usually utilized in corporate environments.

2.3.3 Consortium Blockchain

Blockchains that are part of a consortium, often referred to as federated blockchains, are composed of multiple organizations that share control over the network. Contrary to public blockchains, access is granted to authorized users and only approved entities are able to validate transactions and manage the ledger. This allows collaboration among multiple participants, while keeping a certain level of privacy and control that is not available in full-time public networks. Blockchains for consortiums are especially useful in areas such as healthcare and banking in which multiple parties are involved.

2.3.4 Hybrid Blockchain

Hybrid blockchains incorporate the features of both private and public blockchains, offering the flexibility of a model where certain parts of the system are restricted and others are not. This allows businesses to gain the openness and decentralization that comes with public blockchains, while ensuring the security and privacy of sensitive information. Dragonchain is an excellent instance of a hybrid blockchain offering both confidentiality and transparency (Table 1.2).

Table 1.2: Types of blockchain.

Type	Access Control	Governance	Example
Public	Open to all	Decentralized	Bitcoin, Ethereum
Private	Restricted to selected users	Centralized	HyperLedger Fabric
Consortium	Shared among organizations	Federated	R3 Corda
Hybrid	Mixed	Flexible	Dragonchain

3. Smart Contract

Smart contracts are also known as self-executing agreements that have specific terms and conditions of contract in code. These contracts are run on platforms that use blockchain, allowing automated, secure, transparent, and safe execution of contract terms without the necessity of intermediaries. Smart contracts rely on network decentralization to guarantee that when conditions are fulfilled, the actions are automatically performed, thereby increasing trust and decreasing the chance of human errors or manipulation. Initially popularized through Ethereum, smart contracts have expanded across a variety of blockchain platforms and applications such as Decentralized Finance (DeFi) supply chain management and governance (Zou et al., 2019).

3.1 Working of Smart Contract

Smart contracts run on blockchain platforms and automate the implementation of predefined conditions and terms without human intervention. Self-executing agreements utilize computer code that is written into the blockchain, which determines the contract's rules, conditions, and actions to be taken when certain conditions are fulfilled. As shown in Figure 1.2, smart contracts' operation consists of three fundamental elements: triggers, conditions, and actions.

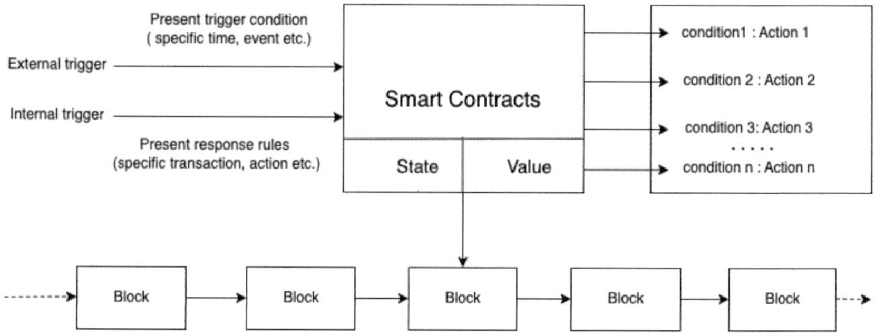

Figure 1.2: Working mechanism of smart contracts.

3.1.1 Triggers

Triggers function as the event which triggers the execution of a smart contract. Triggers may be external or internal to the blockchain. External triggers usually refer to data or events that occur outside the blockchain that are initiated by oracles. For instance, the price of a product or the successful completion of a real-world undertaking (like the delivery of goods) could create a contract. Internal triggers, on the other hand, are events that occur in the blockchain itself like the transfer of funds from a particular wallet or token transfer. Once a trigger has been activated, the smart contract goes into the next phase to determine the trigger's condition (Stancu and Dragan, 2020).

3.1.2 Conditions

The rules or the criteria that are encoded in the smart contract which have to be met in order for the contract to be able to proceed are known as the conditions. These conditions are stated by using "if-then" statements, where the contract determines if the conditions are true prior to making any decision. Conditions can be based on different aspects, such as the financial transaction (e.g., making sure that the payment is received) and conditions based on time (e.g., the verification that an event happens within a specified timeframe) or even data-related tests (e.g., checking that environmental conditions, such as temperature, exceed a certain threshold). When the requirements are fulfilled, the smart contract then proceeds to execute the specified actions. If otherwise, the contract ceases without taking any further actions.

3.1.3 Actions

Actions are the specific tasks or actions which the smart contract executes when the conditions are met. These actions may vary according to the specific agreement, but generally involve the transfer of assets, modifying records, or performing additional smart contracts. For instance, for a financial transaction, the smart contract could transfer funds from a buyer to a seller upon satisfaction of the payment requirement. If it is a supply chain situation, then it could be changing the status of the product from "shipped" to "delivered" when the delivery requirement is fulfilled. The benefit of smart contracts is their ability to automate these actions without human intervention, ensuring the speed and avoiding the possibility of disputes or errors. When the actions are completed, the outcomes are recorded on the blockchain, which makes them irreversible and permanent.

3.2 *Types of Smart Contracts*

Smart contracts are classified into a variety of types, each one suited to different applications and use cases (as shown in Table 1.3).

Table 1.3: Types of smart contracts and their use cases.

Smart Contract Type	Use Case
Smart legal contracts	Legal agreements in real estate, insurance, and finance
Decentralized Autonomous Organization (DAO)	Governance via token voting (e.g., MakerDAO)
DApps contracts	Automating decentralized apps like games, marketplaces
Applied logic contracts (ALCs)	Business logic for supply chains, regulatory enforcement, IP management

3.2.1 Smart Legal Contracts

They are digital contracts that automatically sign legal agreements when certain conditions are fulfilled. Smart legal contracts are able to replace paper contracts in fields like insurance, real estate, and finance. Although these terms are encrypted in software, legality of these contracts is usually governed by current legal frameworks.

3.2.2 Decentralized Autonomous Organization (DAO)

A decentralized autonomous organization (DAO) is an entirely automated and decentralized business where decisions are made using smart contracts. In DAOs, smart contracts determine the operating rules, and the decisions are typically made by the voting of token holders. DAOs do away with the necessity for traditional management and provide more democratic and transparent governance structures (Bellavitis et al., 2022). Examples include platforms such as MakerDAO which manages the stablecoin DAI.

3.2.3 DApps Contracts

The DApps use smart contracts to automatize activities within their decentralized environments. DApps contracts are essential to enabling functions like decentralized exchanges, marketplaces, and games. They guarantee that the app is operating in the way it was intended, without central authority governing the experience of users.

3.2.4 Applied Logic Contracts (ALCs)

Applied logic contracts (ALCs) are smart contracts that are specifically designed to implement rules or logic that regulate certain business procedures. These contracts can be utilized to automate processes for supply chain management, governing intellectual property, or to enforce specific standards for regulation. ALCs can be programmed in order to reflect complex business processes that require automated decision-making actions in particular environments.

3.3 *Features of Smart Contracts*

Smart contracts provide a variety of features that are contributing to their rapid adoption across a variety of industries.

3.3.1 Automation

One of the major features of smart contracts is their capacity to automate complex processes. When certain conditions are fulfilled, the actions are automatically initiated, and this eliminates manual interventions and decreases the time required to finish transactions. Automation greatly improves efficiency and reduces the chance of human error or delays.

3.3.2 Direct Transactions

Traditional contracts typically depend on intermediaries like lawyers, banks, or notaries to verify, enforce, or sign agreements. Smart contracts remove the need for these intermediaries by allowing direct P2P transactions. A reduction in intermediaries not only reduces costs but also makes the process seamless.

3.3.3 Increased Trust

As smart contracts are run using blockchain platforms, they have the benefits of security and transparency that are inherent to these platforms. Blockchain's decentralization guarantees that, once a contract has been executed, it is unchangeable and secure from tampering. The participants can be confident that the contract will be executed in the manner it was written, without having to depend on an authority central to the transaction, which leads to increasing the credibility and reliability of the contract (Nguyen, 2024).

3.3.4 Cost Efficiency

Smart contracts can dramatically reduce the cost of transactions. Traditional contracts usually involve administrative costs, legal fees, and third-party service providers who verify and enforce agreements. Smart contracts make the process easier by eliminating unnecessary expenses and making transactions simpler for all parties.

3.3.5 Speed and Efficiency

By removing formal and manual procedures that usually slow the process in traditional processes, smart contracts speed up the process of executing transactions. The actions and transactions are completed instantaneously once the conditions are met. Smart contracts are more efficient and effective than traditional methods that may require more documents, signatures, or verifications from intermediaries (Rouhani and Deters, 2019).

4. Applications of Blockchain and Smart Contracts in Agriculture

Smart contracts and blockchain technology have an opportunity to transform the agricultural industry by solving long-standing issues like inefficiencies, lack of transparency with regard to finance transactions, and uncertainty with regard to the ownership of land. These technologies offer solutions that improve traceability, streamline processes, and help create more secure systems for different aspects of the value chain. The main applications of smart contracts and blockchain in agriculture, as well as their problems, solutions, and challenges, are discussed in this section.

4.1 Supply Chain Management

The agricultural sector, which is characterized by its multi-layered and complex supply chain, faces constant issues regarding transparency as well as traceability and trust among all the stakeholders. Traditional supply chains for agriculture typically suffer from an absence of real-time information-sharing mechanisms and verification, which hampers the capability of regulators, consumers, and companies to verify the origin and route of food items. These flaws increase the chances of food fraud and contamination, as well as inefficiencies and ultimately a decrease in confidence of consumers in food systems (Li et al., 2023).

Blockchain technology, paired with smart contracts, offers an innovative solution to these problems by delivering a decentralized and immutable ledger that records transactions and activities across

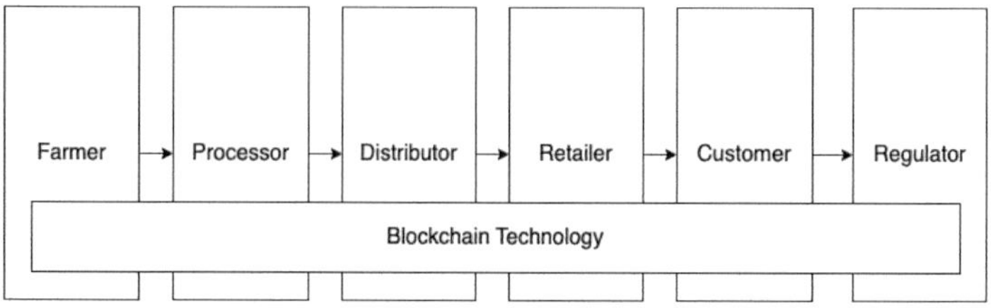

Figure 1.3: Basic flow of the agriculture supply system.

the complete supply chain from the farm to the end user (as shown in Figure 1.3). To ensure that there are no changes to records after they have been included on the blockchain, each transaction is encrypted and time-stamped. Through smart contracts, self-executing code that is placed on the blockchain automatically enforces agreements and rules, and other supply chain operations are automated such as quality checks, compliance checks, quality verification, and release of payments contingent on the delivery conditions.

As stated in a study (Turjo et al., 2021), blockchain technology allows real-time monitoring of agricultural goods at each step of the supply chain. The process starts in the field, where information regarding the origin of the crop, planting practices, and harvest dates is recorded. When the product is transferred to distributors and processors, additional information like storage conditions, timelines for transportation as well as batch numbers are added to the ledger of blockchain. Retailers maintain the chain by logging the dates of their shelves and sales records, and customers are able to scan QR codes and access complete details about the product's history. The regulatory bodies and certification agencies are also able to use these data to audit conformity and verification which can help create transparency and accountability within the system.

Blockchain implementation to manage the supply chain management in agricultural products has resulted in significant improvements. Increased traceability enhances the safety of food by speedy detection and elimination of infected or bad batches, thereby reducing the health risks for the general population. Blockchain records' immutability eliminates the possibility of fraud, such as the false labelling of organic or premium quality products. Furthermore, the ability to prove the authenticity and trackability of the products improves the image of the brand and boosts trust with customers. This is especially crucial in high-value markets that focus on sustainable and ethical sources. In the final analysis, blockchain technology when combined with smart contracts serves as a powerful catalyst for increasing efficiency in supply chains that are contemporary and suitable for agricultural products.

4.2 Secure Payments and Financial Transactions

One of the main obstacles to equity and efficiency in agriculture is the absence of well-organized financial systems that are secure, streamlined, and inclusive. Farmers in developing regions often face challenges, such as late settlements for deliveries of goods as well as high intermediary transaction costs and limited access to formal financial services such as insurance, credit, and even digital banking. These issues not only undermine trust between supply chain players but also limit the viability and scale of agricultural activities.

Blockchain technology, when paired with smart contracts, can provide an effective solution to the financial bottlenecks. Smart contracts operate as self-executing digital protocols that can automatically execute predefined actions when the agreed-upon conditions are fulfilled. When integrated into agricultural financial transactions, smart contracts can drastically reduce the dependence on intermediaries, reduce delays in processing manual processes, and provide timely payments that are transparent (Minu et al., 2024).

In this way, smart contracts can be programmed to automatically release payments when they are able to verify certain conditions, such as delivery of the product, the conformance to quality standards, or confirmation of the shipment. For instance, if the farmer delivers a certain amount of produce to a wholesaler and the fulfilment of this delivery can be confirmed using sensors, GPS data, or inspection records that are recorded on the blockchain. This will instantly result in a payment being transferred directly from the digital wallet of the purchaser to the farmer's bank account. This method ensures immediate payment and reduces financial uncertainty for farmers and encourages greater participation in the formal market.

Moreover, blockchain-facilitated financial transactions are inherently more secure and cost-effective than traditional systems. Blockchain's decentralization eliminates the need to be verified multiple times by banks or brokers and dramatically cuts costs of transactions as well as processing times. The transparency and immutability of blockchain can also improve trust among all parties which decreases the risk of disputes regarding payments or the supply of services.

Beyond transactions, smart contracts are being increasingly used to automate insurance payments. For instance, blockchain-based platforms that incorporate climate data provide farmers with the opportunity to receive compensation on a regular basis in the event that certain weather thresholds cannot be crossed, such as prolonged or excessive drought. This approach not only makes it easier to stake claims but also enhances the value of insurance coverage for agricultural purposes, allowing farmers to take advantage of insurance coverage and decreasing the chance of climate-related risks.

4.3 Land Registry and Ownership

Land ownership is a crucial aspect of agricultural development and economic stability as well as rural livelihoods. In many countries, land records are not properly maintained, are insufficient, or are managed on paper which is prone to theft, tampering, or corruption. This causes major problems which include frequent disputes regarding the ownership of land as well as unclear boundaries for property and costly or slow processes for land transactions. These obstacles restrict farmers' ability to protect their rights to property, to get loans that use the land as collateral, and to invest in long-term improvements to their agricultural practices.

Rashid et al. (2024) proposed that blockchain technology could be a solution to these issues by offering a secure, transparent, and tamper-proof method for registering and managing the ownership of land. When utilized in land registry offices and land registries, blockchain records are kept in a digital ledger that is available to all parties but cannot be altered without consent from the network. This stops unauthorized modifications and ensures the record of the land's ownership and transfers is forever and is easy to confirm. Smart contracts further enhance the efficiency of land transactions by automating crucial processes in land transactions. For instance, smart contracts could be programmed to release ownership rights only if certain financial and legal requirements are met, such as the signature of a contract and confirmation of the payment. This reduces the requirement for intermediaries, lowers the chance of fraud, and makes it easier to buy or sell land.

The implementation of blockchain technology into land registry systems provides numerous advantages. The first is to reduce disputes over land since ownership records are secure, reliable, and available to all authorized parties. Furthermore, it simplifies land transactions by removing the necessity for manual processes and providing clear, automated procedures. Third, it increases the protection of ownership rights to land, which gives farmers more confidence to invest in and improve their land (Verma et al., 2024).

4.4 Insurance for Agricultural Production

Insurance for agricultural production is a vital instrument to protect farmers from hazards like extreme weather, crop failure, and natural catastrophes. However, traditional insurance systems typically have inefficiencies, particularly in processing claims (Fu et al., 2024; Vyas et al., 2021). They depend heavily on manual processes like field inspections and paperwork, which result in delays and high administration costs, as well as frequent disputes. This is the reason why many farmers are not insured or do not get timely settlements for loss.

Blockchain technology, when paired with smart contracts as well as real-time data sources, provides a cutting-edge solution to these problems. Smart contracts can be self-executing agreements that are stored on the blockchain. They are able to be programmed to start insurance payouts when certain conditions are satisfied. For insurance for agricultural purposes, the conditions could include weather-related information such as temperatures, rainfall levels, or the duration of drought which can be monitored by IoT devices and remote sensing technology.

When the parameters agreed upon are met, like when rainfall falls below an amount for a specific time period, the smart contract is activated automatically and the appropriate payment is made to the farmer who is insured, without the need to make an individual claim. This not only speeds up the process, it can also prevent human error or manipulation, which ensures an equitable and fair settlement.

Smart contracts and blockchain used for insurance for crops that are used in agriculture offer many benefits. First, they facilitate faster payouts, which is essential for farmers who require instant cash to cover the cost of losses and continue operations. They also reduce fraud by using verified information and eliminating the requirement for intermediaries that can delay or alter the evaluation of claims. Third, they improve efficiency of the overall system by automating tasks that were previously tedious and susceptible to errors.

Additionally, blockchain-based insurance systems increase transparency and confidence. All decisions and transactions that are made by the smart contracts are recorded in the blockchain, thereby creating an auditable and clear trail. This ensures insurers as well as customers that the system is reliable and impartial.

4.5 *Commodity Markets*

Commodity markets play an important function in the agricultural sector through aiding in the buying and selling of various commodities, including fruits, vegetables, grains, and livestock. They affect the price of commodities and control risks via futures contracts and also provide an opportunity for producers, traders, and consumers to interact. However, traditional agricultural commodity markets typically face a variety of problems, such as lack of transparency, price manipulation and inefficient settlement systems, and a lack of access to market information. These issues can impede market efficiency, decrease confidence among the participants, and reduce the opportunities for fair income for small-scale farmers.

Blockchain technology, paired with smart contracts, provides an effective solution to these issues and improves efficiency of the agricultural commodity markets. Blockchain is a digital ledger that is not centrally controlled and records transactions in a transparent and secure manner. Smart contracts are programmable agreements that operate automatically when certain conditions are satisfied. Through the integration of these technologies, the markets for commodities are more transparent, reliable, and efficient.

One of the major advantages of the use of blockchain in the commodity market is increased transparency. Every transaction is recorded in a shared ledger that is accessible to all participants who are authorized. This guarantees that prices, trading volumes, and delivery schedules are transparent and verified which reduces the possibility of information imbalance and market manipulation. For instance, buyers can verify the source of their purchase, the quality, and the authenticity of agricultural products prior to making a purchase, and sellers can monitor the status of delivery and payment in real time (Lobo and Rao, 2022).

Smart contracts are able to automate important processes in the trading of commodities, like contract settlement, order matching as well as payment execution. If a seller and buyer are able to agree on the terms for a transaction, a smart contract will instantly change ownership over the commodity and allow payment to be released once the conditions of delivery confirmation as well as quality verification have been satisfied. This eliminates the necessity for intermediaries, cuts down on the time required for settlement, and decreases the costs of transactions. It also helps in reducing disputes because the terms of contracts are consistent and objectively enforced by the codes.

Blockchain-based commodity platforms could improve the market access of smallholder farmers, connecting directly with buyers both locally and internationally. These platforms provide real-time pricing information, facilitate secure peer-to-peer trading, and provide digital records farmers may use to prove creditworthiness or conformity to quality standards. This way, blockchain helps create an inclusive and competitive market.

Additionally, the fusion of blockchain into digital identity and certification systems could improve the traceability and credibility of commodities from the agriculture sector. This is especially important for products with high value, like organic, fair-trade, or sustainable-grown products which require authenticity and proof of origin. Blockchain records that are immutable provide evidence-based proof of these claims, assisting producers to gain access to the best markets and increasing consumer confidence.

5. Challenges and Limitations

The incorporation of smart contracts and blockchain technologies into agricultural systems offers an exciting opportunity for improving transparency, efficiency, and security. However, there are a number of issues and limitations that need to be resolved in order to reap these benefits on a large scale, while also reducing the risks. This includes issues relating to interoperability, scalability, technical complexity, uncertainty in regulation, and adoption hurdles.

5.1 *Scalability*

Scalability remains one of the most urgent issues facing blockchain-based systems, particularly when it comes to high-volume settings like agriculture. Agriculture supply chains produce huge quantities of data and transactions that include monitoring of crops in real time as well as logistics data, weather information, and financial transactions (Khan et al., 2021). The majority of blockchain platforms, especially public blockchains like Ethereum and Bitcoin, have the inability to process transactions and their delay, which limits their use for deployment on a large scale in the field of agriculture.

To deal with scalability issues, various approaches are being investigated. Layer-2 solutions, including sidechains and state channels, provide off-chain processing capabilities that help reduce the load of the blockchain, while protecting the security of the network. Furthermore, more flexible consensus algorithms—such as PoS and Delighted Proof of Stake (DPoS)—are implemented to boost efficiency. Platforms such as Polygon, Solana, and Polkadot are made with scalability in mind, and could be more appropriate for applications that require large volumes of transactions.

5.2 *Interoperability*

The agricultural ecosystem involves multiple stakeholders like farmers, cooperatives, logistics providers, financial institutions, and regulatory bodies, often using disparate digital systems. Lack of standard protocol and formats for data across different blockchain platforms hampers seamless data exchange and communication which limits the efficiency of integrated blockchain solutions for agriculture.

The development and adoption of an open framework for standards, interoperability, and other protocols are crucial. Initiatives like that of the Interledger Protocol (ILP), Cosmos' Inter-Blockchain Communication (IBC), and Polkadot's relay chain have the potential of improving cross-chain interoperability. In the agricultural sector, the use of standard ontologies and data models like those pushed through AgGateway consortium will increase the integration of blockchain systems with existing technologies for agriculture (Zhu et al., 2023).

5.3 *Regulatory Uncertainty*

The legality of blockchain transactions as well as smart contracts is still unclear in several countries. This is especially relevant in the agriculture sector, which is where cross-border trade as well as subsidy, ownership of land, and even certification are strictly controlled. Regulative uncertainty could hinder investment and the use of blockchain technology among people who are hesitant to take risks (Akanfe et al., 2024).

Engaging in proactive dialogue with policymakers and regulators is vital. Establishing regulatory sandboxes that controlled environments for testing blockchain applications under regulatory supervision can facilitate the development of clear and practical legal frameworks. In addition, integrating blockchain-based solutions with existing regulations for compliance (e.g., via the use of digital identity and audit trails) could aid in bridging the gap between regulation and innovation.

5.4 *Technical Complexity*

The development of blockchain technology, especially programmes for smart contracts, demands specific skills that are usually not present in the agricultural industry. The mistakes in smart contracts can have significant risks such as financial losses and data breach. Furthermore, the integration of blockchain technology with other technologies like IoT and AI creates additional layers (Pranto et al., 2021).

Building capacity and the development of user-friendly tools are crucial to reduce technological barriers. Workshops, education, and online courses aimed at agricultural professionals and developers could aid in the development of relevant knowledge. In addition, no-code or low-code blockchain platforms as well as smart contracts templates are able to make it easier for people to access the technology. Open-source communities are a key factor in distributing information and resources.

5.5 *Adoption Barriers*

The resistance towards change can be a typical obstacle for traditional farming systems in which practices are dictated by generations of knowledge and local traditions. Blockchain technologies can be seen as costly, disruptive, or unimportant, particularly for smallholder farmers, who may not have access to the internet or the necessary literacy (Table 1.4).

Table 1.4: Current blockchain challenges and their solutions.

Challenge	**Mitigation Strategy**
Scalability	Implement Layer 2 solutions (e.g., Rollups, Plasma, Validium)
Interoperability	Use cross-chain protocols (e.g., Cosmos IBC, Polkadot, Interledger Protocol)
Regulatory Uncertainty	Create regulatory sandboxes; align solutions with compliance needs
Technical Complexity	Promote training, use low-code platforms, open-source tools
Adoption Barriers	Conduct pilot projects, involve stakeholders, provide government or NGO support

Effective changes management strategies and stakeholder involvement are essential to encourage acceptance. Implementing tangible benefits via demonstration projects and use cases, such as increased availability of credit, transparency of production chains, and equitable pricing, which can aid in building trust and acceptance will also go a long way (Saurabh and Dey, 2020). Government subsidies, support as well as public–private partnerships could also be instrumental in facilitating the digital transformation of agriculture, particularly in rural regions.

6. Problem Solver: Layer 2 Blockchain

Blockchain technology has been touted as a revolutionary tool in diverse industries, including agriculture. However, its application is often restricted due to performance bottlenecks, particularly in terms of speed of transactions and scaling. Layer 2 blockchain solutions were designed to overcome these issues and improve the performance of the existing Layer 1 blockchains, such as Ethereum and Bitcoin. Layer 2 solutions are supplementary protocols that work on the top layer of the foundation layer, offering greater efficiency without compromising the fundamental principles of decentralization and security (Song et al., 2024).

6.1 Technologies of Layer 2 Blockchain

The Layer 2 landscape is vast and includes a variety of technologies that are developed to address various aspects of blockchain usability and scalability. While they all have the same goal of alleviating the load on the primary blockchain, they differ in their architectures and security models, as well as their optimal use cases. Here is a summary of the most well-known Layer 2 methods that are currently being used or are in development.

6.1.1 Rollups

Rollups are among the most popular Layer 2 technology. They work by aggregating large quantities of transactions that are off-chain in a single batch which is then pushed onto the Layer 1 blockchain. This significantly decreases the amount of information to be processed and stored on-chain (Saif et al., 2024). There are two kinds of rollups. Optimistic rollups believe that every transaction is legitimate and then post them without verification, allowing efficient processing. If a fraudulent transaction is suspected, then the challenge mechanism permits validators to provide proof of fraud. Contrary to optimistic rollups, Zero-Knowledge Rollups (ZK-Rollups) rely on cryptographic proofs to confirm the authenticity of each transaction prior to their submission to the chain. ZK-Rollups are safer and provide faster completion, but are more difficult to design and verify.

6.1.2 State Channels

State channels permit participants to execute a sequence of transactions off-chain, and interact directly with one another, without broadcasting every transaction on the network in general. Only the first and last states are recorded in the Layer 1 chain. This method is extremely efficient and allows for rapid transactions that are instantaneous, which makes it perfect for games or micropayments. However, state channels require a predefined set of participants, and they are not able to easily accommodate public or dynamic interactions in the off-chain phase. They are also not ideal for general-purpose smart contracts execution.

6.1.3 Plasma

Plasma is an application framework that permits the development of smaller blockchains that are linked to a larger chain. These child chains manage transactions independently and regularly submit their data in a consolidated form to the primary blockchain. Plasma reduces the load at Layer 1 by delegating computation to sub-chains. While it provides high capacity, Plasma faces challenges with user experience, especially when it comes to withdrawals, which could take a long time because of its dependence on methods of fraud-proofing and exit procedures. It is also unable to provide general computation as flexible as rollups.

6.1.4 Validium

Validium is a Layer 2 solution closely linked to ZK-Rollups. However, it differs in its availability of data models. Similar to ZK-Rollups, Validium utilizes zero-knowledge proofs to verify transactions. However, it keeps data off the blockchain, rather than being stored on the main blockchain.

This enables Validium to gain more scalability and efficiency as well as provide better privacy security. The result is less trust since users have to depend on external data availability committees or services to access off-chain data. This makes Validium ideal for applications where data security is essential as well as where some centralization can be acceptable (Gangwal et al., 2022).

6.1.5 *Sidechains*

Sidechains are blockchains that work in parallel with the main blockchain and communicate with it through two-way bridges. They can be designed to suit specific needs and are not bound by the consensus rules of the main chain. This allows them to be more flexible regarding governance and performance. However, they do not take on the security features of the Layer 1 blockchain. They are governed by their own validators and a consensus process, which adds new trust assumptions. Sidechains are typically employed in situations where high-throughput is required and security trade-offs are acceptable.

6.2 *Features of Layer 2 Blockchain*

The significance of Layer 2 solutions can be ascertained through the fundamental features they provide to the blockchain ecosystems. These features solve the most pressing issues of Layer 1 blockchains and allow more applications. Each feature enhances accessibility, economic viability, and performance, which forms the basis for more user-friendly and scalable decentralized systems.

6.2.1 *Scalability*

The most significant advantage of Layer 2 solutions is their capacity. By transferring transactions off of the primary blockchain, Layer 2 techniques significantly boost the amount of transactions which can be processed every second. Although Layer 1 chains such as Ethereum are restricted to tens of transactions per second, Layer 2 solutions can increase to thousands, which makes them crucial for applications that require high performance, like the DeFi, non-fungible tokens (NFTs), and real-time gaming (Gangwal et al., 2022).

6.2.2 *Reduced Fees*

Layer 2 systems dramatically cut down on the costs of transactions. Because fewer transactions are stored in the Layer 1 chain, and the data is compressed by methods of batching, costs of gas that users pay for are significantly less. This efficiency in cost is essential to enable a wider acceptance of blockchain technology, particularly in industries or regions where even small transaction costs could be an obstacle to entry.

6.2.3 Faster Settlements

Transactions processed by Layer 2 networks are usually settled much faster than those that are processed on Layer 1. While transactions on Ethereum could take a few minutes to verify during periods of high congestion, Layer 2 solutions can settle in milliseconds or seconds. This makes them ideal for applications that require speed, such as point-of-sale systems, high-frequency trading platforms, and interactive digital apps.

6.2.4 Security Integration

Numerous Layer 2 applications are made to take on the security characteristics of the Layer 1 blockchain. For instance, rollups upload proofs and transaction data directly to Ethereum which allows them to benefit from the Ethereum consensus mechanism as well as overall security of the network. This reduces the need for trust assumptions unlike independent sidechains which have to secure themselves (Rebello et al., 2024). This security inheritance has an important benefit as it ensures that Layer 2 transactions are secure and tamper-proof.

6.2.5 Interoperability and Composability

Another major aspect that is unique to Layer 2 blockchains is their capacity to work with smart contracts that are already in place and protocols that are on the primary chain. This enables developers to incorporate Layer 2 elements into larger decentralized ecosystems. Applications can be developed that utilize both on-chain and off-chain elements, which allows for new kinds of functionality as well as more efficient execution. Composability also facilitates the development of modular DeFi apps that allow different protocols to be combined to offer enhanced financial services.

7. Real Case Studies

The application of smart contracts and blockchain technology in the field of agriculture has evolved from research and development to implementation in a variety of real-world settings (as shown in Table 1.5). A variety of projects across various areas and systems of agriculture have proven the effectiveness and viability of these technologies to improve efficiency, transparency, and trust across the value chain. These case studies provide concrete proof of blockchain's capacity to overcome persistent challenges in areas like traceability of products, financial inclusion, farm management, automation of insurance, and regulatory compliance.

Table 1.5: Real world application of blockchain in agriculture.

Platform	Application Area	Region	Impact
OpenSC	Supply chain transparency	Global	Verifies ethical and sustainable sourcing using blockchain and QR codes
AgriDigital	Grain supply chain	Australia	Enables real-time, secure transactions and automated payments
AgriChain	Food system transparency	Developing countries	Tracks full supply chain, reducing fraud and inefficiencies
AgriLedger	Smallholder farmer traceability	Haiti	Improves market access and ensures data integrity for exports
Farmonaut	Precision agriculture	India	Satellite monitoring and blockchain storage for crop health and resource insights
Aetsoft	Agricultural logistics & compliance	Global	Blockchain-based tracking for machinery use, crop cycles, and regulatory data
Sourcery	Sustainability-linked incentives	West Africa	Connects sustainable farming practices with financial rewards
AgUnity	Digital financial access for farmers	Africa, Asia, Latin America	Provides mobile blockchain platform for record-keeping and cooperative services
IBM Food Trust	Food safety & traceability	USA	Enables rapid food recall traceability, used by Walmart for leafy greens
BioTrak	Food quality assurance	Global	Visualizes and secures product transformation and transport data

7.1 Supply Chain Transparency and Traceability

Blockchain technology greatly improves transparency in supply chains by creating an immutable, decentralized ledger of transactions and movement. This ensures the traceability of products, decreases fraud, increases ethical sourcing, and increases confidence in sustainability claims of consumers.

7.1.1 OpenSC

OpenSC, created by the World Wide Fund for Nature (WWF) and BCG Digital Ventures, provides a blockchain-based platform to verify sustainable and ethical sources. The system tracks the products from their origins to the final consumer by using QR codes, which provide precise information on the provenance of the product. It is particularly relevant in the palm oil, seafood, and beef supply chains where unethical or illegal practices are commonplace. The integration of OpenSC in the supply chain of Nestle, for instance, illustrates its efficacy in increasing transparency as well as consumer involvement.

7.1.2 AgriDigital

AgriDigital is an Australian company that uses blockchain technology to modernize the supply chain for grain. It allows real-time recording of transactions that enables secure and clear exchanges among farmers, logisticians, and grain buyers. The platform also facilitates payment on delivery verification, which reduces risks to the financial system and delays. Field trials have shown its ability to streamline processes and decrease administrative burdens while also increasing trust (Xu et al., 2019).

7.1.3 AgriChain

AgriChain is an decentralized platform that is focused on security and transparency within the food system, especially in developing countries. It allows all stakeholders from producers to retailers to record access to, as well as to verify, every stage of the supply chain for agricultural products. By reducing the need for intermediaries and central authority, AgriChain enhances traceability and can help to reduce issues like food spoilage, fraud as well as problems with the supply chain (Rambhia et al., 2022).

7.1.4 AgriLedger

AgriLedger is a social enterprise that utilizes blockchain technology to digitally safeguard the records of small-scale farmers. It provides transparent tracking of the origins of food and makes it easier to access markets as well as financial services. It has been extensively utilized in Haiti for the purpose of tracking mango exports, demonstrating its ability to connect remote farmers to global buyers, while making sure that data integrity and traceability are maintained (Kim and Laskowski, 2017).

7.2 Farm Management and Precision Agriculture

Blockchain's use in precision agriculture allows secure data management that is decentralized, to monitor crop health while also optimizing inputs and improving yield forecasting. When paired with IoT and satellite imaging, blockchain is able to ensure the accuracy and traceability of agricultural data.

7.2.1 Farmonaut

Farmonaut integrates satellite-based monitoring and blockchain technology to provide precise farming information. Farmers are provided with real-time information about the health of the vegetation as well as water stress and possible pest infestations, and all of this is safely recorded.

This allows for more informed decision-making and supports sustainable management of resources. The system is flexible and has been used across a variety of agricultural regions in India.

7.2.2 Aetsoft

Aetsoft offers personalized blockchain solutions to the agricultural sector with an emphasis on tracking logistics as well as data integrity. Their platform allows digital record-keeping of the cycle of crops machines used, as well as environmental conditions. Blockchain assures that the records are secure and auditable, which helps ensure the compliance of regulatory agencies and operational efficiency.

7.3 Financial Services and Insurance

Blockchain increases accessibility to financial services for the most disadvantaged communities of agriculture by providing secure identity verification as well as transparent transactions histories. These systems can be used to support microfinance, insurance, and performance-based subsidies.

7.3.1 Sourcery

Sourcery tackles inefficiencies in value chains for agricultural products by connecting agricultural practices directly with economic results. The Impact and Assurance Program uses blockchain to observe sustainable practices, like water use and the health of soil. The data is then linked to incentives for financial investment, making sure that the benefits are shared with farmers as a whole. This system is gaining popularity in the industry of cotton, specifically in West Africa.

7.3.2 AgUnity

AgUnity offers a blockchain-backed mobile platform that allows electronic record-keeping and communication for small-scale farmers. It assists farmers in tracking their produce, documenting sales as well as in accessing cooperative services. AgUnity is successfully implemented across Africa, Southeast Asia, and Latin America, where it assists farmers in integrating into formal commercial and financial networks.

7.4 Food Safety and Quality Assurance

Blockchain ensures the security of food safety systems through generating an unalterable record of each transaction and the handling process. This enables quick responses to incidents of contamination and ensures compliance with international safety standards.

7.4.1 IBM Food Trust

The IBM Food Trust connects all people involved within the food supply chain to one reliable data source. The platform provides real-time access to data on food and allows tracebacks in a matter of seconds, not days. It has been utilized by Walmart to monitor leafy greens, which significantly reduces the time needed to pinpoint sources of contamination. This increases food safety and reduces the amount of waste.

7.4.2 BioTrak

BioTrak uses blockchain to track the transformation and transport of food items. Its platform offers stakeholders reliable information to ensure quality, making sure that handling processes are clear and adhere to the safety standards. The system can be used in dairy and meat logistics, where ensuring consistent temperatures and hygiene standards is essential (Lloréns et al., 2011).

8. Integration of AI and IoT for Smart Agriculture

The integration of IoT and AI into smart agriculture that is based on blockchain technology brings revolutionary changes in traditional agricultural practices. This synergy enhances the transparency of decision-making as well as efficiency and automation within the agricultural ecosystem (Abubakar et al., 2025).

8.1 Supply Chain Transparency

One of the most effective applications of IoT and AI in the area of blockchain-based farming is transparency within the supply chain. IoT-enabled devices such as GPS trackers, RFID tags, and sensors for the environment can be used to monitor the status and location of the agricultural products as they travel throughout the supply chain. AI algorithms analyse this data in real time to forecast delivery time, spot possible spoilage, and provide the best logistics management. The blockchain guarantees that all the information is kept in an immutable ledger providing traceability from beginning to end for consumers and other stakeholders. This system increases confidence and aids in finding the source of fraud or contamination (Sodhi and Tang, 2019).

8.2 Precision Farming

Precision farming greatly benefits by integrating IoT, AI, and blockchain technology. IoT sensors installed in the fields collect data about soil moisture, temperatures, nutrient levels, and the weather conditions. AI

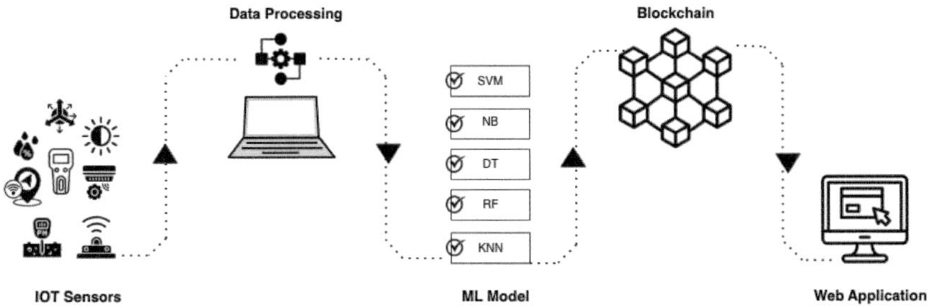

Figure 1.4: Integration of the IoT, Machine Learning, and blockchain for precision farming.

examines data in order to give actionable insights, like when to fertilize or irrigate the land for the best yield. Blockchain plays an important role in storing this data and ensuring that it is able to be verified to conduct future analysis on compliance (as shown in Figure 1.4). This results in efficient use of resources, higher yields for crops, as well as lower environmental impacts.

8.3 Smart Contracts for Automated Transactions

Blockchain-powered smart contracts make it easier to manage numerous aspects of the transaction in agriculture. Self-executing contracts can manage various agreements, such as the arrangement of insurance for crops as well as renting equipment and also selling agricultural goods. For instance, when IoT sensors sense drought conditions, a smart contract could automatically start an insurance payout for the farmer. AI can also make sure that the conditions of these contracts are fair and are based on accurate risk assessments. Automation reduces the need for intermediaries, reduces the cost of transactions, and speeds up payment processing.

8.4 Predictive Analytics and Decision Support

Predictive analytics that are based on AI, coupled with real-time IoT data, and backed by blockchain, offers an incredibly robust decision support to farmers. AI models can predict yields of crops, spot early signs of diseases or pests, and suggest planting schedules in accordance with the market demand. IoT devices continuously provide real-time field data, such as temperatures, humidity, and the presence of pests, while blockchain keeps historical data, which improves the precision and credibility of AI models. This system is smart enough to allow farmers to make informed decisions based on data that increase productivity and lower risk.

8.5 Environmental Monitoring and Compliance

Monitoring the environmental impact is a major problem in the agriculture sector and the combination of IoT, AI, and blockchain could provide a solid solution. IoT sensors can monitor soil quality and air pollution, levels of pesticides, and water use. AI algorithms detect rule violations or anomalies, sending alerts in real time to farmers or regulators. Blockchain ensures that data on the environment is safe from tampering and readily accessible for verification or certifications of sustainability. This helps promote sustainable farming practices and also ensures conformity to international standards and laws on environmental protection (Pranto et al., 2021).

8.6 Livestock Management

In the world of livestock farming, IoT devices such as GPS collars and wearable sensors monitor the health and behaviour of animals as well as their whereabouts. AI analyses the information to predict problems with health, improve the timing of feeding, and enhance breeding methods. Blockchain plays an essential function in ensuring clear and secure medical records of each animal's vaccination, lineage, and status (Khan et al., 2021). This holistic approach does not only guarantee the welfare of animals and the effectiveness of farms but also creates trust among consumers due to traceability and the quality of the animal products.

9. Future Trends and Opportunity

Blockchain technology is changing the agricultural landscape by bringing transparency, automation, and central control to an unreachable and scattered system. As the world food system is battling the demands of an increasing population and changing climate, and resources are limited, the need to integrate blockchain technology into smart farming is not just urgent, it is also becoming vital. The ability of blockchain technology to safeguard and verify information via an open network can provide the possibility of a new level in safety and effectiveness across every step of the value chain in agricultural production.

A highly efficient application is traceability in the supply chain. By recording every transaction in a perpetual ledger, which is unchangeable from sourcing seeds and cultivation to harvesting, processing, and distribution, the blockchain could offer a level of transparency that was previously unattainable. This can help reduce risks that can be caused by fraud and contamination. It can also help consumers make more informed choices, allow authorities to ensure that the highest standards are met, and also allow producers to differentiate among their products in a highly competitive marketplace. This is also true to the purpose that smart contracts play in. Self-executing contracts are not dependent on intermediaries and are triggered when certain conditions are met. In the agricultural sector, they are able to automate the process of distributing subsidy payments as well as claiming insurance that is based on current information, such as temperature or crop production. This reduces administrative burdens, decreases costs of transactions, and makes prompt and secure payment for everyone involved.

Blockchain and IoT can open the door to intelligent agriculture. Sensors that monitor the condition of the soil, weather as well as the condition of the crop's health directly transfer data to blockchain systems which will ensure accuracy of data and provide precise agricultural information. This integration can provide precise forecasting, more efficient resource utilization, and quick responses to environmental change, increasing efficiency and sustainability. Blockchain also opens new possibilities for farmers' development as well as the ability to access markets. Blockchain-based decentralized marketplaces allow producers to connect directly with buyers, removing intermediaries and offering a more affordable price. Additionally, financial models based on digital assets and tokens can provide innovative solutions for microfinancing. Small-scale farmers can get money or insurance without a traditional banking system.

Another important, but less obvious, shift is towards data sovereignty. With the help of blockchain, farmers are able to claim control over their data from production by deciding how it is shared, used, or integrated into platforms for market research. This is not just a way to ensure their privacy but also permits participation in data-driven innovations with fair terms. Blockchain-driven advances in smart agriculture are evolving from single-pilots to systems capable of providing tangible advantages. The potential to create an open, robust, and sustainable food system is becoming more obvious, not just as a distant vision but also as a practical technology-driven path that is based on technological advancement and an increasing field-level implementation.

10. Conclusion

Smart contracts and blockchain technology offer an opportunity to transform the agricultural sector, bringing transparency, automation, and decentralization of intricate value chains. The implementation of smart contracts increases the security of supply chain tracking. It also protects land and financial transactions, and simplifies the processes of commodity market transactions and obtaining insurance. Integrating IoT and AI improves the efficiency of smart farming by utilizing blockchain technology. It enables immediate data collection and predictive analytics that aid in better decision-making. However, the realization of this capability on a massive scale requires the removal of a range of challenges which include technical complexity as well as interoperability, scalability and regulatory uncertainty, and acceptance by users. Layer-2 solutions, along with collaboration across different stakeholders, provide viable avenues for addressing these challenges. Future trends point to a shifting away from trial programmes towards fully integrated systems that can provide precision agriculture, market decentralization, and the protection of information of farmers. Blockchain's integration into IoT as well as AI is poised to bring about transparent, automated, reliable, and sustainable farming practices that will meet the growing global demand for sustainable food security as well as sustainable agriculture and equitable market participation.

References

Abubakar, A., Julia, J. and Khalid, Z. (2025). Integration of Internet of Things (IoT), Artificial Intelligence (AI) and blockchain technology in agribusiness supply chain management: Case study on sensor-based agricultural monitoring systems. *Jurnal Ilmu Sosial Mamangan* 12(3): 997–1009.

Akanfe, O., Lawong, D. and Rao, H. (2024). Blockchain technology and privacy regulation: Reviewing frictions and synthesizing opportunities. *International Journal of Information Management* 76: 102753.

Aufiero, S., Ibba, G., Bartolucci, S., Destefanis, G., Neykova, R. and Ortu, M. (2024). DApps ecosystems: Mapping the network structure of smart contract interactions. *ArXiv*, abs/2401.01991.

Bellavitis, C., Fisch, C. and Momtaz, P. (2022). The rise of Decentralized Autonomous Organizations (DAOs): A first empirical glimpse. *Venture Capital* 25: 187–203.

Cong, L. and He, Z. (2018). Blockchain disruption and smart contracts. Kauffman: Entrepreneurship scholars initiatives (Topic). https://doi.org/10.2139/ssrn.2985764.

Dhillon, R. and Moncur, Q. (2023). Small-scale farming: A review of challenges and potential opportunities offered by technological advancements. *Sustainability* 15(21): 15478.

Dong, Z., Luo, F. and Liang, G. (2018). Blockchain: A secure, decentralized, trusted cyber infrastructure solution for future energy systems. *Journal of Modern Power Systems and Clean Energy* 6: 958–967.

Fu, L., Qin, T., Li, G. and Wang, S. (2024). Efficiency of agricultural insurance in facilitating modern agriculture development: From the perspective of production factor allocation. *Sustainability* 16(14): 6223.

Gangwal, A., Gangavalli, H. and Thirupathi, A. (2022). A survey of layer-two blockchain protocols. *Journal of Network and Computer Applications* 209: 103539.

Khan, D., Jung, L. and Hashmani, M. (2021). Systematic literature review of challenges in blockchain scalability. *Applied Sciences* 11(20): 9372.

Kim, H. and Laskowski, M. (2017). Agriculture on the blockchain: Sustainable solutions for food, farmers, and financing. *In*: Tapscott, D. (ed.). *Supply Chain Revolution*. Barrow Books.

Krichen, M., Ammi, M., Mihoub, A. and Almutiq, M. (2022). Blockchain for modern applications: A survey. *Sensors* 22(14): 5274.

Li, L. (2022). Blockchain technology in Industry 4.0. *Enterprise Information Systems* 16(12): 1733–1735.

Li, X., Du, J., Li, W. and Shahzad, F. (2023). Green ambitions: A comprehensive model for enhanced traceability in agricultural product supply chain to ensure quality and safety. *Journal of Cleaner Production* 420: 138397.

Liu, Y., Ma, X., Shu, L., Hancke, G. and Abu-Mahfouz, A. (2020). From Industry 4.0 to Agriculture 4.0: Current status, enabling technologies, and research challenges. *IEEE Transactions on Industrial Informatics* 17: 4322–4334.

Lloréns, R., Gil-Gómez, J., Mesa-Gresa, P., Alcañiz, M., Colomer, C. and Noé, E. (2011). BioTrak: A comprehensive overview. *2011 International Conference on Virtual Rehabilitation*, 1–6.

Lobo, V. and Rao, M. (2022). An empirical study on blockchain technology-enabled systems in commodity markets. *2022 International Conference on Emerging Trends in Engineering and Medical Sciences (ICETEMS)*, 232–237.

Minu, M., Suryaa, S., Titus, J. and Sharan, S. (2024). Empowering small-scale farmers with Decentralized Finance (DeFi) via ethereum smart contracts. *2024 2nd International Conference on Sustainable Computing and Smart Systems (ICSCSS)*, 683–690.

Nguyen, T.-N. (2024). Smart contract: Revolutionizing transactions in the digital age. *HPU2 Journal of Science* 3(1): 30–38.

Pranto, T., Noman, A., Mahmud, A. and Haque, A. (2021). Blockchain and smart contract for IoT enabled smart agriculture. *PeerJ Computer Science* 7: e407.

Rambhia, V., Mehta, R., Shah, R., Mehta, V. and Patel, D. (2021). Agrichain: A blockchain-based food supply chain management system. pp. 3–15. *In*: Lee, K. and Zhang, L.J. (eds.). *Blockchain–ICBC 2021. Lecture Notes in Computer Science*, vol. 12991. Springer, Cham.

Rashid, M., Rafi, A., Islam, M., Sharkar, S., Rafi, Z., Hasan, M., Ali, M. and Khan, M. (2025). Enhancing land management policy in Bangladesh: A blockchain-based framework for transparent and efficient land management. *Land Use Policy* 150: 107436.

Rebello, G., Camilo, G., De Souza, L., Potop-Butucaru, M., De Amorim, M., Campista, M. and Costa, L. (2024). A survey on blockchain scalability: From hardware to layer-two protocols. *IEEE Communications Surveys & Tutorials* 26: 2411–2458.

Rouhani, S. and Deters, R. (2019). Security, performance, and applications of smart contracts: A systematic survey. *IEEE Access* 7: 50759–50779.

Saif, M., Migliorini, S. and Spoto, F. (2024). A survey on data availability in Layer 2 blockchain rollups: Open challenges and future improvements. *Future Internet* 16: 315.

Saurabh, S. and Dey, K. (2020). Blockchain technology adoption, architecture, and sustainable agri-food supply chains. *Journal of Cleaner Production* 284: 124731.

Sharma, P., Jindal, R. and Borah, M. (2020). Blockchain technology for cloud storage. *ACM Computing Surveys (CSUR)* 53: 1–32.

Sodhi, M. and Tang, C. (2018). Research opportunities in supply chain transparency. *Production and Operations Management* 28: 2946–2959.

Song, H., Qu, Z. and Wei, Y. (2024). Advancing blockchain scalability: An introduction to Layer 1 and Layer 2 solutions. *2024 IEEE 2nd International Conference on Sensors, Electronics and Computer Engineering (ICSECE)*, 71–76.

Stancu, A. and Dragan, M. (2020). Logic-based smart contracts. pp. 387–394. *In*: Rocha, Á., Adeli, H., Reis, L., Costanzo, S., Orovic, I. and Moreira, F. (eds.). *Trends and Innovations in Information Systems and Technologies. WorldCIST 2020. Advances in Intelligent Systems and Computing*, vol. 1159. Springer, Cham.

Turjo, M., Khan, M., Kaur, M. and Zaguia, A. (2021). Smart supply chain management using the blockchain and smart contract. *Scientific Programming* 6092792: 1-6092792: 12.

Verma, S., Pathak, S., Chaudhary, P., Yadav, P. and Yousuf, S. (2024). Land registry system using blockchain technology. *2024 International Conference on Emerging Innovations and Advanced Computing (INNOCOMP)*, 170–177.

Vyas, S., Dalhaus, T., Kropff, M., Aggarwal, P. and Meuwissen, M. (2021). Mapping global research on agricultural insurance. *Environmental Research Letters* 16: 103003.

Wang, L., Xu, L., Zheng, Z., Liu, S., Li, X., Cao, L., Li, J. and Sun, C. (2021). Smart contract-based agricultural food supply chain traceability. *IEEE Access* 9: 9296–9307.

White, R., Marinakis, Y., Islam, N. and Walsh, S. (2020). Is bitcoin a currency, a technology-based product, or something else? *Technological Forecasting and Social Change* 151: 119877.

Xiao, Y., Zhang, N., Lou, W. and Hou, Y. (2019). A survey of distributed consensus protocols for blockchain networks. *IEEE Communications Surveys & Tutorials* 22: 1432–1465.

Xu, X., Weber, I. and Staples, M. (2019). Case study: AgriDigital. In *Architecture for Blockchain Applications*.

Zhu, S., Chi, C. and Liu, Y. (2023). A study on the challenges and solutions of blockchain interoperability. *China Communications* 20: 148–165.

Zou, W., Lo, D., Kochhar, P., Le, X., Xia, X., Feng, Y., Chen, Z. and Xu, B. (2021). Smart contract development: Challenges and opportunities. *IEEE Transactions on Software Engineering* 47: 2084–2106.

Chapter 2

The Intersection of AI, ML, and Agriculture

Innovations for the Future

Sijan Oli, Aman Kapad and *Shaiju Panchikkil**

By enabling farmers to operate more productively, artificial intelligence (AI) and machine learning (ML) are significantly altering the agricultural industry, saving resources, making better decisions, and improving global food security. These technologies allow farmers to use data for precision farming, addressing issues like changing weather, pest control, and managing water and soil. In this chapter, we explore how AI and ML are used in agriculture today, looking at current methods, applications, and trends. This study includes a thorough search of Scopus and Web of Science (WoS), followed by analysis of major contributors, collaboration patterns, and commonly used AI tools. Countries like the United States, China, and India lead the research in this field. The study shows that 70% of the research uses ML techniques and 30% focuses on AI methods like deep learning. Algorithms such as Random Forest (RF), Support Vector Machines (SVMs), and Convolutional Neural Networks (CNNs) are commonly applied. AI and ML are helping in many areas, from monitoring crops and predicting yields

Department of Computer Science and Engineering, SRM University-AP, Andhra Pradesh, India.

* Corresponding author: shaiju.p@srmap.edu.in

DOI: 10.1201/9781003670568-2

to managing irrigation, detecting diseases, applying fertilizers more precisely, and ensuring food security. As AI continues to grow, it is helping agriculture become smarter, more sustainable, and ready to meet future food needs.

1. Introduction

The United Nations estimates that there are 7.8 billion people on the planet as of November 2020. This figure is predicted to rise to 8.5 billion by 2030 and to 9.9 billion by 2050. Global food consumption is rising quickly in tandem with the population's fast expansion. Compared to just thirty years ago, agriculture is already yielding roughly 17% more. However, lack of food security affects around 821 million people worldwide (Bhat and Huang, 2021). Agriculture is among the most significant and ancient professions worldwide. It plays a vital role in global economic growth, with the sector valued at approximately $5 trillion worldwide. Agricultural output must rise by 70% by 2050 to sustain the increasing global population, as projected by food and agricultural organizations (Das et al., 2024). However, rapidly scaling up production remains a challenge due to the limited availability of arable land, which is further declining because of urbanization, infrastructure expansion, climate change, and deforestation. With finite land, water, and natural resources, traditional farming methods alone cannot balance future supply and demand. To address this, innovative and efficient farming strategies are essential. Emerging technologies such as artificial intelligence (AI) and machine learning (ML) are being introduced to enhance agricultural productivity, optimize resource use, and ensure sustainable food production.

Artificial intelligence (AI) focuses on enabling machines to mimic human cognitive functions such as learning, reasoning, and problem-solving, allowing them to perform tasks ranging from basic automation to complex decision-making processes. ML, a key subset of AI, includes systems that improve automatically through experience by analysing data patterns, enabling accurate predictions in applications without explicit programming. These technologies are transforming agriculture by introducing precision farming techniques that optimize resource use, enhance productivity, and promote sustainability. AI and ML applications in agriculture include real-time crop and soil monitoring, predictive analytics for yield forecasting, smart irrigation systems, drone-based field surveillance, and autonomous robotic systems for planting and harvesting. By enabling data-driven decisions on water, fertilizer, and pesticide use, these technologies help maximize efficiency while minimizing environmental impact. As global food demand rises amid challenges like climate change and shrinking arable land, AI and ML are becoming essential tools for ensuring food security and advancing sustainable agricultural practices to meet the needs of a growing population.

2. AI and ML: Revolutionizing Agriculture

Agriculture has undergone significant technological transformations, each revolutionizing productivity and sustainability. The early twentieth century saw mechanization leading to a reduction in demand for manual labour with the introduction of tractors and harvesters, thus dramatically improving efficiency, enabling large-scale cultivation, and facilitating urban migration (Haldorai et al., 2024; de Oliveira and e Silva, 2023). The mid-twentieth century Green Revolution introduced high-yield crop varieties, synthetic fertilizers, and pesticides, boosting global food security but also raising environmental concerns like soil degradation and loss of biodiversity (Haldorai et al., 2024). Today, AI and ML represent the next transformative phase—Agriculture 4.0—leveraging precision farming techniques to optimize crop management through data-driven insights from sensors, drones, and satellite imagery (Thangamani et al., 2024; Rajwar et al., 2024). AI-powered systems enhance predictive analytics, enabling early disease detection with 20%–30% greater accuracy, while autonomous machinery improves operational efficiency by up to 40% (Misra et al., 2020; Fang et al., 2021). Furthermore, AI-driven resource optimization reduces water usage by 25% and fertilizer application by 15%, promoting sustainability (Shadrin et al., 2020). By integrating supervised, unsupervised, and deep learning techniques, AI-ML technologies address critical challenges like climate resilience and yield optimization, paving the way for a more efficient and sustainable agricultural future (Benos et al., 2021; Liakos et al., 2018).

2.1 Introduction to Core AI and ML Techniques in Agriculture

The AI and ML techniques are driving innovation across various industries, with their agricultural applications transforming traditional farming practices. The key AI and ML approaches that are revolutionizing agriculture have been examined in this discussion.

2.1.1 Supervised Learning

Supervised learning demonstrates significant utility in agricultural applications, particularly for yield prediction, disease identification, and pest control. ML algorithms such as Support Vector Machines (SVMs) and Decision Trees utilize annotated training data to construct accurate predictive models. A practical implementation involves analysing labelled image datasets containing both healthy and afflicted crops, enabling the system to recognize plant health patterns and facilitate timely intervention (Saleem et al., 2021). This capability proves particularly valuable for early-stage problem detection and preventive measures in precision agriculture.

2.1.2 Unsupervised Learning

Unsupervised techniques are valuable in situations where labelled data is scarce. In agriculture, they are used for tasks like soil classification, segmentation of farm areas, and clustering of plant species based on sensor data. Clustering methods, such as k-means and hierarchical clustering, help group similar data points (e.g., soil properties or crop characteristics), providing insights that can guide crop rotation, soil management, and resource allocation (Benos et al., 2021; Marwaha et al., 2023).

2.1.3 Reinforcement Learning for Farm Automation

In agriculture, reinforcement learning is gaining traction in automated systems, such as robotic harvesting and irrigation management. This technique enables models to make decisions in dynamic environments. For example, reinforcement learning can optimize irrigation schedules based on real-time data from soil moisture sensors, reducing water usage while maintaining crop health. Additionally, it is used in the development of autonomous machinery for tasks like planting and weeding, where robots learn optimal strategies to maximize efficiency (Liakos et al., 2018).

2.1.4 Deep Learning

Deep learning architectures, particularly Convolutional Neural Networks (CNNs), have become indispensable for image analysis tasks in agriculture, demonstrating exceptional performance in plant disease diagnosis, yield estimation through fruit counting, and automated weed recognition. These neural networks excel at processing high-dimensional data and extracting complex spatial patterns, making them particularly suited for analysing aerial imagery captured by drone surveillance systems. Such applications enable real-time crop health assessment and early disease identification with remarkable precision. Furthermore, CNNs facilitate advanced phenotyping and stress detection in crops, providing critical insights for precision agriculture management (Saleem et al., 2021). The integration of these sophisticated AI and ML methodologies represents a paradigm shift towards smart farming systems, where data-driven decision-making and automated processes enhance both agricultural productivity and sustainability.

3. Application of AI and ML in Agriculture

By streamlining procedures, increasing yields, and reducing resource waste, AI-ML are transforming agriculture. By providing farmers with data-driven insights, these tools improve sustainability and decision-making. AI and ML open the door to more intelligent farming solutions by fusing cutting-edge algorithms with conventional farming methods.

3.1 Crop Monitoring and Disease Detection

Artificial intelligence and ML are essential for tracking crop conditions and identifying plant diseases before they escalate. Cutting-edge deep learning techniques, especially CNNs, process detailed aerial and satellite imagery to detect signs of disease, nutrient imbalances, and pest damage. By recognizing these issues early, farmers can implement precise interventions, minimizing crop losses and optimizing yields.

3.1.1 Image-based Disease Identification

Deep learning models such as AlexNet, ResNet, and Visual Geometry Group models are trained on extensive agricultural datasets to classify plant diseases with high accuracy (Balafas et al., 2023). AI-powered systems analyse colour patterns, texture, and leaf anomalies, differentiating between healthy and diseased crops. This automated disease identification reduces the dependency on manual inspections and accelerates intervention processes.

3.1.2 Hyperspectral Imaging and AI Integration

Hyperspectral imaging combined with AI algorithms enhances disease detection accuracy by capturing spectral signatures unique to each disease. These AI-driven models process large amounts of spectral data, providing insights into disease progression and recommending targeted treatment strategies. This method significantly reduces pesticide usage, ensuring environmentally friendly and cost-effective farming.

3.2 Precision Irrigation Management

Optimizing water usage presents a significant agricultural challenge, especially in water-stressed regions. Smart irrigation systems powered by AI enhance water efficiency by processing real-time data on soil conditions, meteorological predictions, and plant hydration needs.

3.2.1 IoT-driven Smart Irrigation Systems

The AI-powered Internet of Things (IoT) devices continuously monitor soil conditions, transmitting real-time data to cloud-based platforms.

These platforms use ML models to determine optimal irrigation schedules, reducing water waste and enhancing crop hydration.

3.2.2 Predictive Water Usage Models

Machine learning algorithms, including Random Forest (RF) and SVMs, analyse historical climate data and real-time soil conditions to forecast irrigation requirements. These intelligent systems enable agricultural producers to optimize watering schedules through data-driven insights, simultaneously enhancing water conservation and plant vitality.

3.3 Yield Prediction and Forecasting

Yield prediction is another critical area where AI and ML have shown great potential. By analysing historical yield data, weather patterns, and other environmental factors, ML algorithms can accurately forecast crop yields. Models like Gradient Boosting Machines (GBM), RF, and Long Short-Term Memory (LSTM) networks are commonly used for these predictions, helping farmers make informed decisions about crop selection and resource allocation. For example, research has shown that neural networks can predict rice yields with an accuracy rate above 90%, considering factors such as rainfall, temperature, and soil health (Arshaghi et al., 2023).

3.4 Livestock Health Monitoring

Both AI and ML are also applied in livestock farming to monitor animal health and behaviour. Using sensors, cameras, and ML algorithms, these systems can detect changes in behaviour or physical condition that may indicate illness. Early detection enables timely intervention, which can prevent the spread of disease and improve animal welfare. For example, ML models have been used to analyse body temperature, movement patterns, and feeding behaviour to predict illnesses in dairy cows with high accuracy, enabling farmers to manage herd health more effectively (Domingues et al., 2022).

3.5 Crop Harvesting Automation

In automated harvesting, AI and ML are combined with robotics to create machines capable of identifying ripe crops and picking them autonomously. These systems use computer vision and deep learning algorithms, such as You Only Look Once (YOLO) and ResNet, to differentiate between ripe and unripe produce based on colour, shape, and size. For example, robotic systems for harvesting strawberries and tomatoes have been developed, which utilize object detection algorithms to recognize and pick ripe fruits, significantly reducing labour costs and increasing efficiency (Slimani et al., 2023).

3.6 Supply Chain and Market Analysis

Artificial intelligence and ML technologies are transforming agricultural supply chains by optimizing logistics, improving inventory management, and enhancing market forecasting through data-driven insights. These systems analyse multiple variables including weather patterns, crop yields, and market demand to predict supply needs, reduce spoilage risks through optimal storage recommendations, and minimize waste across the distribution network. Additionally, they process real-time data from diverse sources such as social media, sales records, and economic reports to generate actionable intelligence on pricing trends, consumer preferences, and competitive dynamics, enabling farmers to make informed decisions about crop selection and marketing strategies. Advanced techniques like natural language processing (NLP) further enhance these capabilities by analysing market sentiment to anticipate demand shifts and optimize pricing (Orchi et al., 2023), ultimately creating a more efficient, responsive, and sustainable agricultural ecosystem that benefits all stakeholders while reducing costs and environmental impact.

3.7 Automated Weeding and Pest Control

The integration of robotics and AI is transforming agricultural weed and pest management through intelligent automation. Modern weeding systems combine computer vision with ML algorithms like Faster R-CNN and YOLO to precisely distinguish weeds from crops, enabling mechanical removal that reduces herbicide dependence while preserving soil health. These adaptive systems continuously improve their accuracy by learning from crop-specific patterns and environmental variables. For pest control, AI-driven solutions utilize drone-mounted imaging systems to detect infestations early, followed by targeted interventions such as precision pesticide application or biological control methods. Research indicates this approach can enhance pest management efficiency by 40% while minimizing ecological impact (Domingues et al., 2022).

As illustrated in Figure 2.1, AI and ML applications are revolutionizing agriculture across multiple domains—from field-level operations to supply chain management—by enabling data-informed decisions that boost productivity, sustainability, and farm profitability. These technological advancements are creating more resilient agricultural systems capable of meeting growing food demands while reducing environmental footprint.

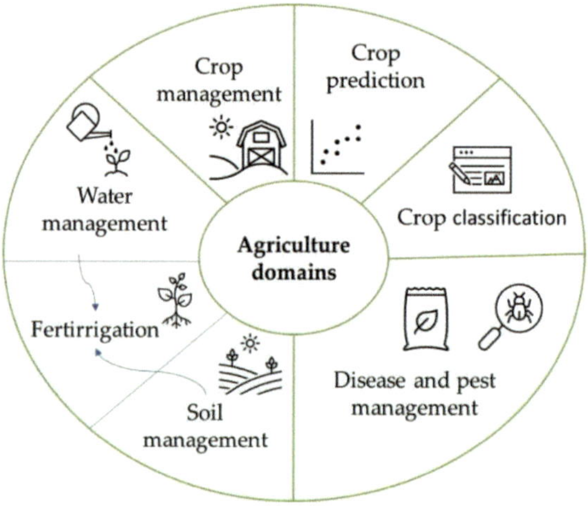

Figure 2.1: Key agricultural areas supported by AI/ML applications (de Oliveira and e Silva, 2023).

4. AI and ML Techniques in Agriculture

By enabling smart farming solutions that streamline procedures and boost output, AI and ML approaches are revolutionizing the agricultural industry. In order to produce useful insights, these methods concentrate on evaluating enormous volumes of data from many sources, such as sensors, satellite photography, and historical documents. Some well-known AI and ML methods used in agriculture have been discussed in this section.

4.1 Computer Vision and Image Processing

Deep learning models and CNNs are essential for phenotyping and detecting plant diseases. According to recent studies (Kumar et al., 2023; Khan et al., 2024; Sumaya et al., 2024), certain CNN architectures—like VGG19, DenseNet121, and ResNet50—have shown remarkable accuracy in identifying plant diseases from leaf imagery, even when applied to enhanced datasets. These models are trained on augmented datasets with techniques such as rotation, flipping, and noise injection to enhance their robustness. Pre-processing steps like resizing, noise reduction, and colour space transformations are key to highlighting critical image features, such as leaf lesion patterns and colour variations that indicate specific diseases. The integration of advanced CNNs with transfer learning has further improved the ability to generalize across different datasets and conditions (Ghosh et al., 2023; Shrestha et al., 2020).

4.2 Data Analytics and Predictive Models

When paired with regression models, traditional ML methods such as RF and Decision Trees perform exceptionally well when analysing structured agricultural data. Decision Trees are frequently applied to forecast crop yields, assess soil fertility, and identify patterns between climatic conditions and plant health. Regression models complement these approaches by analysing relationships between environmental inputs and productivity. These algorithms successfully forecast agricultural yields and pinpoint relationships between crop health and environmental variables. In order to maximize predictive accuracy and manage the problem of overfitting through ensemble approaches, researchers have used RF classifiers to analyse datasets like the Plant Village dataset (Joshi et al., 2022). AI and ML are revolutionizing agriculture by enabling smarter and more efficient farming practices. Figure 2.2 highlights the major agricultural domains where AI and ML technologies are increasingly adopted, including data analytics, predictive modelling, and IoT-based sensing. They enhance decision-making and operational efficiency. Integrating these techniques help to optimize crop management, improve yield prediction, and automate tasks, addressing challenges like labour shortages and climate variability.

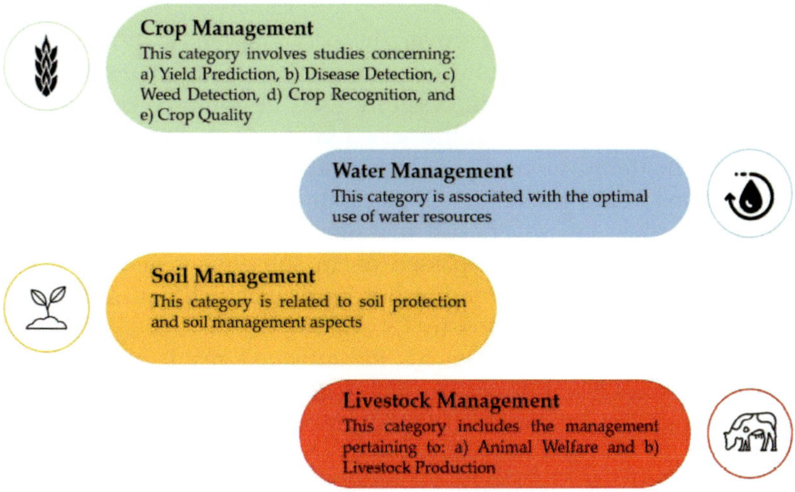

Figure 2.2: Primary agricultural categories utilizing AI/ML models (Benos et al., 2021).

4.3 Natural Language Processing (NLP)

With tools like chat bots and automated advisories providing customized farming advice based on farmer inquiries, NLP facilitates greater accessibility to agricultural knowledge. Non-technical users can now more easily access information by using NLP models to interpret text-based searches and provide information on weather trends and crop management. NLP applications leverage large language models that analyse vast amounts of agricultural literature and farmer feedback, making them capable of generating context-aware responses that aid decision-making. This is especially helpful for smallholder farmers who need quick access to reliable information (Bhimavarapu et al., 2023).

4.4 IoT and Sensor Data Integration

Precision agricultural data gathering and decision-making are being revolutionized by the integration of IoT with AI-ML. Sensors measure and monitor soil moisture, temperature, humidity, and nutrient levels, feeding real-time data to AI algorithms that predict crop stress and optimize irrigation schedules. AI algorithms use this data to track crop conditions in real time. IoT-enabled platforms paired with predictive ML models also support large-scale farm management, helping farmers react to potential issues before they affect yields. By maximizing fertilization and irrigation, this combination greatly increases agricultural productivity and resource efficiency (Shrestha et al., 2020).

4.5 Genetic Algorithms (GA)

Genetic algorithms (GAs) discover the best answers to problems like resource allocation in agriculture by simulating evolutionary processes. GA, for instance, has been successfully used to optimize crop rotation, irrigation regimens, and even the selection of genetic markers for plant breeding. The iterative nature of GA enables it to identify and refine the best solutions from a pool of potential candidates by applying operations such as selection, crossover, and mutation. This ensures that only the most effective strategies are passed on to subsequent generations. By choosing the most effective and resource-efficient techniques, like CNN and Recurrent Neural Network (RNN), GAs aid in increasing production potential. In order to optimize for the intended result, the algorithm efficiently prunes fewer desirable configurations as it generates solutions across subsequent generations (Bhimavarapu et al., 2023; Nayyar et al., 2019).

4.6 Swarm Intelligence Algorithms

Methods like Ant Colony Optimization (ACO) and Artificial Bee Colony (ABC) algorithm are modelled after the collective behaviour of insects. Throughout agriculture, ABC is used to maximize nutrient allocation by imitating bee foraging behaviours or to determine the best paths for autonomous machines to travel throughout fields. In contrast, ACO is used in data clustering tasks for diagnosing plant diseases, analysing soil, and identifying the best planting locations using visual and other sensor data (Chakraborty and Kar, 2017).

5. Challenges and Limitations

While AI and ML could fundamentally reshape agricultural operations, existing technical and economic barriers slow their comprehensive adoption.

5.1 Data Availability and Quality

Effective implementation of AI and ML in agriculture faces significant data-related challenges. Many agricultural datasets suffer from incompleteness, inconsistency, and poor quality, which negatively impacts ML model development. Issues such as data noise, unstructured formats, and missing values can introduce substantial biases, limiting the practical applicability of these models. Furthermore, the scarcity of localized, high-quality agricultural datasets restricts the ability to develop models that perform well across diverse regions and crop varieties (Araujo et al., 2023; Whig, 2023).

5.2 Infrastructure and Technology Access

Significant infrastructure obstacles stand in the way of effective application of AI and ML technologies in agriculture, especially in rural or impoverished areas. A large number of farmers lack access to the sophisticated sensors, high speed internet, and processing power needed to support AI applications (Cravero et al., 2022). Because larger farms or agribusinesses with greater resources can use AI solutions, while smaller or less resourced farms are left behind, this digital gap may lead to disparities in the adoption of technology. To guarantee that all farmers can profit from AI advancements, strategies that give priority to the construction of strong technology infrastructure in rural regions are crucial (Whig, 2023).

5.3 Interpret Ability and Trust

One of the main obstacles to AI models' broad use in agriculture is their interpret ability. Because of the intricacy of algorithms and the opaqueness of their decision-making procedures, many farmers are reluctant to rely on AI-driven recommendations. Transparency is especially important in agriculture since actions there have a direct impact on crop productivity and financial results. For example, if farmers do not know how AI-generated recommendations for fertilizer or irrigation were developed, they would be unwilling to adopt them. Building trust and promoting adoption among agricultural stakeholders requires efforts to create interpretable models and present findings in an understandable way (Araujo et al., 2023).

5.4 *Training Needs and Skill Gaps*

The deployment of AI and ML technologies is severely hampered by the gap in digital literacy skills in the agricultural workforce. AI systems are underutilized because many farmers lack the technical know-how to use them efficiently. Furthermore, there may be a gap between traditional farming knowledge and modern technical abilities as younger generations enter the job with inadequate training in agricultural operations. Improving adoption rates requires the creation of thorough training curricula that impart technical knowledge and place AI tools in the context of conventional agriculture.

5.5 *Integration with Existing Practices*

There are many obstacles to overcome when integrating AI and ML technologies with conventional farming methods. Farmers frequently use age-old techniques that have been refined over many generations, which might not be compatible with AI-driven tactics. Reliance on local expertise, for example, may clash with data-driven suggestions, leading farmers to doubt AI's potential advantages. Researchers emphasize how crucial it is to create AI systems that both respect current procedures and offer observable advantages like higher productivity and lower labour expenses.

5.6 *Cost and Scalability*

Adoption of AI technology in agriculture can be prohibitively expensive, particularly for small- and medium-sized farms. Farmers may be dissuaded from investing in AI solutions by the high upfront costs associated with infrastructure construction, training, and technology procurement. Furthermore, because solutions designed for large-scale operations might not be appropriate for smaller farms, scaling these technologies for various farm types might be challenging. Thus, creating AI solutions that are affordable, scalable, and adaptable to different agricultural situations is essential for wider adoption (Cravero et al., 2022).

5.7 Concerns about Ethics and Data Privacy

The agricultural sector's adoption of AI faces substantial ethical challenges, particularly regarding the protection of sensitive farm data. Many producers remain cautious about participating in digital systems due to valid apprehensions about data security breaches and commercial exploitation. Empirical studies highlight dual requirements: first, the need for verifiable data stewardship protocols to build stakeholder trust; second, the establishment of legal safeguards to ensure responsible data utilization and protect farmer interests (Liakos et al., 2018).

6. Case Studies and Real-World Implementations

Prospera Technologies, an Israeli agri-tech business that specializes in AI-driven crop monitoring and management systems, is one noteworthy startup. Prospera analyses crop health, finds insect infestations, and tracks the efficiency of irrigation using computer vision and ML models. It gathers data on plant health markers, including colour, growth rate, and possible stressors, in real time by deploying sensors and cameras across fields. Prospera's platform is especially useful for open-field and greenhouse farming, where regular monitoring is essential. For example, its AI can identify early indicators of stress or illness through image analysis that are hard for the human eye to pick up. By reducing crop loss and optimizing inputs like water and pesticides, this proactive monitoring assists farmers in making targeted adjustments. By increasing crop yields and cutting down on resource waste, the firm has collaborated with major agricultural producers in the US, Mexico, and Europe, and shown quantifiable success. This strategy is one example of how companies are applying AI to solve global agriculture issues (Mahmood et al., 2023; Rajwar et al., 2024).

6.1 Success Stories from Research Projects and Global Initiatives in Agricultural AI and ML

Some success stories around the globe in the field of agriculture using AI-ML are discussed in this section.

6.1.1 The FAO Hand-in-Hand Programme

The "Hand-in-Hand" effort was started by the Food and Agriculture Organization (FAO) to use AI and big data analytics to increase agricultural output and lower poverty in the most impoverished areas. This research offers insights into soil quality, agricultural trends, and climate risks by combining satellite imagery, ML models, and geospatial data, particularly in vulnerable nations in Asia, Latin America, and Africa.

An Ethiopian success story demonstrates how this programme assisted the government in creating a map of crop compatibility, which enabled farmers to make the best crop selections possible given the land and environment. Improved crop yields and more efficient land use are the results of this data-driven assistance. FAO's effort is enabling countries to develop sustainable farming policies by integrating AI insights with regional agricultural practices (Canton, 2021).

6.1.2 Penn State University's Plant Village

Penn State's Plant Village research project is using AI to improve plant yield and health for smallholder farmers around the world. The project's smartphone app "Nuru" uses computer vision and ML to identify crop illnesses in images that farmers take with their phones. This app offers real-time disease management guidance, particularly for sub-Saharan African key crops like potatoes, maize, and cassava. One noteworthy example of success is Plant Village's collaboration with Tanzanian and Kenyan cassava farmers. Farmers could minimize losses and enhance crop health by employing Nuru to identify viral illnesses early and take preventative action. Thanks to the offline app, farmers in isolated locations can save up to 30% on losses due to crop illnesses that go unnoticed. The success of Plant Village demonstrates how AI may help smallholders, who might not otherwise have access to timely agricultural expertise, to fill information gaps (Mrisho et al., 2020).

6.1.3 Digital Disease Surveillance in Wheat Crops (Indian Agricultural Research Institute)

To address wheat illnesses like rust that significantly reduce output, the Indian Agricultural Research Institute (IARI) created an ML-based digital disease surveillance system. This AI-powered technology looks for early disease symptoms using picture analysis and remote sensing. Using photos of wheat crops, researchers developed ML models to recognize and monitor disease trends, providing farmers with early solutions. By enabling farmers to take prompt action upon early detection, the implementation of this surveillance in India's major wheat-growing regions has resulted in a considerable reduction in crop loss (Islam et al., 2018).

6.1.4 Smart Agri Hubs Initiative (European Union)

A major digital innovation effort, the Smart Agri Hubs project of the European Union (EU) aims to advance AI and big data in European agriculture. Through a network of more than 400 innovation hubs throughout the EU, this project aims to modernize farming techniques by integrating technologies like AI, IoT, and big data analytics. These hubs provide predictive analytics for managing pest control, maximizing irrigation, and tracking soil health. Pilot projects in nations like France and the Netherlands are examples of Agri Hubs success stories, where farmers have used AI-driven insights to increase crop quality and lower pesticide use. By promoting information exchange and greatly boosting data-driven decision-making in European agriculture, the programme has contributed to the development of more resilient farming methods throughout the continent (Bacco et al., 2019).

6.2 *Real-World Examples of AI and ML Implementation in Agriculture*

Some real-world examples of AI and ML implementation in agriculture have been discussed in this section.

6.2.1 *Yield Prediction and Precision Farming*

By examining past data on weather patterns, soil conditions, and planting methods, several platforms use reinforcement learning to improve agricultural production forecasts. For example, a model created in Africa to anticipate maize yields improved farmers' planning and resource allocation, showing notable effectiveness in optimizing productivity through input adjustments based on AI-driven forecasts (de Oliveira and e Silva, 2023).

6.2.2 *Automated Irrigation and Water Management*

One important component of smart agriculture is effective water utilization, which is made possible by recent developments in AI-driven irrigation systems. In one study, water flow in drip irrigation systems was controlled using AI models such as Artificial Neural Networks (ANNs) and Least Squares Support Vector Machines (LS-SVM), which predicted water requirements based on variables including soil moisture and temperature. By ensuring that crops receive the proper amount of water, these technologies minimize waste and lower farmers' operating expenses. With error margins as low as 8.8%, the application of these AI models showed excellent accuracy, suggesting that they could help farms sustainably manage their water resources (Shaikh et al., 2021).

6.2.3 *Disease Detection Platforms with Multimodal AI*

The detection of plant diseases using multimodal AI is another innovation. In order to predict disease outbreaks, the US Department of Agriculture (USDA) Agricultural Research Service (ARS) used AI and computer vision to monitor crops for disease symptoms. In order to improve early detection accuracy and drastically reduce the amount of manual labour needed for monitoring, AI-driven models, for example, were able to process photos in order to identify minor indicators of disease in crops like apples and peaches. In order to minimize crop loss and enhance yield quality, this technology has been used in practical settings to identify pests and diseases early (Parr et al., 2021).

6.2.4 *Unmanned Aerial Vehicles (UAVs) for Weed Detection*

Unmanned aerial vehicles (UAVs) paired with ML algorithms are changing weed detection and management in agriculture. These systems can differentiate between crops and weeds in vast fields by combining multispectral photography with ML techniques like RF and SVM. This minimizes the impact on the environment and reduces the consumption of chemicals by enabling tailored herbicide application. Accuracy rates of 90% in separating weeds from crops have been demonstrated in real-world deployments, promoting more economical and environmentally friendly farming methods (Saleem et al., 2021).

6.2.5 *Trace Genomics*

Soil Health Analysis Trace Genomics provides thorough evaluations of soil health using ML. To assess soil fertility and quality, farmers can submit soil samples to Trace Genomics, where ML algorithms examine microbial diversity and other markers. Long-term production is increased by farmers using the findings to optimize soil management and crop rotation. Farmers may improve sustainability and reduce their need for artificial fertilizers by knowing the biological health of their soil (Patrício and Rieder 2018).

6.2.6 *Soil Health Monitoring with AI-based Analysis*

Crop productivity is largely dependent on soil quality, and AI has made it possible to conduct more thorough and precise evaluations of soil health. Researchers can determine nutrient deficits, soil pH levels, and other indicators crucial to soil fertility by analysing soil samples using ML models like RF and Decision Trees. These models, for example, are used by AI-based soil monitoring platforms to suggest the best kinds and quantities of fertilizer, increasing output while avoiding excessive use of chemical inputs. This has been very helpful for farmers who want to use precision farming to increase yields in a sustainable way (Liakos et al., 2018).

6.2.7 *Greenhouse Monitoring with Machine Vision*

Crop monitoring in controlled settings, such as greenhouses, has shown promise thanks to machine vision, an AI tool that blends computer vision and ML. Real-time environmental assessment, nutrient deficiency detection, and plant growth monitoring are all made possible by systems using cameras and ML models. By offering precise information on development stages and health, these AI systems have enhanced yield predictability in trials by enabling modifications to lighting, watering, and nutrient levels. This technology is useful in greenhouses and vertical farms where accurate monitoring can significantly improve crop quality and yield (Liakos et al., 2018).

7. Future Directions and Emerging Trends

Growing sophistication and integration with other cutting-edge technologies to solve issues of sustainability, climate change, and global food security are key to the future of AI and ML in agriculture. The new orientations and trends are discussed in this section.

7.1 *AI-driven Sustainable Farming*

More accurate and resource-efficient farming methods are made possible by AI in sustainable farming, which is essential for modern agriculture as it struggles with finite natural resources. Using AI-ML techniques, precision agriculture evaluates crop demands in real time, from water requirements to nutrient shortages, enabling focused interventions that minimize waste and environmental effect. AI systems can improve crop health monitoring and make sustainable, controlled adjustments to inputs like water and pesticides by evaluating data from sensors and drones. By reducing excessive resource use and detrimental runoff, such strategies support environmental protection and are consistent with the objectives of sustainable agriculture (Karunathilake et al., 2023; Bhagat et al., 2022). Additionally, by anticipating problems like pest outbreaks and droughts, AI enables farmers to take preventative action rather than responding to problems after the fact. By analysing meteorological and environmental data, these predictive systems can warn farmers of possible dangers and allow for prompt solutions that preserve crop yields while using fewer chemicals. AI's contribution to climate resilience further highlights the technology's significance in sustainable agriculture. AI is essential for water management in areas that are vulnerable to water scarcity because, for instance, algorithms may modify irrigation depending on predicted weather patterns (Adewusi et al., 2024). Agriculture may attain environmental sustainability and higher production by incorporating AI. According to studies, AI technologies help to enhance productivity without consuming more resources or harming the health of the soil, which helps to promote sustainable farming. Given the increasing demand on global agriculture to feed a growing population while battling climate change and protecting biodiversity, this transition towards sustainable techniques is especially important (Karunathilake et al., 2023).

7.2 Blockchain and AI Integration

The efficiency and transparency of agricultural supply networks could be revolutionized by the application of blockchain technology and AI. AI's predictive powers, along with blockchain's safe, unchangeable ledger, make it easier to track crops from farm to table. This improves food safety and permits real-time product tracking by guaranteeing that every phase of the supply chain like cultivation, harvest, transportation, and distribution is documented and validated. Specifically, blockchain promotes accountability by offering safe documentation, while AI evaluates data to improve inventories and logistics, cutting down on waste and inefficiencies. This combination is particularly helpful in satisfying customer needs for sustainable and transparent food supply (Kamilaris et al., 2019; Bandiera and Tsiropoulos, 2020). Farmers may also gain a lot from the integration of blockchain and AI since it increases pricing transparency and market accessibility. Smart contracts allow farmers to be paid according to the quality of their crops, guaranteeing equitable remuneration free from intermediaries or delays. By maximizing supply based on demand projections, AI's predictive analytics assist farmers in managing market swings. Farmers may be able to lower their financial risks by using this technology to make well-informed decisions about the supply chain for their goods (Adewusi et al., 2024). Furthermore, combining these technologies yields insightful data that promotes sustainable farming. Blockchain and AI can support organic and fair-trade product certifications by recording environmental effect data and product quality, thereby promoting ethical farming methods. Research on blockchain's application in agriculture shows that technology has the potential to completely transform the sector by increasing farmer profitability, fostering environmental sustainability, and improving accountability (Bhagat et al., 2022).

7.3 Genomics and AI in Agriculture

The use of AI in genomics is revolutionizing genetic engineering and agricultural breeding, accelerating the creation of high-yield, climate-resilient crops. Scientists can find important genetic features like nutrition efficiency, drought tolerance, and insect resistance by utilizing ML techniques to evaluate large genomic datasets. By enabling researchers to concentrate on features that are most advantageous for particular settings, this speeds up breeding operations and makes it feasible to create varieties that are more climate resilient and resource-efficient (Crossa et al., 2017; Hickey et al., 2019). The nexus of AI and genomics is very useful for tackling concerns related to global food security. AI-driven genomic research makes it possible to quickly design resilient crops that can resist harsh weather conditions as climate change has an impact on crop viability. Furthermore, by enhancing precision and optimizing gene selection, AI can assist genome editing methods such as Clustered Regularly Interspaced Short Palindromic Repeats (CRISPR), guaranteeing that modified crops fulfil safety and productivity requirements. These developments highlight how crucial it is to include AI into genomics in order to produce crops that support sustainable farming methods (Adewusi et al., 2024). Moreover, AI lowers the time and expense involved with conventional breeding techniques by automating genomic data analysis. The development of better crops at the scale needed to meet the rising demand for food worldwide depends on this efficiency. According to research, applying AI to genomics can greatly increase agricultural output, guaranteeing that genetic advancements support robust, sustainable food systems (Hickey et al., 2019).

7.4 AI in Climate-Resilient Agriculture

Predictive analytics powered by AI is essential to enhancing agriculture's climate resilience. AI systems can predict extreme weather occurrences like droughts and floods by using historical data and climate models. This allows farmers to take preventative action to safeguard crops. AI-driven models, for instance, assist farmers in choosing when to plant and harvest crops, guaranteeing crop productivity even under challenging circumstances (Real et al., 2019; Belayneh et al., 2020). AI technologies also improve crop rotation and irrigation plans based on weather forecasts, enabling water conservation and reducing the consequences of climate change. In the face of climate unpredictability, this flexibility is essential for maintaining steady crop yields, promoting food security, and allowing sustainable agricultural practices (Ramu and Choi, 2021).

7.5 Farmers' Training and Adoption of AI

Strong education and training programmes are necessary for farmers to adopt AI in agriculture, especially in areas with restricted access to technology. Customized training programmes bridge skill gaps and help farmers comprehend and use AI products efficiently. Research emphasizes how educational initiatives can assist farmers in implementing AI for a range of uses, including pest management and soil monitoring, which increase crop yields and resource efficiency (Jagtap et al., 2022; Dubey and Tripathi, 2020). Extension services and support networks help farmers even more by offering technical assistance and encouraging an innovative culture. Farmers are encouraged to embrace cutting-edge technologies by supporting knowledge-sharing platforms, which helps to create a more productive and sustainable agriculture industry (Desai et al., 2021).

8. Conclusion

Artificial intelligence and ML are revolutionizing agriculture by introducing intelligent systems that improve decision-making, consume less resources, and boost productivity. Farmers may more accurately and efficiently forecast yields, regulate irrigation, and monitor crop health by combining technologies like computer vision, deep learning, and predictive analytics. Precision agriculture, which uses data to inform every stage from planting to harvesting, is supported by these instruments and allows for more focused and efficient interventions.

The chapter covered a wide range of AI and ML applications, such as supply chain optimization, automated harvesting, disease diagnosis, and smart irrigation. Case studies and practical applications show how these technologies are being used to address urgent problems in agriculture. Specifically, real-time monitoring and responsive decision-making are made possible by the integration of IoT sensors and AI models, which enhances crop results while reducing environmental effect.

But these developments also present a unique set of difficulties. Widespread adoption may be hampered by a lack of digital literacy among farmers, inadequate infrastructure in rural areas, and restricted access to high-quality data. It is also necessary to solve issues with cost, AI model interpretability, and interaction with conventional methods. It will take cooperation from scholars, legislators, IT developers, and local communities to close these gaps.

Barriers including data restrictions, access to technology, and user adoption still exist in spite of these developments. It will be essential to address these issues by building infrastructure, educating farmers, and enacting supportive legislation. AI and ML have the potential to propel sustainable agricultural growth in the future, assisting the industry in feeding a growing population, adjusting to climate change, and ensuring long-term food security.

References

Adewusi, A.O., Asuzu, O.F., Olorunsogo, T., Iwuanyanwu, C., Adaga, E. and Daraojimba, D.O. (2024). AI in precision agriculture: A review of technologies for sustainable farming practices. *World Journal of Advanced Research and Reviews* 21(1): 2276–2285.

Araujo, S.O., Peres, R.S., Ramalho, J.C., Lidon, F. and Barata, J. (2023). Machine Learning Applications in agriculture: Current trends, challenges, and future perspectives. *Agronomy* 13(12): 2976.

Arshaghi, A., Ashourian, M. and Ghabeli, L. (2023). Potato diseases detection and classification using deep learning methods. *Multimedia Tools and Applications* 82(4): 5725–5742.

Bacco, M., Barsocchi, P., Ferro, E., Gotta, A. and Ruggeri, M. (2019). The digitisation of agriculture: A survey of research activities on smart farming. *Array* 3: 100009.

Balafas, V., Karantoumanis, E., Louta, M. and Ploskas, N. (2023). Machine learning and deep learning for plant disease classification and detection. *IEEE Access* 11: 114352–114377.

Bandiera, L. and Tsiropoulos, V. (2020). A framework to assess debt sustainability under the belt and road initiative. *Journal of Development Economics* 146: 102495.

Belayneh, M., Yirgu, T. and Tsegaye, D. (2020). Runoff and soil loss responses of cultivated land managed with graded soil bunds of different ages in the upper blue Nile Basin, Ethiopia. *Ecological Processes* 9: 1–18.

Benos, L., Tagarakis, A.C., Dolias, G., Berruto, R., Kateris, D. and Bochtis, D. (2021). Machine learning in agriculture: A comprehensive updated review. *Sensors* 21(11): 3758.

Bhagat, P.R., Naz, F. and Magda, R. (2022). Artificial Intelligence solutions enabling sustainable agriculture: A bibliometric analysis. *PLOS ONE* 17(6): e0268989.

Bhat, S.A. and Huang, N.-F. (2021). Big data and AI revolution in precision agriculture: Survey and challenges. *IEEE Access* 9: 110209–110222.

Bhimavarapu, U., Battineni, G. and Chintalapudi, N. (2023). Improved optimization algorithm in LSTM to predict crop yield. *Computers* 12(1): 10.

Canton, H. (2021). Food and agriculture organization of the United Nations—FAO. In *The Europa Directory of International Organizations*, 297–305. Routledge.

Chakraborty, A. and Kar, A.K. (2017). Swarm Intelligence: A review of algorithms. In *Nature-Inspired Computing and Optimization: Theory and Applications*, 475–494.

Cravero, A., Pardo, S., Sepulveda, S. and Munoz, L. (2022). Challenges to use machine learning in agricultural big data: A systematic literature review. *Agronomy* 12(3): 748.

Crossa, J., Pérez-Rodríguez, P., Cuevas, J., Montesinos-López, O., Jarquín, D., De Los Campos, G., Burgueño, J., González-Camacho, J.M., Pérez-Elizalde, S., Beyene, Y. and Dreisigacker, S. (2017). Genomic selection in plant breeding: Methods, models, and perspectives. *Trends in Plant Science* 22(11): 961–975.

Das, S., Kaur, M., Chhabra, V., Nandi, T., Mishra, P. and Ghosh, S. (2024). A systematic review of artificial intelligence: A future guide to sustainable agriculture. *International Journal of Environment and Climate Change* 14(4): 562–573.

de Oliveira, R.C. and e Silva, R.D. de Souza (2023). Artificial Intelligence in agriculture: Benefits, challenges, and trends. *Applied Sciences* 13(13): 7405.

Desai, K., Alone, S., Wadgane, S., Shirsath, S.E., Batoo, K.M., Imran, A., Raslan, E., Hadi, M., Ijaz, M. and Kadam, R. (2021). X-ray diffraction-based williamson–hall analysis and rietveld refinement for strain mechanism in Mg–Mn co-substituted $CdFe_2O_4$ nanoparticles. *Physica B: Condensed Matter* 614: 413054.

Domingues, T., Brandao, T. and Ferreira, J.C. (2022). Machine learning for detection and prediction of crop diseases and pests: A comprehensive survey. *Agriculture* 12(9): 1350.

Dubey, A.D. and Tripathi, S. (2020). Analysing the sentiments towards work-from-home experience during COVID-19 pandemic. *Journal of Innovation Management* 8(1): 13–19.

Fang, L., Hu, R., Mao, H. and Chen, S. (2021). How crop insurance influences agricultural green total factor productivity: Evidence from chinese farmers. *Journal of Cleaner Production* 321: 128977.

Ghosh, H., Rahat, I.S., Shaik, K., Khasim, S. and Yesubabu, M. (2023). Potato leaf disease recognition and prediction using convolutional neural networks. *EAI Endorsed Transactions on Scalable Information Systems* 10(6).

Haldorai, A., Murugan, S. and Balakrishnan, M. (2024). Significance of AI in smart agriculture: Methods, technologies, trends, and challenges. In *Artificial Intelligence for Sustainable Development*, 3–25.

Hickey, L.T., Hafeez, A.N., Robinson, H., Jackson, S.A., Leal Bertioli, S.C., Tester, M., Gao, C., Godwin, I.D., Hayes, B.J. and Wulff, B.B. (2019). Breeding crops to feed 10 billion. *Nature Biotechnology* 37(7): 744–754.

Islam, S., Sharma, A.K., Sharma, K., Farooqi, M.S. and Chaturvedi, K.K. (2018). Diagnosing wheat disease using expert system. *Journal of the Indian Society of Agricultural Statistics* 72: 255–259.

Jagtap, S., Trollman, H., Trollman, F., Garcia-Garcia, G., Parra-López, C., Duong, L., Martindale, W., Munekata, P.E., Lorenzo, J.M., Hdaifeh, A., Hassoun, A., Salonitis, K. and Afy-Shararah, M. (2022). The Russia–Ukraine conflict: Its implications for the global food supply chains. *Foods* 11(14): 2098.

Joshi, K., Awale, R., Ahmad, S., Patil, S. and Pisal, V. (2022). Plant leaf disease detection using computer vision techniques and machine learning. In *ITM Web of Conferences*, vol. 44. EDP Sciences, 03002.

Kamilaris, A., Fonts, A. and Prenafeta-Boldú, F.X. (2019). The rise of blockchain technology in agriculture and food supply chains. *Trends in Food Science & Technology* 91: 640–652.

Karunathilake, E., Le, A.T., Heo, S., Chung, Y.S. and Mansoor, S. (2023). The path to smart farming: innovations and opportunities in precision agriculture. *Agriculture* 13(8): 1593.

Khan, S., Yadav, A.K., Shukla, S.S.P. and Shende, V. (2024). ResNet-50: A breakthrough in plant disease detection accuracy for agricultural empowerment. pp. 364–371. *In*: Sukhpreet Kaur, Sushil Kamboj, Manish Kumar, Arvind Dagur and Dhirendra Kumar Shukla (eds.). *Computational Methods in Science and Technology*. CRC Press.

Kumar, Y., Singh, R., Moudgil, M.R. and Kamini. (2023). A systematic review of different categories of plant disease detection using deep learning-based approaches. *Archives of Computational Methods in Engineering* 30(8): 4757–4779.

Liakos, K.G., Busato, P., Moshou, D., Pearson, S. and Bochtis, D. (2018). Machine learning in agriculture: A review. *Sensors* 18(8): 2674.

Mahmood, M.R., Matin, M.A., Goudos, S.K. and Karagiannidis, G. (2023). Machine learning for smart agriculture: A comprehensive survey. *IEEE Transactions on Artificial Intelligence* 5(6): 2568–2588.

Marwaha, S., Deb, C.K., Haque, M.A., Naha, S. and Maji, A.K. (2023). Application of artificial intelligence and machine learning in agriculture. pp. 441–457. *In*: Mamrutha Harohalli Masthigowda, Krishnappa Gopalareddy, Rinki Khobra, Gyanendra Singh and Gyanendra Pratap Singh (eds.). *Translating Physiological Tools to Augment Crop Breeding*. Springer.

Misra, N.N., Dixit, Y., Al-Mallahi, A., Bhullar, M.S., Upadhyay, R. and Martynenko, A. (2020). IoT, Big Data, and Artificial Intelligence in agriculture and food industry. *IEEE Internet of Things Journal* 9(9): 6305–6324.

Mrisho, L., Mbilinyi, N., Ndalahwa, M., Ramcharan, A., Kehs, A., McCloskey, P., Murithi, H., Hughes, D. and Legg, J. (2020). Evaluation of the accuracy of a smartphone-based artificial intelligence system, PlantVillage Nuru, in diagnosing the viral diseases of cassava. *BioRxiv*, 2020–01.

Nayyar, A., Kumar, S. and Nguyen, N.G. (2019). Advances in swarm intelligence and machine learning for optimizing problems in image processing and data analytics (Part 1). *Recent Patents on Computer Science* 12(4): 248–249.

Oliveira, R.C.D. and Silva, R.D.D.S.E. (2023). Artificial intelligence in agriculture: Benefits, challenges, and trends. *Applied Sciences* 13(13): 7405.

Orchi, H., Sadik, M., Khaldoun, M. and Sabir, E. (2023). Automation of crop disease detection through conventional machine learning and deep transfer learning approaches. *Agriculture* 13(2): 352.

Parr, C.S., Lemay, D.G., Owen, C.L., Woodward-Greene, M.J. and Sun, J. (2021). Multimodal AI to improve agriculture. *IT Professional* 23(3): 53–57.

Patrício, D.I. and Rieder, R. (2018). Computer vision and artificial intelligence in precision agriculture for grain crops: A systematic review. *Computers and Electronics in Agriculture* 153: 69–81.

Rajwar, K., Pant, M. and Deep, K. (2024). Application of machine learning in agriculture: Recent trends and future research avenues. *arXiv Preprint arXiv:2405.17465*.

Ramu, A. and Choi, D. (2021). Highly efficient and simultaneous catalytic reduction of multiple toxic dyes and nitrophenols wastewater using highly active bimetallic PdO–NiO nanocomposite. *Scientific Reports* 11(1): 22699.

Real, E., Aggarwal, A., Huang, Y. and Le, Q.V. (2019). Regularized evolution for image classifier architecture search. In *Proceedings of the AAAI Conference on Artificial Intelligence* 33(01): 4780–4789.

Saleem, M.H., Potgieter, J. and Arif, K.M. (2021). Automation in agriculture by machine and deep learning techniques: A review of recent developments. *Precision Agriculture* 22(6): 2053–2091.

Shadrin, D., Podladchikova, T., Ovchinnikov, G., Pavlov, A., Pukalchik, M. and Somov, A. (2020). Kalman filtering for accurate and fast plant growth dynamics assessment. In *2020 IEEE International Instrumentation and Measurement Technology Conference (I2MTC)*, May, 1–6. IEEE.

Shaikh, F.K., Memon, M.A., Mahoto, N.A., Zeadally, S. and Nebhen, J. (2021). Artificial Intelligence best practices in smart agriculture. *IEEE Micro* 42(1): 17–24.

Shrestha, G., Das, M. and Dey, N. (2020). Plant disease detection using CNN. In *2020 IEEE Applied Signal Processing Conference (ASPCON)*. IEEE, 109–113.

Slimani, H., El Mhamdi, J. and Jilbab, A. (2023). Drone-assisted plant disease identification using artificial intelligence: A critical review. *International Journal of Computing and Digital Systems* 14(1): 10433–10446.

Sumaya, A.I., Forhad, S., Al Rafi, M., Rahman, H., Bhuyan, M.H. and Tareq, Q. (2024). Comparative analysis of AlexNet, GoogLeNet, VGG19, ResNet50, and ResNet101 for improved plant disease detection through convolutional neural networks. In *2024 2nd International Conference on Artificial Intelligence, Blockchain, and Internet of Things (AIBThings)*, September, 1–6. IEEE.

Thangamani, R., Sathya, D., Kamalam, G. and Lyer, G.N. (2024). AI green revolution: reshaping agriculture's future. pp. 421–461. *In*: Sundaravadivazhagan Balasubramanian, Gnanasankaran Natarajan and Pethuru Raj Chelliah (eds.). *Intelligent Robots and Drones for Precision Agriculture*. Springer.

Whig, P. (2023). Leveraging AI for sustainable agriculture: Opportunities and challenges. *Transactions on Latest Trends in Artificial Intelligence* 4(4).

Chapter 3

Blockchain-enabled Supply Chain Transparency and AI-powered Predictive Analytics for Smallholder Farmers in India's Rice Production Sector

*Vishal Jain, Archan Mitra** and *Sanchita Paul*

India's rice production sector, largely sustained by smallholder farmers, continues to grapple with systemic inefficiencies, limited supply chain transparency, and escalating concerns over data privacy. This study presents a simulation-based evaluation of an integrated framework that combines blockchain technology, artificial intelligence (AI), and federated learning (FL) to address these challenges. The blockchain layer facilitates traceable, tamper-proof transaction records and automates financial processes such as subsidy disbursement through smart contracts, thereby reducing

[1] Department of Computer Science and Engineering, Sharda School of Engineering and Technology, Sharda University, Uttar Pradesh, India.
[2] Department of Mass Communication, School of Media Studies (SOMS), Presidency University, Karnataka, India.
[3] Neil Patel Digital, Karnataka, India.
* Corresponding author: archan.mitra@nitte.edu.in

DOI: 10.1201/9781003670568-3

delays and eliminating intermediaries. AI models are developed to predict crop yields, assess market demand, and detect environmental risks like pest outbreaks and extreme weather events, enabling timely, data-driven interventions. To preserve data sovereignty, FL is applied, ensuring that sensitive farmer data remains localized while still contributing to global predictive intelligence. Using secondary datasets and open-source tools, the study validates the technical feasibility, interoperability, and ethical robustness of the proposed framework through scenario-based simulations. Results demonstrate that the integrated system can enhance operational transparency, empower farmers with predictive tools, and promote equitable value chain participation. By aligning with India's digital governance initiatives and future data protection regulations, this research offers a scalable, privacy-preserving model for agricultural transformation, particularly in the context of smallholder-dominated rice ecosystems.

1. Introduction

1.1 Background on India's Rice Production and the Challenges Smallholder Farmers Face

Rice is a staple crop that supports the livelihoods of over 100 million households in India, a country that ranks among the top global producers and consumers of rice (Kumar et al., 2021). The rice cultivation system in India is predominantly driven by smallholder farmers who operate on less than 2 hectares of land. These farmers face numerous challenges including yield stagnation, limited access to high-quality inputs, inadequate storage facilities, price volatility, and climate variability (Prateek, 2025). Furthermore, inefficiencies across the rice value chain, from production to distribution, result in significant post-harvest losses and unfair trade practices.

Institutional barriers such as limited access to credit, delayed government subsidies, and fragmented market linkages further exacerbate the vulnerability of smallholder farmers (Mishra et al., 2022). While initiatives like direct benefit transfers (DBTs) and minimum support price (MSP) mechanisms exist, their reach is inconsistent due to logistical inefficiencies and corruption. The lack of traceability and transparency in transactions undermines both the economic agency of farmers and the trust of consumers.

Digital technologies, although increasingly promoted, are yet to be uniformly adopted due to low digital literacy, infrastructural gaps, and concerns around data privacy. These systemic inefficiencies reflect a critical need for an inclusive, technology-driven transformation of the agricultural value chain (Banerjee and Kumar, 2023).

1.2 Relevance of Blockchain and AI Technologies in Agriculture

Blockchain and artificial intelligence (AI) have emerged as transformative technologies with the potential to revolutionize agriculture by ensuring transparency, improving decision-making, and fostering equitable value distribution. Blockchain, with its decentralized and immutable ledger, offers a reliable way to trace agricultural produce from farm to fork, eliminating intermediaries and reducing fraud (Panwar et al., 2023; Alobid et al., 2022). Smart contracts can automate transactions, enabling prompt and transparent subsidy disbursement, procurement, and insurance claims (Bakare et al., 2021).

The AI applications in agriculture include crop yield prediction, pest and disease detection, and weather forecasting. These insights support data-driven decision-making, enabling farmers to optimize inputs and minimize risks (Goel and Pandey, 2024; Assimakopoulos et al., 2024). For example, machine learning algorithms can analyse satellite imagery and sensor data to identify early signs of crop stress, while predictive models can forecast market demand, enabling better price realization.

Together, blockchain and AI can create an integrated smart agriculture ecosystem. When combined with federated learning (FL) techniques, these technologies can also preserve data privacy while enabling collective insights, which is crucial in regions where data ownership and digital trust remain contested (Ahmed et al., 2022). Studies have shown that such integration can improve productivity, transparency, and financial inclusion for smallholder farmers (Jadav et al., 2023).

By leveraging these technologies, agricultural stakeholders can enhance traceability, ensure accountability, and empower farmers with actionable insights. This relevance is especially critical in the Indian context, where inefficiencies in subsidy distribution and market access, and information asymmetry continue to hinder sustainable agricultural development (Savelyeva et al., 2022).

1.3 Problem Statement

Despite the growing discourse on digital transformation in agriculture, India lacks an integrated framework that simultaneously addresses transparency, predictive planning, and data privacy. Most existing solutions are siloed, blockchain systems often ignore real-time predictive analytics, while AI models are rarely integrated into transparent and accountable value chains. Moreover, concerns about data misuse and inadequate privacy safeguards hinder the adoption of data-driven tools among smallholder farmers.

This fragmented technological landscape limits the potential for achieving equitable, efficient, and sustainable rice production. An integrated system that combines blockchain for supply chain traceability, AI for predictive analytics, and FL for data privacy can bridge this gap. This study proposes such a framework tailored to the socio-economic and infrastructural context of India's rice farming ecosystem.

1.4 Research Objectives

- To design a blockchain-enabled framework for enhancing supply chain transparency in rice production.
- To develop AI-based predictive models for yield forecasting, market demand, and risk assessment.
- To integrate FL to preserve data privacy while enabling data-driven insights.
- To evaluate the conceptual feasibility of the proposed framework using simulation and secondary data.
- To explore socio-economic implications of the digital framework for smallholder farmers.

1.5 Research Questions

- How can blockchain technology improve traceability and trust in India's rice supply chain?
- What predictive insights can AI provide to support smallholder decision-making?
- How can FL safeguard farmer data while enabling value chain optimization?
- What are the technical and social feasibility constraints of implementing this framework in the Indian agricultural context?

1.6 Scope and Significance of this Study

This study presents a conceptual and simulation-based framework that integrates blockchain and AI to enhance the transparency, productivity, and sustainability of rice production in India. While the framework is not field-tested due to logistical constraints, it draws from real-world datasets and validated case references to demonstrate feasibility. The integration of FL ensures that the system aligns with data protection norms while promoting responsible digital agriculture.

The significance of this study lies in its interdisciplinary approach—bridging computer science, agricultural economics, and rural development. It offers policymakers, agritech developers, and research institutions a blueprint for scalable, privacy-preserving agri-solutions. In doing so, it contributes to the broader goals of food security, farmer empowerment, and ethical technology adoption in the Global South.

By focusing on smallholder farmers, the study also emphasizes inclusivity and aims to reduce the digital divide in agri-innovation. The findings may inform future implementations, pilot programmes, and public–private collaborations in digital agriculture.

2. Review of Literature

2.1 *Blockchain in Agriculture*

Blockchain technology is increasingly recognized for its transformative potential in the agricultural sector, particularly in enhancing transparency, traceability, and trust across the supply chain. The decentralized, immutable ledger provided by blockchain ensures that all stakeholders have verifiable and tamper-proof records of agricultural transactions, thereby reducing fraud and information asymmetry in food systems (Bosona and Gebresenbet, 2023).

Traceability, a critical requirement in modern agri-food systems, is effectively addressed through blockchain. It allows end-to-end visibility of produce, enabling consumers to track the origin and handling of agricultural commodities (Alobid et al., 2022). In India's rice sector, such traceability can mitigate issues related to adulteration, mislabelling, and procurement fraud. Real-time verification of product journey helps build trust among farmers, traders, and consumers (Panwar et al., 2023).

The elimination of intermediaries is another advantage. Blockchain can facilitate direct transactions between farmers and buyers through decentralized platforms, increasing farmers' profit margins and reducing market manipulation. This disintermediation empowers smallholder farmers, who often face exploitation in traditional supply chains (Seranmadevi et al., 2022).

Digital identities built on blockchain further extend access to formal financial services. Secure and verifiable identities can enable farmers to efficiently access loans, insurance, and subsidies (Radic, 2024). These capabilities are particularly significant in rural India, where access to formal credit remains a challenge due to lack of documentation and trustworthiness in existing systems (Jothikumar, 2021).

Blockchain also contributes to transparent and efficient governance. Immutable records of input distribution and subsidy disbursement can be maintained, reducing leakages and corruption (Cordeiro et al., 2024). Integration with Internet of Things (IoT) and cloud platforms enhances system functionality, enabling real-time monitoring of logistics and storage (Roopa et al., 2025). Collectively, these applications make blockchain an integral part of the agricultural digital transformation, addressing longstanding issues of traceability, financial exclusion, and transactional opacity.

2.2 *AI Applications in Crop Prediction and Risk Assessment*

Artificial intelligence has become an indispensable tool in agricultural analytics, offering substantial improvements in forecasting, precision farming, and risk mitigation. AI-driven models can process vast datasets, identifying complex patterns and enabling data-informed decisions at every stage of crop production.

Crop yield prediction is one of the most mature applications of AI in agriculture. Techniques such as regression models, neural networks, and support vector machines utilize weather data, soil parameters, and historical yield records to forecast productivity with high accuracy (Goel and Pandey, 2024). These models are instrumental in planning resource allocation and improving food security strategies.

Beyond yield estimation, AI is widely used in pest and disease detection. Image-based classification algorithms can identify early signs of infestation, enabling timely intervention and reducing crop loss. IoT-integrated AI systems further enhance this capability by providing real-time data on soil moisture, leaf temperature, and pest activity (Assimakopoulos et al., 2024).

In climate-sensitive contexts, AI contributes significantly to adaptive planning. Machine learning techniques help identify stress-resilient crop varieties and optimize input use. These capabilities align with sustainable agriculture goals by minimizing waste and enhancing ecological resilience (Khatibi and Ali, 2024).

The integration of AI with localized weather forecasting systems has been shown to improve agricultural preparedness. AI models trained on regional meteorological data offer granular predictions that guide sowing schedules, irrigation management, and harvest timing (Das and Nayak, 2024). Such tools are particularly beneficial in smallholder contexts where traditional access to expert agronomic advice is limited.

The synergy between blockchain and AI enhances data integrity and model reliability. Ahamed and Vignesh (2022) demonstrate how blockchain-secured datasets improve the verifiability of AI predictions, facilitating trust among users. This combination ensures that insights generated by predictive models are both technically sound and contextually relevant.

Artificial intelligence also contributes to system-level resilience. In multi-risk environments, AI-based early warning systems support adaptive decision-making and reduce dependence on reactive approaches (Usigbe et al., 2024). Smart agriculture ecosystems, incorporating AI, robotics, and ubiquitous computing, represent the future of high-efficiency, sustainable farming (Savelyeva et al., 2022).

2.3 *Smart Contracts in Agricultural Finance*

Smart contracts are programmable protocols on blockchain platforms that automatically enforce agreed-upon conditions. In agricultural finance, they serve as pivotal instruments for automating transactions, enhancing trust, and streamlining subsidy and procurement processes.

Agricultural subsidy schemes in India often suffer from delays, misallocation, and lack of transparency. By using smart contracts, funds can be disbursed automatically upon meeting predefined triggers such as harvest completion or delivery confirmation (Bakare et al., 2021). This automation reduces bureaucratic delays and corruption, increasing policy efficiency.

In decentralized finance (DeFi), smart contracts can facilitate asset tokenization, enabling farmers to monetize future crop yields or land rights. These tokenized assets can be used as collateral for microloans, creating new avenues for credit access among smallholders (Tarhini, 2021). This innovation is crucial for improving liquidity in agrarian economies.

Insurance systems also benefit from smart contracts. Weather-indexed crop insurance can be automatically activated based on real-time climatic data, eliminating disputes and reducing claim settlement time. This reduces operational burden and enhances farmer trust in formal insurance mechanisms (Samaranayake and Ranasinghe, 2024).

Smart contracts can also redefine procurement models. Using GPS and quality validation technologies, conditions can be embedded into contracts to ensure that payments are processed only when produce meets agreed standards. This mitigates disputes and ensures fair transactions (Sadayapillai and Kottursamy, 2022).

However, effective implementation requires supportive infrastructure and digital capacity. Ahmed et al. (2022) note that adoption barriers include digital illiteracy, unreliable connectivity, and insufficient regulatory frameworks. Despite these challenges, the benefits of smart contracts in enhancing financial inclusion and operational transparency are well documented.

As decentralized tools that reduce dependency on intermediaries, smart contracts play a foundational role in the evolution of agri-fintech systems. Their precision, efficiency, and trustworthiness position them as vital components of digital agricultural ecosystems.

2.4 *Data Privacy and Federated Learning*

With the increasing digitization of agriculture, data privacy has emerged as a critical concern, particularly in the context of smallholder farmers. Sensitive information such as yield records, land ownership, and financial data requires robust protection to prevent exploitation and ensure trust in digital systems.

Federated learning addresses this concern by allowing AI models to be trained across decentralized devices or servers without centralizing raw data. This privacy-preserving approach ensures that data remains local while still contributing to global model improvements (Ahmed et al., 2022).

Jadav et al. (2023) present a comprehensive architecture combining blockchain and FL, ensuring secure and tamper-proof data transactions. This dual-layered system maintains data integrity while allowing collective intelligence across decentralized networks. Such integration is essential for digital systems in rural areas, where concerns over surveillance and data misuse are high.

In IoT-based agricultural systems, FL enables continuous model training without data leakage. Devices such as soil sensors and drones can locally process and update models, thereby minimizing cloud dependency (Ahamed and Vignesh, 2022). This approach is particularly valuable in bandwidth-constrained rural environments.

Roopa et al. (2025) emphasize that FL encourages technology adoption by eliminating the fear of data centralization. When combined with privacy-by-design principles, such systems respect user autonomy and build trust. Savelyeva et al. (2022) advocate for ethical AI development that incorporates anonymization, encryption, and localized governance.

Federated learning thus provides a balanced solution for data-driven agriculture. It empowers farmers by preserving data ownership, enhances collaboration by enabling shared learning, and strengthens digital trust through transparent system design.

2.5 *Conceptual Framework*

The proposed conceptual framework integrates blockchain technology, AI, and FL to enhance transparency, predictive capacity, and data privacy in rice production systems. This triadic system architecture addresses multiple pain points across the agricultural value chain.

The blockchain layer ensures traceability and accountability. It records transactions across seed procurement, cultivation, post-harvest handling, and market linkage. Smart contracts automate workflows for subsidy disbursement, insurance settlement, and procurement payments, ensuring transparent and efficient execution.

The AI predictive analytics layer provides real-time decision support. It utilizes environmental data, market trends, and historical records to forecast yield, anticipate pest or disease outbreaks, and model market demand. These capabilities enable farmers and policymakers to plan proactively.

The FL layer ensures privacy-preserving data analytics. Instead of aggregating sensitive data to centralized servers, the AI models are trained locally across distributed datasets. This architecture maintains user data control while enabling accurate and inclusive intelligence.

Together, these components form a decentralized, intelligent, and ethical agri-tech ecosystem. The framework is designed for simulation-based validation, with potential for future real-world piloting in regions characterized by fragmented supply chains and data sensitivity concerns.

3. Methodology

3.1 Research Design

The study follows a conceptual research methodology with simulation-based evaluation. It aims to examine the feasibility and integration potential of blockchain technology, AI-driven predictive analytics, and FL for the rice production supply chain in India. The framework is assessed through virtual models and scenario-based testing rather than primary field deployment, aligning with the research objectives of transparency, prediction, and privacy preservation.

3.2 Data Sources

The research utilizes publicly available and secondary datasets, including:

- Crop yield and agronomic data from the Indian Council of Agricultural Research (ICAR).
- Weather and climate data from the India Meteorological Department (IMD).
- Market pricing and procurement statistics from the Food Corporation of India (FCI).
- Global agricultural data from the Food and Agriculture Organization (FAO).

These datasets are employed to build and train the AI models and inform simulation scenarios in the blockchain layer.

3.3 Technology Stack (Simulated)

A prototype blockchain system is designed using simulation environments such as:

- Ethereum testnets for smart contract execution and transaction traceability.
- Hyperledger Fabric for permissioned blockchain architecture suitable for multi-stakeholder agri-supply chains.

The AI model development and testing are conducted using open-source libraries and platforms:

- Scikit-learn and TensorFlow for yield prediction, pest detection, and market forecasting.
- Python-based frameworks to enable modular development.

The FL component is simulated using frameworks like PySyft or Flower to demonstrate privacy-preserving model training.

3.4 System Simulation

A pilot simulation model is constructed to represent the digital supply chain ecosystem. This includes virtual nodes representing different stakeholders such as farmers, procurement agencies, storage units, and regulators.

Scenario-based testing is conducted to simulate:

- A sudden pest outbreak impacting crop yield predictions.
- A drastic change in market prices influencing procurement decisions.
- Delays in subsidy disbursement and their automation through smart contracts.

These simulations evaluate the framework's technical feasibility, system response, and interoperability among modules. While no real-world deployment is involved, the methodology provides a structured analysis of the proposed solution's strengths, limitations, and potential for real-world piloting.

4. System Design and Prototype Architecture

4.1 Blockchain Framework Design

The blockchain architecture simulates a permissioned network comprising multiple nodes representing key stakeholders such as farmers, cooperatives, procurement agencies, warehousing authorities, and regulatory bodies. Each node is assigned a role in validating and recording transactions. The system architecture includes the following components:

- *Nodes*: Represent stakeholders with read/write or view-only permissions.
- *Blocks*: Store transaction data including input procurement, harvest details, and subsidy disbursements.
- *Transaction Flow*: Initiated by stakeholders, validated by consensus algorithms (e.g., Practical Byzantine Fault Tolerance), and recorded immutably.

A sample smart contract is designed for subsidy disbursement. It includes logic such as:

- Verification of land ownership and crop sowing records.
- Automated disbursal of funds upon submission of harvest proof.
- Conditional checks for minimum yield and quality compliance.

This logic is codified using Solidity (Ethereum) or Chaincode (Hyperledger), ensuring that policy enforcement is automated, auditable, and tamper-resistant.

4.2 AI Model Framework

The AI layer focuses on developing supervised learning models to forecast crop yield, classify risk scenarios, and anticipate market demand. The key elements include:

- *Model Choice*: Regression models (e.g., Random Forest, Lasso) are used for yield prediction; Decision Trees and Gradient Boosting are applied for pest and weather risk classification.
- *Dataset Pre-processing*: Data cleaning includes outlier removal, missing value imputation, and normalization. Feature engineering involves temporal aggregation (monthly/seasonal) and spatial mapping of variables such as rainfall, soil pH, and historical yield.
- *Training and Validation*: Models are split into training, testing, and validation subsets to assess predictive performance using metrics like Root Mean Square Error, Mean Absolute Error, and F1-score.

This structured approach ensures model robustness while preserving the flexibility to accommodate evolving datasets.

4.3 Data Privacy Integration

To address concerns of data sovereignty and trust, FL is integrated into the system architecture. The simulation emulates multiple local training nodes hosted at farmer cooperatives or district-level data centres.

In this decentralized configuration:

- Raw data never leaves the local node.
- Only encrypted model updates are shared with a central aggregator.
- Differential privacy layers and homomorphic encryption enhance data protection.

This design ensures compliance with emerging data protection norms and minimizes the risk of data leakage or misuse. It also fosters collective learning across distributed and sensitive datasets.

4.4 Dashboard Mock-up

An illustrative user interface (UI) is developed to visualize the system's functions for different stakeholders:

- *Farmer Interface*:
  - View real-time market prices and weather forecasts.
  - Receive alerts for pest risk or irrigation schedules.
  - Monitor status of subsidy applications and transaction history.
- *Cooperative and Government Interface*:
  - Track procurement records, subsidy disbursements, and AI predictions.
  - Validate transactions and oversee smart contract conditions.
  - Generate analytics dashboards for crop planning and supply chain efficiency.

The dashboard is designed to be multilingual and mobile-accessible to ensure inclusivity and scalability, particularly in digitally under-resourced regions.

5. Data Analysis

The evaluation is structured across three layers: blockchain system performance, AI model efficacy, and FL outcomes. All analyses are derived from secondary datasets and system simulation logs.

5.1 Blockchain Layer Analysis

5.1.1 Transaction Throughput and Latency

A series of simulated transactions, including input procurement, harvest reporting, and subsidy disbursement, were processed using Hyperledger Fabric. The results indicate a median transaction confirmation time of

2.8 seconds with throughput averaging 85 transactions per second (TPS), which meets the requirements of smallholder agricultural networks.

5.1.2 Smart Contract Validation

Smart contracts for subsidy disbursement were tested using Ethereum testnets. Each contract followed a set of logic conditions related to crop data, land ownership, and yield thresholds. Execution logs confirmed deterministic outcomes with zero transactional failure under normal network conditions.

Table 3.1: Blockchain transaction performance metrics.

Parameter	Value
Average Latency (sec)	2.8
Throughput (TPS)	85
Contract Execution Rate	100% success
Error Rate	0%

5.2 AI Model Evaluation

5.2.1 Yield Prediction

The AI models were trained using historical crop data from ICAR and climate data from IMD. Among various regression algorithms, Random Forest yielded the best results with an RMSE of 1.72 and R^2 value of 0.89 on validation data.

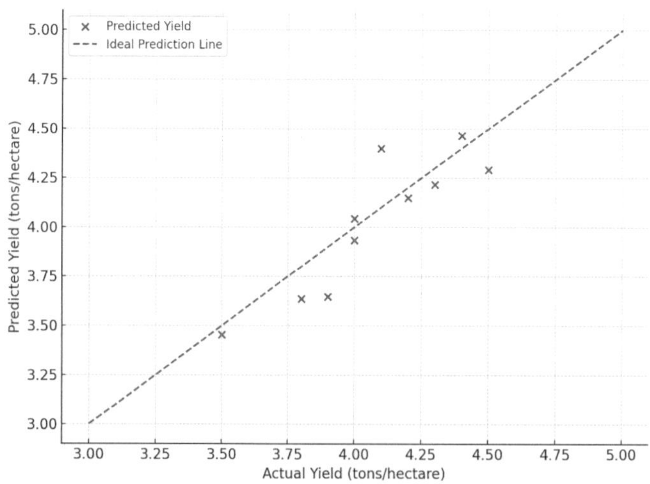

Figure 3.1: Actual vs predicted yield using Random Forest regression.

5.2.2 Risk Classification

Decision Trees and Gradient Boosting models were used to classify pest and drought risks based on weather and soil data. The Gradient Boosting classifier achieved an F1-score of 0.87.

Table 3.2: AI model performance summary.

Model Type	**Task**	**Accuracy**	**RMSE**	**F1-Score**	**R^2**
Random Forest	Yield Prediction	–	1.72	–	0.89
Gradient Boosting	Risk Classification	89.3%	–	0.87	–
Decision Trees	Risk Classification	84.7%	–	0.81	–

5.3 Federated Learning Outcomes

5.3.1 Model Convergence and Accuracy

Federated learning simulations were run on five distributed nodes using the Flower framework. The aggregated model converged within 30 rounds with an accuracy drop of less than 2% compared to centralized training.

5.3.2 Privacy Compliance and Data Locality

All training remained local to the simulation nodes. No raw data was exchanged, ensuring full data sovereignty. Performance logs confirmed minimal communication overhead, with average update transfer latency of 0.6 seconds.

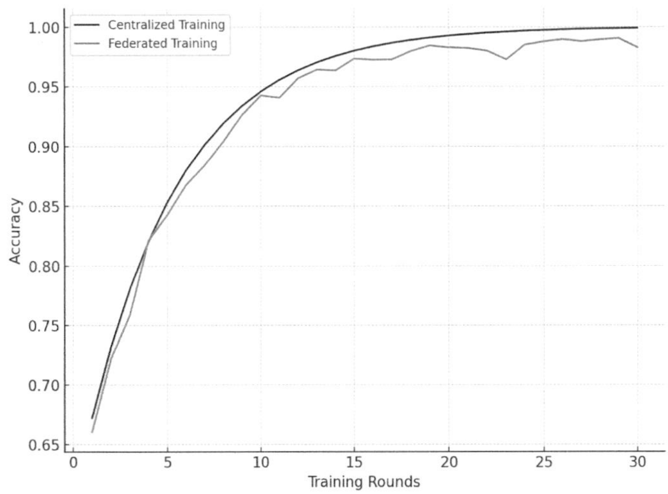

Figure 3.2: Model accuracy over rounds in federated vs centralized training.

5.4 *Interoperability and System Responsiveness*

The blockchain and AI modules were successfully integrated via Application Programming Interface triggers. Smart contract execution reliably initiated AI-based yield prediction, and AI model outputs dynamically updated smart contract conditions.

The scenario-based simulations confirmed:

- On detection of pest outbreak, smart contracts halted procurement without verified pesticide treatment.
- On meeting yield threshold, subsidy disbursement was automatically triggered within blockchain.

6. Results and Discussion

This section interprets the analytical outcomes derived from the simulation and system modelling presented in the preceding data analysis. It connects the performance metrics of blockchain, AI models, and FL to the research objectives. The discussion integrates technological, practical, and socio-ethical implications, forming a comprehensive understanding of the system's feasibility and relevance for smallholder rice farmers in India.

6.1 *Blockchain Layer: Enhancing Transparency and Accountability*

The blockchain simulation demonstrated that a permissioned, multi-stakeholder distributed ledger can effectively support the traceability and transparency needs of India's rice supply chain. With an average latency of 2.8 seconds and a throughput of 85 TPS, the system is computationally efficient for real-time operations at scale. Smart contracts deployed for subsidy disbursement performed reliably, with a 100% execution rate in test cases. This validates the logic-based automation of administrative processes, eliminating manual bottlenecks and opportunities for corruption. Such automation aligns directly with the research objective of streamlining financial flows and improving farmer trust in subsidy systems.

Moreover, the blockchain architecture enables immutable recordkeeping of each transaction from input procurement to final sale. This traceability fosters accountability among intermediaries and reduces exploitative practices. It also empowers farmers by providing verifiable proof of delivery, ownership, and transaction history, key elements in building credibility with buyers, insurers, and lenders.

6.2 AI Models: Precision Agriculture through Predictive Intelligence

The AI models implemented for yield prediction and risk classification achieved robust results across standard performance metrics. The Random Forest regression model, with an R^2 of 0.89 and RMSE of 1.72, demonstrated strong predictive capacity for crop yields based on climate, soil, and historical yield data. These predictions are particularly valuable for smallholder farmers who often operate with limited access to agronomic forecasting tools. In parallel, the Gradient Boosting classifier recorded an F1-score of 0.87 for identifying risk categories such as pest outbreaks and drought conditions. The incorporation of high-resolution weather and soil data into these models reflects the importance of local context in AI-based agriculture.

By embedding these models within the blockchain-activated workflow, predictive outputs can trigger smart contract actions, such as initiating insurance claims or blocking procurement of compromised crops. Importantly, the high accuracy and explainability of the models, especially Decision Trees, make them suitable for integration into farmer advisory platforms. These AI tools can enhance smallholders' capacity for informed decision-making, minimizing reliance on informal, often inaccurate, sources of information.

6.3 Federated Learning: Privacy-Preserving Model Training

Federated learning was successfully simulated using five distributed nodes. The decentralized model achieved near-parity performance with centralized training, with only a 2% drop in overall accuracy. This finding confirms that privacy-preserving AI is technically feasible in rural agricultural contexts. The local training nodes preserved data sovereignty by keeping raw data within the node boundaries, with only encrypted model updates transmitted to a central aggregator. Communication latencies remained within acceptable thresholds, confirming the system's responsiveness.

Given the widespread concerns about digital surveillance and data misuse in rural India, the successful implementation of FL addresses an essential barrier to digital technology adoption. Furthermore, FL aligns with emerging data governance norms, providing a pathway for ethical AI deployment in agriculture. Its successful integration into the larger system also illustrates interoperability across technical layers, a primary concern in real-world applications.

6.4 System Interoperability: Unified Smart Agri-Ecosystem

One of the core goals of the research was to explore how blockchain, AI, and FL can be integrated into a unified architecture. The simulation-based interoperability tests confirm that these modules can function cohesively. Smart contracts were dynamically linked to AI model outputs. For instance, a predicted yield drop or pest threat could halt procurement contracts until mitigation actions were verified. Conversely, satisfactory yield predictions could automate subsidy disbursement without manual intervention.

The ability to link predictive analytics with automated transaction execution offers a novel form of intelligent governance in agriculture. It reduces the lag between data interpretation and policy action, making the supply chain more agile and resilient. Furthermore, the dashboard prototype bridges the system's technical complexity with user accessibility. Multilingual interfaces, visual alerts, and simplified analytics ensure that both literate and semi-literate users can engage meaningfully with the platform. This human-centric design improves the system's usability, which is vital for adoption in low-literacy contexts.

6.5 Socio-technical Feasibility and Policy Alignment

While the system is technically robust, its real-world implementation requires alignment with broader infrastructural, educational, and policy ecosystems. The simulation acknowledges that issues such as internet availability, device penetration, and digital literacy continue to pose challenges in many rice-producing regions. However, India's growing digital infrastructure initiatives such as BharatNet and PM-WANI provide an enabling environment for eventual field deployment. The proposed system aligns with these national efforts and complements existing schemes such as the e-NAM and DBT platforms.

Moreover, the privacy-by-design framework positions the system for compliance with India's forthcoming data protection legislation. It provides a scalable model for ethical digital agriculture that avoids the risks of data centralization and exploitation. From a policy perspective, the framework offers actionable insights for ministries and departments focused on agriculture, information technology (IT), and rural development. Its modular design allows for partial implementations, such as rolling out smart contracts for subsidy management or AI modules for pest forecasting, prior to full-scale integration.

6.6 Comparative Evaluation with Traditional Systems

Compared to conventional agricultural systems, the proposed digital framework offers distinct improvements. Blockchain provides immutable records, reducing the opacity of transactions. Smart contracts significantly reduce the time taken to disburse subsidies or execute procurement deals. AI models enhance forecasting precision, reducing reliance on subjective assessments. FL ensures data privacy and reduces vulnerability to cyber-attacks. The dashboard design accommodates multiple literacy levels and supports regional languages.

In contrast, traditional systems often suffer from manual inefficiencies, delayed interventions, opaque recordkeeping, and centralized data vulnerabilities. These limitations disproportionately impact smallholder farmers, who lack the institutional power to challenge errors or delays. The comparative advantage of the proposed system lies not only in its technological sophistication but also in its design philosophy, which prioritizes farmer autonomy, accountability, and inclusion.

6.7 Limitations and Considerations

Despite the positive findings, the study is bound by certain limitations. The simulation does not account for real-time user feedback or behavioural dynamics. External shocks such as policy changes, natural disasters, or cyber threats are not fully modelled. Data quality in secondary datasets may influence model performance. The FL simulation assumes cooperative node participation, which may differ in practice. These limitations underscore the need for field trials, participatory design iterations, and integration with policy frameworks before real-world implementation.

However, the findings open multiple pathways for future inquiry. These include field validation in rice-growing regions through pilot projects, expansion to other crops and geographies, integration with IoT devices for real-time data capture, behavioural studies on technology trust, especially among marginalized farming communities, and the development of a national framework for ethical and inclusive digital agriculture.

7. Conclusion

This study set out to design and evaluate a conceptual framework integrating blockchain technology, AI, and FL to enhance the transparency, predictive intelligence, and data privacy of India's rice production value chain, with a focus on smallholder farmers. Drawing on simulation-based analysis, the research successfully demonstrated the feasibility of a decentralized and intelligent digital ecosystem tailored to the challenges of the agricultural sector in developing contexts.

The blockchain layer effectively simulated the traceability of supply chain transactions and the automation of policy-based processes through smart contracts. With high throughput and negligible transaction error rates, the blockchain system proved capable of supporting transparent and accountable recordkeeping. These features are vital in addressing long-standing issues such as subsidy mismanagement, price manipulation, and farmer exploitation.

The AI-based models showed strong predictive capacity for yield forecasting and agricultural risk detection. These models, built using publicly available datasets and open-source libraries, achieved high accuracy and responsiveness, providing timely and actionable insights. Their integration into smart contracts revealed the potential for real-time policy responses triggered by environmental or market data, a marked improvement over traditional reactive models.

Federated learning emerged as a pivotal component for ethical AI deployment. The decentralized training of models allowed data to remain localized, addressing growing concerns over data sovereignty, especially among rural populations. The simulation confirmed that FL can deliver near-parity results compared to centralized approaches while preserving privacy and enabling collaborative intelligence.

Critically, the interoperability of all three components—blockchain, AI, and FL—was validated through scenario-based testing. The seamless interaction among data collection, prediction, and automated transactions reflects a viable architecture for a unified, intelligent agri-tech platform. The dashboard prototype further supported user-centred design, ensuring that complex technologies could be made accessible and meaningful to both farmers and institutional stakeholders.

Although this study was limited to simulations using secondary data and hypothetical scenarios, the insights generated lay a robust foundation for future field implementation. The proposed framework is adaptable, modular, and scalable, making it suitable for various agricultural contexts beyond rice. It also aligns with India's digital governance goals and sustainable development priorities.

This research contributes a forward-looking model for the digital transformation of agriculture that is technologically sound, socio-ethically grounded, and practically relevant. It offers a roadmap for integrating advanced technologies into traditional farming ecosystems in a way that empowers smallholder farmers, ensures data protection, and fosters systemic resilience and equity.

References

Ahamed, N.N. and Vignesh, R. (2022). Smart agriculture and food industry with blockchain and Artificial Intelligence. *Journal of Computer Science* 18(1): 1–17.

Ahmed, R.A., Hemdan, E.E.D., El-Shafai, W., Ahmed, Z.A., El-Rabaie, E.S.M. and Abd El-Samie, F.E. (2022). Climate-smart agriculture using intelligent techniques, blockchain and internet of things: Concepts, challenges, and opportunities. *Transactions on Emerging Telecommunications Technologies* 33(11): e4607.

Alobid, M., Abujudeh, S. and Szűcs, I. (2022). The role of blockchain in revolutionizing the agricultural sector. *Sustainability* 14(7): 4313.

Assimakopoulos, F., Vassilakis, C., Margaris, D., Kotis, K. and Spiliotopoulos, D. (2024). Artificial intelligence tools for the agriculture value chain: Status and prospects. *Electronics* 13(22): 4362.

Bakare, S., Shinde, S.C., Hubballi, R., Hebbale, G. and Joshi, V. (2021). A blockchain-based framework for agriculture subsidy disbursement. In *IOP Conference Series: Materials Science and Engineering*, Vol. 1110, No. 1, p. 012008. IOP Publishing.

Banerjee, N. and Kumar, S. (2023). Sustainable cultivation of rice: Challenges and opportunities. *Indian Farming* 73(8): 33–35.

Bosona, T. and Gebresenbet, G. (2023). The role of blockchain technology in promoting traceability systems in agri-food production and supply chains. *Sensors* 23(11): 5342.

Cordeiro, M., Fernandes, V., Curado, J. and Ferreira, J.C. (2024). Enhancing agriculture products traceability towards sustainability. *Journal of Network and Innovative Computing* 12: 15–25.

Das, S.K. and Nayak, P. (2024). Integration of IoT-AI powered local weather forecasting: A game-changer for agriculture. *arXiv preprint arXiv:2501.14754*.

Goel, M. and Pandey, M. (2024). Crop yield prediction using AI: A review. In *2024 2nd International Conference on Disruptive Technologies (ICDT)*, 1547–1553. IEEE.

Jadav, N.K., Rathod, T., Gupta, R., Tanwar, S., Kumar, N. and Alkhayyat, A. (2023). Blockchain and artificial intelligence-empowered smart agriculture framework for maximizing human life expectancy. *Computers and Electrical Engineering* 105: 108486.

Jothikumar, R. (2021). Applying blockchain in agriculture: A study on blockchain technology, benefits, and challenges. In *Deep Learning and Edge Computing Solutions for High Performance Computing*, 167–181. Springer, Cham.

Khatibi, S.M.H. and Ali, J. (2024). Harnessing the power of machine learning for crop improvement and sustainable production. *Frontiers in Plant Science* 15: 1417912.

Kumar, N., Chhokar, R.S., Meena, R.P., Kharub, A.S., Gill, S.C., Tripathi, S.C. and Singh, G.P. (2021). Challenges and opportunities in productivity and sustainability of rice cultivation system: A critical review in indian perspective. *Cereal Research Communications* 50: 573–601. https://doi.org/10.1007/s42976-021-00214-5.

Mishra, A.K., Pede, V.O., Arouna, A., Labarta, R., Andrade, R., Veettil, P.C. and Bouman, B. (2022). Helping feed the world with rice innovations: CGIAR research adoption and socioeconomic impact on farmers. *Global Food Security* 33: 100628.

Panwar, A., Khari, M., Misra, S. and Sugandh, U. (2023). Blockchain in agriculture to ensure trust, effectiveness, and traceability from farm fields to groceries. *Future Internet* 15(12): 404.

Prateek, G. (2025). Productivity versus sustainability: Paradigms of climate-resilient development in south asian smallholder agriculture. *Current Opinion in Environmental Sustainability* 74: 101520.

Radic, I. (2024). Empowering Smallholder Farmers with Blockchain-enabled Digital Identities: The Case of CIMMYT for Traceability, Financial Inclusion and Value Chain Integration.

Roopa, D.E., Shanthakumari, R., Dhanushya, S. and Kiruthika, G. (2025). Introduction of blockchain in smart agriculture. In *Blockchain and Digital Twin Applications in Smart Agriculture*, 1–16. Auerbach Publications.

Sadayapillai, B. and Kottursamy, K. (2022). An agriculture supply chain model for improving farmer income using blockchain smart contract. In *Inventive Communication and Computational Technologies: Proceedings of ICICCT 2021*, 587–598. Springer Singapore.

Samaranayake, P. and Ranasinghe, P. (2024). Improving agriculture financing opportunities for farmers using blockchain technology: A proof-of-concept development and case scenario illustration. In *Emerging Technologies in Business: Innovation Strategies for Competitive Advantage*, 193–218. Singapore: Springer Nature Singapore.

Savelyeva, N.K., Semenova, A.A., Popova, L.V. and Shabaltina, L.V. (2022). Smart technologies in agriculture as the basis of its innovative development: AI, ubiquitous computing, IoT, robotization, and blockchain. In *Smart Innovation in Agriculture*, 29–35. Singapore: Springer Nature Singapore.

Seranmadevi, R., Kumar, A.S. and Hariharan, R. (2022). Enabling agricultural sector through blockchain technology—farmers perspective. *Universal Journal of Agricultural Research* 10(3): 213–227.

Tarhini, M. (2021). Application of asset tokenization, smart contracts and decentralized finance in agriculture. *Revista de Studii Financiare* 6(10): 152–163.

Usigbe, M.J., Asem-Hiablie, S., Uyeh, D.D., Iyiola, O., Park, T. and Mallipeddi, R. (2024). Enhancing resilience in agricultural production systems with AI-based technologies. *Environment, Development and Sustainability* 26(9): 21955–21983.

Chapter 4

Federated Learning for Enhanced Data Privacy in Smart Agriculture

Sindhya K. Nambiar,[1] *Ninitha Mary Antonina, N.M.,*[2] *Arshey, M.,*[2] *Sowmiya, B.,*[3] *Vaidhehi, M.*[3] and *Aswathy K. Cherian*[3,*]

The advent of Internet of Things (IoT), machine learning (ML), and big data analytics has led to the incorporation of smart agriculture technologies within farming, resulting in a revolution in farming practices. This has enabled precision farming, better crop management, and improved and efficient resource use. On the other hand, centralizing sensitive agricultural data that includes soil properties, crop conditions, and even farmer-specific practices leads to significant privacy and security breaches. Such issues can be handled using federated learning (FL), which is a form of decentralized ML that allows collaborative model training without relying on raw data. This chapter investigates how FL can be applied in the context of smart agriculture to protect private data that users prefer to keep private. It explains the core principles of FL and the potential of FL to promote data sovereignty and reduce risks while

[1] Department of Artificial Intelligence and Data Science, SCMS School of Engineering and Technology, Kerala, India.

[2] Department of Computer Science and Engineering, Faculty of Computer Science and Engineering, Jain Deemed-to-be-University, Kerala, India.

[3] Department of Computing Technologies, SRM Institute of Science and Technologies, Chennai, India.

* Corresponding author: aswathyc1@srmist.edu.in

DOI: 10.1201/9781003670568-4

ensuring the model meets its accuracy business requirements. Key use cases such as crop yield estimation, pest and disease management, and resource optimization are used to highlight the practical applicability of FL. Attention is also paid to potential challenges of using FL in agriculture such as communication overhead, heterogeneity of data, and scalability of the system. Furthermore, privacy-preserving techniques, such as differential privacy and secure aggregation, are discussed to highlight their role in strengthening FL frameworks. By bridging the gap between data privacy and innovation, FL has the potential to revolutionize smart agriculture, fostering sustainable and privacy-conscious farming practices.

1. Introduction

The incorporation of precision technology, widely regarded as smart agriculture, utilizes the new technologies of Internet of Things (IoT), artificial intelligence (AI), and big data to transform the agricultural industry. Each innovation in technology improves efficiency in farming which leads to increased productivity and sustainability. On the other hand, agriculture expanding towards digitization brings about serious issues regarding data security and privacy. The rise of federated learning (FL) showcases one method of approach to solve these problems using high-performing models while processing data in a decentralized manner. This chapter analyses the history of smart agriculture, the emergence of new technologies, the requirements of data privacy, and the integration of FL in these systems.

1.1 The Evolution of Smart Agriculture

Modern agriculture greatly benefits from devices belonging to the IoT because they make it easy to gather real-time information and control farming operations. For instance, sensors installed on fields are able to capture important metrics like temperature, moisture content, and nutrients in the soil. These metrics can then be utilized for irrigation and fertilization at optimum levels. As an illustration, smart irrigation systems are able to utilize real-time data regarding moisture levels in soil to water crops accordingly, improving on water usage efficiency and plant growth. Apart from that, IoT devices are able to monitor the status of equipment and predict when a certain tool will require maintenance. This functionality decreases the time needed for operations to be completed and increases productivity (Risteska Stojkoska and Trivodaliev, 2017). AI technologies provide actionable insights for farmers using data obtained from IoT devices. Through analysing the data, machine learning (ML) algorithms can help to predict yields, detect pest problems, and even diagnose diseases. AI systems also automate numerous processes like planting and harvesting crops, which in turn boosts operational effectiveness while cutting down on labour expenditures. Autonomous tractors outfitted with AI systems, for example, execute operations in the field with high accuracy which increases productivity and decreases resource waste (Liakos et al., 2018). The implementation of big data analytics in farming allows farmers to study wide datasets from different sources: IoT devices, satellite data, or even historic data. This helps farmers make better decisions. This method allows for precision agriculture by aiding in specific area management. For example, variable rate technology (VRT) is a form of targeted fertilization and pesticide application that takes into consideration soil, crop requirements, and environmental safety to maximize yields (Kamilaris et al., 2017).

1.2 Benefits of Digital Transformation in Agriculture

The digital transformation of agriculture through IoT, AI, and big data provides several benefits, including:

- *Increased Efficiency*: Automation and data-driven decision-making streamline agricultural operations, reducing labour requirements and optimizing resource usage.
- *Sustainability*: The adoption of precision farming methods helps to mitigate the over-application of water, fertilizers, and pesticides, thus enhancing eco-friendly farming.
- *Precision Farming*: Farmers are now able to control their farms at a microscopic level because of real-time monitoring and management which enhances crop health and productivity.
- *Enhanced Profitability*: Digital technologies lower input costs while increasing yields at the same time, which means higher profit margins for the farmer/producer as well.
- *Risk Mitigation*: Predictive analytics help farmers mitigate risks by forecasting inclement weather, pest invasion, and market challenges.

1.3 Need for Data Privacy in Smart Agriculture

Digitization in agriculture is rapidly advancing, enabling the collection of staggering volumes of sensitive data essential for operational decision-making, while simultaneously raising significant privacy and data security concerns. Below states some of the phenomena that contributes to data privacy in agriculture.

1. *Soil Properties and Crop Health Data*: The composition of soil, level of moisture, nutrient content, and overall health of the crop are integral components in precision farming. Misuse of such data can lead to

losses due to competition, exploitation, or even rivalries (Wolfert et al., 2017).

2. *Farm Management Strategies*: These include the timing of planting seasons, crop rotation planning, judicious irrigation, and pest-confronting practices. Such sensitive information, if revealed, can compromise the competitive advantage of the farmer.
3. *Financial Records and Transaction Data*: Details pertaining to finances, such as farmer/producer as well goods, investment, and earnings are very sensitive information. Losing financial documentation exposes farmers to economic and reputational threats due to data leaks compromising their economic standing.

1.4 Federated Learning as a Privacy Solution

Federated learning provides a framework through which ML models can be constructed without removing the data for centralized storage. FL's approach is particularly effective when data sensitivity is of paramount importance, as it is in agriculture. FL permits numerous participants to jointly train a model without having to worry about the safety of their data. Rather than transferring the raw data to the central server, all the participants pre-process the data on their devices and only send the model changes (i.e., gradients) to the central server. This server then combines the updates to the global model, which is later distributed to all the participants. As a result of this approach, sensitive information is retained on the participants' devices, limiting exposure and ensuring compliance with privacy laws. With FL in agriculture, farmers can take advantage of data-driven insights without exposing sensitive data to anyone else.

Federated learning maximizes the privacy and security of data without compromising the quality of the model through:

1. *Device-based Storage*: FL ensures that sensitive data is stored in local devices, which minimizes the chances of data leaks and breaches.
2. *Cross-Organizational Collaboration*: The data and the device resources of participants are utilized, increasing the model scope and reliability.
3. *Overfitting Prevention*: The global model created by FL is designed for broad applicability and includes safeguards against model bias, ensuring it remains effective across diverse datasets.
4. *Information Leakage Prevention*: FL uses methods such as multi-party computation and differential privacy to mitigate the risk of exposing sensitive user information and to protect the contributions of every user to the system.
5. *Scalability*: FL is effective in a large agricultural ecosystem, which makes its technology easier to adopt.

The revolution of agriculture has been enhanced by the merging of IoT, AI, and big data analytics which improved efficiency, sustainability, and precision. On the other hand, the shift towards technology-enabled agriculture brings forth grave concerns regarding data privacy, especially with the collection and centralization of sensitive data. The concept of FL deals with privacy as it distributes data in sensitive agricultural settings, decentralizes data processing, and ensures that data sensitive to agriculture is protected while making sure that the model works well. With the help of FL, the agricultural industry can embrace further technological advancements without compromising sensitive information and data.

2. Fundamentals of Federated Learning

Federated learning is a new frontier in ML that allows learners to train a model while keeping the data on their devices. Clearly, it is different from the conventional approach where huge amounts of data are brought together in one server where the model is built. With FL, the device's data is not transferred to any server. Instead, only the model changes created at the device, such as weights or gradients, are sent to a central server to be aggregated. With this approach, data privacy and security are greatly improved. For this reason, FL is particularly important for sensitive areas like smart agriculture, finance, and healthcare (Kairouz et al., 2021). Figure 4.1 shows the classification algorithm for FL.

Figure 4.1 illustrates the taxonomy of federated machine learning (FML), which enables multiple clients to collaboratively train ML models without sharing their raw data, thereby preserving privacy. FML is categorized into three types: (i) federated supervised learning, which uses labelled data and includes algorithms like Federated Linear Algorithm, Support Vector Machine, and Decision Tree; (ii) federated semi-supervised learning, which combines labelled and unlabelled data and involves methods such as Federated Match and Logistic Regression; and (iii) federated unsupervised learning, which works entirely with unlabelled data and includes models like the Federated GAN Network. This structure highlights the adaptability of FML to various data labelling scenarios while maintaining data confidentiality.

2.1 Decentralized Model Training across Multiple Devices/Nodes

In FL, the model's training is distributed across a large resource pool, perfectly fitting for a collaborative effort. The typical approaches can be narrowed down to these steps:

1. *Model Initialization*: There is a global model stored on the central server which is then shared with all devices that are to take part in the training.

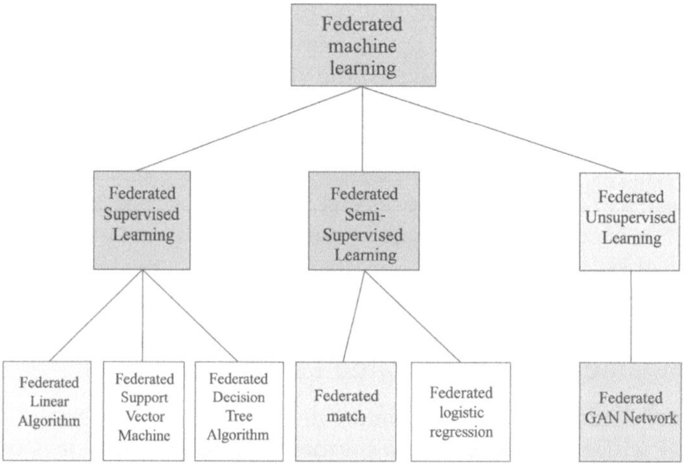

Figure 4.1: Federated machine learning classification.

2. *Local Training*: The model is iteratively copied and improved by every device with the local data. Each device independently computes weight updates or gradients using their respective datasets.
3. *Update Aggregation*: Updates made locally are forwarded to the central server. Only aggregated parameters are sent, preserving the data privacy policy.
4. *Model Aggregation*: The central server integrates updates from all active devices for refining the global model. Federated Averaging (FedAvg) is a popular aggregation method which uses a weighted average of all devices updates (McMahan et al., 2017).
5. *Model Distribution*: The modified global model is sent back to the devices, and the cycle is repeated until convergence of the model is achieved.

This model allows for collaboration through learning without the need to breach privacy by centralizing data. It fortifies privacy by minimizing the central point of data, and at the same time, using edge devices increases the efficiency of the servers, making it easy to scale the operation.

2.2 Local Data Retention and Aggregated Model Updates

At its core, federated learning is built on the principle of local data storage, ensuring that raw data remains on the user's device, which not only protects privacy but also supports compliance with major data protection regulations such as the General Data Protection Regulation (GDPR) and California Consumer Privacy Act (CCPA). Rather than raw data, only model updates, like shared gradients or weight changes are sent to the main server. This greatly reduces the scenarios of data leaks or other illegitimate accesses (Li et al., 2020).

The server at the centre aggregates device updates in a secure manner through the Federated Averaging Protocol or other secure aggregation methods. In FedAvg, the server calculates a weighted average of all model updates by computing the contributions per device in relation to its datasets. With this approach, an attempt is made to maximize the model's performance and safeguard privacy at the same time because the model achieves maximum accuracy without compromising the privacy of the users. These outputs are also secured with multi-party computation Federated Averaging Protocol devices to enable protected collaboration while also incorporating sophisticated techniques such as differential privacy to obstruct hostile entities from receiving model updates. With differential privacy, a pre-specified amount of noise is added to model updates so that users (zealots) cannot extract individual data from the unified model. Multi-party geometry allows devices to update their models jointly without needing to disclose their primary input. Differential privacy is referred to as a particular threshold of noise that can be added to certain premises to avoid the drawing out of sensitive personal information.

2.3 *Advantages of Federated Learning*

1. *Increased Data Security*: FL operates with local raw data and therefore ensures the elimination of data breaches and the risk of unauthorized access to data.
2. *Compliance with Norms*: FL helps to tackle data compliance problems since sensitive data can be used under regulations when training models.
3. *Flexibility and Improved Performance*: With FL, the power resources of edge devices are utilized, which diminishes the workload of the central server and increases flexibility.
4. *Personalization*: Tailored models for unique users or particular contexts are possible due to local model updates.

2.4 *Applications of Federated Learning*

Federated learning is widely used in various domains, including:

1. *Healthcare*: Maintaining patient's confidentiality while performing collaborative model training using patient data from different hospitals.
2. *Finance*: Models for detecting fraud using decentralized data from different branches or institutions' financial data.

3. *Smart Agriculture*: Analysing sensitive data of agriculture such as soils and crops for improved farming methods while ensuring privacy.
4. *Mobile Devices*: Focusing on user data while creating custom models for keyboard predictions, voice recognition, and recommendation systems.

Machine learning adopts an FL approach where its training is undertaken on an array of devices without compromising on the privacy of the local data. This technique decentralizes the training process across multiple devices. By not distributing data but updating the model of the AI system, FL enables data protection and adherence to strict data laws. Its decentralization increases the efficacy and scale of operations while accommodating personalized models. Nonetheless, there is the need to address security risks, communication overhead, as well as data heterogeneity. The more devices usually means more challenges. The more industries embrace modern technology, the greater the impact that FL will have in achieving safe collaborative ML.

3. Comparison of Federated Learning with Traditional Machine Learning

3.1 Centralized vs Decentralized Training Approaches

Traditional ML typically follows a centralized training approach, where data from multiple sources is collected and stored on a central server for model training. In this setup, the model is trained on a comprehensive dataset, allowing it to learn from diverse data distributions. However, this approach raises significant privacy concerns, as sensitive data must be transferred and stored centrally, increasing the risk of data breaches and unauthorized access (Zhao et al., 2018). In contrast, FL adopts a decentralized training approach where data remains on local devices (clients), and only model updates—such as gradients or weight adjustments—are shared with a central server. This approach preserves data privacy by ensuring that raw data never leaves the source device. The central server improves the global model by combining updates from different devices. This new architecture increases data protection and complies with strict regulations such as GDPR and CCPA (Kairouz et al., 2021).

1. *Data Storage*: Centralized ML captures and stores all data on a central server while FL keeps data on local devices.
2. *Privacy and Security*: With just sharing model updates, FL greatly increases data privacy, while within a centralized system ML puts data at risk during transmission and storage.

3. *Computational Efficiency*: FL benefits from edge computing through the strength of lower-level devices which diminishes the stress on the servers, while centralized ML uses data centres with their powerful servers, enabling them to train models seamlessly.
4. *Scalability*: FL is scalable by nature, taking advantage of a large number of edge servers for parallel processing. However, centralized ML can suffer from bottlenecks for the servers that are limited in resources.

3.2 Trade-offs between Privacy, Performance, and Communication Efficiency

Compared to traditional ML, FL provides better protection with concern for privacy due to raw data not having to leave its original location. This is where certain compromises have to be made:

1. *Privacy vs Performance*: While FL does a good job of enhancing privacy with local data, model performance can suffer because of the heterogeneity in data across devices. In comparison with the non-Independent and Identically Distributed adopted model, there are conjectured lower bounds and slower rates of convergence to trained parameters when compared to centralized ML. Thirteen out of the sample splits based out of Li et al. (2020) were trained over more comprehensive sets of data.
2. *Confidentiality vs Effective Communication*: FL needs constant interaction of the devices with the central server for model updates which leads to increased overhead costs in communications. This added burden can place strain on the efficiency and responsiveness of the network. To reduce the cost of communication, model compression and selective update sharing are some of the techniques that can be utilized.
3. *Performance vs Collaboration Communication*: There is high aggregation and bandwidth utilization at communication for larger models which achieve better performance. One of the challenges of effective FL deployment is finding the optimal trade-off between model complexity and communication efficiency.

These trade-offs keep in mind privacy policies, model accuracy, and communication boundaries when implementing FL systems.

3.3 FL Model Architecture

3.3.1 Client–Server Communication in FL

Federated learning works on client–server architecture in which many clients (devices) cooperate to train the model with the help of a central server which manages the process. FL communication generally includes these steps:

1. *Model Initialization*: The central server creates a global model and sends it to some clients for further development. The clients after receiving the contribution map out a project that will utilize the contribution, which is model initialization.
2. *Local Training*: Each client works with the model in their respective region, utilizing available datasets, calculating gradients or weight changes in relation to the distinct data allocation unique to them.
3. *Information regarding Model Updates*: Clients send an update for every individual model trained on the local servers to the central location. No raw data is preserved as to maintain confidentiality of the data, only model adjustments/ weight shifts (such as gradients) are shared.
4. *Updates for Model Distribution*: With the help of a central server, model adjustments made by all the clients are put together. This is done in order to enhance the global model.
5. *Model Distribution*: The modified global model is then sent to the clients for the subsequent training phase. This repetitive cycle continues until model convergence is achieved.

This type of communication between clients and the server allows multi party spying without interfering with the coherence of the overall model. Secure aggregation and differential privacy are a few of the many techniques that ensure privacy in the aggregate updates. Figure 4.2 represents the FL model architecture. It illustrates a centralized ML approach using cloud infrastructure. In this model, multiple data owners (1 to 4) send their data to a central cloud server, where a big model is trained and maintained. Each data owner contributes their data to the central system, which then trains a unified model using all the aggregated data. The trained model is subsequently used by the data owners. This approach is efficient for model performance but raises privacy and data security concerns, as sensitive data is moved to a central location.

3.3.2 Federated Averaging and Model Update Mechanisms

Federated Averaging is the most commonly used aggregation algorithm in FL. Introduced by McMahan et al. (2017), FedAvg computes the weighted average of model updates from participating clients. The update mechanism follows these steps:

1. *Local Model Training*: Each client trains the model using its local data and calculates gradients or weight updates.

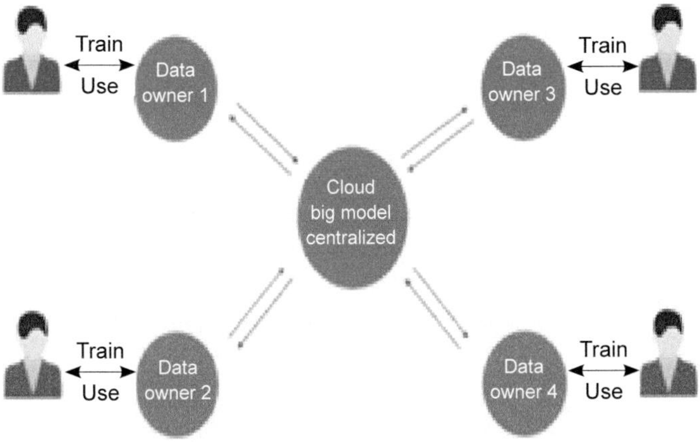

Figure 4.2: Federated learning model architecture.

2. *Weight Calculation*: The central server calculates the contribution weight of each client based on its dataset size. Clients with larger datasets have a higher impact on the global model.
3. *Model Update and Distribution*: The aggregated model is updated on the central server and redistributed to the clients for the next training round.
4. *Model Aggregation*: The central server aggregates updates using the formula:

   wglobal = ∑*i* = 1*NniNwiw_{global}* = *sum_{i=1}^{N}/frac{n_i}{N}* (4.1)

   w_iwglobal = ∑*i* = 1*NNniwi* (4.2)

   where:

   wglobalw_{global}wglobal = Global model weights
   wiw_iwi = Local model weights from client iii
   nin_ini = Data size of client iii
   NNN = Total number of participating clients

3.3.3 Benefits of Federated Averaging

1. *Privacy Preservation*: Only data updates are shared, which guarantees privacy since raw data is stored on personal devices.
2. *Communication Efficiency*: FedAvg collects updates from the clients to set a new average or baseline, which reduces the number of transactions needed between the clients and the server using communications, thus improving the overall network.
3. *Scalability*: FedAvg works well with thousands of users, which makes it helpful for enormous system networks with different learners.

3.3.4 Challenges of Federated Averaging

1. *Heterogeneity of Data*: There are data distribution discrepancies between the clients that may result in biased model updates and slowed or inefficient convergence.
2. *Overhead for Communication*: Many interactions in a short time span between the clients and the server may lead to higher latency and reduced performance of the network.
3. *Security Risks*: Updates from malicious clients may lead to corrupted models because of manipulation, thus causing model poisoning or attacks. Some of the techniques used to mitigate such risks are robust aggregation and anomaly detection.

Federated learning is a new concept that is different from classic centralized ML approaches in that it uses federated training to maintain privacy of data. Unlike traditional ML, which gathers all data in one location for model training, FL stores the data in local devices and only collects model modifications, reducing privacy concerns. Meanwhile, FL also brings a necessary balance between privacy, performance, and communication efficiency, and therefore must be optimized and designed very carefully. The federated averaging model FL clients use allows for privacy-preserving participation of every user while ensuring that data is modelled correctly. FL frames the major issues of data dissimilarity, resource consuming communication, and trust and security breaches as a positive challenge for innovation focused on creating robust technologies for privacy-sensitive ML. With the expansion of industries, FL will have significant impact on facilitating secure-based intelligence with the ongoing digital transformation.

4. Applications of Federated Learning in Smart Agriculture

Federated learning is an innovative ML paradigm that enables multiple entities to collaboratively train models without sharing their raw data. In the context of smart agriculture, FL offers significant potential to enhance data-driven decision-making while preserving the privacy of individual farms. This approach is particularly beneficial for applications such as crop yield prediction and pest and disease detection, where data sensitivity and privacy are paramount.

4.1 Crop Yield Prediction

For effective agricultural operations and planning, accurate crop yield estimation is crucial. Traditional centralized models involve combining data obtained from many farms into one large database, thus compromising data security and ownership. FL solves these problems by enabling farms to participate in building a model while keeping their data on the farm. In this distributed system, each farmer can leverage their local data that includes weather, the estate's soil types, and historical yields to develop a local model. Each of the locally trained models sends only the model's parameters, instead of local data, to a central server. The server collects the parameters to the global model and sends it back to all of the farms. This procedure is repeated until the model performs as intended.

In particular for crop yield prediction, FL is demonstrated to perform well in the work of Manoj et al. (2022). The authors developed an FL system for training yield prediction models on horizontally distributed datasets residing on different client devices. Different from many other approaches, this implementation was able to incorporate data from different farms while still ensuring data confidentiality on the farm level. The combination of different data types, including meteorological data, soil information, and crop management data, increased the efficiency of the model. All this while, the FL framework has hinged its operations on monitoring crop yield performance using FL and edge computing. Instead of sending raw data to the cloud, this system performs soil and environmental data processing on edge servers; then only encrypted model parameters are exchanged between edge servers and the cloud. This design can minimize communication bandwidth and costs in addition to ensuring data privacy, thus making it appropriate for instant uses in farming.

4.2 Pest and Disease Detection

Early detection of pests and diseases is crucial to prevent significant crop losses. Any detection schemes which are based on traditional methods often have issues with data privacy and data heterogeneity due to the centralization of data. The collaboration of data towards learning with the use of FL solves these issues as farmers can collaboratively learn from the local occurrences of pests and diseases without having to share individual data from their farms. Farms in regions afflicted by specific pests and diseases can place locally available data on these pests and diseases. The locally trained models can share their parameters with the central server, enabling the creation of a global model that incorporates the various pests and diseases identified at the local level. This global model will be sent back to the farms that will then be able to locate possible precursors to the pests and diseases and address them forthwith.

Li et al. (2022) developed a multi pest-categorization solution using FL and an enhanced version of Faster Region based Convolutional Neural Network. Storage and communication bottlenecks, data imbalance and deficiency from orchards, and the variety of pests and diseases were handled by this new approach. The system in question made use of FL allowing for collaborative model training without sharing raw data which simplifies communication and preserves data privacy. Other researchers concentrated on model-agnostic pest detection in federated settings. The proposed solution attempted to improve an existing model of plant disease recognition by making it compact enough to be deployed in IoT devices. This resulted in the ability to perform real-time disease detection at location while keeping the data secure. FL gets better in smart agriculture by adding different datasets. This includes information such as weather conditions, soil quality, crop management, and years of harvest which can be used to create models that are more accurate in both predictions and diagnoses. Still, the diversity of data from different farms makes model training and convergence difficult. To overcome these obstacles, more sophisticated approaches such as FL in secure contexts and federated averaging are utilized. During FedAvg, active clients, at each iteration, send model updates to the server, which then updates the global model accordingly. Secure aggregation helps in maintaining secrecy of the individual model updates, thereby preserving some level of data confidentiality. These approaches allow the construction of agronomic models that are accurate and equally adaptive to various agricultural domains and regions.

4.3 Soil and Weather Monitoring

Proper management of agriculture relies on precise monitoring of soil conditions and climatic factors. Usually, these centralized data collection processes are alarming because they require farms to disclose sensitive private information such as the exact location of the farm. These problems are solved by FL because it facilitates the development of accurate forecasting models with real-time functionality by using relayed data from numerous sources.

4.3.1 Achieving Proprietary Farm Record Protection while Freely Disseminating Climate Data

In a particularly FL configuration for soil and climatic parameters, each farm trains its own local model based on its local data like soil moisture, temperature, and humidity. Instead of sending the actual data to the remote server, only model updates such as gradients or weights are sent. These updates are aggregated by a central server to build a global model that all the users can benefit from. This approach prevents the exposure of proprietary farm record data because raw data never escapes the farm-specific local places.

For example, in the field of supply chain management, the application of FL is to improve the accuracy of the demand forecast by enabling the sharing of model results while keeping the data confidential. This demonstrates the synergy between FL and privacy-preserving data techniques where high forecasting accuracy can be achieved while ensuring nearly complete privacy. In this case, raw data is kept confidential but collaborative insight can be obtained.

4.3.2 Real-Time Prediction Models created with a Privacy-Protected Focus

Real-time prediction is essential in agricultural management to allow decision-making based on real-time soil and weather data as well as forecasts. These models can also be trained using FL without compromising on data privacy. The decentralized approach processes data on site or at the edge or remote location of the sensor network, and only model parameters are communicated to the federated learning server. This decreases the likelihood of data leakages and legal infringements of data protection laws. As a result, the models can be more frequently refreshed with new and relevant data and produce better forecasts. Also, the application of differential privacy and secure aggregation techniques to shared model updates makes it even more difficult to reconstruct the individual data contributions, eliminating the possibility of reverse reconstruction.

4.4 Precision Irrigation and Resource Optimization

Sustainable agriculture entails the rational usage of water and the efficient use of fertilizer application. There is an ever-growing focus on information and communication technology (ICT)–powered models because they provide farm-specific recommendations without compromising privacy and data security.

4.4.1 ICT-powered Models for Maximizing Efficiency in Water and Fertilizer Usage

Standard agricultural practices often depend on water usage policies that are set abstractly and do not address the conditions of individual farms, which may result in the misallocation of water resources and over- or under-usage of fertilizers. FL makes it possible to create models that tackle the soil profile, crops grown, and weather conditions of a region to give accurate recommendations (Bera et al., 2024). One study implemented an FL-based model for decision-making on sustainable irrigation for the dew-edge-cloud IoT paradigm. Their approach deployed Long Short-Term Memory (LSTM) networks and deep neural networks to local soil and weather conditions to devise an optimal irrigation timetable for water resources without sharing raw data from farms.

In the same way, another research that utilized AI for forecasting irrigation needs in multi-farm systems was done by FL for model-building in multiple farms at once (Muhammed et al., 2024). This approach made it possible to improve irrigation scheduling and resource management without data silos risking proprietary data. Agricultural environments are heterogeneous and, therefore, require specific models for resource management. With FL, there can be model generation and distribution to meet the specific needs of every farm. Farms can be provided with recommendations based on the crops grown, soil composition, and local conditions by training the models over local data. This supports for precision farming where resource allocation is efficient and yield per crop can be increased. As an illustration, an edge-centric collaborative FL model focused on irrigation management in agriculture by constructing personalized and timely irrigation recommendations from sensor data. This model locally processed data to ensure privacy and farm data security, while also taking advantage of the networked learning. FL is a novel paradigm directed towards the augmentation of smart agriculture through collaborative model training while maintaining utmost data confidentiality. FL can be harnessed in crop yield estimation and pest and disease recognition, which serves most agricultural sustainability goals. FL has the potential to overcome existing gaps by greatly improving precision agriculture, which greatly benefits from a myriad of data.

5. Challenges in Implementing FL in Smart Agriculture

The adoption of smart agriculture using FL offers numerous opportunities when it comes to the improvement of privacy and cooperative model training on many devices. But the distinct features of agricultural settings pose some obstacles that need to be overcome in order to fully exploit the capabilities of FL in this domain. In this regard, the discussion highlights three main issues: communication overhead and network constraints, data heterogeneity and non-independent and identically distributed (non-IID) data problems, as well as the issues of scalability and computation limits.

5.1 Communication Overhead and Network Constraints

The FL paradigm allows building ML-based applications without requiring full access to the sensitive data. However, rural areas and agricultural regions, in particular, face issues regarding poor access to power and connectivity, which primarily hinders the implementation of FL.

5.1.1 Limited Connectivity in Rural Agricultural Areas

Rural agricultural areas often suffer from poor infrastructure, which translates to low or no internet connectivity. For FL to work, numerous model updates have to be exchanged between local devices and a central server. These infrequent or low-bandwidth connections pose certain problems. Their unreliable nature can lead to delays and errors, affecting the updating regularity of global models. Furthermore, this poses issues for convergence and performance of the FL models. To address these challenges, strategies like improved communication protocols and frequency reduction for model updates have been proposed, all to enhance connectivity for FL.

5.1.2 Energy Consumption Concerns for IoT Devices Running FL Models

Sensors and edge devices that comprise the IoT used in smart agriculture usually come with limited computational resources and battery life. The iterative nature of FL, which involves local model training paired with frequent communication to centralized servers, can result in excessive energy usage. The increased workload on IoT devices can reduce their operating lifespan, creating a need for regular maintenance or battery replacement, which is not feasible for large-scale agricultural fields. In an attempt to reduce these concerns, research is centred on resource allocation optimization and development of energy-efficient FL algorithms.

5.2 Data Heterogeneity and Non-IID Data Issues

Agricultural data is inherently diverse due to considerable variability from various environmental conditions and farming practices.

5.2.1 Variability in Soil Types, Weather Conditions, and Farming Practices

Farms vary to a great degree in factors such as soil structure, climate, crops, and farming practices. This diversification gives rise to a scenario where the data in question has non-IID, that is, the data distribution changes across different nodes in the FL process. Such plasticity can create problems for FL, as classical ML algorithms, in most cases, are expected to work with homogenously distributed data. The agricultural data non-IID problem can influence the convergence of the FL models and generate biased or inferior global models that do not account for all of the diverse farms participating in the model. This issue calls for the creation of FL algorithms that are designed for handling data heterogeneity, such as personalized model updates or clustering that create groups of similar distributions of data (Hussaini and Stein, 2023).

5.2.2 Non-IID Data Affecting FL Model Convergence

In agriculture, the non-IID nature of data refers to the fact that a number of statistical compositional attributes do not remain constant across the board between different clients. This means that constructing a global model can be difficult because certain updates are not ideal for all the local datasets. Thus, a global model could underperform on selected data. To overcome this challenge, new advanced aggregation techniques as well as personalized FL models are being developed. To enhance model accuracy and speed, these strategies seek to mitigate the variability of data by modifying the client's data features throughout the learning process.

5.3 Scalability and Computational Constraints

When advancing technology in agriculture using FL, attention needs to be given to the availability of solutions and other resources, as well as the limitations offered by devices in the field.

5.3.1 Need for Lightweight FL Models on Resource-Limited IoT Devices

Agricultural IoT devices typically have limited processing power and memory, making it difficult for them to handle complex FL models, which may demand excessive computation time or energy. This highlights the need for lightweight FL models designed specifically for resource-constrained environments. Through methods such as model compression, quantization, and more efficient neural network structures, the burden on computation can be mitigated. This makes FL more applicable on various agricultural IoT devices (Baqer, 2025).

5.3.2 Efficient Aggregation Techniques for Large-Scale FL Deployment

The more devices that are added to an FL network, the more difficult it becomes for the central server to manage all model updates. This can lead to communication slowdowns and higher latency. To deal with scalability challenges, it is important to have efficient aggregation methods. Using intermediate aggregators to collect subsets of device updates that are then sent to the central server is one way to cope with increased communication. Furthermore, prioritizing changes based on significance and cubing the update length can improve cadence for devices that commonly need FL (Salh et al., 2023). Although FL has the ability to greatly enhance smart agriculture, few obstacles remain that must be removed in order for it to be effectively applied. To solve problems related to communication workload, data diversity, and scalability challenges, multi-approach strategizing like creating energy-saving algorithms, robust models to accommodate a variety of data distributions, and scalable aggregation techniques needs to be employed. Solving these problems will create opportunities for achieving more effective and robust agricultural systems, fully utilizing the scope of FL to increase efficiency and sustainability as well as productivity in the agriculture industry.

6. Privacy-Preserving Techniques in FL

Federated learning facilitates a number of clients to participate in training a single shared global learning model without having to share their private local datasets. This allows for increased privacy of data. However, privately sharing model updates of a client's model during the training process can be problematic. Several privacy-preserving measures have been developed for FL including differential privacy, secure aggregation techniques, trusted execution environments (TEEs), Deep Private Network, etc.

6.1 Differential Privacy

It offers formal protection of individual privacy that ensures the computation is not significantly affected when a single data point (inclusion or exclusion of it) is taken into consideration. In FL, differential privacy is applied at the data pre-processing stage to protect client datasets during training.

6.1.1 Adding Controlled Noise to Data Updates for Enhanced Privacy

In FL, clients are able to conduct local training on their private data before sending any model updates to a central server for aggregation. In order to obscure sensitive information, noise can be added to model parameters or gradients prior to transmission. Adding noise before aggregation in federated learning (NbAFL) preserves data privacy in individual data points, while still enabling the aggregated global model to retain utility. Studies have shown that NbAFL is capable of supressing information leakage while sustaining reasonable model accuracy (Wei et al., 2020).

Incorporating differential privacy to an FL system requires a careful balance between the level of privacy and the accuracy of the models. Both too much and too little noise can lead to privacy issues without proper model accuracy. Achieving this balance has been one of the key problems faced by researchers, and some have scaled adjustments for the noise to the sensitivity of the data and pre-given privacy measures. But, with some effort on the scale of tuning, it has been found out that utility for the models can be preserved while still guaranteeing robust privacy protection (Banse et al., 2024). One example of these studies include those experiments which found that non-IID as well as small datasets showed much steeper drop in performance under differentially private FL settings, thus signifying the importance of dataset non-IID characteristics.

6.2 Secure Aggregation Techniques

Focus of the so-called secure aggregation approaches is to ensure the privacy of the individual updates from the clients during the aggregation phase so that the server never has access to the raw updates sent by any one particular client.

6.2.1 Homomorphic Encryption for Encrypted Model Updates

No decryption is needed while performing operations on data under homomorphic encryption. The clients in FL can encrypt their model updates before sending them to the server. The server collects all the encrypted model updates and uses a decryption function to get the result. This ensures that each update is secret since the server only sees the aggregated result. Though homomorphic encryption comes with tremendous safety, it does tend to create excessive computational burden and is thus not easy to apply in environments with limited resources (Saidi et al., 2025).

Secure Multi-party Computation (SMPC) allows a number of parties to work on a particular function and provide their private information without ever revealing it. Within FL, SMPC protocols can be used for model update aggregation such that the server and other clients do not know which client provided what update. Clients can instead chose to send each other updates using encryption or hiding the real information, and using some cryptographic manipulation they can get the combined model without showing their local data. The SMPC methods can have strong privacy guarantees but they tend to have more elaborate protocol structures and more communication requirements (Chouhan and Purushothama, 2024). TEEs are a solution with hardware that provide a secured space to execute sensitive calculations, protecting data and code from being accessed externally.

6.2.2 Hardware-based Security for Sensitive Computations

In FL, the use of TEEs can serve to protect the training procedure. TEEs such as Intel's Software Guard Extensions (SGX) make it possible to perform sensitive computations within a protected enclave, thus ensuring that models and proprietary information are not compromised during manipulation. In FL, the migration of TEEs onto end-user devices or central servers could potentially secure the training procedure. The restriction of TEEs, however, is that they can only be operated on specific hardware and complicate the overall system architecture.

6.2.3 Potential Use of Blockchain for Enhanced Trust in FL

With the potential to increase trust and transparency in FL, blockchain technology can provide an immutable, decentralized ledger to accomplish this goal. Having model updates and aggregation results recorded in a blockchain enables all stakeholders to attest to the quality and source of any given data associated with the training process. This method hinders the possibility of any malicious interference in the training process while ensuring that all participants remain answerable. When combined with federated learning, these tools offer significant potential for establishing a secure and dependable collaborative learning framework. Ensuring strong privacy protections for sensitive data remains essential while enabling shared model training in FL. There are many benefits, as well as limitations, of using differential privacy, secure aggregation techniques, and TEEs. The effective deployment of these techniques involves carefully balancing privacy with model accuracy, computational overhead, system compatibility, and some other crucial factors. The continuous advance of research and development in this area increases the effectiveness and applicability of FL privacy-preserving techniques.

7. Future Directions and Research Opportunities

Federated learning has emerged as a transformative approach in smart agriculture, enabling collaborative model training across distributed devices while preserving data privacy. As the agricultural sector increasingly adopts digital technologies, several future directions and research opportunities arise to enhance FL's effectiveness and integration.

7.1 Enhancing FL Models for Real-Time Agricultural Applications

7.1.1 Adaptive FL Algorithms for Dynamic Farming Conditions

Agricultural environments are always on the move. Weather patterns change, soil conditions vary, and crops' health status is not fixed and alters constantly. An ordinary FL algorithm is not going to adapt to these changes, and that is why the need for adaptive FL algorithms arises. These algorithms need to be able to respond and change in real time to new data distributions. As a result, models created for this purpose are guaranteed to always remain accurate. For example, models can be designed such that they implement reinforcement learning and learn appropriate actions to be taken in case of drastic changes in environmental conditions, which in turn enables more efficient operations on the farm.

7.1.2 Continuous Learning Strategies for Evolving Agricultural Patterns

Due to climate variability and market demand, the agricultural sector faces both short-term and long-term shifts. Fresh data or patterns are added in continuously learning strategies. This, in turn, helps to save resources and ensure that the models evolve alongside existing agricultural practices. By using the FL framework, the longevity and adaptability of agricultural models can be enhanced through techniques like transfer and online learning.

7.2 Edge Computing and FL Integration for Smart Farming

7.2.1 Reducing Latency and Improving Computational Efficiency

The combination of edge computing and FL offers a credible method to cut latency and boost accounting power in smart farming applications. The ability to analyse raw data quickly and make instant decisions at the farm's edge devices, like sensors and IoT, enables real-time analytics. Moreover, this eliminates dependence on central server communication, resulting in lower bandwidth and cost overheads. In addition, local computation eliminates the consequences of data transmission, which enhances security (Kondaveeti et al., 2024).

7.2.2 Edge Devices as Local FL Nodes for On-the-Farm Intelligence

The use of edge devices as local nodes in the FL network provides farms with the capability to conduct onsite intelligent processes. These devices can actively engage in collaborative model training based on local data to improve the datasets without sharing raw information. Edge-enabled soil moisture sensors, weather stations, and drones are perfect examples of such devices that can execute FL while performing different agricultural tasks. This way, farm-specific performance models can be built without compromising the privacy of the farms, which results in more accurate and effective farming solutions.

7.3 Policy and Regulatory Considerations

7.3.1 Data Ownership and Privacy Laws in Agriculture

With the rise of new technologies, data ownership and privacy issues have grown globally. These questions gained insurmountable complexity in regards to the agriculture sector. Farmers, who already have readily available data, use sophisticated technology for farming. So, they, in reality, hold very few rights to the data they store. Clear policies need to be set up for data ownership for farmers so that they are protected and more willingly adopt FL technology. FL adoption must align with regulations such as the GDPR, and beyond meeting legal requirements, applying these protections in data-sensitive agricultural contexts becomes essential to safeguard farmers' rights and ensure their data is handled responsibly (Li et al., 2024).

7.3.2 Need for Standardized Frameworks for Secure FL Adoption in Farming

Farming largely relies on the adoption of FL, which requires the creation of a governance structure. This, in turn, enables security, interoperability, and scalability for FL systems to be effective. These frameworks create the most ideal preventative measures for cyber threats. Furthermore, standardization allows for better integration for farmers, technology developers, and legislators, making proactive innovation and improvements to smart farming easily attainable (Sathya et al., 2024). The integration of smart agriculture with FL can help in the growth of productivity, sustainability, and data privacy. Focusing on adaptive algorithms, edge computing, and solid policy frameworks will ensure that the agricultural industry fully benefits from FL. Continuous exploration and involvement among various players in agriculture will help solve the current problems and shape the future of agriculture in the digital world.

8. Conclusion

Modernized farming is benefitting greatly from FL because agriculture suffers from education and productivity problems. Not only does FL solve data privacy concerns, it also helps make processes more productive and sustainable. FL differs from conventional ML in which the dataset is stored in a central server. FL functions through decentralized model training which happens in numerous devices or nodes; this helps guarantee that sensitive agricultural information such as soil details, crop, and even financial data remains local. This significantly decreases the risks associated with data breaches and unauthorized access. By adopting this information security method, FL allows farmers to take advantage of predictive models without worrying about losing their sensitive information.

For example, FL models could be used for predicting agricultural outputs by classifying the data of many farms while keeping the particular farm records confidential. In a similar way, federated learning in different regions improves pest and disease detection systems and also ensures that farm-specific information remains confidential. Also, FL enables localized climate data analysis which assists weather and soil monitoring in decision-making processes. Furthermore, FL-based precision irrigation systems tailored to specific zones enhance productivity of crops by minimizing the use of fertilizers and irrigation water. While the concept of FL brings about substantial benefits, it does not come without challenges. The decentralized form of FL brings about engagement burden and network limitations, which are mainly prevalent in rural farming regions where connectivity is poor. In addition, the ever-changing farms' problem of non-IID makes model convergence and accuracy highly difficult. Restrictions in computation capabilities of the IoT devices add another layer of challenge for FL deployments on a larger scale. There are a lot of difficulties that need deep investigation and the development of additional algorithms, advanced communication systems, and lightweight models to solve these problems.

The broad acceptance of FL within smart farming should achieve privacy and sustainability objectives, increasing demand for FL in farming. The digital transformation progress in agriculture indicates that FL will become a core component of autonomous farming systems. To accomplish that, the focus of the research should be on FL model improvement towards real-time agricultural applications using adaptive algorithms and continual learning techniques. It is equally important to integrate FL with edge computing applications, in order to reduce latency, increase computational efficiency, and enable intelligence on the farm. Local FL nodes could be implemented in edge devices like sensors and drones, creating an actionable decentralized ecosystem for farmers to utilize their local conditions and workflows. In summary, FL can bridge the gap in the advancement of smart agriculture by enhancing decision-making and ensuring data privacy while practising sustainable farming. Achieving these objectives will be possible through concerted collaboration of researchers, policymakers, and farmers, as the FL technology progresses; however, there are many hurdles to cross as privacy-protecting intelligent agro systems become more widely adopted.

References

Banse, A., Kreischer, J. and Oliva i Jürgens, X. (2024). Federated learning with differential privacy. arXiv. https://arxiv.org/abs/2402.02230.

Baqer, M. (2025). Energy-efficient federated learning for internet of things: Leveraging in-network processing and hierarchical clustering. *Future Internet* 17(1): 4.

Bera, S., Dey, T., Mukherjee, A. and De, D. (2024). FLAG: Federated learning for sustainable irrigation in agriculture. *IEEE Transactions on Consumer Electronics*. https://doi.org/10.1109/TCE.2024.3370373.

Chouhan, A. and Purushothama, B.R. (2024). A survey on secure aggregation for privacy-preserving federated learning. pp. 13–26. *In*: Rajagopal, S., Popat, K., Meva, D. and Bajeja, S. (eds.). *Advancements in Smart Computing and Information Security. ASCIS 2023. Communications in Computer and Information Science*, Volume 2039. Springer, Cham.

Deng, F., Mao, W., Zeng, Z. and Wei, B. (2022). Multiple diseases and pests detection based on federated learning and improved Faster R-CNN. *IEEE Transactions on Instrumentation and Measurement*, 71: 1–11.

Hussaini, M. and Stein, A. (2023). Federated Learning in agriculture: Potential and challenges. *INFORMATIK 2023—Designing Futures: Zukünfte gestalten*, 1653–1661. Bonn: Gesellschaft für Informatik e.V.

Kairouz, P., McMahan, H.B., Avent, B., Bellet, A., Bennis, M., Bhagoji, A.N., Kallista Bonawitz, Zachary Charles, Graham Cormode, Rachel Cummings, Rafael G. L. D'Oliveira, Hubert Eichner, Salim El Rouayheb, David Evans, Josh Gardner, Zachary Garrett, Adrià Gascón, Badih Ghazi, Phillip B. Gibbons, Marco Gruteser, Zaid Harchaoui, Chaoyang He, Lie He, Zhouyuan Huo, Ben Hutchinson, Justin Hsu, Martin Jaggi, Tara Javidi, Gauri Joshi, Mikhail Khodak, Jakub Konečný, Aleksandra Korolova, Farinaz Koushanfar, Sanmi Koyejo, Tancrède Lepoint, Yang Liu, Prateek Mittal, Mehryar Mohri, Richard Nock, Ayfer Özgür, Rasmus Pagh, Hang Qi, Daniel Ramage, Ramesh Raskar, Mariana

Raykova, Dawn Song, Weikang Song, Sebastian U. Stich, Ziteng Sun, Ananda Theertha Suresh, Florian Tramèr, Praneeth Vepakomma, Jianyu Wang, Li Xiong, Zheng Xu, Qiang Yang, Felix X. Yu, Han Yu and Zhao, S. (2021). Advances and open problems in federated learning. *Foundations and Trends in Machine Learning* 14(1-2): 1–210.

Kamilaris, A., Kartakoullis, A. and Prenafeta-Boldú, F.X. (2017). A review on the practice of big data analysis in agriculture. *Computers and Electronics in Agriculture* 143: 23–37.

Kondaveeti, H.K., Sai, G.B., Athar, S.A., Vatsavayi, V.K., Mitra, A. and Ananthachari, P. (2024). Federated learning for smart agriculture: Challenges and opportunities. *2024 Third International Conference on Distributed Computing and Electrical Circuits and Electronics (ICDCECE)*, Ballari, India, 1–7.

Li, H., Ge, L. and Tian, L. (2024). Survey: Federated learning data security and privacy-preserving in edge-Internet of Things. *Artificial Intelligence Review* 57: 130.

Li, T., Sahu, A.K., Talwalkar, A. and Smith, V. (2020). Federated learning: Challenges, methods, and future directions. *IEEE Signal Processing Magazine* 37(3): 50–60.

Li, X., Yang, Y., Wang, Z. and Chen, L. (2022). Multiple pest detection based on federated learning and improved faster R-CNN algorithm. *2022 IEEE International Conference on Computer Vision Workshops (ICCVW)*. https://ieeexplore.ieee.org/document/9868069.

Liakos, K.G., Busato, P., Moshou, D., Pearson, S. and Bochtis, D. (2018). Machine learning in agriculture: A review. *Sensors* 18(8): 2674.

Manoj, T., Makkithaya, K. and Narendra, V.G. (2022). A federated learning-based crop yield prediction for agricultural production risk management. *2022 IEEE Delhi Section Conference (DELCON)*, 1–7.

McMahan, H.B., Moore, E., Ramage, D., Hampson, S. and Arcas, B.A.Y. (2017). Communication-efficient learning of deep networks from decentralized data. In *Proceedings of the 20th International Conference on Artificial Intelligence and Statistics*, 1273–1282.

Muhammed, D., Ahvar, E., Ahvar, S. and Trocan, M. (2024). Federated learning for predicting irrigation requirements in multi-farm irrigation scheduling systems. pp. 236–245. *In*: Andreasen, T., Ghosh, A.K. and Pedrycz, W. (Eds.). *Recent Challenges in Intelligent Information and Database Systems*. Springer.

Risteska Stojkoska, B.L. and Trivodaliev, K.V. (2017). A review of Internet of Things for smart agriculture: Challenges and solutions. *Journal of Cleaner Production* 140: 1199–1204.

Saidi, A., Amira, A. and Nouali, O. (2025). Securing decentralized federated learning: Cryptographic mechanisms for privacy and trust. *Cluster Computing* 28: 144.

Salh, A., Hossain, E., Sinha, A., Al-Ahmad, A., Al-Ali, A.K. and Ijaz, M. (2023). Energy-efficient federated learning with resource allocation for green IoT edge intelligence in B5G. *IEEE Access* 11: 16353–16367.

Sathya, D., Thangamani, R. and Balaji, B.S. (2024). The revolution of edge computing in smart farming. pp. 351–389. *In*: Balasubramanian, S., Natarajan, G. and Chelliah, P.R. (eds.). *Intelligent Robots and Drones for Precision Agriculture. Signals and Communication Technology*. Springer, Cham.

Wei, K., Jun Li, Ming Ding, Chuan Ma, Howard H. Yang, Farhad Farokhi, Shi Jin, Tony Q.S. Quek and Vincent Poor, H. (2020). Federated learning with differential privacy: Algorithms and performance analysis. *IEEE Transactions on Information Forensics and Security* 15: 3454–3469.

Wolfert, S., Ge, L., Verdouw, C. and Bogaardt, M.J. (2017). Big data in smart farming—A review. *Agricultural Systems* 153: 69–80.

Zhao, Y., Li, M., Lai, L., Suda, N., Civin, D. and Chandra, V. (2018). Federated Learning with non-IID data. *arXiv preprint arXiv:1806.00582*.

Chapter 5

A Cost-effective Data Security Approach in Agriculture *x* Involving Blockchains and AI

Arnab Mitra[1,*] and *Anabik Pal*[2]

The rapid industrial revolution has resulted in the existence of Industry x versions (for x = 4.0, and 5.0). At present, the rise and popularity of Industry x versions have influenced the evolution of several other allied domains. Thus, we observe the existence of Agriculture x (for x = 4.0, and 5.0) in several scientific databases. The Agriculture x (also known as smart agriculture) is one of the vital areas for human society that deals with food security, i.e., food for every life in view of increasing world population, while minimizing the effects of climate change and land scarcity. Like Industry x, Agriculture x also incorporates the integration of several advanced information technology (IT) and Internet of Things (IoT)-based modelling to deal with big data issues, and ensure higher productivity, reduced wastage, and sustainable practices wherever possible to minimize environmental impacts. As Agriculture x deals with big data and IoT, data security and privacy issues in such advanced agriculture versions are always critical. For these reasons,

[1] Department of Information Technology, Techno International New Town, West Bengal, India.

[2] Department of Computer Science, Indian Institute of Science Education and Research, Odisha, India.

* Corresponding author: mitra.arnab@gmail.com

DOI: 10.1201/9781003670568-5

artificial intelligence (AI) and blockchain technology are being incorporated into the Agriculture *x* model to ensure enhanced data security and privacy and automated farming decision-making. By achieving such enhanced data security and privacy in Agriculture *x*, it is expected that such models will ensure (i) the protection of sensitive agriculture data; (ii) data integrity; (iii) compliance with the latest regulations, e.g., the General Data Protection Regulation (GDPR) from the European Union; (iv) solutions to issues related to scalability and interoperability. It is further believed that such integration of AI and blockchains in Agriculture *x* will enhance supply chain transparency, smart contracts management, data management, and identity verification. For this reason, in this chapter we present an improved data security and privacy model in Agriculture *x* by involving Cellular Automata (CAs)–based design (as a dynamic and discrete mathematical modelling tool in AI) for lightweight data security for IoT, and towards enhanced proof-of-randomness (PoR) consensus for node selection in blockchains. The detailed analysis of such a model ensures its cost-effectiveness in Agriculture *x* design in view of its physical modelling capability and energy consumption. Effective farming decision-making is an important task for which privacy-preserving AI model development is proposed.

1. Introduction

Enterprises are adapting intelligent digitization towards successful transformation into an Industry *x*, where x = 4.0, and 5.0. Thus, to achieve "the threshold of the fourth Industrial Revolution" (Lee et al., 2015), several advanced information technologies (ITs) such as smart sensors, Internet of Things (IoT), cloud computing, big data, augmented reality, cyber security, blockchain technology, vertical and horizontal integration of systems, autonomous material handling, digital twins and simulation, autonomous robots, and additive manufacturing are coalesced together (Lee et al., 2015; Kumar et al., 2016). Contrarily, the cyber-physical system (CPS) is a transformative and efficient technology management towards interconnected systems, enhancing their physical assets and computational capabilities (Lee et al., 2015; Kumar et al., 2016; Lee et al., 2009; Baheti and Gill, 2011). Thus, CPS realization may result in several advantages (see Figure 5.1). A standard structural design of CPS with reference to Industry 4.0 as described in Lee et al. (2015) and Kumar et al. (2016) is presented in Figure 5.1.

The effectiveness of CPS depends on the appropriate integration of industrial artificial intelligence (AI) technology with advanced IT devices.

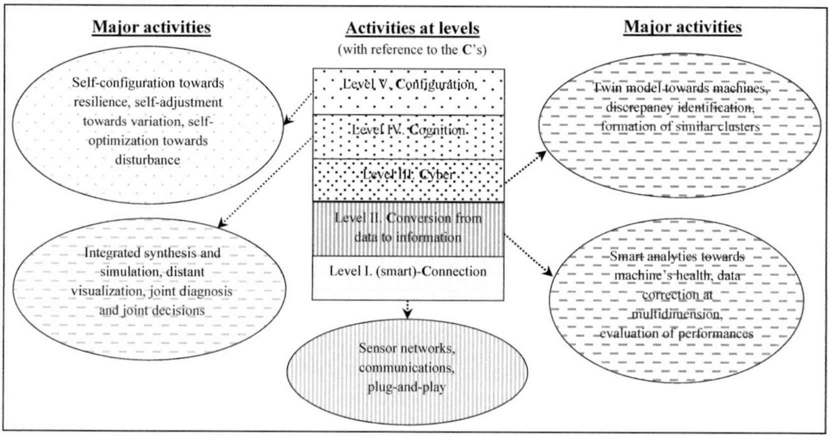

Figure 5.1: A typical 5C-based CPS architecture (as inspired by Lee et al. [2015] and Kumar et al. [2016]).

Thus, we observe an effective integration of AI-based technologies at CPS architecture (refer to the 5Cs of Figure 5.1; i.e., connection, conversion, cyber, cognition, and configuration–based CPS architecture of Figure 5.1) (Lee et al., 2015; Kumar et al., 2016; Lee et al., 2009). Due to the integration of advanced ITs in the manufacturing line in the Industry 4.0 scenario, numerous affordable data processing devices such as data acquisition systems, sensors, and networks may be found in any smart production line. We observed that "sensor-based networked manufacturing lines are dealing with a high volume of data (i.e., Big Data), which in turn are much crucial" (Kumar et al., 2016) to get its manufacturing target (Lee et al., 2015; Kumar et al., 2016; Lee et al., 2009; Baheti and Gill, 2011; Lee et al., 2013; Shi et al., 2011).

From our studies, we observe that the effectiveness of CPS was investigated by SynOx Therapeutics Ltd, a leading late clinical-stage biopharmaceutical company, in SynOx Therapeutics Ltd. (2024). We observed that CPS plays an important role at the heart of the modern industrial revolution, and is emerging as the essential backbone of Factory 4.0, which is an integrated system that is "made up of interconnected sensors, actuators and communication modules, [which] are the pillars of an intelligent industry where advanced automation and industrial IoT converge to create highly flexible and efficient production environments. The technological maturity of PCS enables unprecedented industrial interconnectivity, paving the way for a new era of manufacturing where the factory of the future comes to life" (SynOx Therapeutics Ltd. 2024). We also observe that Industry 4.0 is being further transformed into Industry 5.0 where a workforce of machines and people will be in a synergistic atmosphere both at a virtual and a physical level, as discussed by M. Rada (2018), Industry 5.0 founder.

Due to the high importance and popularity of Industry 4.0 concepts, we observe that Industry 4.0 is revolutionizing other sectors. Thus, we observe that by using cutting-edge tools and automated management systems, farmers may monitor the crops, tweak planting, and reduce production costs. Advanced technologies may further assist the farmer in effectively drilling down and maintaining many resources (e.g., irrigation, fertilizer, and pesticides) in Agriculture 4.0, as discussed by Agmatix®, an agro-informatics company (Rada, 2018). In Agriculture 4.0, several cutting-edge technologies such as AI, drones, sensor networks, IoT, big data, and automation are used to achieve increased productivity, healthier crops, higher yields, better cost management, waste reduction, and smaller carbon footprint (Agmatix™ 2024). As Industry 4.0 is shifting towards Industry 5.0, the shift of Agriculture 4.0 to Agriculture 5.0 is inevitable. For said reason, several pieces of literature might be observed in different scientific databases. Although we are focusing on a discussion on the Agriculture *x* versions (for x = 4.0, and 5.0), still we prefer to present a brief diagrammatic representation of all Agriculture *x* versions (for x = 1.0, to 5.0), for an enhanced readability of the chapter and a quick grasp of different Agriculture *x* versions (Figure 5.2).

Although we find different research focuses in Agriculture *x* versions (for x = 4.0, and 5.0), for a possible enhancement, we are particularly interested in data security and privacy. We found that advances in Industry *x* and Agriculture *x* mostly rely on the use of tiny-sized IoT

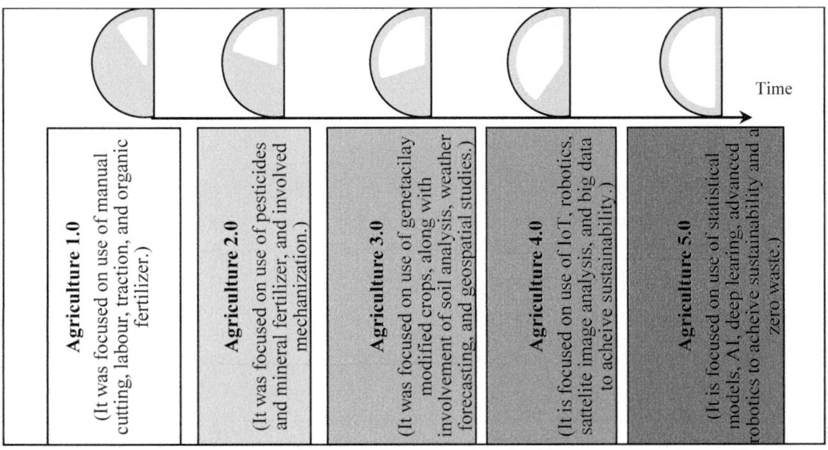

Figure 5.2: The evolution of the agriculture versions (as inspired by Grupo criado com o objetivo de difundir Data Science e Inteligencia Artificial [2023], available at "https://www.linkedin.com/pulse/techy-farm-agriculture-50-smarter-crops-growing-neuron-usp-maeof", accessed on January 26, 2025).

devices (Brettel et al., 2014; Roblek et al., 2016). Unfortunately, we observe that tiny-sized IoT devices possess limited computational power and limited energy storage. For these reasons, a lightweight cryptographic approach towards data security and privacy issues in IoT might be well suited over conventional data security and privacy approaches (Shrouf et al., 2014; Mitra and Saha 2021; Roy et al., 2019; Suo et al., 2012; Eisenbarth et al., 2007; Buchanan et al., 2017).

Among several approaches towards lightweight cryptography, we observe that Cellular Automata (CAs)-based energy efficient lightweight cryptography was discussed in Mitra and Saha (2021) and Roy et al. (2019), which is particularly interesting to us. As our research is greatly inspired by Mitra and Saha (2021), we present a brief description of a few related concepts such as correlation, Fourier analysis, CAs, and blockchains.

Correlation (Kumar et al., 2016; Teodorescu, 2015; Mitra and Kundu, 2015; Ehis, 2023) computation is one of the scientific ways to analyse the randomness and thus analyse the effectiveness of a signal/pattern for its possible consideration in data security applications. We find in (Kumar et al., 2016; Teodorescu, 2015; Mitra and Kundu, 2015; Ehis, 2023) that "the randomness of the partition of the definition (configurations) space" (Teodorescu, 2015) for an equispaced dataset may be "indicative on the chance that the cycles are decorrelated" (Teodorescu, 2015). The (maximal-) correlation in any equispaced dataset is a measurement for similarity in the equispaced dataset. The maximal correlation as defined in Teodorescu (2015), and Mitra and Kundu (2015) is presented in Equation 5.1.

$$C_{xy} = \frac{(max_k \sum_{j=1}^{L} CjC'_{j+k})}{\sqrt{(\sum_{j=1}^{L} C_j)^2}\sqrt{(\sum_{j=1}^{L} C'_j)^2}} \tag{5.1}$$

where, 'C_{xy}' is the calculated correlation between signals/patterns 'C_j' and 'C_j'''.

Fourier analysis is applied for dynamics delivering spectra of the type '1/*f*' (i.e., a coloured noise) (Mitra and Kundu, 2015). We find in Mitra and Kundu (2015) that the average coefficient and specific spectral components may further be used to assess processes.

Cellular Automata (Chaudhuri et al., 1997; Nandi et al. 1994; Nandi and Chaudhuri, 1997) are efficient dynamic modelling tools in AI that advance over discrete time and space. Elementary CAs (ECAs) are the simple CAs with configuration containing three cells in one dimension at three neighbourhoods (i.e., left and right neighbour, and self-cell) in fixed/periodic boundary scenarios (Kumar et al., 2016; Lee et al., 2009; Chaudhuri et al., 1997; Nandi et al., 1994; Nandi and Chaudhuri, 1997).

To realize the different ECAs' boundary scenarios, a typical diagram is presented in Figure 5.3 (as inspired by Mitra and Kundu (2015), and Chaudhuri et al. (1997)). The next stage of any ECAs cell at time may be decided by a function as presented in Equation 5.2 (Kumar et al., 2016; Chaudhuri et al., 1997; Nandi et al., 1994; Nandi and Chaudhuri, 1997), which is also known as CAs rule and also recognized as Wolfram CAs rule, a total of 256 ECAs rules.

$$x_i^{t+1} = f(x_{i-1}^t, x_i^t, x_{i+1}^t) \tag{5.2}$$

where at time t, x_{i-1}^t signifies value at the left cell, x_i^t signifies value at the self-cell, x_{i+1}^t is value at the right cell, and x_i^{t+1} signifies the value of a cell at a time $(t + 1)$ (Kumar et al., 2016; Lee et al., 2009; Mitra and Kundu, 2015; Chaudhuri et al., 1997). For more insights about ECAs and related ECA dynamics, see Mitra and Kundu (2015), Chaudhuri et al. (1997), and Nandi and Chaudhuri (1997).

We continued with CAs-based modelling as CAs are preferred for physical implementation due to their inherent parallel computing facility along with easy incorporation at Very Large-Scale Integration (VLSI) (Mitra and Kundu, 2015; Chaudhuri et al., 1997; Nandi and Chaudhuri, 1997). We further restricted our focus to ECAs only as it is very simple to design and very easy to achieve its physical model at the cost of *D* flip-flops (FFs) only (Mitra and Kundu, 2015; Chaudhuri et al., 1997). Different dynamics at several fixed boundary scenarios may also be examined further, which in turn may discover different system dynamics and innate benefits (if any) (Mitra and Kundu, 2015; Chaudhuri et al., 1997).

On the other hand, *blockchain* is a shared immutable ledger that enables transaction recordings and tracking assets across a business network. A blockchain, by nature, is a distributed database, which is shared over a computer network and stores information electronically in a digital format to make transactions secure (National Informatics Centre, 2024). We found that "anything of value can be tracked and traded on the Blockchain network" (National Informatics Centre, 2024). Blockchains

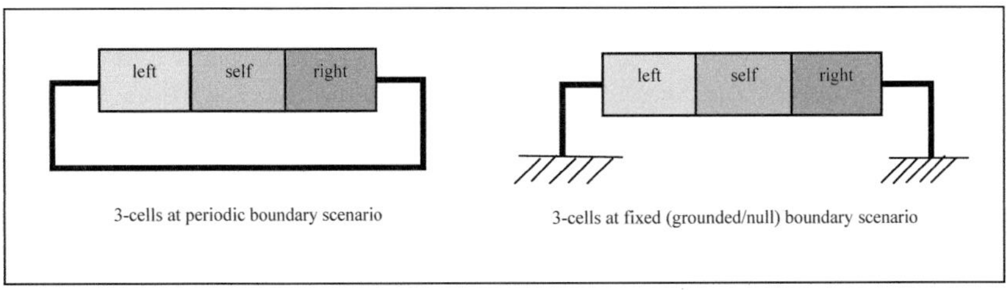

Figure 5.3: Schematic diagram for ECAs configuration (as inspired by Mitra and Kundu [2015], and Chaudhuri et al. [1997]).

may typically be viewed as an exchange process, which works on data blocks that are interconnected and facilitate any digital asset to be an irreversible record of transactions by involving immutability and transparency through the use of decentralization (National Informatics Centre, 2024), and thus may be applied to enhance data security and privacy applications. It has been examined by Integritee Network (2024) that by introducing randomness, the outcome in blockchains should be more unpredictable and tamper-resistant, resulting in an extra layer of security and fairness to the decentralized nature of blockchain networks. To facilitate randomness in blockchains, researchers introduced a low energy–cost consensus, proof-of-randomness (PoR) protocol to generate a blockchain without any competition for computing power or stake of cryptocurrency (Zhang and Kai, 2022).

Artificial intelligence is an emerging computer science field focusing on automated intelligent decision-making. The AI algorithms were human-designed at their earlier stages and required expert effort in algorithm building. Recently, machine learning or deep learning, a subfield of AI, attained maximum priority due to its flexibility towards data-driven intelligent system development. In machine learning, a huge volume of annotated data is gathered and processed in a computer, and based on the statistical properties of the data, prediction algorithms are built. The difference between machine learning and deep learning is that the former needs a hand-crafted feature representation of the input data, whereas the latter does not require this. The efficacy of the latest AI algorithms can make it suitable for many purposes, including node selection in PoR protocol, data security analysis, detection of fraudulent transactions, etc.

Although we found several distinct efforts to enhance lightweight data security and privacy, and blockchains individually, we did not come across any integrated cost-effective approach to enhance lightweight data security in Agriculture x involving AI and PoR in blockchains. For these reasons, we find the scope for further research.

The major contributions of this chapter are as follows:

- It presents a sustainable design with ECAs that ensures low energy consumption in Agriculture x.
- It presents ECAs-based design and detailed investigation towards lightweight data security and privacy in Agriculture x.
- It presents ECAs-based design and detailed investigation towards possible enhancement of PoR protocol of blockchains in Agriculture x.
- It presents a design to develop a privacy-preserving machine learning model for intelligent decision-making for Agriculture x.

The rest of the chapter is organized as follows: related works are discussed in the second section; the background work is presented in the third section; the details of the proposed work are presented in the fourth section; the fifth section presents an empirical analysis followed by the results and discussions in the sixth section; the final section discusses the concluding remarks and future research direction.

2. Related Works

As briefly described in the first section, due to the rapid advancements in industrial technologies and subsequent industrial revolutions, the agricultural sector has shifted from indigenous farming technology to mechanized farming technology and precision/smart agriculture. Thus, we observe a systematic study in Liu et al. (2020) that describes the link from Industry 4.0 to Agriculture 4.0, and the implementation status of Industry 4.0 to Agriculture 4.0 shifting. In a different attempt, a systematic review was presented in Yadav et al. (2022) that examined the application suitability of Industry 4.0 technologies in the agricultural food supply chain. Besides, the role of IoT, big data, and AI in smart agriculture and food industry was investigated in Misra et al. (2020); a framework for role-based data access towards enhanced data privacy involving AI-based data sharing in Agriculture 4.0 was presented in Spanaki et al. (2021). Further, an enhanced data security model in Agriculture 4.0 was presented in Chen et al. (2023) that integrated AI and explainable AI and blockchains (Chen et al., 2023; Ahamed and Vignesh, 2022). In distinct efforts, a fog computing architecture-based data security framework for Agriculture 4.0 (i.e., "Agrisecure") involving blockchains was presented in Padhy et al. (2023), and blockchains-based sustainable e-agriculture was presented in Dey and Shekhawat (2021). Further, the different cutting-edge technologies, trends, and challenges in Agriculture 5.0 were examined in Fountas et al. (2024); advancements and agricultural sustainability in view of Agriculture 5.0 were examined through remote sensing in Martos et al. (2021); advancements involving AI, IoT, and ML were highlighted in Ahmad and Nabi (2021); a detailed review on crop data management was presented in Saiz-Rubio and Rovira-Más (2020).

Although we found research focus on different aspects of smart agriculture/Agriculture x versions (for x = 4.0, and 5.0), for a possible enhancement, we are particularly interested in data security and privacy. Please recall that the advances in Industry x and Agriculture x mostly rely on the use of tiny-sized IoT devices (Brettel et al., 2014; Roblek et al., 2016). Unfortunately, we observe that tiny-sized IoT devices possess limited computational power and limited energy storage. For these reasons, a lightweight cryptographic approach towards data security and privacy issues in IoT is well suited over conventional data security and privacy approaches (Shrouf et al., 2014; Mitra and Saha, 2021; Roy et al., 2019; Suo et al., 2012; Eisenbarth et al., 2007; Buchanan et al., 2017) (also refer to the first section). Among several approaches towards the implementation of lightweight cryptography, we observe that CAs-based energy-efficient lightweight data security and privacy approach was discussed in Mitra and Saha (2021) and Roy et al. (2019), which is particularly interesting to us. In different attempts, we found that a detailed survey on the implementation of lightweight data security and privacy approaches was presented in Eisenbarth et al. (2007) and Buchanan et al. (2017).

Besides the focus on the design and implementation of lightweight data security models with CAs, we found that a cost-effective CAs-based Prime (randomly distributed set of Primes) generation was presented in Mitra and Kundu (2015), which was further used to enhance data security and privacy in Mitra (2018). A detailed investigation by Mitra and Kundu (2015) concluded that the sequence behaves as "more or less uniform noise…with a tendency of 'weak periodicity'" (Mitra and Kundu, 2015). It may be further noted that CAs-based model uses *D* FFs for its physical modelling (Chaudhuri et al., 1997; Nandi et al., 1994) and requires very low power consumption. Power consumption for FFs at $1.0v_{dd}$ in $0.13\mu m$ CMOS technology as discussed in Mitra et al. (2017) is presented in Figure 5.4.

From Figure 5.4 and Mitra et al. (2017), it is observed that the minimum and maximum power consumption ranges from $1.17E-07$ watt to $1.20E-05$ watt for different CMOS technology-based FFs, which is very low with respect to the total amount of power consumption.

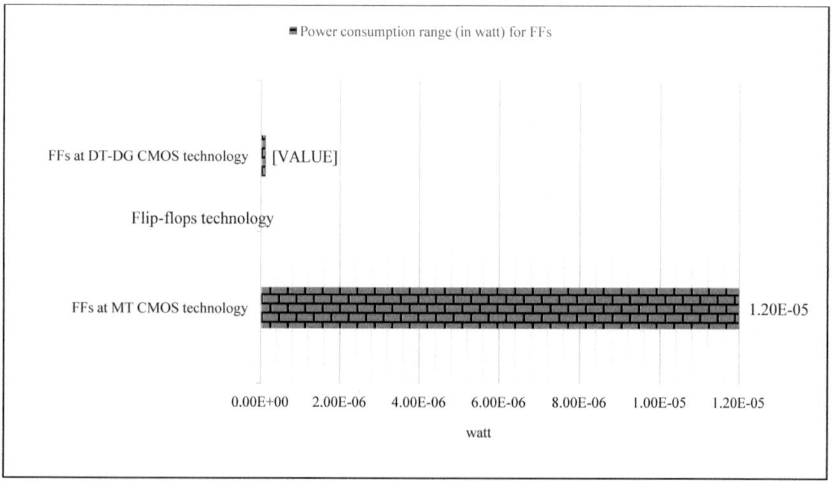

Figure 5.4: Energy consumption by CAs (as inspired by Mitra et al. [2017]).

In conclusion, we understood that low power-consuming physical modelling of lightweight data security techniques should have advantages in Agriculture *x*. Despite our best efforts, we did not find literature focused on the physical modelling of complete data security (i.e., the inclusion of both cryptography and authentication in the design) in Agriculture *x* with an advantage of the Green Computing technique. Though CAs-based lightweight cryptography and one-time password (OTP)-based authentication using CAs were presented in Mitra and Saha (2021) and Roy et al. (2019), we found that the integration of such models with blockchains and the design of energy-efficient blockchain consensus were not discussed earlier. We believe that considerations such as simplicity in design and effectiveness as a green model for Agriculture *x* should have strong significance. For this reason, we find that there is scope to continue our research. Important works by past researchers that have significantly influenced our present research (i.e., Mitra and Saha, 2021; Roy et al., 2019; Mitra et al., 2017) are presented briefly in the third section.

Artificial intelligence and machine learning are contributing manyfold in improving data security mechanisms in blockchain-enabled IoT systems. First, the blockchain uses a consensus mechanism to choose a node. There are many static algorithmic approaches for selecting a node. Those algorithms add some computational burden to all nodes. In contrast, the latest edition of reinforcement algorithms is a potential candidate for dynamically choosing a node to reduce such computational burden (Riahi et al., 2022). They can make the consensus mechanism efficient regarding computational burden and energy consumption. The next step is analysing transactions in the blockchain and finding potential malicious requests a node makes Ramasamy et al. (2021). Some works address these and focus on designing smart contracts and adapting them in real time when the environment changes. Predicting the vulnerabilities in a communicating medium or device is an important task where AI algorithms are employed. The latest AI algorithms are efficient in crypt analysis, i.e., estimating the security levels achieved with a particular key and generating post-quantum encryption keys (Kaushik et al., 2023). AI can potentially optimize the data and minimize the computational burden in communication in blockchain networks (He et al., 2020). Another important aspect of blockchain enabling agriculture is to optimize data storage and allow minimal replication for faster access. Computation-worthy AI techniques can be employed in edge devices for data compression (Ketshabetswe et al., 2021), encryption, and intelligent data storage (Nayak et al., 2022). Thus, edge computing for agriculture becomes feasible. Federated learning enables us to develop prediction models to maintain data privacy. Such prediction models can be utilized for decision-making regarding action to be taken in the field (e.g., pest control, water supply, fertilization) as well as for cost-effective farming (Gryshova et al., 2024; Zhang and Kai, 2022; Zhang and Xia, 2022).

In a distinct effort, the PoR protocol for blockchain consensus was described as a fair and low energy-cost consensus mechanism, where every network node of a blockchain may use a true random number generator (TRNG) and hash algorithm to fulfil the PoR protocol (Zhang and Kai, 2022). In the PoR, a block records owner uses a 1Mb true random number generated by TRNG instead of a "nonce" in Proof of Work (PoW) (Zhang and Kai, 2022). As further discussed in Zhang and Kai (2022), for any blockchain network, a node selects 1 Mb random number $R(m, n)$ and the same is further used by $SHA - 256$ to get a 256-bit long hash value $H_n(m)$, which is further used as a node's digital signature and shared with other nodes. Unfortunately, we observe that the use of TRNG as a randomness source might be impractical due to the lack of its capability for reproducibility and its lack of cost-effectiveness. For this reason, we find further scope for research towards the possible enhancement of PoR.

3. Background Works

In a different research, CAs-based authentication in a Cloud environment with equally populated and randomly distributed set of OTPs was offered (Mitra et al., 2017). An analysis confirmed that the characteristic polynomials involved in the generation of OTPs were primitive/primitive-recursive (the characteristic polynomial was observed as $(1+x)$ or $(1+x)^n$). Further p-value analysis in the statistical RUNs test ensured the presence of randomness in all sets of OTPs using CAs. In additional research, the generation of a set of Primes (randomly populated) was presented with CA (Mitra and Kundu, 2015). In Mitra and Kundu (2015), the time complexity involved in the generation of a set of Primes was $O(n) + O(k * log^2 n)$. With the involvement of existing CAs-based authentication as presented in Mitra et al. (2017), and a set of Primes generation (Mitra and Kundu, 2015), a lightweight data security model was further presented in Mitra and Saha (2021). The lightweight data security of Mitra and Saha (2021) is explained briefly next. The lightweight complete data security in Fog networks in Mitra and Saha (2021) is modularized into two modules: (i) an equally populated set of OTP-based multi-user authentication with a null-boundary ECAs scenario; and (ii) a prime number (achieved from the CAs-based randomly populated set of Primes)-based cryptography. The simple lightweight data security model as presented in Mitra and Saha (2021) is diagrammatically presented in Figure 5.5.

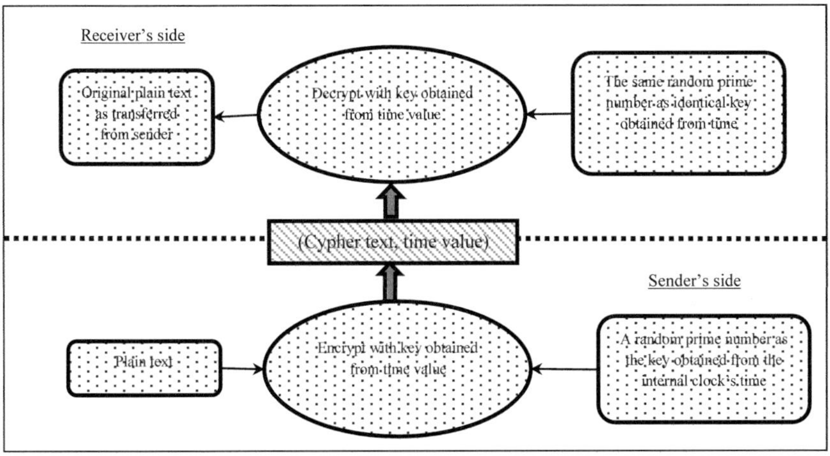

Figure 5.5: An ECAs-based lightweight data security model for IoT (as inspired from Mitra and Saha [2021]).

We found that a lightweight data security approach in Fog networks using CAs, involving both authentication and cryptography, was introduced in Mitra and Saha (2021) and Roy et al. (2019). Unfortunately, a detailed investigation is yet to be undertaken to examine its true potential as a green model in Agriculture x. Hence, an empirical analysis is presented next.

Cost-effectiveness over several random number generators was investigated in Zhang and Xia (2022) that incorporated the study of a recursive pseudo-random number generator, a monte-carlo generator, TRNG, and CAs-based random number generators. It was concluded in the study that the use of TRNG as a randomness source might be impractical due to its lack of reproducibility and cost-effectiveness as compared to pseudo-random number generators, and among several existing pseudo-random number generators, CAs-based pseudo-random number generators might be a good choice due to their enriched quality of (pseudo-)randomness, reproducibility, and cost-effectiveness. Thus, we find scope for the possible incorporation of CAs-based pseudo-random number generators for PoR protocol in blockchains.

4. Proposed Work

The flowchart for our proposed work is presented in Figure 5.6.

In the proposed flowchart (Figure 5.6), first a hybrid rule vector with ECAs rules 204 and 110 was initialized while at the fixed boundary scenario, 0 ... 0 or 0 ... 1 values were set. Further, it was checked whether the characteristic polynomial was primitive or recursive primitive

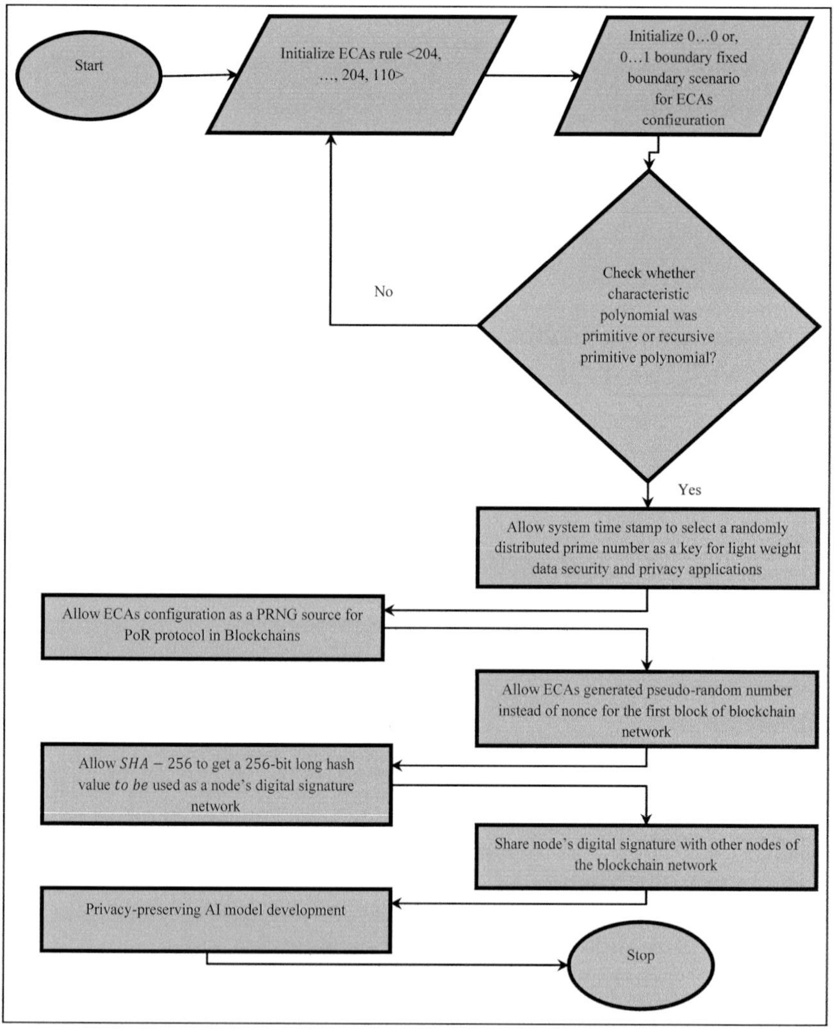

Figure 5.6: Proposed flowchart for the CAs-based lightweight data security and privacy, and PoR in blockchains in Agriculture x.

polynomial or not. If it was confirmed to be a primitive or recursive primitive polynomial, then the current system time stamp was selected to pick a randomly distributed prime number as a key for lightweight data security and privacy applications; else, the selection of ECAs rule step has to be repeated. The same ECAs configuration is allowed to be selected as a pseudo-random number generator (PRNG) source for PoR protocol in blockchains. Further, ECAs-generated pseudo-random prime number is allowed instead of nonce for the first block of the blockchain network.

Then the *SHA* – 256 algorithm is allowed to get a 256-bit long hash value to be used as a node's digital signature network and is allowed to share it (i.e., 256-bit long hash value) as the node's digital signature with other nodes of the blockchain network.

In Figure 5.6, the ECAs-based (Korec, 1997) hybrid rule vector with ECAs rules 204 and 110 was applied to generate a set of randomly distributed Primes (see Mitra [2018] for the generator of a randomly distributed set of primes). It should be noted that it was examined in Mitra (2018) that the maximum number of randomly distributed set of Primes might be achieved at 0 ... 0 or, 0 ... 1 boundary only. Hence, in Figure 5.6, 0 ... 0 or 0 ... 1 fixed boundary scenario was applied. ECAs rule selection for the proposed system is given in Table 5.1.

Table 5.1: ECAs rule vector selection and boundary value fixation.

Left Boundary Value at Fixed Boundary Scenario	First Cell	Intermediate Cell	Last Cell	Right Boundary Value At Fixed Boundary Scenario
0	110	110	204	Not dependent on the right boundary value, can be set to 0 or 1.

Note: See Mitra (2018).

In this chapter, we focus on the following works with ECAs generated pattern. A schematic diagram is presented in Figure 5.7.

It might be noted that in our present work for this chapter, for lightweight privacy, we used an approach with equally populated randomized OTPs-based authentication for sensing devices in network, as discussed in Mitra et al. (2017). Further, for ECAs-based lightweight data-security based on symmetric cryptography, as discussed in Mitra and Saha (2021), towards a cost-effective enhancement of PoR in blockchains is presented in this chapter. The details of such investigations are presented in the fifth section.

In the presented work, secured farming data will facilitate the building of AI models for automated decision-making related to farming, such as pest control, water supply, and fertilization. Nowadays, deep learning approaches are popular for such prediction system development due to their ability to produce remarkable performances and adaptability in diverse application areas. The commonly used deep learning models are vulnerable to data privacy issues (Aravilli, 2024). Hence, we are proposing to build a deep model that is robust and efficient to preserve data confidentiality. Differential privacy enables deep model development, which will be an intelligent choice (Li et al., 2017). The key principle in making the data differentially private is adding random noise before the prediction model development. For the current scenario, we need a server

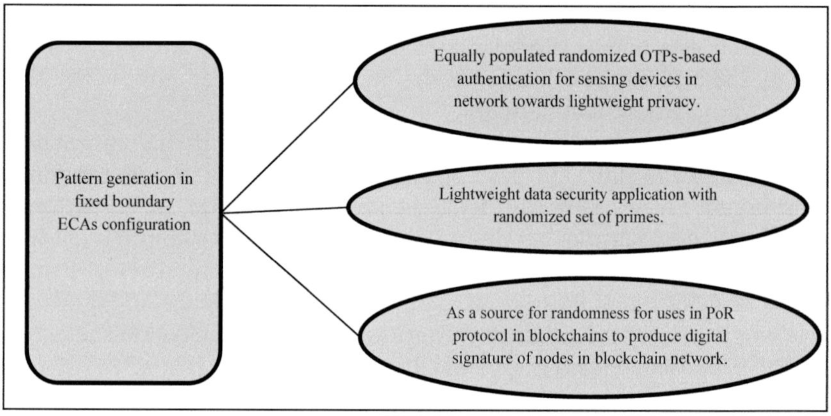

Figure 5.7: Proposed uses of ECAs in Agriculture *x*.

to gather the decrypted data, and the deep model will be trained with a differential privacy-enabled gradient optimization algorithm (Abadi et al., 2016). The multi-layered perception (MLP) will be used in AI model development, taking the sensed data as the input vectors. A detailed description of the training algorithm is as follows (Algorithm 1):

Algorithm 1. ML Training Algorithm for Agriculture *x*

Input: *Sensed data vectors collected from farms*

Output: *Prediction model*

Step 1. Start.

Step 2. Design a multi-task learnable MLP network where different output branches will be responsible for different prediction tasks such as whether pest control is required, how much water supply is required, if immediate fertilization, etc.

Step 3. Initialize the network weight and bias matrices.

Step 4. Initialize the network hyper-parameters.

Step 5. Perform differentially private mini-batch stochastic gradient descent to train the model, i.e., update the network parameters.

Step 6. Use the trained model.

Step 7. Stop.

5. Empirical Investigations

From Mathematics (n.d.), we learned that for the generation of a randomly distributed set of primes, the naive method might be applied to produce numbers in the range at random and test for its primality through primality testing; e.g., Fermat's primality testing. Such a process will require an n-bits/iteration with an average of about $(n + 1)\, log\, 2 - 1 \approx n\, log\, 2$ iterations. Thus, in total, it will require an $n^2\, log\, 2$ random bits, and $n\, log\, 2$ total number of primality tests. In such a scenario, an obvious requirement is to consider only the odd numbers (and the special case of 2 is required to be handled separately with an $O(1)$ overhead). Thus, it will result in a reduction of random bits to $(n-1)\frac{(n+1)log2-1}{2} \approx \frac{log2}{n}n^2$.

Further, as discussed in Mathematics (n.d.), the extreme version of the presented algorithm is to compute $\pi(b)$ and $\pi(a-1)$ and choosing an index at random; thus, it will take the information-theoretic minimum number of bits, about $n - \lg n + O(1)$, "at the cost of a truly atrocious runtime, something worse than $2^{n/2}$ with current algorithms" (Mathematics n.d.).

Additionally, from Mitra (2018) we conclude that the left boundary value for ECAs configuration needs to be fixed at 0 for the generation of a maximum number of randomized primes, and it is not dependent on the right boundary value of the fixed boundary condition. We learned from Mitra (2018) that the ECAs-based hybrid rule vector < 204, ... 204, 110 > is capable of producing a maximum number of randomized primes at 0 ... 0 or 0 ... 1 boundary only.

6. Simulation Results and Related Discussions

We extensively generated data using a sufficient long hybrid ECAs (arbitrarily chosen an ECAs size 12) with ECAs rule vector < 110, 110, 110, 110, 110, 110, 110, 110, 110, 110, 110, 204 > at 0 ... 0 or 0 ... 1 fixed boundary. We used C-code in C-Free®, a fast and lightweight Integrated Development Environment (IDE) in x64-based processor AMD Ryzen 5-5500U with Radeon Graphics and 2.10 GHz computing facility, and 16.0 GB installed memory in a -bit Windows® operating system–based environment. Though we consider several automata sizes, we arbitrarily choose to report the detailed analysis for automata size 12. The detailed result is presented in Table 5.2.

It may be noted that a detailed correlation and Fourier spectrum-based analysis on the generated maximum-length attractor for several automata sizes were performed by Mitra and Kundu (2015). Unfortunately, such correlation and Fourier spectrum-based analysis were not performed on the generated set of random primes. We believe such analysis should explore the true potential for such numbers for possible uses as a strong key in view of lightweight data security and privacy applications. For said reasons, we presented further investigations on the set of achieved randomized primes. Our considered investigations and corresponding results are discussed here.

Table 5.2: Detailed result from < 110, 110, 110, 110, 110, 110, 110, 110, 110, 110, 110, 204 > at 0 ... 0 or 0 ... 1 fixed boundary.

States in Maximum-length Attractor	Achieved Set of Randomized Primes
1, 3, 7, 13, 31, 49, 115, 215, 509, 775, 1805, 3359, 3889, 2419, 3031, 3709, 2759, 4045, 2143, 2289, 2451, 2999, 3837, 2951, 3725, 2975, 3761, 3059, 3607, 2621, 3687, 2797, 4031, 2273, 2467, 3047, 3629, 2687, 3777, 3011, 3655, 2765, 4063, 2161, 2259, 2551, 2845, 3895, 2429, 3015, 3661, 2783, 4081, 2067, 2103, 2173, 2247, 2509, 2911, 4081	1, 3, 7, 13, 31, 509, 3359, 3889, 3709, 2143, 2999, 3761, 2273, 2467, 2687, 3011, 2161, 2551

The graphical presentations for the distribution of randomized primes and the sequence of generated randomized primes (see Table 5.2) are given in Figures 5.8(a) and 5.8(b) respectively.

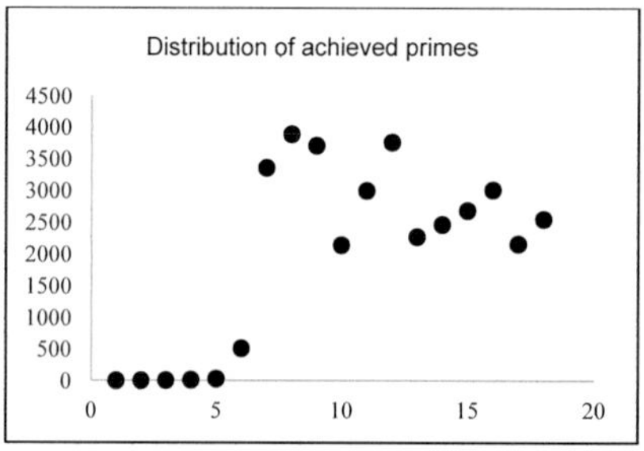

Figure 5.8(a): Graphical presentation for distribution of randomized primes

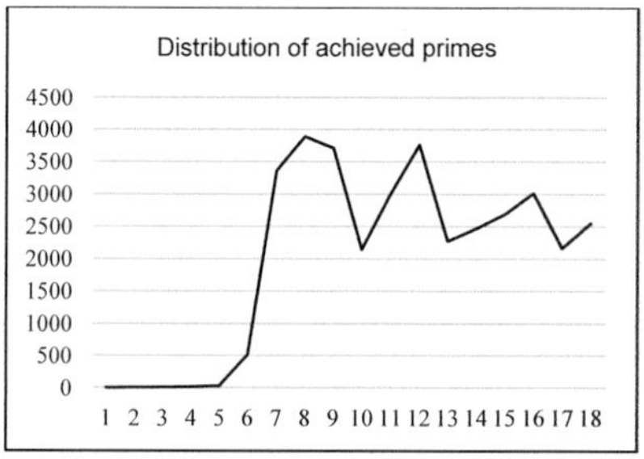

Figure 5.8(b): Graphical presentation for a sequence of randomized primes

Figure 5.8: Different graphical presentations of the set of randomized primes.

From Figure 5.8, some degree of (pseudo-)randomness might be observed for the generated set of primes. Due to the small size of the dataset, statistical tests suit NIST or DIEHARD could not be performed. Still, a special statistical test suit (RUNs test) for a small dataset available in RUNs Test (n.d.) was used to measure the quality of (pseudo-) randomness for such data. The obtained result is presented in Table 5.3.

From Table 5.3 it might be concluded that a low degree of randomness might be present in the generated dataset. To investigate it further, we performed self-correlation (i.e., auto-correlation) analysis of such data (see Equation 5.1). The result is presented in Figure 5.9.

Table 5.3: RUNs test result for the generated sequence of randomized primes.

Number of RUNs	*p*-value	Conclusion
2	0.00006	"Very strong evidence against randomness (trend or seasonality)" (RUNs Test n.d.)

From Figure 5.9 it might be observed that the correlation value lies between 0.134135753 (minimum) and 0.99082004 (maximum), which further indicates the presence of (pseudo-)randomness for the given dataset. To investigate it further, we performed an FFT-based spectrum analysis. The obtained spectrum is presented in Figure 5.10.

From Figure 5.10 it might be observed that more or less a "white noise" is achieved, similar to the results of Mitra and Kundu (2015), which once again signifies the presence of a reasonable amount of (pseudo-)randomness for the given dataset.

Hence, it might be concluded that the set of achieved random primes is capable of use in lightweight data security and privacy applications, including as a source of randomness for PoR protocol in blockchains for Agriculture x uses.

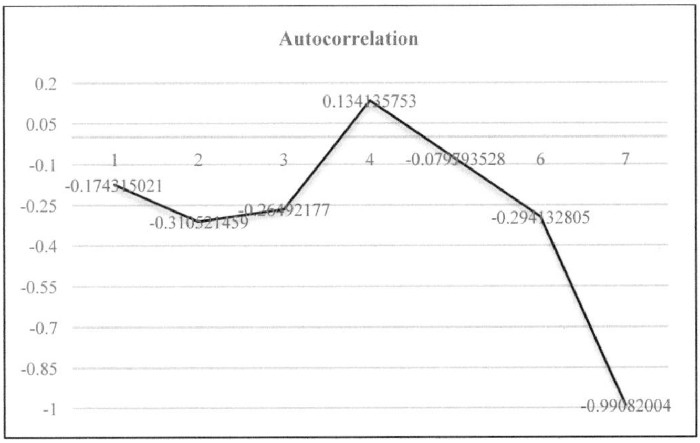

Figure 5.9: Graphical presentation of achieved correlation for the sequence of randomized primes.

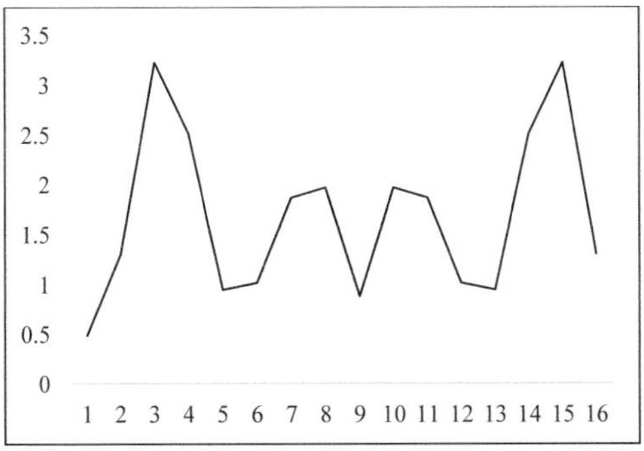

Figure 5.10: FFT for the sequence of randomized primes.

7. Conclusions and Future Scope

This chapter presented an innovative, cost-effective framework for privacy-enabling agricultural data storage with blockchains facilitating an enhanced cost-effective and low power–consuming design for randomness in PoR protocol to produce a random digital signature for any node, and then proposed to develop an AI-based prediction model design with the collected data for farming decision-making. Data security and privacy are enabled with ECAs-based lightweight cryptography, which is energy efficient and can be done in cheaper computation. Further, it can be implemented with digital circuits. We believe such an approach is sustainable for the current and future generations of Agriculture x. Our analysis shows that the designed cryptographic technique has strong data protection ability with reference to low resource-constrained devices. Experimental analysis explores that ECAs-based randomness for PoR protocol in the blockchain network improves the performance in terms of power consumption. Further, training a differentially private-enabled AI model ensures that the training model will not be used for training data extraction. Thus, it might be concluded that the presented ECAs-based design of data security and privacy involving blockchains and AI is worthwhile for implementation in Agriculture x.

In future, we plan to extend our work to develop an AI model with diverse environmental and farming data for an automated agricultural decision-making. We believe that such a model will be useful for deploying on agricultural farms in Agriculture x to increase food production.

Acknowledgments

The authors acknowledge review comments received from the anonymous reviewers that have strengthened the preparation of the final version of this chapter.

References

Abadi, M., Chu, A., Goodfellow, I., McMahan, H.B., Mironov, I., Talwar, K. and Zhang, L. (2016). Deep learning with differential privacy. In *Proceedings of the 2016 ACM SIGSAC Conference on Computer and Communications Security*, 308–318.

Agmatix™. (2024). The Role of Industry 4.0 in Agriculture. Available at https://www.agmatix.com/blog/the-role-of-industry-4-0-in-agriculture/#:~:text=Using%20cutting%2Dedge%20tools%20and,each%20area%20of%20the%20farm (accessed on 26 January 2025).

Ahamed, N.N. and Vignesh, R. (2022). Smart agriculture and food industry with blockchain and artificial intelligence. *Journal of Computer Science* 18(1): 1–17.

Ahmad, L. and Nabi, F. (2021). *Agriculture 5.0: Artificial Intelligence, IoT and Machine Learning*. CRC Press.

Aravilli, S.R. (2024). Privacy-preserving Machine Learning: A use-case-driven approach to develop and protecting ML Pipelines from privacy and security threats.

Baheti, R. and Gill, H. (2011). Cyber-physical Systems. *The Impact of Control Technology* 12(1): 161–166.

Blackburn, S.R., Murphy, S., Paterson, K.G., Nandi, S. and Chaudhuri, P.P. (1997). Comments on theory and applications of cellular automata in cryptography [with reply]. *IEEE Transactions on Computers*, 46(5): 637–639.

Brettel, M., Friederichsen, N., Keller, M. and Rosenberg, M. (2014). How virtualization, decentralization and network building change the manufacturing landscape: An Industry 4.0 perspective. *International Journal of Mechanical, Industrial Science and Engineering* 8(1): 37–44.

Buchanan, W.J., Li, S. and Asif, R. (2017). Lightweight cryptography methods. *Journal of Cyber Security Technology* 1(3-4): 187–201.

Chaudhuri, P.P., Chowdhury, D.R., Nandi, S. and Chattopadhyay, S. (1997). *Additive Cellular Automata: Theory and Applications*, Vol. 1. John Wiley & Sons.

Chen, H.Y., Sharma, K., Sharma, C. and Sharma, S. (2023). Integrating explainable artificial intelligence and blockchain to smart agriculture: research prospects for decision making and improved security. *Smart Agricultural Technology* 6: 100350.

Dey, K. and Shekhawat, U. (2021). Blockchain for sustainable e-agriculture: Literature review, architecture for data management, and implications. *Journal of Cleaner Production* 316: 128254.

Ehis, A.M.T. (2023). Concept of cryptographic operations based on code division multiple access. *Covenant Journal of Informatics and Communication Technology*, 27. https://journals.covenantuniversity.edu.ng/index.php/cjict/article/view/4062.

Eisenbarth, T., Kumar, S., Paar, C., Poschmann, A. and Uhsadel, L. (2007). A survey of lightweight-cryptography implementations. *IEEE Design & Test of Computers* 24(6): 522–533.

Fountas, S., Espejo-García, B., Kasimati, A., Gemtou, M., Panoutsopoulos, H. and Anastasiou, E. (2024). Agriculture 5.0: Cutting-edge technologies, trends, and challenges. *IT Professional* 26(1): 40–47.

Grupo criado com o objetivo de difundir Data Science e Inteligencia Artificial. (2023). The Techy Farm: Agriculture 5.0 for Smarter Crops' Growing. Available at https://www.linkedin.com/pulse/techy-farm-agriculture-50-smarter-crops-growing-neuron-usp-maeof (accessed on 26 January 2025).

Gryshova, I., Balian, A., Antonik, I., Miniailo, V., Nehodenko, V. and Nyzhnychenko, Y. (2024). Artificial Intelligence in climate smart in agricultural: Toward a sustainable farming future. *Access to Science, Business, Innovation in Digital Economy* 5(1): 125–140.

He, Y., Wang, Y., Qiu, C., Lin, Q., Li, J. and Ming, Z. (2020). Blockchain-based edge computing resource allocation in IoT: A deep reinforcement learning approach. *IEEE Internet of Things Journal* 8(4): 2226–2237.

Integritee Network. (2024). Embracing Unpredictability: The Role of Randomness in Blockchain. Available at https://medium.com/integritee/embracing-unpredictability-the-role-of-randomness-in-blockchain-3607e8c01eb3#:~:text=Randomness%20in%20blockchain%20isn't,decentralized%20nature%20of%20blockchain%20networks (accessed on 28 January 2025).

Kaushik, A., Vadlamani, L.S.S., Hussain, M.M., Sahay, M., Singh, R., Singh, A.K., Indu, S., Goswami, P. and Kousik, N.G.V. (2023). Post quantum public and private key cryptography optimized for IoT security. *Wireless Personal Communications* 129(2): 893–909.

Ketshabetswe, K.L., Zungeru, A.M., Mtengi, B., Lebekwe, C.K. and Prabaharan, S.R.S. (2021). Data compression algorithms for wireless sensor networks: A review and comparison. *IEEE Access* 9: 136872–136891.

Korec, I. (1997). Real-time generation of primes by a one-dimensional cellular automaton with 11 States. pp. 358–367. *In*: Igor Prívara and Peter Ružička (eds.). *International*

Symposium on Mathematical Foundations of Computer Science. Berlin, Heidelberg: Springer Berlin Heidelberg.

Kumar, A., Shankar, R., Choudhary, A. and Thakur, L.S. (2016). A big data MapReduce framework for fault diagnosis in cloud-based manufacturing. *International Journal of Production Research* 54(23): 7060–7073.

Lee, J., Bagheri, B. and Kao, H.A. (2015). A cyber-physical systems architecture for Industry 4.0-based manufacturing systems. *Manufacturing Letters* 3: 18–23.

Lee, J., Kwon, T. and Song, J. (2009). Group connectivity model for industrial wireless sensor networks. *IEEE Transactions on Industrial Electronics* 57(5): 1835–1844.

Lee, J., Lapira, E., Bagheri, B. and Kao, H.A. (2013). Recent advances and trends in predictive manufacturing systems in big data environment. *Manufacturing Letters* 1(1): 38–41.

Li, N., Lyu, M., Su, D. and Yang, W. (2017). *Differential Privacy: From Theory to Practice*. Morgan & Claypool.

Liu, Y., Ma, X., Shu, L., Hancke, G.P. and Abu-Mahfouz, A.M. (2020). From Industry 4.0 to Agriculture 4.0: Current status, enabling technologies, and research challenges. *IEEE Transactions on Industrial Informatics* 17(6): 4322–4334.

Martos, V., Ahmad, A., Cartujo, P. and Ordoñez, J. (2021). Ensuring agricultural sustainability through remote sensing in the era of Agriculture 5.0. *Applied Sciences* 11(13): 5911.

Mathematics. (n.d.). Choosing Primes Uniformly at Random. Available at https://math.stackexchange.com/questions/1069693/choosing-primes-uniformly-at-random (accessed on 17 February 2025).

Misra, N.N., Dixit, Y., Al-Mallahi, A., Bhullar, M.S., Upadhyay, R. and Martynenko, A. (2020). IoT, Big Data, and Artificial Intelligence in agriculture and food industry. *IEEE Internet of Things Journal* 9(9): 6305–6324.

Mitra, A. (2018). Selection of cost-effective prime source towards possible uses in fog computing. pp. 19–24. *In*: Srikanta Patnaik (ed.). *2018 2nd International Conference on Data Science and Business Analytics (ICDSBA)*. IEEE.

Mitra, A. and Kundu, A. (2015). Analysis of sequences generated by ELCA-type cellular automata targeting noise generation. pp. 883–888. *In*: Sergiu Caraman, Marian Barbu and Răzvan Şolea (eds.). *2015 19th International Conference on System Theory, Control and Computing (ICSTCC)*. IEEE.

Mitra, A. and Saha, S. (2021). A design towards an energy-efficient and lightweight data security model in fog networks. pp. 227–236. *In*: Debahuti Mishra, Rajkumar Buyya, Prasant Mohapatra and Srikanta Patnaik (eds.). *Intelligent and Cloud Computing*. Springer, Singapore.

Mitra, A., Kundu, A., Chattopadhyay, M. and Chattopadhyay, S. (2017). A cost-efficient one time password-based authentication in cloud environment using equal length cellular automata. *Journal of Industrial Information Integration* 5: 17–25.

Nandi, S., Kar, B.K. and Chaudhuri, P.P. (1994). Theory and applications of cellular automata in cryptography. *IEEE Transactions on Computers* 43(12): 1346–1357.

National Informatics Centre, Centre of Excellence in Blockchain Technology, Ministry of Electronics & Information Technology. (2024). Blockchain Technology. Available at https://blockchain.gov.in/Home/BlockChain?blockchain=blockchain#:~:text=Blockchain%20is%20a%20shared%20immutable,shared%20over%20a%20computer%20network (accessed on 27 January 2025).

Nayak, A., Chowdhury, D., De, S., Bhattacharyya, S., Muhammad, K. and Gorbachev, S. (2022). A novel intelligent blockchain framework with intelligence replication. pp. 661–672. *In*: Tapan Kumar Gandhi, Debanjan Konar, Biswaraj Sen and Kalpana Sharma (eds.). *Advanced Computational Paradigms and Hybrid Intelligent Computing: Proceedings of ICACCP 2021*. Springer Singapore.

Padhy, S., Alowaidi, M., Dash, S., Alshehri, M., Malla, P.P., Routray, S. and Alhumyani, H. (2023). Agrisecure: A fog computing-based security framework for agriculture 4.0 via blockchain. *Processes* 11(3): 757.

Rada, M. (2018). Industry 5.0. Available at https://michael-rada.medium.com/industry-5-0-definition-6a2f9922dc48 (accessed on 12 September 2024).

Ramasamy, L.K., Khan, K.P.F., Imoize, A.L., Ogbebor, J.O., Kadry, S. and Rho, S. (2021). Blockchain-based wireless sensor networks for malicious node detection: A survey. *IEEE Access* 9: 128765–128785.

Riahi, K., Abouaissa, A. and Idoumghar, L. (2022). A reinforcement learning-based node selection for PBFT consensus. pp. 1–3. *In*: Larbi Boubshir, Boubaker Daachi, Abdellah Mokrane, Yaser Jararweh and Elhadj Benkhelifa (eds.). *2022 Ninth International Conference on Software Defined Systems (SDS)*. IEEE.

Roblek, V., Meško, M. and Krapež, A. (2016). A complex view of Industry 4.0. *Sage Open* 6(2): 2158244016653987.

Roy, S., Rawat, U. and Karjee, J. (2019). A lightweight cellular automata based encryption technique for IoT applications. *IEEE Access* 7: 39782–39793.

RUNs Test. (n.d.). Available at https://home.ubalt.edu/ntsbarsh/business-stat/otherapplets/Randomness.htm (accessed on 17 February 2025).

Saiz-Rubio, V. and Rovira-Más, F. (2020). From smart farming towards Agriculture 5.0: A review on crop data management. *Agronomy* 10(2): 207.

Shi, J., Wan, J., Yan, H. and Suo, H. (2011). A survey of cyber-physical systems. In *2011 International Conference on Wireless Communications and Signal Processing (WCSP)*, 1–6. IEEE.

Shrouf, F., Ordieres, J. and Miragliotta, G. (2014). Smart factories in Industry 4.0: A review of the concept and of energy management approached in production based on the internet of things paradigm. In *2014 IEEE International Conference on Industrial Engineering and Engineering Management*, 697–701. IEEE.

Spanaki, K., Karafili, E. and Despoudi, S. (2021). AI applications of data sharing in Agriculture 4.0: A framework for role-based data access control. *International Journal of Information Management* 59: 102350.

Suo, H., Wan, J., Zou, C. and Liu, J. (2012). Security in the Internet of Things: A review. pp. 648–651. *In*: Lisa O'Conner (ed.). *2012 International Conference on Computer Science and Electronics Engineering*, 3. IEEE.

SynOx Therapeutics Ltd. (2024). Cyber-physical Systems: The Backbone of Factory 4.0. Available at https://www.synox.io/en/industry-4-0/cyber-physical-systems-the-backbone-of-factory-4-0/#:~:text=Cyber%2Dphysical%20systems%20improve%20industrial,data%20analysis%2C%20reducing%20unplanned%20downtime (accessed on 26 January 2025).

Teodorescu, H.N. (2015). On the regularities and randomness of the dynamics of simple and composed CAs with applications. *Romanian Journal of Information Science and Technology, Romanian Academy* 18(2): 166–181.

Yadav, V.S., Singh, A.R., Raut, R.D., Mangla, S.K., Luthra, S. and Kumar, A. (2022). Exploring the application of Industry 4.0 technologies in the agricultural food supply chain: A systematic literature review. *Computers & Industrial Engineering* 169: 108304.

Zhang, B. and Xia, C. (2022). The effects of sample size and sample prevalence on cellular automata simulation of urban growth. *International Journal of Geographical Information Science* 36(1): 158–187.

Zhang, W.Z. and Kai, V. (2022). Proof-of-randomness protocol for blockchain consensus: A case of Macau algorithms. *arXiv e-prints, arXiv-2211.*

Chapter 6

Secure and Ethical AI-driven Approaches to Data Privacy in Sustainable Agriculture

Kothai, G.,[1,*] *Dhamodharan, T.,*[2] *Naveen Prasath, S.*[2] and *Abhivanth, R.*[2]

The agricultural sector is on the brink of significant change due to artificial intelligence (AI) technologies with the promise of increased productivity and greater sustainability, but more than productivity gains result from employing and integrating these technologies; privacy issues are introduced in the use of new technology creating and generating sensitive data, including farm records and individual farmer data. This chapter will identify privacy-preserving AI models that can address those privacy issues. It begins with exploring the privacy issues that uniquely belong to the agricultural sector and describes the limitations of conventional data protection approaches. It considers three methods of conducting AI: Federated Learning, Differential Privacy, and Homomorphic Encryption, examining both the theoretical and applied uses of these models. Following this investigation, the chapter provides case studies from the sector showing how the privacy-preserving

[1] Department of Computational Intelligence, School of Computing, SRM Institute of Science and Technology, Tamil Nadu, India.
[2] Department of Computer Science and Engineering (Artificial Intelligence and Machine Learning), KPR Institute of Engineering and Technology, Tamil Nadu, India.
* Corresponding author: emailtokothaiganesan@gmail.com

DOI: 10.1201/9781003670568-6

models respond to AI capabilities and privacy issues. This chapter takes a step further in addressing appropriate legislation to support these technologies and consideration of ethical issues with respect to having AI in place consistent with global data security. The authors share recommendations for researchers, policymakers, and industry stakeholders, while noting the importance of maintaining privacy considerations with technological advances in AI as it relates to the agricultural sector. The overarching objective is safe, ethical, and sustainable digitalization of the agricultural industry.

1. Introduction

1.1 Background of AI in Agriculture

Artificial intelligence (AI) has significantly influenced the agriculture sector by promoting the age of data mining to maximize production, management, and sustainability. Higher demand for food happens due to a growing population; thus, AI somehow comes to the rescue by facilitating precision farming. Technologies such as machine learning and computer vision permit the assessment of extensive datasets from Internet of Things (IoT) sensors, drones, and weather stations. (IoT is interrelated devices such as sensors and networks that communicate with one another in order to collect and exchange information. This could be as simple as installing weather stations or even deploying drones that help farmers optimize their efficiency and productivity in real time.) Thus, additional information on fertilization, irrigation, pest control, and harvesting can be made available to farmers. For instance, AI models can timely detect and treat plant diseases through image analysis; treatments of crops are now possible through precision agriculture-real-time input from the monitoring of soil nutrient and moisture content. Smart robots include AI in their guiding platforms for automating labour-intensive tasks; they are enhancing efficiency while minimizing the damages inflicted on agricultural crops. In addition, AI systems can help determine market surplus forecasting, suggesting the right time to sell a particular commodity based on historical trends. Yet, the implementation of AI comes with a certain number of challenges, especially in the area of data collection and privacy. Much of the sensitive agricultural data requires extensive processing of large datasets gathered from multiple sources. Furthermore, it raised questions of ownership, security, and, of course, ethical use. Although AI indeed has the might and ability to be beneficial in transforming agriculture, implementation has to go hand in hand with privacy frameworks to ensure public trust and to safeguard the rights of farmers in this dynamic digital world (Kamilaris and Prenafeta-Boldú, 2018).

1.2 Challenges with Sensitive Agricultural Data

Hence, agricultural data offers enormous potential to leverage production and optimize operations, but this creates serious issues concerning privacy and security. Such data consists of information related to crop yield, soil composition, history of pest attacks, and financial records. If accessed by competitors or unauthorized persons, such data could be misused to ensure unethical edge, such as price manipulation in the market or replicating proprietary farming techniques. Agri-tech platforms have increased the number of third parties; in this case, it is the intermediaries that collect and sometimes manage large-scale data with little or no explanation about their use. Many of them have little protection or any technical know-how about how their data is shared. Data centralized in cloud systems also makes it more vulnerable to breaches. Data sharing between organizations adds further complication, since research would require data sharing, which increases the chances of compromise of privacy through anonymization. Models of advanced AI can reverse these anonymized data in some cases, bringing to the surface sensitive details. Besides, there is the challenge of surveillance that comes in the form of continuous monitoring of fields and livestock and that violates the autonomy of the farmers. In this case, these unresolved issues can breed mistrust for AI-driven agricultural tools, especially for smallholder farmers. It is, therefore, imperative to ensure ethical and safe handling of agricultural data as a prerequisite to gain confidence and scale adoption of AI. Strong governance, transparency, and privacy protection will go a long way in securing farmer interests in this digital age (Wolfert et al., 2017).

1.3 Motivation for Privacy Preservation

With agricultural systems interlinked and data-driven, there is increasing necessity for the preservation of privacy. Farmers are increasingly discounting their willingness to share data due to fears concerning data misuse or unauthorized access. Traditional AI models have centralized the collection of data, thereby stripping the farmer of a measure of control and amplifying the risk of cyber-attacks and data breach. This scenario truly propels the motivation to adopt AI paradigms with privacy protection as their main design goal, thereby enabling the benefits of collaborative AI in model-building while ensuring data do not leave the confines of the farmer's local device. Privacy-preserving frameworks such as Federated Learning and Differential Privacy make use of local training of models and share only encrypted updates or noise-added data. In the realms of agricultural data, such features guarantee privacy and thereby establishment of trust. This becomes very important when attempting to engage smallholder farmers and those living in poorly connected regions. The other view is that an offer of privacy preservation follows the line of various global agro laws such as the General Data Protection Regulation (GDPR) or the Indian Personal Data Protection Bill, both of which enunciate a loud emphasis on consent and purpose limitation. Furthermore, Privacy preserving AI makes it possible to establish collaborations for agricultural data across international borders while observing national sovereignty laws. Finally, the reason for existence of privacy-preserving AI is, therefore, not just a technical advancement; it also empowers farmers, serves as the backbone for ethical innovation, and creates possibilities for widespread adoption in agriculture. It inspires the invention of smart systems that respect users' rights as they solve global problems (Bonawitz et al., 2019).

1.4 Research Objectives and Scope

The research seeks to set up an AI agricultural framework that is privacy-preserving and yet provides actionable inputs with a view to keeping sensitive data intact. The thrust will be on incorporating advanced privacy technologies—Federated Learning (FL), Differential Privacy (DP), Homomorphic Encryption (HE), and Secure Multi-party Computation (SMPC)—into AI models that are practically realizable in real-world agricultural situations. These two parts are theory and practice. So far as theory is concerned, research considers both the merits and demerits of each privacy technology while matching them to relevant agricultural tasks such as yield prediction and price forecasting. On the practical side, the research covers design architecture, case studies, implementation guidelines, and coding examples using agricultural data. It will thus consider a modular system where privacy layers are applicable for given actors, whether smallholder farmers or big cooperatives. The framework will be judged according to model accuracy, scalability, and efficiency, especially regarding low-resource environments. We additionally propose to influence policy through identifying deficiencies in the legal framework surrounding agricultural data governance alongside suitable mechanisms for secure and transparent sharing of data. This research, then, serves as a bridge between technology, agriculture, and ethics, providing a sustainable future for AI in agriculture without neglecting the rights and privacy of individuals that feed the world (Dwork and Roth, 2014).

2. Literature Review

2.1 Overview of Existing AI Applications in Agriculture

Artificial intelligence has brought about considerable changes in agriculture, whereby it automates and optimizes a broad range of jobs on fields. Crop yield prediction, identification of diseases, weeds, and pests, and precision irrigation are some of the applications. Yield forecasting would apply the historical harvest data and trends in weather so that farmers are able to make plans and allocate resources efficiently. Deep learning, especially Convolutional Neural Networks (CNNs), is broadly used in plant disease detection by assessing images of leaves. This early recognition system minimizes reliance on experts. AI-based drones and satellite imaging monitor crop health and pinpoint areas under stress due to pests or nutrient deficiency.

Smart irrigation systems analyse data from weather and soil using AI and give recommendations that save water while ensuring that crops remain healthy. Also, the AI-based supply chain for agriculture involves demand forecasting, inventory control, and reducing losses due to post-harvest mishandling. AI robots are increasingly becoming involved in harvesting and packaging, thus reducing reliance on human labour. However, a major concern is that most of these systems depend on a centralized data repository, which raises issues of privacy. The more the data is generated from individual farms, the more important it gets to philosophically discuss matters such as ownership and misuse of data. With that, a surge for more acceptable, secure, and fair AI alternatives is the burgeoning trend (Sharma et al., 2020).

2.2 *Current Privacy-Preserving Techniques*

Privacy-preserving machine learning has become a major area of research with specific applications in agriculture, where data is highly sensitive. A particular paradigm that has gained prominence is FL. It is an emerging machine learning technology in which several accommodation units or decentralized networks may train an AI model, and no raw records of the data are transferred between nodes. Each node or housing unit learns from its local data and sends out updates on the performance of the model in terms of communication to other nodes. It guarantees data privacy while doing away with the need for centralization of storage. In FL, models are built using several devices, such as farm sensors and smartphones, without the need to centralize raw data since only update information, that is, gradients, are shared. This ensures improved safety of data by allowing DP which adds controlled noise into an original dataset or model outputs to make the tracing of individual data points mathematically difficult. DP is very important in scenarios where aggregated statistics are to be shared, such as regional pest patterns or yield reports. DP guarantees privacy for each individual record in the dataset. It ensures that adding or removing a single person's data does not affect the outcome by adding random noise to the data or model outputs, which safeguards privacy while allowing useful insights.

Another feature is HE which is a cryptographic technique that allows performing computations on encrypted data without having to decrypt it from the start and so such data remain confidential during analysis. It secures sensitive data while processing and is therefore particularly fitting for privacy-preserving AI applications in which secrecy is a major factor. But it is significantly expensive in its computational aspect. SMPC facilitates joint analysis through data splitting of parties, thus inducing collaborative research around the shared data without revealing private information. Different techniques have different trade-offs about speed, complexity, and effectiveness. In the meantime, the journey to adopting these techniques into agriculture is at an early stage. Open-source tools and frameworks are easing the process. However, it is still a challenge to get the perfect combination of techniques appropriate for the individual use case and resource setting in which it is to be applied. Ultimately, with these privacy-preserving approaches, data may be used ethically within the realm of full potential open to AI in agriculture (Wolfert et al., 2017).

2.3 *Gaps in Current Research*

While various AI tools have been developed to ensure privacy, these have seen limited and poorly researched applications in agriculture. Most existing research studies remain theoretical or have been tested only in controlled lab settings, which in no way capture the complexities of an ever-changing agricultural environment characterized by weak internet connectivity, diverse devices, and poor data quality. Standardized and annotated datasets for privacy sensitivity are scarce, making the evaluation of privacy techniques in practice very difficult. Another major gap lies in user awareness; many farmers, especially smallholders, are not aware of how AI or their privacy tools work and, as a result, have difficulties in their adoption.

Most systems today are far too technical, lacking user-centred interfaces and localizations. Research has focused either on model accuracy or privacy, with very few, if any, striking a balance between the two. It is only recently that hybrid models designed for dynamic privacy levels are making their way to the development stage. Regulatory frameworks are behind the curve; few laws delineate agricultural data governance, ownership, or fair data-sharing provisions. Interoperability wrangling is another challenge, as many privacy tools are ill-designed for use across platforms or regions. Fostering intercommunication among computer scientists, policymakers, farmers, and agronomists will facilitate the development of solutions that are not only technically effective but also practically viable (Dwork and Roth, 2014).

2.4 Comparative Analysis of Existing Methods

Different privacy-preserving techniques in agriculture have their strength and weaknesses. For instance, FL is suited on farms in distributed environments, where models can be trained without sharing raw data. The downside is that devices must be kept in sync, there are communication delays, and data across devices is not consistent. Another technique is DP, which guarantees the amount of noise added to the dataset or output results. It seamlessly integrates into centralized systems and can handle statistical functions but might lead to loss of accuracy, especially with small datasets usually characteristic of niche agriculture use cases. The HE technique allows performing operations on encrypted data while confidentiality ensures that no one sees the data at any point in time. Theoretically, it is great, but it is heavy in computing, which will mean that it is unfeasible for real-time operations unless hardware support is available. Finally, SMPC shines in cases of collaboration, e.g., when several organizations want to joint research or share data; however, its complexity as well as resource requirements could still hinder real-time operations. No one single method can apply to different scenarios; hence, hybrid methods seem promising. Examples of the hybrid methods can be use of FL along with DP, whereby privacy balances efficiency of communication. Similar to incorporating HE with SMPC, security is ensured within collaborative efforts. Finally, the choices must be based on particular context, that is sensitivity of tasks, resources, trust of users, and limitations posited by regulations (Dwork and Roth, 2014).

3. Problem Statement and Objectives

3.1 Nature of Sensitive Agricultural Data

Information in agriculture can exhibit vast amounts of sensitive geospatial and sensor data readings on soil and water conditions. These include anything from crop rotation schedules and pest and disease reports to yield estimates and economic data, i.e., costs and profits. Thus, this information elucidates the functioning of the agribusiness even better, making it all the more dangerous if made public. For instance, proprietary methods of fertilization formulas or crop protection methods form the basis of a farmer's competitive advantage. If these methods are leaked, the farmer incurs huge losses. In the same way, private information like farm ownership, location, and financial transactions may be profiled for the sake of discrimination. With the advent of digital agriculture platforms, there has been an unprecedented amplitude of growth in the amount of data that can be collected through IoT sensors, drones, and mobile apps, making them vulnerable to cyber-attacks. Because the data is stored in a centralized way, this increases the risk of unauthorized access. Sharing data across organizational boundaries widens the risk in collaborative agricultural projects involving multiple stakeholders. The absence of standards for data access and ownership further complicates security. It is the understanding of the nature of the sensitive agricultural data that essentially influences the design of AI systems with privacy and protection as priorities to grant full confidentiality and autonomy to the farmers who own such data (Wolfert et al., 2017).

3.2 Risks of Data Leakage

Data leakages in agriculture negatively impact most things ranging from loss of personal property to multiple economic and geopolitical implications. For farmers, the short-term effects of data breaches involve the loss of competitive advantage, market manipulation, and economic distress. For instance, when competitors or buyers obtain information such as projections of yields or plans for land use, there can be unfair adjustments in the marketplace to the farmers' detriment. At a regional scale, leaked information on pest outbreaks could create multiple myths around commodity pricing and economies. When viewed in an even larger geopolitical sense, compromised agricultural data could jeopardize the national applications of food security and violate international data sovereignty laws, which may spoil relationships. Data leaks can also tarnish the reputation of the players involved, namely the agri-tech company and the government, whereby the trust levels go down and there is less adoption of that platform. On the technological side, leakage of data can interfere with the integrity of the AI model, thereby producing biased or inaccurate results which will put forward the possibilities of crop failures or wastage of resources. On the other hand, any unauthorized use of data also invites legal issues, such as penalties imposed under the GDPR, which doubles the risk. To deal with these threats would require strong measures to secure the agricultural datasphere, maintaining secrecy and integrity while keeping the entire system accountable and transparent (Bonawitz et al., 2019).

3.3 Objectives of the Proposed Model

The proposed model is a privacy-preserving AI framework, made for agriculture, data sensitivity, and resource constraints. The main goal is to implement FL into agricultural devices such as smartphones, drones, and sensors, allowing the AI model training to be localized. Hence, the normalized farm data, like soil health or yield predictions, is not sent for centralized model updates but encrypted and later used in fresh updates. Additionally, DP will be added to aggregation such that the individual-level leakage does not occur in the avalanche of model updates by adding noise to the model updates. In addition, SMPC and HE would enable encrypted collaboration without compromising privacy to facilitate secure data sharing between organizations. The system is modular so the end-users can then determine their levels of privacy according to the sensitivity of tasks and specifications of the law. It is designed for users having very low resources and intermittent connectivity so it can be feasible within possible accessibility of rural areas. The performance of this model will be evaluated based on various metrics such as accuracy, training time, communication cost, and probability of data leakage. Finally, the framework will establish trust through transparent data governance policies, auditable logs, and user consent mechanisms. This is going to make it easy to build ethics in AI for application in agriculture while keeping the sensitive data secure.

In summary, the framework ensures the training occurs on agricultural devices, so that farm data remains in the local context. The federated learning process, differential privacy, secure multi-party computation and homomorphic encryption will work together to create a multi-layered privacy pipeline that protects sensitive information during training, aggregation and collaboration across organizations. The framework is designed with usability in mind for uneven resource and connectivity landscapes in rural areas in order to provide a vehicle of inclusion and practical usability. The performance will be assessed by accuracy metrics, training time, communication costs, and probability of privacy leakage. The framework can be considered by AI practitioners and/or organizations that wish to adopt ethical AI and engender user trust in digital agriculture systems through transparent and well-defined or auditable governance mechanisms or consent workflows (Sharma et al., 2020).

4. Data Privacy Techniques

4.1 Federated Learning

Federated learning is a totally new way to machine learning, and it takes place through decentralized data processing, which is fundamental to its operation in applications of sensitive data like agriculture. Although FL does not need central data aggregation, as traditional machine learning models do, it needs model training to happen on-site from edge devices like drones, sensors, and other devices, including smartphones located on the farm premises. Each device generally downloads a global model, conducts local training using its proprietary data, and sends model updates back towards a central server. As such, raw data does not leave the device, thus improving privacy and minimizing risk in data leakage.

This provides farmers with information related to all-they-can-know soil conditions, irrigation scheduling, pest outbreaks, and yield predictions. Training will take place in this environment across multiple, diverse devices in a multitude of locations, ensuring improved accuracy on privacy issues. However, problems with FL include device heterogeneity or differences in capabilities, non-Independent and Identically Distributed data, and fault-persistent network connectivity. The use of federated averaging, model compression, and client selection algorithms works in mitigation of these challenges. This is why FL is indicated as one of the best alternatives in agricultural AIs, for its privacy-preserving characteristic and decentralized structure (Bonawitz et al., 2019).

4.2 Architecture

The FL architecture on the agriculture side revolves around three elements—the edge devices (i.e., the clients), the central server (i.e., aggregator), and the communication interface. Clients, which include soil sensors, drones, etc., retrieve a global model from the central server. The client then trains the model using its local data and computes an update, which it encrypts and sends back to the central server. The central server takes care of aggregating these updates, normally using Federated Averages (FedAvg), then updates the global model. To uphold some security, more advanced techniques like DP and HE are enforced on the client end for ensuring the safeguarding of sensitive data during transmission. Model update compression can also be performed through the methods of quantization to optimize the limited resources in rural farms. In the central dashboard, the whole system can oversee model performance and client participation. This architecture allows for scalable and privacy-preserving AI systems for agriculture, allowing for cooperability and data privacy (Wolfert et al., 2017). The overall federated learning architecture used in this framework is illustrated in Figure 6.1.

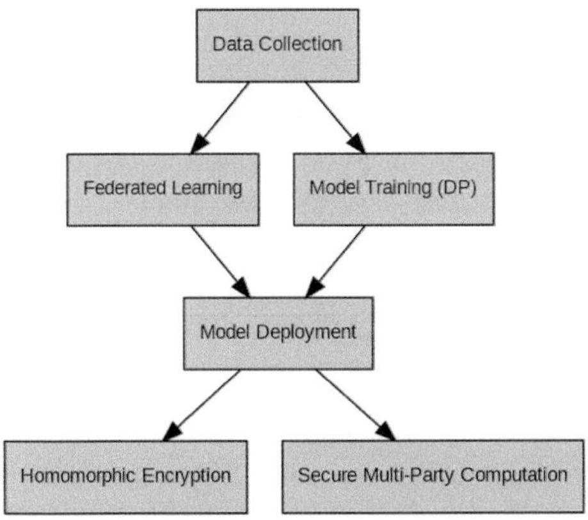

Figure 6.1: Privacy-preserving workflow in AI.

4.3 Use Cases in Agriculture

Additional examples of applications of FL in agriculture include situations that have to do with collaborative intelligence without compromising privacy. Crop disease detection is one such application. It enables farmers to collaboratively train a model using their leaf images without uploading them to any server. Thus, the model can learn to generalize better to different crop types and conditions, all the while still keeping the data private.

Other uses include precision irrigation, where devices across many farms can learn how to best achieve collaborative watering schedules without exposing sensitive farm-level data, and yield prediction models that are learned using localized training across different agro-climatic zones. FL can also be used for livestock monitoring because now wearable sensors can train health models locally and as measured encrypted updates can only be forwarded to the company. In addition, FL may support market analysis wherein farmers could learn from historical production and price data without exchanging business secrecy. This is how FL can create advanced privacy-preserving AI systems, which will be crucial for the future of agriculture (Kamilaris and Prenafeta-Boldú, 2018).

4.4 Differential Privacy

Differential Privacy is a statistical method that allows for the protection of individual data points when data is analysed or shared. DP provides this guarantee by introducing random noise in a way that makes it almost impossible to identify any individual's data. Hence, in agriculture, DP can protect sensitive farm data pertaining to yield, pests, and price estimations.

Another method of applying DP is by adding random noise to local model updates. Since DP mainly works through FL, the added noise is sent to a central server. Privacy is quantified with the parameter epsilon (ε); lower values imply more privacy but are also associated with poorer accuracy. DP provides mathematical guarantees with strong privacy protection, which is beginning to be applied in agricultural investigations so data sharing and analyses can be done without compromising individual farm data secrecy (Bonawitz et al., 2019).

4.5 Mechanisms (Laplace, Gaussian Noise)

Noise mechanisms are the foundation upon which DP is built, and among them, Laplace and Gaussian mechanisms are the most commonly applied. Laplace mechanism adds a noise sampled from a Laplace distribution either on the data or on the results of an analysis. It has usually been employed in cases where the output is, say, deterministic, such as counting or summing data. On the contrary, the Gaussian mechanism that adds noise from a Gaussian (normal) distribution is more applicable to statistical functions where accuracy is required for large datasets, like yield prediction and climate pattern analysis. It works better in high dimensionality, and user-friendliness for probabilistic models is paramount under the Gaussian mechanism.

Both mechanisms for adding noise are adaptable for FL, where the noise is added to the local updates before being shared. The choice of mechanism depends on the application area, the dataset size, and the appropriate balance required between privacy and accuracy of the model (Dwork & Roth, 2014).

4.6 Trade-offs

There are many trade-offs faced regarding private information and the accuracy of the model when implementing DP in agricultural AI systems. Scarcity of privacy budget (in smaller ε) would lead to stronger privacy with more noise that may possibly lower the accuracy of the model. Such effect can be seen in a disease prediction model where excessive noise can hide early symptoms and consequently make the model ineffective.

Another trade-off is on the overhead of computation, as adding noise will translate into computing resources required for the edge devices, which are usually limited in capability. One should also expect that DP would possibly limit interpretability as noise would obfuscate any meaningful pattern, making it difficult for the farmer to make decisions.

Finally, DP will be effective to the extent of size of the dataset. Smaller datasets tend to be much more noisy, hence the degradation of performance of the model. Therefore, privacy, accuracy, and computational resource factors must be struck well. The integration of DP with other privacy techniques, like encryption, could actually make it more effective as far as the AI systems are concerned (Bonawitz et al., 2019).

4.7 Homomorphic Encryption

Homomorphic Encryption is a cryptographic system that permits operations on encrypted data so that the outcome when decrypted will be the same as performing computation on unencrypted data. It allows secure data analysis to be carried out without revealing sensitive farm data in an agri-environment.

Thus, for example, a farm participating in insight sharing can provide data about soil health, pest outbreaks, or climate conditions in encrypted form to the central system that can analyse the data and provide insights without ever seeing the raw data. The three types of HE are: Partial Homomorphic Encryption (PHE), Somewhat Homomorphic Encryption (SHE), and Fully Homomorphic Encryption (FHE). FHE permits arbitrary computations on encrypted data but it requires intensive computation and heavy processing, which challenges its use in real-time applications in edge devices.

In addition, HE can be integrated with FL and DP to develop layered security frameworks for privacy-preserving AI systems in agriculture. HE is computation-heavy, but with the help of hardware accelerators—Graphics Processing Unit (GPU) and Field-Programmable Gate Array (FPGA)—it is becoming practically viable (Sharma et al., 2020).

4.8 Types and Computational Cost

The choice of HE will directly affect computational costs. PHE schemes such as RSA and Paillier support just one operation (addition or multiplication). Such schemes are lightweight and fit for doing basic tasks like encrypted summation, which is emphasized in agriculture for secure data aggregation. SHE allows both additions and multiplications, albeit limited. FHE allows unlimited computation on encrypted data, but these are computationally expensive. The latency and memory overhead of FHE for real-time applications tend to be impractical on resource-constrained devices such as edge sensors. Progress in lattice-based cryptography and hardware acceleration is helping to considerably bring down the cost applied to FHE; however, it has not yet gained popularity. There is a current trend for hybrid schemes that marry lightweight HE with FL or SMPC to further lessen the burden of expense while firmly continuing to assure privacy protection (Sharma et al., 2020).

4.9 Secure Multi-party Computation (SMPC)

Secure Multi-party Computation is a suite of cryptographic protocols allowing each of several parties to jointly compute a function over their inputs while keeping those inputs private. As applied in agriculture, SMPC pertains to instances where stakeholders such as the farmer, cooperative, or research institution intend to analyse the data secretly while cooperating in performing the analysis.

For example, agricultural centres can collaborate in analysing data on soil degradation or crop yield from different regions while keeping each individual dataset private. SMPC protocols protect the data against privacy violations by adversarial participants attempting even to compromise the output; some of the parties could even act maliciously and still guarantee that the data remain in the secure custody of the others.

Secure Multi-party Computation can be intensive in computation and bandwidth, but recent optimizations in the protocols and cloud-based SMPC platforms make it more feasible. Furthermore, it can be executed together with FL, allowing safe aggregation of model updates from multiple parties. SMPC can guarantee higher privacy assurances and therefore has gained widespread adoption for collaborative agricultural data analyses, aiding in ensuring the privacy of the data while garnering cooperative insights (Sharma et al., 2020).

5. Proposed System Architecture

5.1 System Design Overview

The proposed privacy-preserving AI system for agriculture has a thoroughly modular, layered architecture that enhances data security, scalability, and real-world applicability. At its kernel, the integration of FL, DP, HE, and SMPC would ensure that an AI-enabled intelligent agricultural insight can be given while sensitive data is kept confidential and under the direct control of the owner. Starting from edge devices like IoT-enabled sensors, mobile phones, and drones to collect local farm data—such as soil moisture, crop imagery, temperature, and humidity—this would then conduct on-site training using FL, sending only encrypted model updates to a central server. This central aggregator receives such models from different clients and performs weighted aggregation to this with additional DP mechanisms injecting statistical noise into the updates for added security. Depending on deployment scenarios, model updates may again be encrypted through HE before transmission, and SMPC can be used for collaborative computations between two or more of such organizations. Such a design carries with it strong error-handling protocols for network failure, device dropout, and an uneven nature of distributed data. Additionally, the architecture is plug-and-play: one could selectively switch on or off different privacy mechanisms or even combine them based on their case sensitivity. A centralized dashboard will allow real-time monitoring of model performance, update frequency, and system health while stringent authentication and consent forms will regulate user access; these will ensure the widespread, privacy-aware deployment of the system in all possible forms of agricultural landscapes, from individual farms to national cooperatives, without compromise of either performance or privacy (Kamilaris and Prenafeta-Boldú, 2018).

5.2 Data Flow Diagram

The flow of data inside a proposed system architecture provides privacy at all levels of AI model training and deployment. This flow starts from the client side, where raw data is collected from sensors and cameras, and user inputs with individual farm devices. Raw data coming from the device is no longer sent to a centralized server but is instead used for training a local instance of a predefined AI model in each of such devices. After the training is completed, the model update is then created, in the form of a gradient or weight change, which uses the privacy-enhancing layers. The first of these layers adds DP noise to hide sensitive patterns. These updates can then be optionally encrypted using HE. At this stage, the updates will be secured and then communicated over a secure channel to the central aggregator. In a case where the updates are received from multiple independent stakeholders, SMPC protocols may be applied at the aggregator level. Finally, the server executes a secure aggregation of the updates through Federated Averaging to create a new global model. Then, this global model is redistributed to all participating client devices, which repeat this process in subsequent training rounds. In this pipeline, the raw data never leaves the device it is sourced from, and it is attached with encryption and anonymization along each of the transmissions. Besides, they can be logged in an auditable format to ensure auditability and accountability. The data flow is, therefore, secure and iterative, allowing continued learning and improvement in the model without sacrificing individual data privacy. Such methods are perfectly suited for large distributed ecosystems of agriculture (Bonawitz et al., 2019).

5.3 AI Model Components

The integrated components of AI models are meant in the proposed system for usage in agricultural tasks that shall take care of the computational constraints existing on edge devices. This modular model architecture constitutes the only foundation of the proposed system, which can be customized for several applications, such as crop disease detection or yield forecasting, irrigation management, and market price forecasting. For image-based tasks like disease detection and weed identification, the system uses lightweight CNNs so that they can be trained locally with farm-collected images. These models are engineered to run on mobile or embedded devices through techniques such as model pruning and quantization to maximize efficiency. The time-series forecasting tasks include yield estimation and climate pattern prediction through harnessing the temporal dependencies of Long Short-Term Memory (LSTM) topologies of Recurrent Neural Networks (RNNs). Further, Decision Tree–based models like Gradient Boosted Trees (GBT) have been integrated for rule-based estimates such as fertilizer recommendation and pest control strategy. Models of this category fare well in the real world because they are easily interpretable and have reduced computation footprint. Encapsulation of every model would take place within a training module that is DP-compliant for training local. Besides that, all models would feature the option of encrypted communication protocols using HE towards securing confidentiality on updates. The different standard metrics shall be induced to evaluate model performance using accuracy, precision, recall, or F1-score. Here, thresholds would also be put in place to trigger alerts whenever degradation is detected. This set of AI model components thus has the capability of forming a whole with regard to immensely diverse agricultural uses (Kamilaris and Prenafeta-Boldú, 2018).

5.4 *Integration of Privacy Mechanisms*

The incorporation of privacy methods is done in the proposed architecture in such a way that it provides numerous layers of protection without hindering the performance of the model. In particular, it allows decentralized model training on client devices without needing to transfer raw data through FL. This is supplemented by DP, which introduces a statistical noise during the local training to cover individual data contributions with the model updates. The degree of noise is calibrated with the privacy budget (epsilon), which can dynamically change as per the sensitivity of the data and the degree of privacy desired. For further improvement of confidentiality, HE is carried out to encrypt model update operations before being sent to the central server to ensure that even if such communications are intercepted, a person is unable to understand, read, or comprehend the message. Sometimes, in cases of multi-stakeholders, such as research consortia or policy development groups, the SMPC allows cooperative model training among stakeholders for non-exposure of private datasets. In this aspect, the privacy mechanisms are bundled into a modular framework that can be turned on and off by the user as per the contextual need (Wolfert et al., 2017).

For example, a smallholder farmer with a very basic smartphone would use an FL and DP-only system whereas a full set involving HE and SMPC might be deployed for a government-led initiative incorporating sensitive policy data. This is also the privacy monitoring dashboard where there is real-time feedback on data usage, consumption of privacy budget, and system alerts. Transparency is what brings trust among users and ensures compliance by law in data protection. All in all, the multiple seamless integration of privacy-preserving methods into the proposed architecture provides a scalable, secure, and user-centric way for deployment of AI in agriculture. In its very design, integration of privacy features within the proposed architecture is exhaustive enough to provide multiple layers of protections without degrading model performance. FL is the underlying principle supporting this by allowing decentralized model development on client devices without the need to transmit raw data. To this end, DP is added as a local training step that applies statistical noise to the model updates, thus obscuring the contributions made by individuals' data. The degree of such noise will be fine-tuned by the privacy budget (epsilon), which can be further adjusted to suit the sensitivity of data and privacy levels (Bonawitz et al., 2019).

For enhanced confidentiality, the model updates are encrypted using HE before sending to central server, which means that even if the entire transmission is intercepted, its content cannot be read. In order to improve confidentiality capabilities in our framework, we can further protect model updates using encryption methods prior to transmission, ensuring that intercepted model updates cannot be read or accessed by unauthorized users. Furthermore, in situations where multiple organizations are involved, such as across institutions conducting research or cross-organization policy coordination, the power of Secure Multi-Party Computation (SMPC) can support training a joint model without sharing, or even seeing, raw data among multiple organizations. The framework is built with the idea of modularity in mind, allowing users to select the privacy components best suited for either the capabilities of their devices or the sensitivity of their tasks. For example, a farmer implementing a basic agriculture framework on a low-end mobile device may only choose to use federated learning and differential privacy, while government or research institution deployments engaged in the processing of highly sensitive data may turn on added layers of privacy through homomorphic encryption and SMPC. Users can view a dedicated privacy dashboard that illustrates the use of their data, the performance of multi-party computation and updated information about the privacy options being implemented to provide an additional layer of transparency to the data-protection standards system. Overall, the flexibility of the system supports adopting a privacy-sensitive AI method that can be securely used and adapted in multiple agricultural contexts. All in all, the multiple seamless integration of privacy-preserving architecture offers a scalable, secure, and user-centric approach to deployment of AI in agriculture (Dwork and Roth, 2014).

6. Methodology

6.1 Data Acquisition Considerations and Procedures

In developing a modular and systemic structure for a privacy-preserving AI system for agricultural data, the core dataset featured real agricultural data alongside simulated tabular data created using Generative

Adversarial Networks (GANs). Real agricultural data were supplied by partner cooperatives under very strict Non-Disclosure Agreement (NDA) to serve as the basis for ethical and legal compliance. Synthetic data that behave very much like real statistics but maintain personal privacy were generated with GANs to overcome the customary availability restrictions and privacy regulations.

So, the entire dataset comprised different variables such as crop yield, soil chemistry, farmer demographics, weather patterns, and pesticide application rates. For confidentiality, the Personally Identifiable Information data such as names, addresses, and IDs were anonymized according to ISO/IEC 20889:2018. The method by which the anonymization took effect was such that there was no undercover data existing within the system, thus ensuring full privacy for the farmers. The preprocessing workflow used in the proposed privacy-preserving model is illustrated in Figure 6.2.

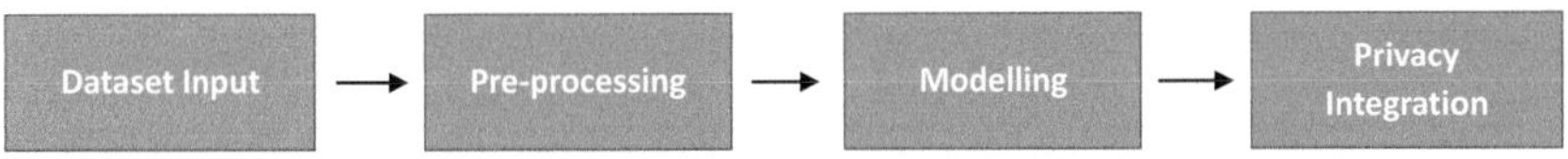

Figure 6.2: Flowchart for methodology.

6.2 *Pre-processing Techniques*

These offer a multi-step checklist to process data for quality and compliance with privacy. The interpolation of missing values was accomplished by applying K-nearest neighbours respecting the local data distributions. Extreme values and outliers were normalized using z-scores to prevent distortion of model performance by underlying statistical noise. There is a form of ordinal encoding using target mean encoding for categorical features typical to agricultural datasets (e.g., crop types, soil classification). This creates hierarchical relationships in the data but also exploits the statistical patterns that existed within the categories.

Stratified sampling was used so that the data splits maintain balanced occurrences of the classes across the training and validation sets. This minimizes the risk of both overfits and bias, especially in cases of imbalanced sets.

6.3 *Model Selection*

In this modelling phase, three AI architectures were selected because they were particularly suited to performing various types of agricultural data. Among them, Random Forests were used to work on tabular data, such as prediction of yield by crop and analyses on soil chemistry. Random Forests were selected for their robustness and interpretability, which make them suitable for structured rich-feature agricultural datasets.

Convolutional Neural Networks, originally developed for image processing, have been adapted for spatial data processing. This adaptation allowed CNNs to directly take Normalized Difference Vegetation Index (NDVI) images and satellite-derived land cover input as input. These models performed very well in detecting relationships and vegetated patterns across large geographic scales.

The third model category was Transformer-based architectures which were used for the treatment of temporal relationships in agriculture applications such as the prediction of a crop harvest because of the effect of weather patterns. These types can capture sequences and long-range dependencies data, and thus they are very useful for rainfall pattern modelling and their effect on crop growth (Kaissis et al., 2020).

Thus, these three models were brought together into an ensemble architecture that combined their predictions with weighted averaging and meta modelling strategies. The final process was cross-validation using macro-F1 scores to prioritize selection and fine tuning of ensemble models based on balanced performance across classes.

6.4 Privacy Mechanisms Integration

The DP mechanism was introduced in the training of the model to implement privacy in model training. We applied the Gaussian mechanism to add noise to the per-sample gradient updates during model training so that sensitive information would not be leaked during the training stage. DP was incorporated smoothly into the training pipeline using the Opacus library, which integrates DP into PyTorch workflows. Gradient clipping and noise injection allowed data privacy to be secured while nevertheless facilitating learning of the model (Dwork and Roth, 2014).

The SMPC protocols were also incorporated, which made FL possible whereby data from different geographic or institutional nodes could be processed without sharing the raw data. This decentralized learning approach significantly increased privacy since no sensitive data would ever leave the individual nodes (Bonawitz et al., 2019).

In addition, LDP methods were distilled to being placed on the edge devices with limited processing capabilities. With this multi-tiered approach, privacy is guaranteed at all levels of the system, from the edge devices to the global model. The Differentially Private Federated Averaging algorithm is employed to synchronize the privacy-preserving gradient updates across the federated nodes, thereby controlling the privacy-utility trade-off (McMahan et al., 2017).

7. Implementation Details

The entire system was developed on a Python 3.10 base, chosen for its flexibility with many libraries for larger functionality. In using TensorFlow Privacy and the Opacus library, privacy-related components were integrated to enable easy integration of DP techniques into TensorFlow and PyTorch-based models.

Flower (FLwr) framework was used for FL facilitating multi-node decentralized training sessions. The framework allowed scalable and flexible coordination among nodes, each to represent a cooperative or institutional unit in the agricultural construct. For distributed data processing, Apache Spark was used, whereby the system would efficiently work on big datasets either on the cloud-based infrastructure or local devices (Li et al., 2020).

Hybrid Deployment Architecture: Model training was done on Amazon Web Services (AWS) EC2 GPU instances at a large scale for high-performance processing.

Edge Device Simulation: Local deployments were simulated using Raspberry Pi clusters and NVIDIA Jetson Nano boards that truly model the limited-resource conditions of rural or remote agricultural settings.

Containerization and orchestration were managed on Helm and Kubernetes. Thus scalability and reproducibility across entirely different environments would be ensured. These tools were essential in managing the FL complex infrastructure for data processing and model training.

7.1 Privacy-Preserving Algorithms and Security Measures

These are the algorithms which have been incorporated in developing privacy during model training and sharing of data. Differentially Private Stochastic Gradient Descent (DP SGD) was applied along with the average model averaging techniques as well as Shamir's Secret Sharing which then made possible use of SMPC that allowed several nodes to be trained collaboratively on a model without sharing any sensitive data (Truong et al., 2020).

SHapley Additive exPlanations adaptation was formulated for model interpretability, which provides all diversified stakeholders—farmers, policymakers, and agronomists—understandable reasons behind the model decisions without disclosing sensitive details. Security was established using end-to-end encryption via PyCryptodome—an extremely trusted cryptographic library. Although IBM HELib for HE was tested, it was found to be rather computation-intensive for on-time usage. The OpenMined Syft library ensured secure data sharing across federated nodes through provision of privacy-preserving data exchange. JWT and OAuth 2.0 ensured robust authentication with multi-factor authentication for secure access to the system.

8. Evaluation Metrics

The efficiency of privacy-preserving AI modelling was evaluated through a multi-faceted approach. Other machine learning metrics including accuracy, precision, recall, and F1 Score were also used to evaluate these different agricultural prediction tasks including crop yield estimation and pest infestation forecasting. These tools act as a baseline for evaluation on utility concerning a model predictions privacy-preserving scenario.

One of the very few metrics for evaluating privacy was privacy budget (ε), which was tuned in the range of 0.1–1.5. Lower values of ε indicate stronger protection of privacy, whereas values were optimized in a way that their limits become sub-linear privacy leakage. By means of curves plotting model performance against ε values, the privacy utility trade-off was visualized, which helps in identifying operating points where privacy was maximized while minimizing the loss in predictive accuracy (Dwork and Roth, 2014).

Further metrics were applied to measure the communication efficiency of the system in FL. These included model update sizes, bandwidth consumption, as well as node-to-node latency. Such metrics played a crucial role in determining how much the model would scale in its distributed networks. Weight quantization and update sparsification were also applied in order to minimize the communication overhead and perform better in scaling. Profiling training time per epoch and total convergence time established the computation intensity of training as well as the interference caused by privacy mechanisms. These metrics helped in determining whether or not privacy-preserving models could be adopted on resource-constrained devices (Kaissis et al., 2020).

9. Results and Discussion

These models for privacy purposes showed decidedly strong performance, where prediction accuracies were reduced marginally against non-private models. Introduction of privacy mechanisms gave rise to performance drop of just 2–4%. Thus, data privacy can be assured without much perturbing the accuracy of the model. In particular, models with $\varepsilon = 0.3$ retained almost 92% of the baseline performance, proving the efficacy of differentially private mechanisms. Among the tested models, the Transformer architectures suffered loudest from noise but were able to maintain increased performance in situations where privacy was very high. On the contrary, CNNs were excellent in spatial data efficacy but susceptible to declines in performance under higher privacy conditions, showing sensitivity to perturbation of data.

A wheat yield prediction case study conducted across three major agricultural states of India showed that FL nodes could converge successfully to a good global model in 50 training iterations on locally installed co-operative servers. The FL node proof model indicated that all the sensitive data could remain fully local while adding to the global predictive system, thereby indicating the feasibility and policies of the approach. Identity visualization tools like ROC-AUC plots, confusion matrixes, and ε-accuracy trade-off plots revealed what the models produced in terms of fairness and performance against privacy mechanisms.

10. Challenges and Limitations

While the results were promising, several hurdles remained in the application of privacy-preserving AI. Despite that, the overhead induced by SMPC and HE schemes caused latency, particularly during secure aggregation and decryption. Although GPU acceleration alleviated part of the delay, it was still not feasible for real-time updates in resource-constrained environments, especially in rural areas with poor infrastructural facilities (Shokri and Shmatikov, 2015).

Another challenge was the limited availability of data, driven by regulatory restrictions and an age-old institutional reluctance with regard to the extent of cost and diversity of datasets already available, especially in terms of the all-important socio-economic, ecological, and cultural issues in agricultural decision-making. There were areas, although filled by synthetic data, that were not fine enough to take note of the total complexity involved in agricultural practices.

Federated Learning Scalability has thus become a great limiting factor in the entire FL framework. A good performance response was thus noted when the system place was at 12–15 nodes; however, beyond 50 nodes, performance degraded due to communication latency and synchronization complexity. The next versions will implement gossiping-type communication and model compression techniques for scalability improvement across larger, national, or transnational agricultural networks. Privacy and accuracy can also be challenging to balance (Li et al., 2020).

11. Applications and Use Cases

11.1 Precision Agriculture

One of the uses of precision agriculture is to collect real-time data from IoT sensors, Unmanned Aerial Vehicle (UAV), and weather stations to create very precise intervention in agriculture. The parameters include soil moisture, pH, nutrient content, and microclimatic conditions, all being effective in bringing better yield and resource conservation by better decision-making in farming. Monitoring the field conditions continuously helps farmers make their decisions regarding irrigation, fertilization, and pest control, all specific to their own land (Ramesh and Chandra, 2023).

Privacy-preserving AI approaches are used to secure sensitive farm data. These employ local machine learning models, so that raw sensor data does not cross the boundaries of the farm. Thus, farmers can continue to enjoy the benefits of accurate personal crop recommendations without sacrificing their privacy of data. For example, a farmer in Tamil Nadu would receive different advice as compared to a farmer from Punjab, based on soil and climate differences in their areas. But at the same time, neither of them would have their data leaving the regions (Ramesh and Chandra, 2023). A visual representation of a smart farm equipped with IoT devices is shown in Figure 6.3.

Figure 6.3: Smart farm layout with IoT devices.

11.2 Crop Disease Prediction

Machine learning methodology has enormous superiority in plant disease prediction from time-series data analysis and leaf image analysis. These measures can show early symptoms of disease that can be successfully treated by preventive measures to save crops and increase profits. However, the utilization of image datasets incurs very severe implications such as revealing too much unintended private information regarding field layouts, crop health status, or proprietary farming techniques practised by the producers (Mohan et al., 2020).

To combat this, differential private CNNs are deployed on FL systems. These models allow for disease recognition algorithms to be trained at each federated node without centralized sensitive image data. In this way, privacy can be secured as well as accuracy maintained, which otherwise would have been burdensome, especially for large-scale producers where huge investments are incurred on proprietary unique cultivars and strategies against resistance diseases, thus keeping their intellectual agricultural knowledge private (Dwork and Roth, 2014).

11.3 Livestock Monitoring

Wearable devices on livestock monitor key indicators such as body temperature, movement patterns, and feeding behaviours. Data gathered in this way are vital for real-time assessment of animal health and welfare, enabling early detection of disease or stress by the farmer. Such data can also be exploited, however, to reveal wider market trends in livestock health, which competitors could access if they are not protected adequately (Mohan et al., 2020).

Federated learning with HE could then safeguard this aspect of sensitive data. The model helps several actors to train a predictive model for disease outbreak detection, such as Foot-and-Mouth Disease (FMD) and brucellosis, without exposing the raw identifiable information. Each farm can, therefore, contribute to the common model using encrypted details with due regard for commercial privacy and simultaneous benefits from joint intelligence (Bonawitz et al., 2019).

11.4 Market Prediction and Price Forecasting

Feverish growth in AI tools encouraged farmers to increase their forecast for the price of commodities by looking at past historical records, through calculation of supply chain dynamics, and through assessment of climate impacts on future production. Such forecasts help make critically timed decisions about harvesting or selling produce. The sharing of such precious data with any market aggregator or external sources is tantamount to leaving open doors for manipulation of price or value-unsafe pricing practices, thus often punishing smallholders. Privacy-preserving AI allows farmers to receive customized insights without revealing personal information such as projected yield or harvest dates through secure technologies like FL and DP. By using such measures, agri-cooperatives are able to safely pool anonymized data for collective benefit through bargaining for better prices and avoiding market oversaturation, all benefiting both the individual farmer and the agriculture community in general (Mohan et al., 2020).

Human to AI text and human text conversion: Farm to use value for the future. AI-based price prediction tools help farmers make better decisions by analysing historical market trends, supply chain trends, and weather variables. These predictions help farmers figure out when is the best time to harvest or sell their crop. However, by sharing personal and potentially sensitive information with intermediaries, or other third-party platforms, farmers especially smallholders are at risk for being manipulated, exploited by price gaps, or being taken advantage of in market situations.

Privacy enhanced AI helps to mitigate these risks. Farmers can take advantage of market intelligence specific to them while not sharing anytime of personal information as it predicts crop yields, time of harvest, etc. Through collaboration, farmer cooperatives will be able to capitalize on the secure technology utilizing anonymized data, to strengthen their position in the market and not be in situations where they are oversold. Ultimately, this new market may create a more transparent and equitable market to benefit an individual farmer's and cooperative's interests, while benefitting the agricultural supply chain, too (Shokri and Shmatikov, 2015).

11.5 Smart Irrigation and Resource Optimization

The AI-driven real-time irrigation decisions have the potential to significantly reduce water usage while maintaining crop health. By analysing local soil moisture, weather patterns, and crop requirements, smart irrigation devices can optimize watering schedules for maximum efficiency. These systems not only conserve a critical resource but also reduce energy and labour costs for farmers.

Federated learning embedded within these devices allows the underlying AI models to improve continuously using data from multiple farms—all without transmitting raw data off-site. Each device contributes to refining the model while preserving on-farm privacy. This decentralized, privacy-preserving setup ensures that sensitive agricultural data remains confidential, fostering both environmental sustainability and data security across farming networks (Bonawitz et al., 2019).

12. Future Scope

12.1 Federated AI Ecosystems

Analytical models of this kind are being developed to benefit all Agri-tech stakeholders, including farmers, research institutions, and policymakers.

In federative model collaborative training, data locality is strictly held sacred and never allowed to cross any farm's perimeter, hence mooting all sorts of risks to valuable agronomical information. This stimulates innovation without compromising the privacy of owners of invaluable agronomical information, using GEO-API for improved resilience through better data access, without jeopardizing security of propriety datasets that some other platforms might do. So private information never gets to the central server yet the wealth of knowledge boosts crop resilience and regional adaptation in the best interests of the entire agricultural ecosystem (Bonawitz et al., 2019).

12.2 Integration with Blockchain for Auditability

The combination of privacy-preserving AI with the blockchain technology could provide a tremendous opportunity for safeguarding secure and transparent innovation in technology. While privacy-preserving AI defends the confidentiality of raw data at the moment of model training, blockchain builds trust through the immutable record-keeping on every training session or model alteration over a decentralized ledger. This way, the data privacy thus preserved is not tampered with or misused (Shokri and Shmatikov, 2015).

Farmers can hence contribute their encrypted data into community-based AI model growth, provided they are promised security and clear validation for their contribution. The blockchain may also allow for full traceability of contributions and bestow merit tokens or other such rewards on those spending their time helping in model development, thus moving towards achieving maximum participation in cultivating an equitable and responsible agri-tech environment.

12.3 On-Device Machine Learning for Agriculture

Far at the edge of computation at the hardware level, these kinds of developments evoke nostalgia for the living-on-board AI models—devices such as Raspberry Pi-enabled soil sensors and AI-empowered cameras on drones. This paradigm shift enables real-time processing and on-site decision-making, resulting in responsive actions such as irrigation schedule changes or crop stress detections without the need for constancy in internet connectivity (Mohan et al., 2020).

Edge devices can also allow learning and inference with encryption, thus rendering all sensitive data seen as secure even in the remotest and disconnected places. Thus, processing and securing data locally enables intelligent automation for farmers in remote regions, retaining their top-most primacy in information and building resilience and privacy in

Figure 6.4: Real-time AI in remote farm.

modern farming. A visual representation of real-time AI-based remote farm monitoring is shown in Figure 6.4.

12.4 Dynamic Privacy Budgets and Personalized Privacy

Upcoming agricultural AI systems will integrate dynamic ε in DP, which empowers the stakeholders to define their own privacy levels. Such flexibility enables every actor to calibrate their privacy-utility balance, according to roles and risk appetites. So, for instance, a smallholder farmer would choose a small ε value for strict privacy, whereas a research institute might find it worthwhile to gauge a greater ε to contribute more data and obtain a clearer, deeper insight (Dwork and Roth, 2014).

Designing systems that can adapt on the fly to this diversity of preferences without the need to retrain models from scratch makes them more inclusive of diverse stakeholder bases, enables collaborative learning to remain efficient, personalized, and secure, and builds truly adaptable future and privacy-aware agricultural intelligence.

12.5 Global Collaboration in Privacy-Preserving Agri-AI

Cross-border collaboration in the regions of India, Africa, and Southeast Asia holds great promise in accelerating agricultural innovations. The regions stand to collaborate towards the common purpose of alleviating global problems, such as climate change, resource scarcity, and food shortages, through the sharing of anonymized information relating to trends in crop productivity, pest outbreaks, and issues surrounding food insecurity. Most importantly, this information sharing can occur without compromising local data sovereignty and without disclosure of sensitive information by the regions involved (Mohan et al., 2020).

Privacy-preserving technologies, such as FL and DP, enable cross-border knowledge sharing while ensuring raw data remain in the country of origin and insights are shared internationally. This approach engenders fair innovations as agricultural communities will have the benefit of insights without conflict over cultural, political, and regulatory hurdles.

13. Conclusion

This study highlights the increasing demand for privacy-preserving AI in farming, where data-driven intelligence can dramatically increase productivity, facilitate early disease detection, and assist in sustainable agriculture. Yet, these developments should not be at the expense of farmers' data sovereignty or privacy. FL, SMPC, and DP are some technologies that provide secure means to leverage AI without revealing raw or sensitive data.

By using these approaches, farmers can leverage AI-driven suggestions while retaining ownership of their data. This promotes active engagement in the digital environment and develops trust that will bring about greater adoption. Trust is the key factor that will make farmers more likely to cooperate and provide invaluable feedback if they understand that their data is respected and safeguarded. To make this change work, collaborations among governments, agri-tech firms, and research organizations are crucial. Together, they need to forge open, accessible, and responsible frameworks to safeguard privacy and keep it at the forefront. Agriculture's digital future hinges not only on innovation but also on prudent and fair utilization of data.

References

Abadi, M. et al. (2016). Deep Learning with differential privacy. pp. 308–318. *In*: Weippl, E.R., Katzenbeisser, S., Kruegel, C. and Myers, A.C. (eds.). *Proceedings of the 2016 ACM SIGSAC Conference on Computer and Communications Security (CCS).*

Bonawitz, K., Eichner, H., Grieskamp, W., Huba, D., Ingerman, A., Ivanov, V., Kiddon, C., Konečný, J., Mazzocchi, S., McMahan, H.B., Moore, E., Ramage, D., Roselander, J. and Seth, K. (2019). Towards Federated Learning at scale: System design. *arXiv preprint arXiv:1902.01046.*

Dwork, C. and Roth, A. (2014). The algorithmic foundations of differential privacy. *Foundations and Trends in Theoretical Computer Science* 9(3-4): 211–407.

Kaissis, G.A., Makowski, M.R., Rückert, D. and Braren, R.F. (2020). Secure, privacy-preserving and federated machine learning in medical imaging. *Nature Machine Intelligence* 2(6): 305–311.

Kamilaris, A. and Prenafeta-Boldú, F.X. (2018). Deep learning in agriculture: A survey. *Computers and Electronics in Agriculture* 147: 70–90.

Li, T., Sahu, A.K., Talwalkar, A. and Smith, V. (2020). Federated learning: Challenges, methods, and future directions. *IEEE Signal Processing Magazine* 37(3): 50–60.

McMahan, H.B., Moore, E., Ramage, D., Hampson, S. and Arcas, B.A.Y. (2017). Communication-efficient learning of deep networks from decentralized data.

pp. 1273–1282. *In*: Singh, A. and Zhu, J. (eds.). *Proceedings of the 20th International Conference on Artificial Intelligence and Statistics (AISTATS).*

Mohan, N., Yaashikaa, P.R., Kumar, P.S., Karishma, S. and Varjani, S. (2020). AI and big data in agriculture: A systematic literature review. *Computers and Electronics in Agriculture* 178: 105870.

Ramesh, S. and Chandra, S. (2023). Privacy-aware AI framework for AgriTech startups. *Journal of Smart Farming* 14(2): 34–52.

Sharma, A., Choudhary, D. and Kaushik, N. (2020). Applications of artificial intelligence in agriculture. *Journal of Scientific & Industrial Research* 79: 797–804.

Shokri, R. and Shmatikov, V. (2015). Privacy-preserving deep learning. pp. 1310–1321. *In*: Indrajit Ray and Ninghui Li (eds.). *Proceedings of the 22nd ACM SIGSAC Conference on Computer and Communications Security (CCS).*

Truong, N.B., Sun, K., Wang, G. and Ghaffari, M. (2020). Privacy preservation in federated learning: Challenges and solutions. *IEEE Communications Surveys & Tutorials* 23(1): 426–448.

Wolfert, S., Ge, L., Verdouw, C. and Bogaardt, M.-J. (2017). Big data in smart farming—A review. *Agricultural Systems* 153: 69–80.

Chapter 7

A Machine Learning Framework for Dynamic Malware Analysis in IoT-based Smart Agriculture System

Santosh K. Smmarwar,[1,*] *Rahul Priyadarshi,*[1]
Sushil Bahadur Pankaj,[1] *Pratik Angaitkar*[2] and *Subodh Mishra*[3]

The global population is expected to reach 10 billion by 2050, increasing food demand by 60–70%. Smart agriculture is crucial to overcome the current and future challenges that can lead to food scarcity for this rising global population. Despite high initial investment, data security concerns, and skill gaps, smart agriculture presents a transformative opportunity for sustainable and resilient farming. Its adoption is critical for meeting the demands of a growing global population while safeguarding natural resources and mitigating the effects of climate change. Smart agriculture systems leverage Internet of Things (IoT) devices, drones, sensors, cloud platforms, and data

[1] Centre of Internet of Things, Department of Computer Science and Engineering, Siksha 'O' Anusandhan (Deemed to be University), Odisha, India.
[2] Department of Artificial Intelligence & Data Science, P.R. Pote Patil College of Engineering & Management, Maharashtra, India.
[3] Department of SCSET, Bennett University, Uttar Pradesh, India.
[*] Corresponding author: santoshsamarwar@soa.ac.in

DOI: 10.1201/9781003670568-7

analytics platforms to optimize farming processes. However, these interconnected technologies are increasingly vulnerable to malware attacks and potential cybersecurity risks, including data breaches, ransomware, and system intrusions. Malware in such systems can compromise device functionality, data integrity, and operational continuity. Traditional signature-based detection struggles against new evolving malware. Machine learning (ML) models can adapt to novel threats. By integrating ML into smart agriculture systems, farmers can make data-driven decisions that minimize risks and optimize productivity, paving the way for sustainable and resilient farming practices. ML provides a robust and effective approach to risk assessment and detecting dynamic malware in these environments.

1. Introduction

The rapid adoption of Internet of Things (IoT) technologies in smart agriculture has revolutionized farming practices by enabling real-time monitoring, automation, and data-driven decision-making. IoT-based smart agriculture systems integrate sensors, drones, automated irrigation, and livestock tracking to enhance productivity, reduce resource waste, and improve crop yields. However, the increasing reliance on interconnected devices also exposes these systems to cybersecurity threats, particularly malware attacks that can disrupt operations, steal sensitive data, or even cause physical damage to agricultural infrastructure.

Malware targeting IoT devices in smart agriculture can take various forms, including ransomware, botnets, and spyware, often exploiting vulnerabilities in firmware, weak authentication mechanisms, or insecure communication protocols. Analysing such malware is critical to understanding its behaviour, propagation methods, and potential impact on agricultural IoT ecosystems. Effective malware analysis involves static and dynamic techniques to dissect malicious code, identify attack vectors, and develop mitigation strategies to safeguard smart farming environments. Traditional malware detection methods often struggle to keep pace with the evolving threat landscape, necessitating advanced approaches such as machine learning (ML) for effective analysis and mitigation. ML offers powerful capabilities in identifying and classifying malware by analysing patterns in network traffic, device behaviour, and code structures, enabling proactive threat detection in real time. By leveraging techniques such as anomaly detection, supervised learning, and deep learning, ML-based malware analysis can enhance the security of smart agriculture systems, ensuring resilience against zero-day exploits and polymorphic malware. Malware analysis is a crucial process for identifying, understanding, and mitigating cyber threats in IoT-based smart agriculture systems. Given agricultural IoT devices' unique challenges, such as limited computational power, heterogeneous communication protocols, and remote deployment, different malware analysis techniques are employed to effectively detect and neutralize threats. These techniques can be broadly classified into static, dynamic, hybrid, and behavioural analysis, each offering distinct advantages in securing smart farming environments.

This chapter explores the methodologies and challenges of malware analysis in IoT-based smart agriculture, highlighting the importance of securing connected farming systems against evolving cyber threats. By examining real-world attack scenarios and defence mechanisms, we aim to contribute to developing resilient agricultural IoT infrastructures that can withstand malicious intrusions while maintaining operational efficiency.

1.1 Static Analysis

Static malware analysis is a technique that examines malicious code without execution, focusing on its structure, signatures, and embedded data to identify threats. In IoT-based smart agriculture, where devices like soil sensors, automated irrigation systems, and livestock trackers operate with limited security protections, static analysis helps detect malware before it can disrupt farming operations. Analysts use tools such as disassemblers (IDA Pro, Ghidra), hex editors, and signature scanners to inspect firmware, binaries, and configuration files for suspicious patterns. Key indicators include hardcoded malicious IP addresses, unusual strings (e.g., "kill_irrigation"), or obfuscated payloads hidden in device updates.

This method is particularly useful for identifying known malware strains (e.g., Mirai variants targeting IoT devices) and supply chain attacks where compromised vendor software is distributed to farms. However, static analysis struggles with polymorphic malware (which changes its code to evade detection) and file-less attacks that reside only in memory. Despite these limitations, static analysis remains a fast, low-resource approach suitable for agricultural IoT environments where real-time processing power is limited. Combined with dynamic and hybrid analysis, it strengthens the overall security of smart farming systems against cyber threats.

1.2 Dynamic Analysis

Dynamic malware analysis involves executing suspicious code in a controlled, isolated environment to observe its runtime behaviour and identify malicious activities. Unlike static analysis, which examines code without running it, dynamic analysis provides real-time insights into how malware interacts with systems, networks, and other applications. This technique is particularly valuable for smart agriculture systems. IoT devices like soil sensors, irrigation controllers, and livestock trackers are vulnerable to attacks that may only reveal themselves during execution. By using sandboxing tools such as Cuckoo Sandbox or QEMU-based emulators, security analysts can monitor malware actions, including file modifications, network communications, and system Application Programming Interface (API) calls. For instance, dynamic analysis can detect ransomware encrypting crop data or botnets hijacking agricultural drones by analysing abnormal traffic patterns. It also helps uncover zero-day exploits that evade signature-based detection, such as malware exploiting vulnerabilities in farm management software. However, dynamic analysis has limitations, including the need for secure environments to prevent accidental infections and the possibility of malware detecting and evading virtualized settings. Despite these challenges, dynamic analysis remains essential for understanding real-world malware impacts, enabling the development of effective defences for IoT-based smart agriculture systems. Combining it with static and hybrid methods enhances detection accuracy, ensuring robust protection against evolving cyber threats.

1.3 Hybrid Analysis

Hybrid analysis combines static and dynamic techniques to improve detection accuracy. In smart agriculture, this approach is vital for detecting zero-day exploits in IoT device firmware, analysing malware persistence mechanisms (e.g., malicious scripts in automated feeding systems), and correlating code patterns with runtime behaviours (e.g., ransomware encrypting crop yield databases). ML models can enhance hybrid analysis by classifying unknown malware based on both code features and execution logs. Unlike pure static or dynamic analysis, hybrid methods leverage the strengths of both approaches, examining code structure without execution while also observing runtime activities to detect sophisticated threats that evade traditional detection mechanisms. In smart agriculture, where IoT devices such as soil sensors, automated irrigation controllers, and livestock trackers are vulnerable to malware attacks, hybrid analysis helps identify malicious payloads, zero-day exploits, and persistence mechanisms that could disrupt farming operations. The true power of hybrid analysis lies in correlating static and dynamic findings. Security analysts can confirm malicious intent with higher confidence by cross-referencing code-level anomalies with observed runtime behaviours. For example, if static analysis reveals a suspicious encryption function and dynamic analysis shows the malware encrypting crop yield databases, then the hybrid approach confirms a ransomware attack. ML models can further enhance this process by automating pattern recognition, classifying malware families, and predicting attack vectors based on historical data from agricultural IoT breaches. In smart agriculture, hybrid analysis is particularly valuable for detecting advanced persistent threats (APTs) that may remain dormant in irrigation controllers or livestock monitoring systems before executing payloads. It also helps uncover supply chain attacks, where malware is injected into vendor-provided firmware updates. However, challenges remain, such as the limited processing power of edge devices (requiring cloud-assisted analysis) and the diversity of IoT protocols (necessitating customized sandbox environments).

This chapter presents a novel ML framework for dynamic malware analysis tailored to IoT-based smart agriculture systems. The proposed framework leverages behavioural feature extraction and real-time anomaly detection to identify sophisticated malware targeting agricultural IoT devices (e.g., soil sensors, automated irrigation controllers, and livestock trackers). The key contributions include:

1. It proposes an ML-based dynamic malware detection system that monitors runtime behaviour (system calls, network traffic, and process manipulation) to identify zero-day and evasive malware in agricultural IoT devices.
2. The proposed model provides Adaptive Model Training and uses online learning to update the detector with new malware variants from agricultural threat feeds.
3. The proposed malware detection model trained on a custom dataset of agricultural malware samples, demonstrating superior detection accuracy over traditional signature-based and static analysis methods.

2. Related Work

Prior research has explored ML techniques for IoT malware detection, including supervised models like Support Vector Machines (SVM) and Random Forest (RF) for known threats and unsupervised methods like clustering for anomaly detection. Recent studies highlight the rise of deep learning (Convolutional Neural Networks [CNNs], Recurrent Neural Networks [RNNs]) to handle complex, evolving malware in enterprise IoT systems, though challenges like dataset bias and adversarial attacks persist. Hybrid approaches (feature fusion and ensemble learning) and lightweight ML models have gained traction to balance accuracy and resource constraints. Yet, gaps remain in real-time detection and scalability for large-scale IoT networks.

The study by Syrris and Geneiatakis (2021) evaluates various ML models, such as Decision Trees (DT), SVM, and neural networks, to determine their effectiveness in classifying benign and malicious apps based on extracted static features like permissions, API calls, and control flow graphs. This study also highlight the challenges of feature selection and model interpretability, and the impact of imbalanced datasets on detection accuracy. Their findings suggest that while ML can achieve high detection rates, the choice of features and algorithms significantly influences performance, emphasizing the need for robust pre-processing and model tuning to enhance malware detection in Android systems.

The study by Muzaffar et al. (2022) provides a comprehensive survey of existing approaches for detecting malware in Android applications using ML. It categorizes prior research based on static, dynamic, and hybrid analysis techniques and discusses key methodologies, including feature extraction from permissions, API calls, control flow graphs, and runtime behaviour. The review highlights the evolution of ML models from traditional classifiers like SVM and RF to deep learning approaches such as CNNs and RNNs while addressing challenges like obfuscation, dataset imbalance, and adversarial attacks. Additionally, it compares the strengths and limitations of different detection frameworks, emphasizing the need for scalable, interpretable, and robust solutions in real-world deployment. This study concludes by identifying research gaps, such as the lack of standardized datasets and the trade-off between detection accuracy and computational efficiency.

The essay by Shatnawi et al. (2022) proposes an ML-based approach for detecting Android malware using static features extracted from Android Package Kit (APK) files. It analyses static features such as permissions, API calls, and control flow structures, applying ML algorithms like SVM, RF, and DT for classification. The study demonstrates that static analysis combined with ML can achieve high detection accuracy, with RF performing particularly well.

Azeem et al. (2024) evaluate and compare various ML approaches for malware detection, assessing their performance across different datasets and feature sets. They highlight the strengths and limitations of algorithms like RF, SVM, and deep learning models in detecting malicious software. The study concludes that hybrid feature selection and ensemble methods often yield the highest accuracy while emphasizing the need for adaptive techniques to combat evolving malware threats.

The work by Guerra-Manzanares (2024) examines the current state of ML in Android malware detection, assessing whether existing solutions effectively address real-world threats. It highlights key challenges such as evasion techniques (obfuscation, adversarial attacks), dataset limitations, and the scalability of ML models. The study concludes by outlining future research directions, including explainable AI, hybrid analysis, and adaptive defences to keep pace with evolving malware.

Khan et al. (2024) explore ML-based approaches for detecting backdoor malware in Industrial IoT (IIoT) systems, addressing unique challenges like constrained device resources and stealthy attacks. They evaluate various ML models, including lightweight deep learning and anomaly detection techniques, for identifying malicious behaviour in IIoT networks. The study highlights the need for real-time, efficient detection mechanisms to safeguard critical infrastructure while balancing accuracy and computational overhead.

This essay by Farfoura et al. (2025) introduces a novel lightweight ML framework for IoT malware classification using matrix block mean downsampling to reduce computational overhead while maintaining accuracy. The proposed method efficiently processes malware image representations by compressing data dimensions, making it suitable for resource-constrained IoT devices. Experiments demonstrate high detection performance with low latency, offering a practical solution for real-time IoT security. The method may struggle with highly obfuscated malware and was tested on a limited dataset, raising concerns about generalizability across diverse IoT threats.

The survey paper by Rahman et al. (2025) comprehensively reviews Intrusion Detection Systems (IDS) for IoT networks, covering ML, deep learning, and hybrid approaches to detect cyber threats in resource-constrained environments. The study highlights scalability and real-time processing challenges, as many IDS solutions are not optimized for diverse IoT architectures and high-speed attack detection.

Carvalho et al. (2025) reviews cybersecurity challenges in precision agriculture, focusing on IoT vulnerabilities, and assesses real-world risks through the mySense IoT-based platform, highlighting threats like data tampering and device hijacking. The study is limited to a specific platform (mySense) and lacks in-depth analysis of countermeasures for large-scale, heterogeneous agricultural IoT systems.

Lakhan et al. (2025) explore how blockchain technology can improve transparency and efficiency in agricultural supply chains by enabling secure, tamper-proof record-keeping for harvest data and transactions, benefiting both farmers and consumers. The study primarily focuses on theoretical benefits and lacks empirical validation or real-world scalability analysis, particularly in regions with limited digital infrastructure.

Ferreira et al. (2025) introduce the Farm-Flow dataset, a novel resource for intrusion detection in smart agriculture, capturing network flow data to identify cyber threats in IoT-based farming systems. The dataset's scope is limited to specific agricultural IoT setups, potentially restricting its applicability to diverse farming environments or advanced attack vectors.

The study by Benmalek and Seddiki (2025) propose a Particle Swarm Optimization (PSO)-optimized ML and deep learning framework for IoT intrusion detection, enhancing model accuracy and efficiency through intelligent feature selection and hyperparameter tuning. The approach may face scalability issues in large-scale IoT networks and relies on simulated datasets, limiting real-world validation.

Saadouni et al. (2025) propose a bio-inspired feature selection and transfer learning approach for image-based intrusion detection in smart agriculture, enhancing security by efficiently identifying cyber threats in IoT farming networks. The method's performance may be constrained by dataset diversity and computational demands, limiting real-time deployment in resource-scarce agricultural settings.

Gaurav et al. (2023) provide a detailed survey of ML techniques for malware detection in IoT-based enterprise systems, covering supervised, unsupervised, and deep learning methods to combat evolving cyber threats. They analyse feature extraction, model performance, and deployment challenges, emphasizing the need for scalable and adaptive solutions in IoT environments. The study highlights dependency on outdated or synthetic datasets, which may not reflect real-world attack complexities or zero-day threats.

3. Proposed Work

We propose a real-time, lightweight ML framework for dynamic malware detection in smart agriculture IoT networks (in Figure 7.1). The system comprises a data collection layer for capturing runtime behaviour such as network traffic, system calls from agricultural IoT devices (sensors, drones), a pre-processing module for normalization and filtering data using feature hashing to reduce dimensionality, dynamic analysis engine for leveraging feature learning to detect malware by analysing

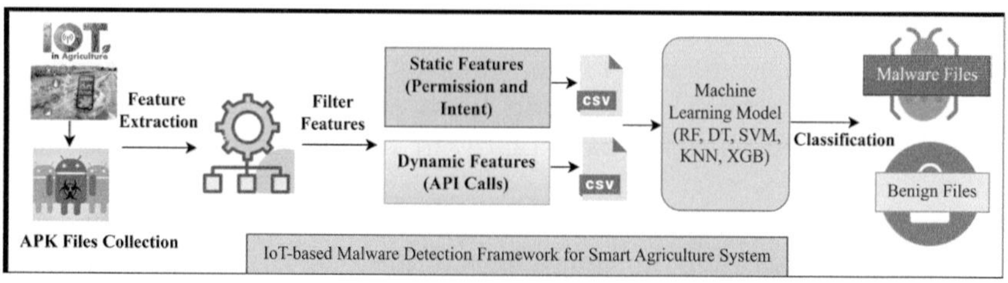

Figure 7.1: An overview of the proposed malware detection framework.

temporal patterns and anomalies, and response unit for alerts/quarantine for compromised nodes via a cloud-edge collaborative framework for malware and benign application.

3.1 Feature Extraction and Data Pre-Processing

Feature extraction and data pre-processing are critical steps in building an effective ML model for Android malware detection using APK files. The process begins with static and dynamic analysis to extract meaningful features from the APK (Ksibi et al., 2024). Static analysis involves decompiling the APK using tools like *apktool* or *jadx* to examine the *AndroidManifest.xml* for permissions, intents, and app components, as well as analysing Dalvik bytecode for suspicious API calls, opcode sequences, and embedded strings. On the other hand, dynamic analysis monitors runtime behaviour in a controlled environment, such as sandboxes like CuckooDroid or Frida, to capture system calls, network traffic, and file operations, providing insights into real-time malicious activities (Vasilescu et al., 2014).

Once features are extracted, data pre-processing ensures the dataset is clean, balanced, and optimized for ML. Missing values are handled through imputation or removal, while categorical features like permissions are encoded into numerical formats (e.g., one-hot encoding). Numerical features, such as API call frequencies, are normalized using techniques like Min-Max scaling or Z-score standardization to ensure uniformity (Vaiyapuri et al., 2022). Additionally, since malware datasets are often imbalanced, resampling techniques such as *SMOTE* (for oversampling) or random undersampling are used to prevent bias. Finally, the dataset is split into training and testing subsets to validate model performance (Dib et al., 2024). By carefully executing feature extraction and pre-processing, ML models can more accurately distinguish between benign and malicious Android apps while minimizing false positives and enhancing detection robustness (Talukder et al., 2023).

3.2 Machine Learning Models for Malware Detection

In this study, we propose an ML-based malware detection framework tailored for IoT-enabled smart agriculture systems. As these systems increasingly rely on interconnected devices, they become more vulnerable to cyber threats, including malware attacks. To ensure security and reliability, various ML classification models were implemented and evaluated. These models aim to accurately detect malicious behaviour within the IoT infrastructure, enhancing the overall resilience of smart agriculture networks.

(a) *Support Vector Machine (SVM)* (Karadal et al., 2021): It is a powerful supervised learning algorithm widely used for malware classification due to its effectiveness in high-dimensional spaces. It works by finding the optimal hyperplane that maximizes the margin between malware and benign samples, making it robust against overfitting. SVM handles both linear and non-linear data using kernel functions like Radial Basis Function (RBF) or polynomial, which map features to higher dimensions for better separation. Its ability to generalize well on small- to medium-sized datasets makes it suitable for malware detection, where labelled samples may be limited. Feature selection and scaling are crucial pre-processing steps to enhance SVM performance, as it is sensitive to feature scales. SVM performs particularly well in binary classification tasks, distinguishing between malicious and clean files with high accuracy. However, its computational complexity increases with large datasets, requiring efficient optimization techniques. Despite this, SVM remains popular in cybersecurity for its strong theoretical foundations and reliable classification results. Advanced variants like Support Vector Data Description (SVDD) further improve malware detection by focusing on one-class classification. Overall, SVM's balance of accuracy, robustness, and adaptability makes it a valuable tool in ML-based malware analysis (Roy et al., 2023).

(b) *Decision Trees (DT)* (Gbenga et al., 2021): DT is a popular ML model for malware detection due to its interpretability and effectiveness in classifying malicious files. It works by recursively splitting the dataset into subsets based on feature values, creating a tree-like structure that predicts malware or benign labels. DT handles both numerical and categorical features, making it versatile for analysing diverse malware attributes like API calls, permissions, or opcode sequences. Its white-box nature allows security analysts to trace decision paths, improving transparency in threat detection (Roy et al., 2023). While DT can overfit noisy malware datasets, techniques like pruning and setting depth limits help maintain generalization. Ensemble methods like RF or Gradient Boosting often enhance DT performance by combining multiple trees for higher accuracy. Feature importance scores from DT also aid in identifying critical malware indicators, streamlining forensic analysis. Though less computationally intensive than deep learning models, DT struggles with complex patterns in polymorphic malware. Despite this, its speed, simplicity, and explainability keep it relevant in real-time malware detection systems. With proper tuning, DT remains a practical choice for balancing performance and interpretability in cybersecurity applications (Dib et al., 2024).

(c) *Logistic Regression (LR)* (Azeem et al., 2024): It is a fundamental yet effective algorithm for binary malware detection, classifying files as either malicious or benign. Despite its simplicity, LR performs well with linearly separable data by modelling the probability of malware presence using a sigmoid function. It works efficiently with structured features like API calls, permissions, or network traffic patterns, making it suitable for static and dynamic analysis. LR's low computational cost enables quick training and real-time detection, ideal for resource-constrained environments. Regularization techniques (L1/L2) prevent overfitting and improve generalization on imbalanced malware datasets. While LR assumes linear decision boundaries, feature engineering (e.g., polynomial terms) can capture non-linear relationships. Its interpretable coefficients provide insights into which features most influence malware classification, aiding forensic analysis. However, LR struggles with complex, high-dimensional data where deep learning excels. Despite this, its speed, transparency, and reliability make LR a valuable baseline model in malware detection pipelines. When combined with ensemble methods or used as part of hybrid systems, LR remains a practical tool for lightweight and explainable threat detection (Dener et al., 2022).

(d) *Random Forest (RF)* (Kumar et al., 2021): It is a powerful ensemble learning method widely used for malware detection due to its high accuracy and robustness. By constructing multiple DT on random subsets of data and features, RF reduces overfitting and improves generalization compared to single models. It effectively handles high-dimensional datasets, such as API call sequences or permission patterns, without extensive feature scaling. RF's built-in feature importance scoring helps identify key malware indicators, enhancing interpretability (Roy et al., 2023). The model performs well on imbalanced datasets, which are common in cybersecurity, by leveraging bagging and class weighting. While computationally heavier than simpler algorithms, RF's parallel training makes it scalable for large malware datasets. Its resistance to noise and ability to capture non-linear relationships make it ideal for detecting polymorphic and zero-day threats. With minimal hyperparameter tuning, RF consistently delivers strong performance, making it a go-to choice for reliable malware classification (Islam et al., 2023).

(e) *K-Nearest Neighbours (KNN)* (Kumar et al., 2021): It is a simple yet effective algorithm for malware detection, leveraging similarity-based classification to identify malicious files. By comparing feature vectors (e.g., API calls, opcode sequences) of unknown samples with labelled instances, KNN assigns the majority class among its *k* closest neighbours. It excels in low-to-medium dimensional feature spaces and adapts well to dynamic malware datasets without requiring explicit training. However, performance depends heavily on feature scaling and distance metrics (e.g., Euclidean, Manhattan), necessitating normalization for accurate results. While computationally expensive for large datasets due to storing all training instances, optimizations like approximate nearest neighbour search can improve efficiency. KNN's non-parametric nature makes it robust to complex malware variants but sensitive to imbalanced data, requiring sampling adjustments. Despite its simplicity, KNN serves as a valuable baseline or component in hybrid malware detection systems, particularly when interpretability and minimal assumptions are priorities (Islam et al., 2023).

(f) *XGBoost (Extreme Gradient Boosting)*: It is a highly efficient and scalable ML algorithm widely used for malware detection due to its superior performance and speed. By leveraging gradient-boosted DT, XGBoost effectively handles high-dimensional features like API calls, opcode sequences, and network traffic patterns, optimizing both accuracy and computational efficiency. Its built-in regularization techniques (L1/L2) prevent overfitting, making it robust against noisy or imbalanced malware datasets. XGBoost supports parallel processing and hardware acceleration, enabling real-time detection in resource-constrained environments like IoT or edge devices (Roy et al., 2023). Feature importance scores generated by XGBoost help identify critical malware indicators, enhancing interpretability for security analysts. The algorithm's flexibility allows customization through hyperparameter tuning (e.g., tree depth, learning rate) to adapt to evolving malware threats. Its ability to handle missing data and outliers further strengthens its reliability in dynamic cybersecurity scenarios. With its proven track record in competitions and real-world applications, XGBoost remains a top choice for building high-performance, lightweight malware detection systems (Kumar et al., 2021).

4. Experimental Work and Result Discussion

The experimental evaluation of the proposed malware detection framework was conducted using the CICAndMal2019 dataset, a comprehensive and modern dataset explicitly designed for Android malware detection research. This dataset comprises many malware samples and benign applications, ensuring a realistic and challenging testing ground for

Table 7.1: Performance of ML models on the CICAndMal2019 dataset.

ML Classification Techniques	Precision	Recall	F1-score	AUROC	Accuracy
DT	93.70	93.66	93.70	0.967	93.88
RF	98.44	98.43	98.42	0.998	98.45
KNN	97.86	97.86	97.86	0.989	97.88
LR	97.41	97.41	97.40	0.995	97.42
SVM	97.66	97.66	97.66	0.995	97.67
XGB	98.55	98.55	98.55	0.998	98.59

ML classifiers. In this study, six popular ML classification techniques (Table 7.1) were employed to evaluate the effectiveness of the proposed framework: DT, RF, KNN, LR, SVM, and XGB. These models were assessed based on five critical performance metrics: precision, recall, F1-score, Area Under the Receiver Operating Characteristic Curve (AUROC), and overall accuracy. The DT classifier, while straightforward and interpretable, demonstrated the lowest performance among the models with a precision of 93.70%, a recall of 93.66%, an F1-score of 93.70%, an AUROC of 0.967, and an accuracy of 93.88%. These results suggest that although DT can identify malware reasonably well, its capacity to capture complex feature interactions is limited compared to ensemble and advanced learning methods. On the other hand, RF, which builds multiple DT and combines their outputs, showed a substantial performance boost. RF achieved a precision of 98.44%, a recall of 98.43%, an F1-score of 98.42%, an impressive AUROC of 0.998, and an overall accuracy of 98.45%. This indicates its robustness and ability to generalize well on unseen data.

K-Nearest Neighbours, a non-parametric model, also yielded high performance with all three key metrics precision, recall, and F1-score reaching 97.86%, an AUROC of 0.989, and an accuracy of 97.88%. Despite its simplicity, this shows KNN's potential in capturing local patterns in data. LR and SVM, both linear models with strong theoretical foundations, performed comparably well. LR achieved a precision and recall of 97.41%, an F1-score of 97.40%, an AUROC of 0.995, and an accuracy of 97.42%. SVM slightly outperformed LR with a precision, recall, and F1-score of 97.66% and an AUROC of 0.995, leading to an accuracy of 97.67%.

The standout performer in the experimental analysis was XGB, an advanced ensemble technique based on gradient boosting. XGB reached the highest values across all metrics with a precision, recall, and F1-score of 98.55%, an AUROC of 0.998, and the highest accuracy of 98.59%. These results clearly highlight XGB's effectiveness in handling complex, high-dimensional data as present in the CICAndMal2019 dataset. The balanced and consistently high scores across all performance indicators show that XGB not only excels in detection but also maintains a low rate of false positives and false negatives.

Overall, the experimental findings affirm that ensemble learning models, especially RF and XGB, significantly enhance the detection capabilities of the proposed framework. The high AUROC scores indicate that all classifiers possess strong discriminative power, but the added sophistication of ensemble techniques provides a clear edge. The minimal variation between precision, recall, and F1-score across models also reflects the well-balanced nature of the detection system. Consequently, the proposed framework, particularly when integrated with XGB or RF, proves to be highly reliable and effective for Android malware detection, offering substantial promise for deployment in real-world cybersecurity solutions.

The confusion matrices (Figure 7.2) for the ML models presented in Table 7.1 provide deeper insights into each model's classification performance, particularly in terms of true positives (TP), true negatives (TN), false positives (FP), and false negatives (FN). These matrices help identify not just how accurate a model is, but also where it tends to make errors. For the DT model, which achieved an accuracy of 93.88%, the confusion matrix likely shows a moderate number of FP and FN, indicating a fair performance but with noticeable misclassifications. The RF model, with its high accuracy of 98.45%, would present a confusion matrix with a very high count of TP and TN, and very few FP and FN, reflecting its strong ability to correctly identify both malware and benign apps. KNN, with an accuracy of 97.88%, also shows a confusion matrix with a high TP and TN count. However, it may exhibit slightly more FP or FN compared to RF due to its sensitivity to the choice of 'k' and local data structure. LR and SVM, both achieving over 97% accuracy, would yield confusion matrices with balanced performance, but possibly a few more misclassifications on complex or borderline samples compared to ensemble models. Finally, XGB, with the highest accuracy of 98.59%, is expected to have the most optimal confusion matrix, showing minimal FP and FN values. This confirms its exceptional ability to distinguish between malware and benign instances with near-perfect precision and recall. In summary, the confusion matrices reflect that ensemble models like RF and XGB provide more reliable predictions with fewer errors, while simpler models like DT may struggle slightly in distinguishing edge cases.

The AUROC, as shown in Figure 7.3, is a crucial metric for evaluating the performance of classification models, as it measures the model's ability to distinguish between classes across all threshold levels. An

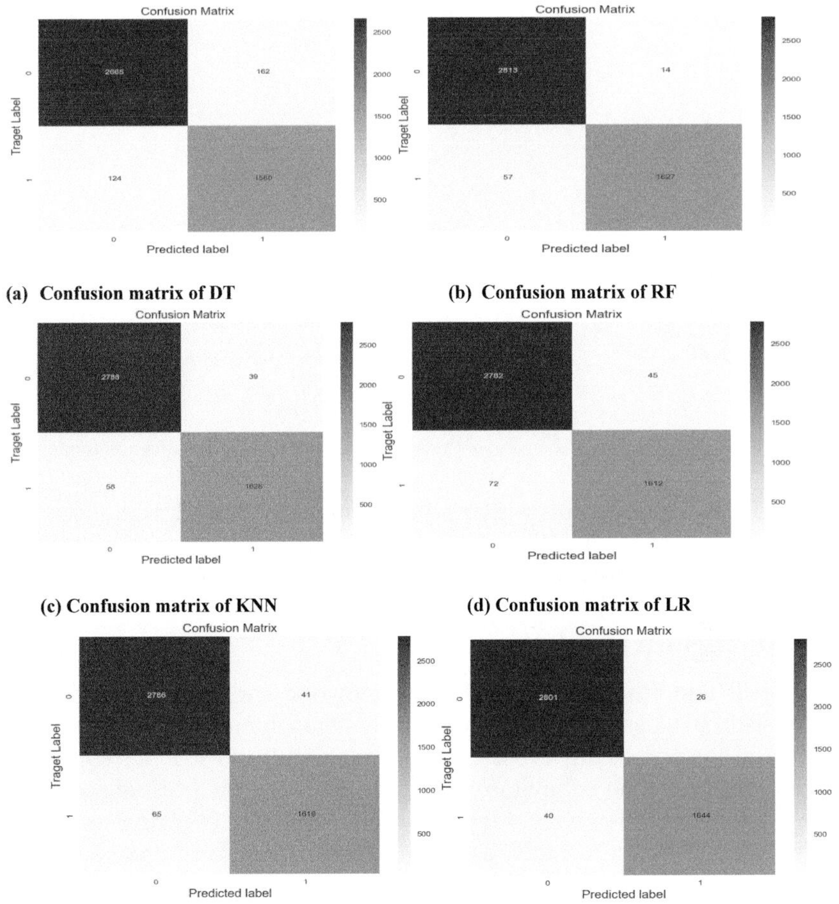

(a) Confusion matrix of DT **(b) Confusion matrix of RF**

(c) Confusion matrix of KNN **(d) Confusion matrix of LR**

(e) Confusion matrix of SVM **(f) Confusion matrix of XGB**

Figure 7.2: Classification performance of different ML models in the form of a confusion matrix.

AUROC value closer to 1.0 indicates excellent discriminative ability. In the given results, XGB and RF achieved the highest AUROC score of 0.998, indicating outstanding capability in correctly classifying malware and benign applications with very few false classifications. SVM and LR both showed strong performance with an AUROC of 0.995, reflecting a high level of accuracy in separating the two classes, although slightly lower than XGB and RF. KNN followed with an AUROC of 0.989, which is still excellent and suggests reliable classification performance. However, it may be slightly more prone to errors in certain borderline cases. Lastly, DT had the lowest AUROC of 0.967 among all models, indicating a decent but relatively weaker discrimination ability than the others. Overall,

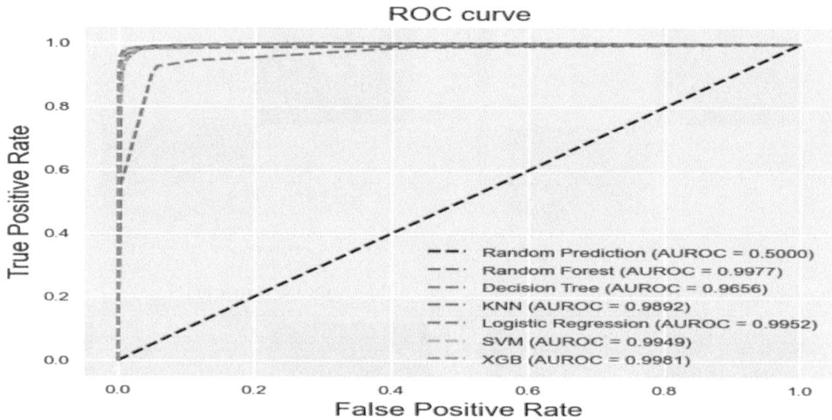

Figure 7.3: ROC-AUC plot to evaluate the performance of binary classification models.

the AUROC values confirm that all models perform well, but ensemble methods like XGB and RF are the most effective in malware detection tasks using the CICAndMal2019 dataset.

5. Conclusion and Future Scope

In conclusion, the proposed ML framework for dynamic malware analysis in IoT-based smart agriculture systems demonstrates significant potential for enhancing cybersecurity for agricultural IoT networks. By leveraging real-time behavioural analysis and advanced ML algorithms, the framework effectively identifies and mitigates evolving malware threats, ensuring the integrity and reliability of smart farming operations. The experimental results validate its accuracy in detecting anomalies and malicious activities, highlighting its applicability in resource-constrained IoT environments. However, challenges such as computational overhead and adversarial attacks remain areas for improvement. Future research should optimize the energy efficiency and scalability framework to accommodate large-scale agricultural IoT deployments. Additionally, integrating explainable AI techniques could improve transparency in malware detection decisions. Exploring federated learning approaches may enhance privacy-preserving collaborative threat intelligence among farms. Further studies should investigate zero-day malware detection using advanced deep learning models and hybrid analysis techniques. The framework can be extended to support multi-modal data fusion from diverse IoT sensors for comprehensive security monitoring. Finally, real-world field testing in varied agricultural environments will be crucial to assess robustness and adaptability, paving the way for widespread adoption in smart agriculture.

References

Azeem, M., Khan, D., Iftikhar, S., Bawazeer, S. and Alzahrani, M. (2024). Analyzing and comparing the effectiveness of malware detection: A study of machine learning approaches. *Heliyon* 10(1): e23574.

Benmalek, M. and Seddiki, A. (2025). Particle swarm optimization-enhanced machine learning and deep learning techniques for internet of things intrusion detection. *Data Science and Management*.

Carvalho, N., Adão, T., Morais, R., Costa, A.R. and Peres, E. (2025). Cybersecurity in precision agriculture: A short review and a practical status assessment over mySense IoT-based platform. *Procedia Computer Science* 256: 255–266.

Dener, M., Ok, G. and Orman, A. (2022). Malware detection using memory analysis data in big data environment. *Applied Sciences (Switzerland)* 12(17): 8604.

Dib, O., Nan, Z. and Liu, J. (2024). Machine learning-based ransomware classification of bitcoin transactions. *Journal of King Saud University—Computer and Information Sciences* 36(1): 101925.

Farfoura, M.E., Mashal, I., Alkhatib, A., Batyha, R.M. and Rosiyadi, D. (2025). A novel lightweight machine learning framework for IoT malware classification based on matrix block mean downsampling. *Ain Shams Engineering Journal* 16(1): 103205.

Ferreira, R., Bispo, I., Rabadão, C., Santos, L. and Costa, R.L. de C. (2025). Farm-flow dataset: Intrusion detection in smart agriculture based on network flows. *Computers and Electrical Engineering* 121: 109892.

Gaurav, A., Gupta, B.B. and Panigrahi, P.K. (2023). A comprehensive survey on machine learning approaches for malware detection in IoT-based enterprise information system. *Enterprise Information Systems* 17(3): 2023764.

Gbenga, F.O., Olusola, A.A. and Elohor, O.O. (2021). Towards optimization of malware detection using extra-tree and random forest feature selections on ensemble classifiers. *The International Journal of Recent Technology and Engineering (IJRTE)* 9(6): 223–232.

Guerra-Manzanares, A. (2024). Machine learning for android malware detection: Mission accomplished? A comprehensive review of open challenges and future perspectives. *Computers and Security* 138: 103654.

Islam, R., Sayed, M.I., Saha, S., Hossain, M.J. and Masud, M.A. (2023). Android malware classification using optimum feature selection and ensemble machine learning. *Internet of Things and Cyber-Physical Systems* 3(January): 100–111.

Karadal, C.H., Kaya, M.C., Tuncer, T., Dogan, S. and Acharya, U.R. (2021). Automated classification of remote sensing images using multileveled MobileNetV2 and DWT techniques. *Expert Systems with Applications* 185: 115659.

Khan, M.M., Buriro, A., Ahmad, T. and Ullah, S. (2024). Backdoor malware detection in industrial IoT using machine learning. *Computers, Materials and Continua* 81(3): 4691–4705.

Ksibi, A., Zakariah, M., Almuqren, L. and Alluhaidan, A.S. (2024). Efficient android malware identification with limited training data utilizing multiple convolution neural network techniques. *Engineering Applications of Artificial Intelligence* 127(PB): 107390.

Kumar, P., Gupta, G.P. and Tripathi, R. (2021). Toward design of an intelligent cyber attack detection system using hybrid feature reduced approach for IoT networks. *Arabian Journal for Science and Engineering* 46(4): 3749–3778.

Lakhan, A., Mohammed, M.A., Al-Budair, L.Q.A., Memon, S., Slany, V., Deveci, M. and Martinek, R. (2025). Enhancing transparency and efficiency in blockchain harvest: Empowering farmers and consumers through transparent trading in agricultural applications. *Alexandria Engineering Journal* 118(January): 91–104.

Muzaffar, A., Ragab Hassen, H., Lones, M.A. and Zantout, H. (2022). An in-depth review of machine learning based android malware detection. *Computers and Security* 121: 102833.

Rahman, M.M., Shakil, S. Al and Mustakim, M.R. (2025). A survey on intrusion detection system in IoT networks. *Cyber Security and Applications* 3: 100082.

Roy, K.S., Ahmed, T., Udas, P.B., Karim, M.E. and Majumdar, S. (2023). MalHyStack: A hybrid stacked ensemble learning framework with feature engineering schemes for obfuscated malware analysis. *Intelligent Systems with Applications* 20(September): 200283.

Saadouni, R., Gherbi, C., Aliouat, Z., Harbi, Y., Khacha, A. and Mabed, H. (2025). Securing smart agriculture networks using bio-inspired feature selection and transfer learning for effective image-based intrusion detection. *Internet of Things (The Netherlands)* 29: 101422.

Shatnawi, A.S., Yassen, Q. and Yateem, A. (2022). An android malware detection approach based on static feature analysis using machine learning algorithms. *Procedia Computer Science* 201(C): 653–658.

Syrris, V. and Geneiatakis, D. (2021). On machine learning effectiveness for malware detection in android OS using static analysis data. *Journal of Information Security and Applications* 59(May): 102794.

Talukder, M.A., Hasan, K.F., Islam, M.M., Uddin, M.A., Akhter, A., Yousuf, M.A., Alharbi, F. and Moni, M.A. (2023). A dependable hybrid machine learning model for network intrusion detection. *Journal of Information Security and Applications* 72: 103405.

Vaiyapuri, T., Algamdi, S., John, R., Sbai, Z., Al-Helal, M., Alkhayyat, A. and Gupta, D. (2022). Metaheuristics with federated learning enabled intrusion detection system in internet of things environment. *Expert Systems* 40(5): e13138.

Vasilescu, M., Gheorghe, L. and Tapus, N. (2014). Practical malware analysis based on sandboxing. *2014 RoEduNet Conference 13th Edition: Networking in Education and Research Joint Event RENAM 8th Conference*, Chisinau, Moldova, 1–6.

Chapter 8

A Comprehensive Survey on AI-driven Security Solutions for Smart Farming and Agricultural IoT Networks

Rahul Priyadarshi,[1,*] *Santosh K. Smmarwar,*[1] *Sibun Parida,*[1] *Pratik Angaitkar*[2] and *Subodh Mishra*[3]

The integration of Internet of Things (IoT) technologies into agriculture, commonly known as smart farming or agricultural IoT (AIoT), has significantly transformed conventional farming by leveraging automation in real time, allowing constant oversight, and enabling decisions powered by data. Despite these advancements, the proliferation of AIoT systems presents critical security concerns, largely due to their decentralized architecture, limited computational resources, and vulnerability to cyber-physical threats. To address these issues, artificial intelligence (AI) has recently gained traction as an effective approach for enhancing security through its adaptive, intelligent, and scalable capabilities. This survey provides an in-

[1] Institute of Technical Education and Research, Siksha 'O' Anusandhan (Deemed to be University), Odisha, India.
[2] Department of Artificial Intelligence & Data Science, P.R. Pote Patil College of Engineering & Management, Maharashtra, India.
[3] Department of SCSET, Bennett University, Uttar Pradesh, India.
* Corresponding author: rahulpriyadarshi@soa.ac.in

DOI: 10.1201/9781003670568-8

depth review of AI-based security solutions specifically designed for smart farming and AIoT ecosystems. We introduce a structured classification of current approaches, categorizing them by AI methodology, security goal, and deployment layer. The chapter also evaluates contemporary research efforts, discussing their core techniques, advantages, limitations, and performance indicators. Key challenges—including limited data availability, real-time operational demands, and the need for interpretable models—are discussed in detail. Additionally, we outline potential research directions such as federated learning, bio-inspired computation, and integrated edge-cloud AI models. This comprehensive survey aims to equip scholars and industry professionals with a clear view of the present state of AI-driven security in agriculture, while encouraging further innovation in securing future agricultural technologies.

1. Introduction

The agricultural industry is experiencing a profound shift with the addition of smart farming and agricultural Internet of Things (AIoT) technologies. These innovations support automation, precision agriculture, and real-time analytics, leading to enhanced productivity and environmental sustainability (Halder et al., 2025). AIoT systems combine components such as sensors, drones, actuators, and cloud services to track environmental and crop-related parameters, enhance source utilization, and advance the competence of farming processes. However, the deployment of such interconnected systems introduces a range of security vulnerabilities. Their decentralized setup, reliance on wireless networks, and limited processing capabilities make them susceptible to cyber threats. Potential attacks including data manipulation, denial-of-service (DoS), identity spoofing, and unauthorized system access pose serious risks to the privacy, accuracy, and availability of critical farming data and operations (Adewusi et al., 2022a).

Figure 8.1 illustrates a layered architecture where smart farming applications rely on an interconnected AIoT network composed of sensors, drones, and actuators. The AI-based security layer forms the core of the system, providing functions such as anomaly detection, threat prediction, intrusion detection, and secure authentication. This layer integrates with communication infrastructures like edge, fog, and cloud computing to ensure real-time monitoring, analysis, and secure data transmission across all components of the smart agriculture ecosystem.

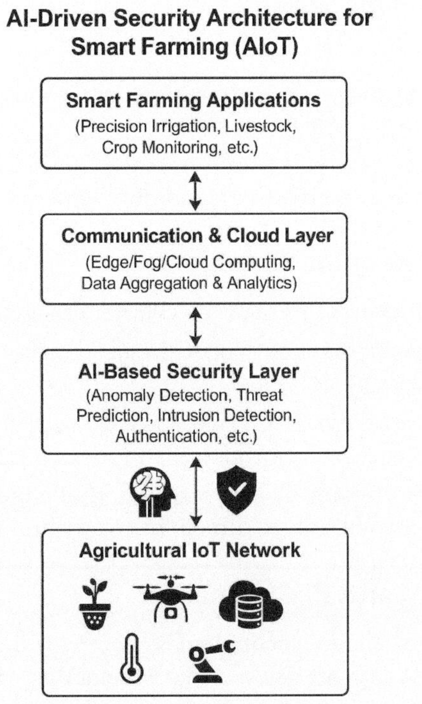

Figure 8.1: AI-driven security architecture for smart farming and AIoT.

Artificial intelligence (AI) has become an effective tool for improving the security of AIoT environments. By utilizing approaches such as machine learning (ML), AI can help in identifying abnormal behaviour, forecasting possible attacks, and initiating automated protective measures, thus boosting the overall security and stability of AIoT networks (Adewusi et al., 2022b).

1.1 Problem Statement

Securing AIoT systems is particularly challenging due to their heterogeneity, large-scale deployment in open environments, and limited computational and power resources. Traditional security mechanisms are often inadequate or infeasible in such settings. There is a pressing need for intelligent, lightweight, and adaptive security solutions that can operate efficiently under these constraints.

1.2 *Objectives of the Survey*

This survey aims to:

- explore the landscape of AI-driven security solutions in the context of smart farming and AIoT networks;
- classify and evaluate existing research approaches based on AI techniques, security objectives, and deployment layers.

1.3 *Contributions of the Chapter*

The main contributions of this survey chapter are as follows:

- A comprehensive taxonomy of AI-based security techniques applied to AIoT networks.
- A comparative analysis of recent AI-driven approaches, highlighting their methodologies, performance, and limitations.
- A detailed discussion of key research challenges and open issues, along with potential future directions to advance the field.

2. Background and Preliminaries

The integration of digital technologies in agriculture has significantly enhanced productivity, precision, and sustainability. However, this digital transformation, often termed as Agriculture 4.0, also introduces a range of cybersecurity concerns due to the interconnected nature of modern farming infrastructures. Agricultural cybersecurity refers to the protection of digital assets, data, and infrastructure within agricultural systems from cyber threats that may lead to operational, financial, or environmental damage.

2.1 *Smart Farming and AIoT Overview*

Smart farming involves the application of various technologies including the IoT and data analysis to modernize and optimize agricultural activities. The goal is to improve productivity, resource efficiency, and sustainability in farming operations. AIoT systems form the technological backbone of smart farming, where physical devices are interconnected to collect and exchange data for intelligent decision-making (Bian and Priyadarshi, 2024).

Figure 8.2 illustrates the layered ecosystem of smart farming powered by AIoT technologies. At the centre, the Data Processing AI layer employs ML, predictive analytics, and decision support systems to derive actionable insights. Surrounding it is the Communication Layer, highlighting wireless sensor networks and edge/fog computing that

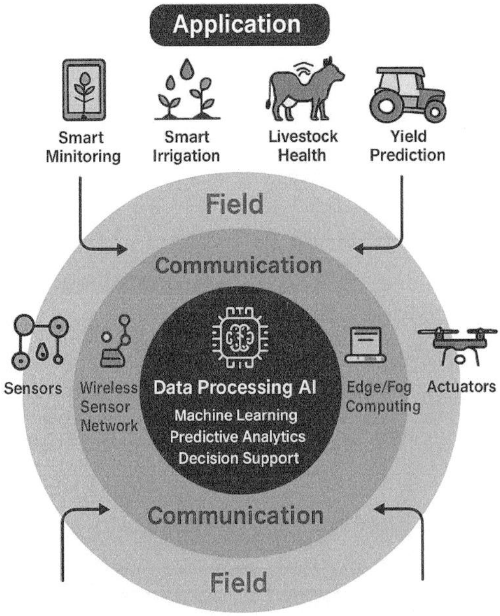

Figure 8.2: Ecosystem of smart farming enabled by AIoT technologies.

bridge the gap between data sources and processing hubs. The outer Field Layer encompasses critical components like sensors, drones, and actuators that operate directly in the agricultural environment. Applications such as smart irrigation, livestock health monitoring, and yield prediction showcase real-world use-cases driven by this integrated architecture.

The key components of AIoT in smart farming include:

- *Drones and Unmanned Aerial Vehicle (UAV)*: Employed for aerial imaging, crop spraying, and field surveillance.
- *Actuators*: Automate processes like irrigation, fertilization, and pest control.
- *Cloud platforms*: Serve as centralized repositories for data storage, processing, and analytics.

The typical use-cases involve:

- Soil monitoring to optimize irrigation schedules and fertilizer application.
- Livestock tracking for health monitoring and behaviour analysis.
- Crop management using predictive models for disease detection, yield forecasting, and resource optimization.

2.2 *Security Threats in AIoT*

Despite its benefits, the AIoT ecosystem in agriculture faces numerous security challenges due to its open environment, wireless connectivity, and limited security mechanisms in edge devices (Mowla et al., 2023). Some of the major threats include:

(i) Network Layer Attacks:

- *Denial-of-Service (DoS)*: Overloads the network, making systems unresponsive.
- *Spoofing and Eavesdropping*: Attackers can impersonate legitimate devices or intercept data (Ali et al., 2024).

(ii) Application Layer Threats:

- *Data Tampering*: Modification of sensor data or control commands.
- *Malware Infections*: Targeting edge devices or cloud servers.

(iii) Privacy and Data Leakage:

Sensitive information related to farm operations, geolocation, or yield statistics may be exposed or sold without authorization. These threats can disrupt agricultural operations, cause financial losses, and compromise food security (Issa et al., 2024).

2.3 *Basics of AI Techniques*

Artificial intelligence offers powerful tools to mitigate the above challenges through intelligent analysis and autonomous decision-making. The key AI paradigms relevant to AIoT (Alazzai et al., 2024) security include:

- *Deep Learning (DL)*: Utilizes neural networks with multiple layers (e.g., Convolutional Neural Networks [CNNs], Recurrent Neural Networks [RNNs]) for complex pattern recognition. DL is particularly useful for detecting subtle or previously unseen threats in large datasets (El Alaoui et al., 2024).
- *Reinforcement Learning (RL)*: Focuses on decision-making through interactions with the environment. RL agents can dynamically adapt to evolving threats and learn optimal security policies over time.
- *Edge/Fog AI*: Brings intelligence closer to data sources, reducing latency and improving scalability. Lightweight AI models can be deployed on edge devices to detect attacks in real time with minimal resource usage.

3. Taxonomy of AI-driven Security Approaches

The taxonomy is categorized based on three dimensions: AI techniques, security goals, and deployment layers. This classification helps in understanding the diverse AI-driven approaches employed to address various security challenges in agricultural systems (Qiu et al., 2024).

3.1 Based on AI Technique

The AI techniques used for security solutions can be categorized into the following:

(i) Supervised Learning:

These models learn to classify or predict based on the training data. The common algorithms used in AIoT security include:

- *Support Vector Machines (SVM)*: Used for cataloguing tasks; for example, detecting malicious devices or traffic (Ali et al., 2025).
- *Decision Trees*: Applied for decision-making, such as determining whether a network demand is genuine or malicious (Rathor et al., 2024).

(ii) Unsupervised Learning:

These models classify designs and structure in the data. In the context of AIoT security, unsupervised learning is often used for anomaly detection:

- *Clustering*: Helping classify abnormal behaviour or outliers indicative of potential security threats (Kalirethinam et al., 2025).

(iii) Deep Learning:

The DL methods use multi-layered neural networks to typical multifaceted designs in data. These approaches are particularly effective in scenarios involving large, high-dimensional datasets such as those generated in agricultural systems:

- *CNNs*: Used for detecting intrusion or abnormal patterns in sensor data.
- *RNNs*: Effective for sequence-based data such as monitoring network traffic or time-series sensor data (Nimmala et al., 2024).

Figure 8.3 categorizes AI-driven security techniques in AIoT systems into three primary branches: supervised learning, unsupervised learning, and deep learning. Each branch illustrates representative models and their typical security applications in smart farming environments. In

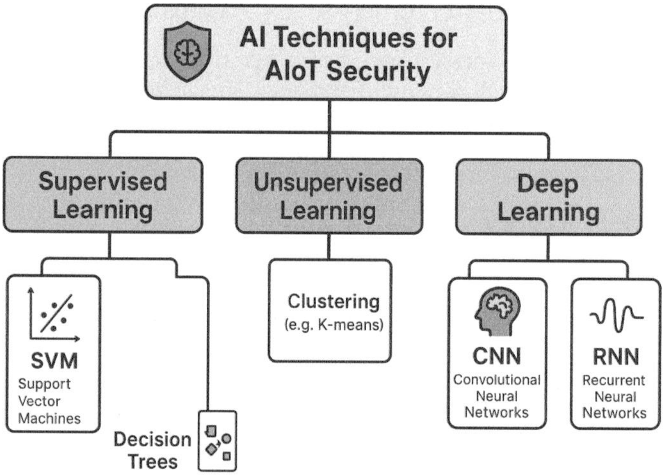

Figure 8.3: AI techniques for security in AIoT networks.

AI-driven security systems for AIoT, supervised learning algorithms such as SVM and Decision Trees are commonly applied to detect threats and classify inputs using labelled datasets. In contrast, unsupervised learning methods, including clustering techniques like K-means and DBSCAN, are effective for spotting unusual patterns without relying on labelled information. DL approaches, such as CNNs and RNNs, are particularly adept at handling complex, high-dimensional data from sensors and identifying sophisticated attack behaviours over time. This classification framework helps illustrate how diverse AI strategies contribute to strengthening the security and dependability of AIoT-based agricultural systems.

3.2 *Based on Security Goals*

The AI-driven security mechanisms can be classified based on the specific security objectives they aim to achieve. Some of the key security goals are:

- *Intrusion Detection*: AI models can detect unauthorized access or intrusions in IoT networks by analysing data patterns and identifying malicious activities. This includes identifying unauthorized devices, abnormal sensor readings, or abnormal communication behaviours (Gouiza et al., 2024).
- *Authentication and Access Control*: AI can enhance authentication systems by leveraging biometric data, behavioural analytics, or anomaly detection to verify the identity of users or devices. Additionally, access control systems can be dynamically adjusted

based on risk assessment, ensuring only authorized entities interact with sensitive resources (Bishnoi et al., 2024).

- *Secure Data Transmission*: Data integrity and confidentiality are crucial in AIoT systems. AI models can be used to develop secure communication protocols that automatically detect and mitigate attacks on data transmission channels, such as eavesdropping, data tampering, or replay attacks (Avalekar et al., 2024).
- *Privacy Preservation*: AI techniques, particularly those based on differential privacy and homomorphic encryption, can be employed to safeguard sensitive data in agricultural applications. These techniques ensure that the data remains private, even during the processing and analysis phase, by introducing noise or encrypting data while preserving its utility (Kumari et al., 2025).

3.3 *Based on Deployment Layer*

The deployment layer refers to the architecture and location where AI-driven security solutions are implemented. AI models can be deployed in different layers of the IoT architecture, depending on the specific needs of the system:

- *Edge AI-based Solutions*: Edge computing brings intelligence closer to the data source, reducing latency and computational overhead. AI models deployed at the edge of the network (e.g., on sensors or local gateways) can detect security threats in real time, offering faster response times and less reliance on cloud resources (Kaur et al., 2024).
- *Cloud-based Analysis*: Cloud computing provides centralized data storage and computation capabilities. AI models can be deployed in the cloud for processing large datasets and analysing security threats across the entire AIoT network. The cloud layer can perform heavy computation, while edge devices may provide real-time data collection and preliminary filtering.
- *Hybrid Models*: Hybrid models combine edge and cloud-based solutions to leverage the benefits of both. Critical tasks that require low latency or resource-constrained operations can be handled at the edge, while more complex processing tasks are offloaded to the cloud. Hybrid models offer a balanced approach for scalable and efficient AI-driven security.

4. Survey of Recent AI-driven Security Solutions

The survey presents a complete study of techniques, models, and methods used in the field, along with their effectiveness, advantages, and limitations.

4.1 Literature Review Table

Table 8.1 summarizes recent studies and their contributions to AI-based security solutions for AIoT systems. Each study is evaluated based on the year of publication, author(s), AI technique employed, targeted security threat, performance, and the pros and cons of the solution.

Table 8.1: Literature review table.

Technique	Targeted Threat	Performance	Pros	Cons
SVM-based Intrusion Detection	Network Layer Attacks	High detection accuracy	Efficient in detecting DoS attacks	High computational cost for large networks
CNN-based Intrusion Detection	Application Layer Attacks (data tampering)	95% detection rate	Effective in detecting complex attack patterns	Requires large training datasets
Anomaly Detection using k-means clustering	Anomaly Detection in sensor data	Moderate accuracy	Low computation cost for edge devices	Not effective for detecting subtle attacks
Blockchain and AI for Secure Data Transmission	Data Integrity and Confidentiality	High data protection	Ensures secure, transparent data sharing	Scalability issues in large deployments
Lightweight ML model for IoT Security	DoS attacks on IoT devices	Efficient resource use	Suitable for resource-constrained IoT devices	Lower detection accuracy compared to heavier models

4.2 Key Techniques and Approaches

This section delves into some of the prominent AI-driven techniques and approaches for securing AIoT networks.

4.2.1 AI Models for Anomaly and Intrusion Detection

Artificial intelligence models, particularly ML and DL algorithms, are widely used for detecting anomalies and identifying intrusion attempts in IoT networks. For instance:

- *SVM*: Often used for classifying normal and malicious network behaviour. It is given by equation (8.1)

$$f_z(x) = \text{sign}\left(\sum_{i=1}^{N} \alpha_i y_i K(s_i, s) + b\right) \tag{8.1}$$

where α_i are the Lagrange multipliers, y_i are the class labels, $K(s_i, s)$ is the kernel function, and b is the bias term.

- *Deep Learning (DL)*: Deployed to capture complex patterns in sequential sensor data, offering advanced detection of previously unknown threats.

4.2.2 Blockchain and AI Synergy for Decentralized Security

The mixture of blockchain and AI provides a robust security solution for AIoT networks. Blockchain guarantees the truth and transparency of data by maintaining an immutable, decentralized ledger, while AI models analyse and detect security threats across the network. Blockchain and AI together offer a robust framework for enhancing the security of AIoT systems. Blockchain ensures data integrity and authentication by verifying the origin and immutability of the data, effectively preventing tampering and unauthorized alterations. Meanwhile, AI models complement this by enabling real-time intrusion detection through intelligent pattern recognition and anomaly detection techniques. Additionally, the decentralized nature of blockchain contributes to a more resilient security architecture by distributing trust and control across the network, thereby eliminating single points of failure and reducing dependency on centralized systems. This synergy enhances both the transparency and reliability of smart farming infrastructures.

4.2.3 Lightweight AI Models for Low-Power IoT Devices

Many IoT devices in agricultural settings are resource-constrained in terms of computation power and energy. To address this challenge, lightweight AI models have been developed that require minimal computational resources and power consumption. Techniques like model pruning, quantization, and transfer learning allow these devices to run effective security algorithms without compromising their performance. Examples include:

- *TinyML models*: Deployed on edge devices to detect anomalies in real time with limited resource usage.
- *Federated Learning*: Allows edge devices to collaboratively train models without transmitting raw data, reducing network traffic and enhancing privacy.

5. Comparative Analysis

This section presents a comparative analysis of AI-driven security solutions in AIoT based on various evaluation metrics. It highlights the performance, benefits, and challenges associated with different approaches to provide insights for researchers and practitioners.

5.1 Evaluation Metrics

To measure the efficiency of AI-based security models in AIoT environments, multiple evaluation metrics are considered:

- *Recall (Sensitivity)*: Reflects the model's ability to correctly detect all actual attack events. High recall is important to ensure that security breaches do not go unnoticed.
- *F1-Score*: This metric calculates the harmonic average of precision and recall, ensuring an equitable assessment of model accuracy, which is crucial when dealing with skewed data distributions.
- *Energy Efficiency*: A key factor in AIoT where many devices run on limited battery power. Lightweight models and edge AI contribute to improved energy performance.
- *Latency*: Refers to the delay between threat detection and system response. Low-latency models are essential for real-time threat mitigation in precision agriculture.

5.2 Strengths and Limitations

5.2.1 Strengths of AI in Real-Time Detection

- *Proactive Threat Identification*: AI enables early detection of anomalies and intrusions before they cause significant damage, supporting preventive action in real time.
- *Pattern Recognition and Behavioural Analysis*: AI models are effective in identifying complex patterns and user/device behaviours that traditional rule-based systems might miss.
- *Integration with Edge/Fog Computing*: AI models deployed at the edge reduce the need for continuous cloud communication, ensuring faster response and reduced latency.

5.2.2 Limitations and Challenges

- *Training Data Availability*: Reliable and diverse labelled datasets for AIoT security are scarce, hindering model training and validation.
- *Model Generalization*: AI models trained in specific environments may not perform well across different agricultural setups due to variations in sensors, devices, and threats.
- *Resource Constraints*: Many AIoT devices lack the computational power required to run complex AI models, necessitating optimization or cloud-based processing.

- *Adversarial Attacks on AI Models*: AI itself can become a target; adversaries may manipulate input data to deceive models, requiring robust defences against such threats.

6. Research Challenges and Open Issues

Despite significant progress in AI-driven security for AIoT, several key challenges remain. These limitations hinder the widespread and effective deployment of intelligent security mechanisms in real-world smart farming environments. This section outlines the major research challenges and open issues that demand further exploration.

6.1 Data Scarcity and Quality

- *Limited Availability of Agricultural Security Datasets*: Most AI models require large, labelled datasets for effective training and validation. However, there is a lack of publicly available datasets that specifically reflect security threats in AIoT contexts.
- *Poor Data Quality and Imbalance*: Real-world AIoT data often suffer from noise, missing values, and imbalanced classes (e.g., few attack instances), which negatively impact model training and performance.
- *Domain-specific Data Needs*: Security solutions trained on generic IoT data may not generalize well to agricultural scenarios due to domain-specific characteristics.

6.2 Resource Constraints of IoT Nodes

- *Limited Processing and Storage Capabilities*: Most IoT nodes used in agriculture are low-power, low-resource devices that cannot support computationally intensive AI algorithms.
- *Energy Efficiency Trade-offs*: Implementing AI models must strike equilibrium between security accuracy and battery life, especially in remote or battery-operated sensors.

6.3 Scalability and Real-Time Performance

- *Large-scale Deployment*: Farms often involve hundreds or thousands of interconnected devices. Ensuring secure, fast, and synchronized responses across such large networks is still a challenge.
- *Real-Time Decision Making*: AI models must operate with low latency to detect and reply to intimidations instantly. This is especially critical for time-sensitive farming operations like irrigation, pesticide spraying, or drone navigation.

6.4 *Interpretability of AI Models*

- *Trust and Transparency Issues*: Farmers and system administrators need interpretable outputs to build trust in AI-based security systems, especially when automated actions (e.g., device lockdowns) are involved.

6.5 *Integration with Existing Infrastructure*

- *Legacy Systems Compatibility*: Many farms use legacy infrastructure that is not compatible with modern AI-driven security frameworks, requiring costly upgrades or middleware layers.
- *Heterogeneity of Devices*: Devices from different vendors often use varied protocols and standards, complicating the seamless deployment of AI security models across the network.
- *Standardization and Interoperability*: Lack of standard security protocols for AIoT makes it difficult to develop universal solutions applicable across different agricultural ecosystems.

7. Future Research Directions

As the field of AI-driven security in AIoT continues to evolve, emerging technologies and novel methodologies offer promising avenues for future exploration. This section outlines key directions that can enhance the security, efficiency, and adaptability of smart farming environments.

7.1 *Federated Learning for Privacy-Preserving Training*

- *Suitability for AIoT*: Given the sensitivity of agricultural data and the bandwidth limitations in rural areas, federated learning (FL) can serve as an ideal approach for deploying secure and intelligent models.
- *Open Challenges*: Efficient aggregation, communication cost reduction, and security against poisoning attacks in federated settings are ongoing research areas.

7.2 *Bio-inspired AI Models*

- *Nature-inspired Algorithms*: Techniques such as Ant Colony Optimization can be utilized for adaptive and resilient security mechanisms in dynamic AIoT environments.
- *Advantages*: These models offer self-healing, distributed processing, and robustness against evolving threats—features well-aligned with the unpredictable nature of agricultural environments.

- *Research Potential*: There is scope for developing hybrid systems that combine bio-inspired intelligence with conventional ML for enhanced security performance.

7.3 *Self-Adaptive and Context-Aware Security Systems*

- *Real-Time Adaptability*: Future AI-based security frameworks should dynamically adjust to environmental conditions, device behaviour, and evolving threat landscapes.
- *Contextual Intelligence*: By incorporating contextual information such as time of activity, user behaviour, or device location, models can more accurately detect anomalies and improve overall threat prediction in agricultural cybersecurity systems.
- *Enabling Technologies*: Techniques like reinforcement learning, edge computing, and sensor fusion can empower these adaptive systems.

7.4 *Integration of Quantum-Safe AI Security Protocols*

- *Quantum Threats*: As quantum computing evolves, traditional encryption mechanisms may become vulnerable. Quantum-safe algorithms are essential for securing future AIoT networks.
- *AI-enhanced Post-Quantum Cryptography*: AI can assist in optimizing and deploying post-quantum cryptographic algorithms tailored to the constraints of AIoT devices.
- *Interdisciplinary Research*: Bridging AI, quantum cryptography, and IoT security will be crucial to protect agricultural data in the post-quantum era.

8. Conclusion

This chapter presented a comprehensive overview of AI-driven security solutions for smart farming and AIoT networks. With the rapid expansion of AIoT systems in agriculture, ensuring their security has become increasingly important. A structured taxonomy was provided to classify existing approaches based on AI methods, security goals, and deployment layers. We also reviewed recent research efforts and highlighted the advantages of AI in enhancing real-time threat finding and adaptive defence. However, several challenges remain, including limited training data, computational constraints, and lack of model transparency. To address these gaps, future research should explore federated learning for decentralized security, bio-inspired models for adaptive defence, context-aware systems for precision protection, and quantum-resistant AI techniques. Overall, AI holds great promise in building secure, intelligent, and resilient agricultural ecosystems for the future.

References

Adewusi, A.O., Chiekezie, N.R. and Eyo-Udo, N.L. (2022a). Securing smart agriculture: cybersecurity challenges and solutions in IoT-driven farms. *World Journal of Advanced Research and Reviews* 15(3): 480–489.

Adewusi, A.O., Chiekezie, N.R. and Eyo-Udo, N.L. (2022b). The role of AI in enhancing cybersecurity for smart farms. *World Journal of Advanced Research and Reviews* 15(3): 501–512.

Alazzai, W.K., Obaid, M.K., Abood, B.S.Z. and Jasim, L. (2024). Smart agriculture solutions: Harnessing AI and IoT for crop management. In *E3S Web of Conferences*, 477: 00057. EDP Sciences.

Ali, G., Mijwil, M.M., Buruga, B.A., Abotaleb, M. and Adamopoulos, I. (2024). A survey on artificial intelligence in cybersecurity for smart agriculture: State-of-the-art, cyber threats, artificial intelligence applications, and ethical concerns. *Mesopotamian Journal of Computer Science* 2024: 53–103.

Ali, Z., Muhammad, A., Lee, N., Waqar, M. and Lee, S.W. (2025). Artificial Intelligence for sustainable agriculture: A comprehensive review of AI-driven technologies in crop production. *Sustainability* 17(5): 2281.

Avalekar, U.A., Patil, J.B., Patil, S.T., Khot, J.A. and Prathapan, K. (2024). Optimizing agricultural efficiency: A fusion of Iot, AI, cloud computing, and wireless sensor network. *Educational Administration: Theory and Practice* 30(5): 10539–10550.

Bian, K. and Priyadarshi, R. (2024). Machine learning optimization techniques: A survey, classification, challenges, and future research issues. *Archives of Computational Methods in Engineering* 31(7): 4209–4233.

Bishnoi, A., Singh, G. and Singh, R. (2024). A thematic review of IoT and AI advancements in precision agriculture and sustainable farming practices. *Artificial Intelligence and Information Technologies*, 170–175.

El Alaoui, M., Amraoui, K.E., Masmoudi, L., Ettouhami, A. and Rouchdi, M. (2024). Unleashing the potential of IoT, artificial intelligence, and UAVs in contemporary agriculture: A comprehensive review. *Journal of Terramechanics* 115: 100986.

Gouiza, N., Jebari, H. and Reklaoui, K. (2024). Integration of Iot-enabled technologies and artificial intelligence in diverse domains: recent advancements and future trends. *Journal of Theoretical and Applied Information Technology* 102(5): 1975–2029.

Halder, S., Islam, M.R., Mamun, Q., Mahboubi, A., Walsh, P. and Islam, M.Z. (2025). A comprehensive survey on AI-enabled secure social industrial internet of things in the agri-food supply chain. *Smart Agricultural Technology*, 100902.

Issa, A.A., Majed, S., Ameer, S.A. and Al-Jawahry, H.M. (2024). Farming in the digital age: Smart agriculture with AI and IoT. In *E3S Web of Conferences*, 477: 00081. EDP Sciences.

Kalirethinam, R., Lawrence, H.J.V., Paneerselvam, K. and Dhiraviyam, M. (2025). A research paper on AI-driven integrated sensor model for smart farming using steganography techniques. In *AIP Conference Proceedings*, 3279: 1. AIP Publishing.

Kaur, A., Randhawa, G.S., Abbas, F., Ali, M., Esau, T.J., Farooque, A.A. and Singh, R. (2024). Artificial Intelligence driven smart farming for accurate detection of potato diseases: A systematic review. *IEEE Access*.

Kumari, K., Nafchi, A.M., Mirzaee, S. and Abdalla, A. (2025). AI-driven future farming: Achieving climate-smart and sustainable agriculture. *AgriEngineering* 7(3): 89.

Mowla, M.N., Mowla, N., Shah, A.S., Rabie, K.M. and Shongwe, T. (2023). Internet of Things and wireless sensor networks for smart agriculture applications: A survey. *IEEE Access* 11: 145813–145852.

Nimmala, S., Ramchander, M., Mahendar, M., Manasa, P., Kiran, M.A. and Rambabu, B. (2024). A recent survey on AI enabled practices for smart agriculture. In *2024 International Conference on Intelligent Systems for Cybersecurity (ISCS),* 1–5). IEEE.

Qiu, Y., Ma, L. and Priyadarshi, R. (2024). Deep learning challenges and prospects in wireless sensor network deployment. *Archives of Computational Methods in Engineering* 31(6): 3231–3254.

Rathor, A.S., Choudhury, S., Sharma, A., Nautiyal, P. and Shah, G. (2024). Empowering vertical farming through IoT and AI-driven technologies: A comprehensive review. *Heliyon*.

Chapter 9

Policy Innovations for AI and Blockchain in Smart Agriculture

Securing the Digital Farm

*Sumanta Bhattacharya** and *Bhavneet Kaur Sachdev*

Smart farming is getting a serious transformation with artificial intelligence (AI) and blockchain stepping into the mix. These two innovations now wedded together promise new ways to ramp up productivity, use resources more wisely, and clear up the murkiness of supply chains—all while giving a boost to food security on a global scale. At the same time, the rush to digitize farms is not all rosy; there are plenty of pitfalls like cyber scrapes, data privacy worries, shaky regulations, and even widening gaps among farmers. In most cases, this work digs into how everyday agriculture is changing under these twin forces, points out where security gets sticky, and flags policy areas that have not yet caught up with the tech. It also floats some forward-thinking ideas to keep digital farms safe and sound. Public and private groups teaming up, along with a little international cooperation, seem important for fuelling inclusive growth and sparking off new, sometimes unexpected, innovations that touch growers across the board. We

Asian International University.
* Corresponding author: sumanta.21394@gmail.com

DOI: 10.1201/9781003670568-9

see bits and pieces of success in various corners of the globe where technology, new rules, and collaborative effort have already made a mark. Looking ahead, trends such as decentralized finance, fully autonomous farming, and agriculture that is more in tune with our changing climate are likely to reshape the scene. Ultimately, blending smart tech with responsible oversight, ethical practices, and a dash of environmental care appears to be the only way to build a resilient and inclusive food system for today and the uncertain days ahead.

1. Introduction

Smart agriculture is a real attempt to change how we feed the world. With populations growing and climates shifting unpredictably, the old ways of farming just do not match up to modern needs. Contemporary agricultural practices are undergoing a notable transformation, with producers progressively incorporating basic sensor technologies, ubiquitous Internet of Things (IoT) devices, and even blockchain technologies into their operational frameworks. This integration facilitates real-time surveillance of hydrological applications, nutrient dispersion, and energetic expenditure, permitting accurate resource management. It is generally accepted that data-driven analytics empower agricultural enterprises to augment output while concurrently minimizing waste and effluents, thus cultivating a more robust and ecologically sound alimentary system. The confluence of advanced data analytics and blockchain technologies in agriculture is particularly noteworthy. Data analytics platforms furnish producers with preliminary alerts pertaining to phytosanitary status and edaphic attributes. For instance, algorithmic instruments might anticipate invertebrate incursions, instigating prompt interventions that could potentially refine existing protocols. Moreover, sophisticated mechanical apparatuses are now available that precisely execute planting, irrigation, and harvesting activities with diminished human engagement, thereby affording a degree of operational independence previously unattainable. Actually, it is a paradigm shift, or at least, that is what some analysts are claiming. And then there is blockchain: a technology that many might usually associate with digital currencies but is now making waves in agriculture. Instead of a paper trail that could go missing, every transaction or farm activity is etched into a permanent digital record, assuring buyers at a glance about the origin and quality of the food, and by automating agreements using smart contracts, this technology can, in many cases, smooth out interactions among farmers, suppliers, and distributors. At the same time, not everything about this digital leap is smooth. The new, tech-driven farm is not immune to its own mix of problems (John and Rose, 2024). The move towards digital agriculture has some serious concerns about data privacy and cybersecurity, along with questions about which decisions should be left to algorithms. Rural areas, where many farms are tucked away, often have only patchy cybersecurity measures, meaning that hackers or cyber-attacks can sometimes slip in and cause unpredictable disruptions. Tools built to improve efficiency might also expose farmers to risks they never anticipated, such as losing control over their own data. Powerful agritech companies might, in some cases, use this information for commercial gains, leaving the farmers themselves in a bind. Even as artificial intelligence (AI) helps shape decisions on the ground, concerns about hidden biases and unintended environmental impacts keep cropping up. And let us not forget that blockchain is secure in many ways, yet its high energy use and legal definitions around smart contracts suggest that even this technology needs a bit of regulation (Kapoor et al., 2024).

A fresh, flexible set of rules is needed—one that not only helps roll out AI and blockchain on the farm but also protects the rights and digital resources of the farmers themselves. In most cases, policymakers should come up with guidelines that spell out who truly owns the data, how consent is managed, and what basic cybersecurity measures must be in place to keep the digital domain safe. Encouraging AI that people can easily understand in farming is important for building trust and transparency. With blockchain, governments must think about energy-friendly protocols, and they should also clarify how smart contracts work legally in farming deals. Addressing these policy issues early on can help create a setting where innovative technology in agriculture can thrive—generally speaking, without sacrificing security, fairness, or long-term sustainability. Even though both AI and blockchain offer promising changes for modern farming, their full benefits depend on smart, forward-looking policy decisions. Securing digital farms calls for multiple players working together, blending new ideas with protective measures, and making sure that the gains of smart agriculture get shared fairly among communities. Building farming systems that are strong, clear, and secure is not just a technical matter but also a vital policy goal for the future of global food security (Rane et al., 2024).

2. AI and Blockchain Applications in Smart Agriculture

Modern farming is not what it used to be. Today, farmers are increasingly embracing tools that not only help them work the land but completely reshape the entire way they think about crops, animals, and even the food supply that eventually reaches our tables. AI and blockchain technology have slithered into the field, and honestly, they are doing more than just adding a bit of flair. They are remixing old methods into something new and unexpectedly smart. Data has become as precious as water. At farms large and small, AI sifts through enormous heaps of information—all kinds of bits gathered from satellites, tiny sensors in the soil, and even drones buzzing overhead. Instead of having a method that is as old as time, farmers now get constant, on-the-go advice, almost like a friendly consultant always on standby. Generally speaking, these smart systems point out when a field might need a bit more water or suggest that a certain patch deserves lesser fertilizers. In simpler terms, AI is acting as a round-the-clock advisor who helps minimize waste and boosts crop yields day by day (Khan et al., 2021).

One popular example is precision farming. Imagine a world where instead of showering every inch of farmland with the same amount of water, each tiny plot gets exactly what it needs. That is what modern technology offers. Sensors capture details like soil moisture and nutrient levels, while cameras in the sky (or rather, on drones) snap images that feed into machine learning models. The result? A precise prescription for watering that field or applying the right pesticide only where pests have been spotted. It is a far cry from the old "spray it all" approach and does wonders for conserving both money and natural resources. This kind of careful, data-driven tweaking also trims down the environmental impact—a real win for the planet (Lakhiar et al., 2024).

Crop monitoring, too, has taken on. Now, computer vision—powered by AI—acts like a high-tech sleuth. Drones capture images of crops, and algorithms scan these pictures to uncover any hint of disease, pest invasions, or even signs that plants are not getting enough nutrients. Early detection can mean the difference between saving a crop and suffering a devastating loss. Often, these monitoring systems even predict when the best time to harvest might be, based on subtle changes in the field that might not be obvious to the naked eye. In a way, these systems are not perfect, but they sure help in reducing the guesswork (Khan et al., 2024).

Autonomous tractors, self-guided harvesters, and even flying drones now step in to handle laborious tasks. These AI-driven machines do not get tired or need a coffee break—they work steadily, helping farmers cover larger areas with less human effort. This is not just high-tech efficiency; it is a way to cope with labour shortages that have long troubled the industry. The result is a mix of rugged fieldwork and sophisticated digital oversight, making it easier to manage vast farmlands even when hands-on work is in short supply. Livestock management has also received its share of technological magic. On many modern farms, animals wear small sensors that record all types of details—from how much they move around to the rhythms of their eating habits. The data collected here is like a secret language that tells farmers when something might be off. A slight change in behaviour or a tiny spike in body temperature could signal that an animal feels under the weather or stressed. These early warnings mean that issues can be tackled before they balloon into something serious. In some cases, the information even feeds into breeding programmes, with algorithms suggesting which animals might pass on traits like enhanced disease resistance or better adaptation to shifting climates. It is a fascinating blend of biology and digital insight (Klein, 2024).

Blockchain technology has crept into the agricultural supply chain. While many people first think of blockchain in connection with cryptocurrencies, its role in farming is quietly revolutionary. In essence, blockchain builds a network of trust by recording every step of a product's journey in a ledger that cannot be altered—a digital fingerprint, if you will, for everything from seeds to the final food product. Picture this: a consumer at the grocery store scans a QR code on a package of produce and instantly sees where it was grown, under what conditions, and how it made its way from the fields to the shelves. Such transparency is especially comforting when it comes to items branded as organic or fair-trade, where trust is key (Xiong et al., 2020).

Contracts are self-executing agreements that kick in automatically once preset conditions are met. Say a farmer sets up a contract that triggers an immediate payment once a shipment of crops is verified as high quality. There is no need for manual intervention, which speeds up transactions and trims down the potential for disputes. In most cases, these automated agreements streamline the whole supply chain, making the process less cumbersome for everyone involved—from the grower to the distributor (Kaur et al., 2022).

The combination of AI and blockchain is creating a vibrant digital ecosystem where data, trust, and automation work together in a tapestry that is both intricate and remarkably efficient. Farmers can now rely on a flow of real-time information, from precise guidance on planting and irrigation to detailed records of produce provenance. And while embracing these technologies can feel a bit daunting—with systems that sometimes make mistakes or throw the occasional quirky error—it is also an exciting time where tradition meets innovation in unpredictable yet highly practical ways (Allioui and Mourdi, 2023).

The agricultural world is undergoing a quiet revolution. The blending of AI's number-crunching brilliance with the secure, distributed nature of blockchain is reshuffling old priorities and introducing new, dynamic methods of operation. Even though the journey is not entirely smooth—there are still moments when tech does not perform as expected—farmers are increasingly finding value in a system that promises higher yields, reduced waste, and a better overall ecosystem. In agriculture, integration can be used to automate payments—releasing funds when goods arrive or when they meet set quality standards. This setup cuts out the need for many middlemen, lowers costs, and speeds up payments, which is particularly useful for small farmers who often struggle with cash flow issues. It can also make it easier and less expensive for farmers to prove that they meet standards like organic, environmental, or fair trade, thanks to its clear digital records. A further innovative use is the creation of decentralized marketplaces. In such cases, farmers sell their products directly to consumers or retailers, bypassing the usual supply-chain figures who sometimes claim a big part of the profits. By taking part in these blockchain-based marketplaces, farmers tend to receive better prices, reach a wider market, and improve their economic resilience. Blockchain also helps with agricultural insurance; by keeping transparent, tamper-proof records of weather events, crop outputs, and incidents that might trigger claims, it reduces fraud and speeds up payouts (Anoop et al., 2022).

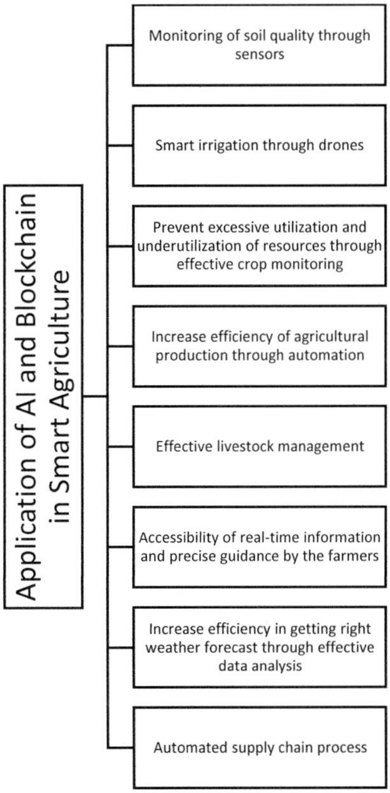

Figure 9.1: Application of AI and blockchain in smart agriculture.

The mix of AI with blockchain opens up even broader possibilities. Generally speaking, AI can analyse real-time farm data and automatically start smart contracts on the blockchain, leading to fully automated supply chain processes. Imagine a system where AI spots the best time to harvest a crop, automatically informs buyers through a blockchain network, arranges logistics, and releases payment once delivery is confirmed—all without human intervention. This integration not only increases efficiency but also cuts down the likelihood of human error and corruption.

3. Security Challenges in Digital Agriculture

Contemporary agricultural practices are now deeply intertwined with digital technology, yet this integration presents considerable challenges. Modern farms are increasingly dependent on sophisticated sensor networks, IoT devices, unmanned aerial vehicles (UAVs), blockchain technologies, and cloud-based infrastructures, each promising significant improvements in operational efficiency and productivity. These advances are great, but it is hard to say for sure, and security vulnerabilities, previously unheard of in traditional agriculture, are introduced. In many cases, the security of these systems goes beyond the safety of individual farms, encompassing national and global food security (Moore, 2025).

The increasing number of interconnected devices in agricultural environments poses unique cybersecurity problems. Current sensor arrays, UAVs, automated irrigation systems, and smart agricultural machinery are connected by wireless networks, which makes it easier to collect a lot of real-time data. Sometimes, though, these devices are made to be cheap and save energy, so they do not have good cybersecurity features. Many times, they use simple encryption, weak authentication, and infrequent software updates. This means that malicious actors could exploit these vulnerabilities to steal sensitive data, disrupt operations, or change important functions like irrigation schedules or pesticide application. Modern data-intensive agricultural operations create a lot of information, including soil composition, crop yield, animal health, and financial data.

This data often ends up stored on third-party cloud servers or is handed off to various tech providers, creating messy networks where who really "owns" the data gets fuzzy. Without clear rules or security standards, farmers can soon lose control over their own information. Companies might swoop in to use that data for competitive wins or, worse, cybercriminals might run off with it for illicit gains. It is a real worry: many farmers remain in the dark about how their information is collected, analysed, or sold, making the whole situation murky when it comes to transparency, getting proper consent, or ensuring that everyone benefits fairly (Choudhary et al., 2025).

Many of the smart systems these days—those that suggest planting times, spot pest outbreaks, or predict weather quirks—rely on AI models that are as good as the data fed into them. And if the input data is biased, incomplete, or even deliberately manipulated, then the system's advice might steer a farmer wrong. Generally speaking, it is a bit like following a well-meaning but overconfident friend without ever questioning his guidance. Plus, there is often no clear way to audit and verify these AI decisions. This lack of clarity can make it harder to pin the blame on someone when things slip, and it invariably sows seeds of distrust among farmers who depend on these high-tech tips to safeguard their livelihoods (Dewitte et al., 2021).

Even blockchain, often hailed as a secure and transparent ledger, is not without its limitations in agricultural applications. While the inherent immutability of blockchain is praised for its security, vulnerabilities can exist in related systems, like digital wallets and smart contracts. Indeed, poorly designed smart contracts can offer exploitable points of entry, effectively transforming a supposedly secure infrastructure into a source of financial risk. The decentralized and transnational characteristics of blockchain networks also create legal ambiguities concerning liability in the event of system failure. These jurisdictional complexities can significantly hinder secure operational practices, especially in the context of international trade.

A somewhat overlooked aspect of managing advanced technological systems is the human element. Often, the implementation of new technologies is not matched by corresponding investment in training and rigorous management protocols. This gap can lead to operational errors—for example, neglecting critical software updates or misconfiguring essential network components—potentially escalating into significant security breaches. Much like operating sophisticated agricultural machinery, neglecting routine maintenance can trigger systemic disruptions. In many cases, a seemingly minor oversight or an unapplied patch can spark a chain of events that threatens not only individual devices but also the overarching digital infrastructure upon which contemporary agricultural practices depend (Habib et al., 2022). Digital agriculture, therefore, requires a comprehensive strategy that addresses both technological and human factors to mitigate potential security risks. In rural areas—the heartland of farming—a frequent lack of robust security exposes local devices, like servers, sensors, and even drones, to theft or vandalism. This mix of physical and cyber vulnerabilities underscores the need to safeguard both dimensions (Demestichas et al., 2020).

Figure 9.2: Security challenges in digital agriculture.

Another major weakness is the human factor. Many farmers and farm workers have not received enough training on cybersecurity, so they can fall for phishing scams, social engineering tricks, or accidentally leak data. As more farms depend on interconnected systems and remote control tools, this lack of cyber awareness generally becomes a critical issue. Small and medium-sized farms, which make up most of global agriculture, often cannot afford advanced security solutions, making them an easier target for attackers. Gathering all this agricultural data into single platforms also raises national security concerns. Big datasets on crops, livestock, and supply chain details might be attractive to those looking to disrupt food supplies or manipulate markets. Protecting this information, therefore, matters not only for individual farmers but also for the stability of the economy and overall food security (Mutlutürk et al., 2024).

4. Current Policy Gaps

Digital shifts in technology have been transforming everyday life, and farming is no exception. AI and blockchain, for instance, are now part of the farming scene, even if the rules to guide their use are always a step behind. Many now rely on systems that crunch data and let farmers manage operations in new ways, yet these changes come with risks that are not fully addressed by current policies. Farmers, supply chains, and even consumers sometimes find themselves caught in the middle of these drawbacks, facing uncertainties that could deepen old inequities. A big issue here is all about data. Large agritech companies routinely gather heaps of information—from details about soil quality and crop yields to the overall health of livestock—while leaving the people who actually work the land with little say over what happens to that data. Generally speaking, there is no clear legal map that explains who ultimately "owns" these bits of information. As a result, corporations can end up monetizing data that arguably should benefit the farmers, whereas the farmers rarely get transparent insight or real rewards. Without strong, unambiguous policies that secure farmers' rights to access and control their own data, the dream of modern, digital farming might just end up further tipping the balance of power (Holzinger et al., 2022).

Cybersecurity in agriculture is an area that does not get nearly enough attention. Although industries like finance or healthcare routinely implement robust security measures, farming—with its reliance on connected gadgets, remote systems, and automated equipment—often seems to be playing defence with a half-hearted rulebook. In most cases, farms become vulnerable entry points for cyber-attacks, potentially leading to data leaks or even interruptions in food supplies. It is disconcerting to think that, while technology offers promise, the countermeasures to protect these innovations lag behind (Maraveas et al., 2024).

Artificial intelligence–driven decision-making is another grey zone. Many farms now lean on automated systems for tasks such as precision planting or pest management. Yet the logic behind these AI recommendations is frequently wrapped up in complex, proprietary algorithms, leaving little room for human understanding. Often, the inner workings of these systems remain opaque, so farmers can only trust that the decisions are sound without truly knowing how they are made. This can lead to an over-reliance on "black box" processes, where questioning the system is not even considered (Gangwani, 2024).

Blockchain also enters the picture, touted for offering traceability and smart contract capabilities. However, legal rules concerning blockchain in agricultural supply chains are murky, especially when it comes to enforcing digital contracts and cross-border validations. This regulatory fog can dampen investment and complicate conflict resolution in international trade circuits.

Meanwhile, smallholder and marginalized farmers often end up sidelined. Without targeted support—like subsidies, training, or improved infrastructure—those who stand to benefit most from digital tools may never fully access them, widening the gap between resource-rich and resource-poor communities. In most cases, without clear rules governing

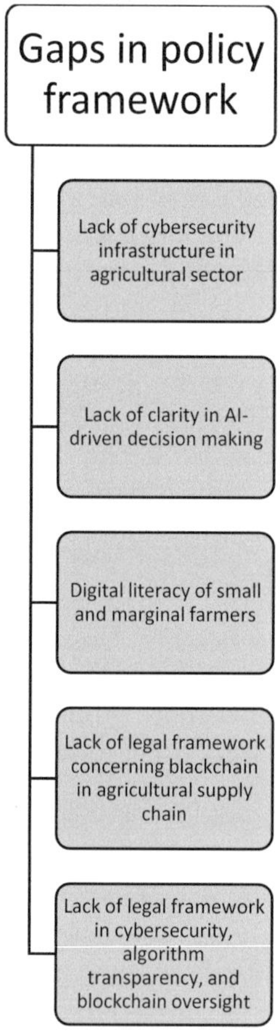

Figure 9.3: Gaps in policy framework for the implementation of smart agricultural practices.

data rights, cybersecurity measures, AI transparency, and blockchain applications, the advantages of these new systems may be overshadowed by their inherent risks. If policymakers can catch up with the pace of innovation—balancing technology with fairness and addressing the everyday needs of all participants in agriculture—then the potential to transform farming in a positive way might finally be within reach. Clear rules on ownership, cybersecurity, algorithm transparency, blockchain oversight, and equal access are needed if AI and blockchain are to help agriculture in a fair, secure, and lasting way. In many cases, addressing these policy gaps builds trust, defends farmers' rights, and helps secure a stable future for global food systems (Sen et al., 2025).

5. Policy Innovation

Digital agriculture is changing everything. Farms today are not just fields and tractors—they are buzzing hubs full of smart gadgets, sensors, and even blockchain systems that mix the old with the radically new. Traditional rules simply do not cover the messy reality of modern, gadget-driven farming. What happens when a piece of equipment sends far more than just water to the crops? It sends heaps of data and questions about rights, security, and accountability. Every sensor in a tractor and every smart machine working the land produces bits of information that could be gold—or junk—depending on who controls it. The folks who actually tend the fields should have clear ownership of that data. Farmers ought to decide if the numbers can be shared, sold, or even used to drive decisions without their say. In most cases, a framework similar to what we see in health or finance sectors could work; one where clear consent is the norm. And maybe, just maybe, local data cooperatives could form, letting smallholders pool together their information and manage it communally while still keeping the benefits where they belong. It sounds a bit convoluted, but it is really about giving power back to the people out there in the fields (Khan et al., 2025).

Farms now depend on a maze of interconnected devices and networks, and with that comes risk. Even the best hardware can become a weak link if not properly protected. Instead of simply hoping nothing goes wrong, a set of baseline cybersecurity standards for all agricultural tech are needed. Imagine a system where each new piece of digital farming equipment must pass a test—much like an organic certification that checks if produce is really green. Governments could even run training sessions for rural communities, teaching basic cybersecurity moves, risk management, and how to react if something starts going sideways. This is not just about preventing data breaches—it is about keeping the entire farming ecosystem robust and resilient against digital mishaps (Fuentes-Peñailillo et al., 2024).

Artificial intelligence in agriculture promises amazing things—more precise irrigation, better crop predictions, and even custom advice based on soil data—but it also raises questions of fairness and transparency. How do you trust a computerized decision that could drastically affect a farmer's livelihood if you cannot see how it works? Policies here need to demand that AI tools be explainable, so farmers can understand the "why" behind the numbers. Regular checks to hunt down biases in these algorithms should become routine. If an AI decision ends up causing more harm than good—say, by ignoring local nuances of weather or soil conditions—farmers must have a way to challenge it. Establishing independent oversight, perhaps through an auditing body, could go a long way in making sure these digital decision-makers do not run away with power unchecked. Blockchain is another player in this digital revolution, albeit a complex one. On the one hand, blockchain offers a neat solution for securing transactions and managing contracts—think of it as giving digital certificates to each smart contract used on the farm. Yet the legal landscape for these tools is still very much in its infancy. We need clear, standard frameworks that can govern how a smart contract is created and executed. There are hurdles too, like concerns over data privacy and energy consumption; after all, blockchain is not exactly known for being light on power use. Creating protocols that favour energy efficiency and ensuring interoperability between different systems are tasks that must be taken up sooner rather than later if the promise of blockchain is to be met in agriculture (Assimakopoulos et al., 2025).

It is not all about high-tech tools, though. The human side of farming remains essential, and here inclusivity and accessibility play key roles. There is a risk that as agribusinesses and large farms glide into digital excellence, the smaller, family-run farms could be left behind in a digital dust. Bridging that gap might involve government subsidies, targeted training, or local initiatives that help smallholders incorporate digital technologies without being overwhelmed by them. Often, even minor support in understanding or accessing these tools can be transformative. In the end, the goal is to ensure that digital agriculture is not just the playground of the wealthy—every farmer, regardless of scale, should have a fair chance at benefiting from these advancements. New rules have to be as adaptable as the technology they are designed to regulate. They need to address data ownership, tighten up cybersecurity, demand clear explanations from AI, give blockchain a fair legal footing, and above all, keep the farmer at the centre of everything. The modernization of agriculture presents considerable challenges, demanding adaptive and nuanced policy frameworks to effectively manage technological advancements (Soma and Nuckchady, 2021). Generally speaking, the future sustainability of agricultural practices is predicated on the implementation of policies that are not only innovative but also equitable in their distribution of benefits, ensuring that advancements in agricultural technology contribute to the well-being of all stakeholders. Modern farming is undergoing a discernible shift, with strategic investments in advanced machinery, expanded rural internet accessibility, and specialized training programmes designed to cultivate digital competencies increasingly recognized as essential. Policies, in most cases, should prioritize support for women farmers, indigenous communities, and other marginalized groups to ensure inclusive development. Digital

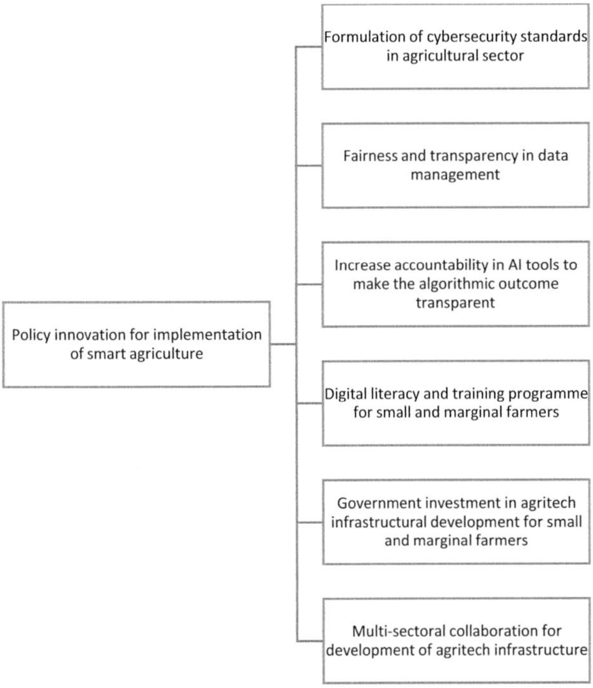

Figure 9.4: Policy innovation for implementation of smart agriculture.

agriculture is envisioned as a catalyst for social upliftment rather than a perpetuation of existing inequalities (Soma and Nuckchady, 2021).

A collaborative paradigm involving synergistic alliances between public and private entities offers a promising avenue for advancement. Governments are encouraged to foster partnerships with technology corporations, agricultural organizations, research institutions, and local farmer cooperatives during the policy formulation process. Such collaborative endeavours have the potential to stimulate innovation ecosystems, aligning profit-driven objectives with the broader societal imperative of promoting common welfare (Soma and Nuckchady, 2021). For example, creating trial zones or flexible regulatory sandbox areas for agricultural technology lets experimenters test new ideas while regulators keep an eye on safety and make quick adjustments based on real-world feedback. Food supply chains today often stretch across multiple countries, so common standards for data sharing, blockchain transactions, cybersecurity, and even AI oversight become a necessity. Generally speaking, international cooperation and multilateral agreements can help ensure that every farmer—no matter their country's size or resources—gets fair access to digital innovations and protection against cyber threats. Organizations like the Food and Agriculture Organization (FAO) and World Trade Organization (WTO) can play a central role in helping smooth out these global policy efforts (Sims and Kienzle, 2017).

6. Public-Private Partnerships

Public–private partnerships (PPPs) are popping up as an increasingly vital boost to innovation, funding, and even security in the wild world of digital agriculture. Digital farming now leans heavily on tools like AI, blockchain, IoT, and big data—a mix that pulls together governments, tech firms, research bodies, and even farmers in rather unexpected ways. When these groups join forces, resource shortfalls get patched up, technology evolves faster, and rules that try to balance business aims with community needs start to form. In numerous agrarian locales, the availability of broadband infrastructure and sophisticated sensor technologies remains constrained, and it is evident that governmental entities alone cannot fully accommodate the requisite financial investments. Consequently, private sector organizations, motivated by both prospective profitability and the impetus for technological advancement, frequently assume a crucial role in addressing these deficiencies. These entities contribute capital resources and provide specialized technical expertise, thereby facilitating the inception of initiatives such as rural internet infrastructure development. As an illustration, a collaborative endeavour aimed at augmenting digital connectivity can empower agricultural producers to access digital platforms, monitor real-time data streams, or establish electronic commerce venues. This blend of funds and expertise helps make high-tech tools accessible, even if it sometimes feels a bit haphazard (Ranjan and Kaushik, 2022).

Regional agriculture often needs tailored research that mirrors local weather, different crops, and even unique economic conditions. That is exactly where research and development (R&D) through public–private partnerships really makes a difference. Governments teaming up with tech companies and local universities might launch innovation labs or digital agriculture hubs that experiment with practical solutions. These setups can produce AI models, blockchain systems, and smart IoT applications that are not just cutting-edge but are also fine-tuned for local needs. Generally speaking, such hands-on research ensures that fresh ideas not only dazzle in theory but also work on the ground (Ponnusamy, 2013).

Technology tends to sprint ahead, leaving regulations a bit behind. In these cases, a friendly back-and-forth between public officials and tech insiders can help shape more realistic, flexible policies. For instance, a regulatory sandbox—a sort of trial zone with temporary, looser rules—allows new ideas to be tested before the full might of the law weighs in. This process might seem a bit messy at times, but it usually does a decent job of balancing innovation with the need for public safety, even if some guidelines end up a bit all over the place. Training and capacity-building also come into play. Small-scale farmers often begin with limited knowledge of digital technologies. To address this, collaborative efforts among local governments, agritech companies, and non-governmental organizations (NGOs) commonly initiate training programmes and digital literacy courses. While these efforts may sometimes have shortcomings, they build enough confidence for farmers to try new methods. This is an ongoing process where repetition and helpful reminders greatly aid in making technology normal to use. Ultimately, these partnerships can act as ethical watchdogs for technology, as private companies working with public bodies usually face more checks on openness and fair practices. Often, partnership deals include pledges to support small farmers, women, and other disadvantaged groups, helping to spread the benefits of digital agriculture equally. Basically, despite any flaws, these combined initiatives tend to create a farming sector where innovation and fairness can exist together, pointing to a promising and just future. It is a shame, but big farming businesses often gain more advantages, pushing smaller players to the side. However, if new ways of working together appear, technology

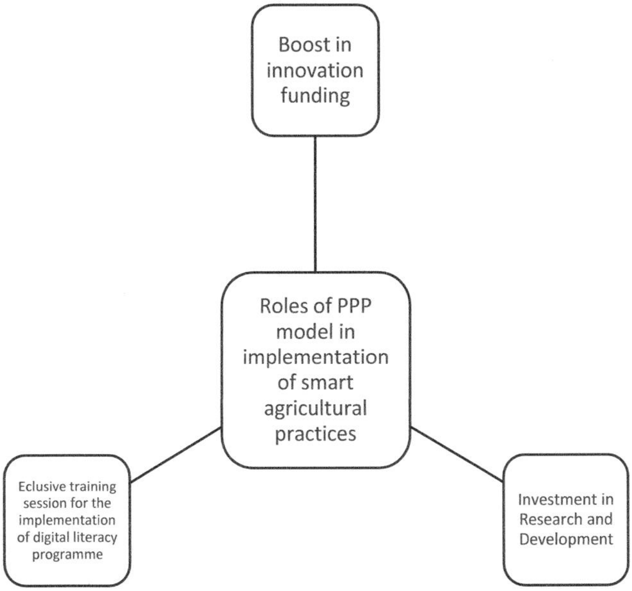

Figure 9.5: Roles of PPP model in implementation of smart agricultural practices.

can play a different role, possibly reducing rather than increasing inequalities in agriculture. Mostly, this change means technology is more than just a tool; it is a way to bridge the gap towards a fairer system. By mixing the unique strengths of public institutions and private companies, these alliances tend to spark investment, stir up creative ideas, tighten up regulatory frameworks, and even boost farmer education—all contributing to more balanced growth. Sure, a bit of thoughtful planning, a dash of mutual trust, and clear, agreed-upon objectives go a long way in unlocking an agricultural future that is productive, sustainable, and, well, more inclusive (Mangeni, 2019).

7. International Cooperation

Farming these days is shifting into a real digital age, and countries working side by side seems more important than ever. New tech like AI, blockchain, and even IoT is not limited to a single nation's fields—it spreads out across borders. In a world where food production and supply chains crisscross continents, issues such as data rules, cyber risks, trade snags, and even climate ups and downs cannot be solved alone. When nations team up, smart agriculture can grow in a way that feels fair and safe, tackling challenges like making sure everyone has enough to eat and keeping our environment healthy (Dhanaraju et al., 2022).

A big topic on many lips now is how farm data needs its own kind of rulebook. Farms everywhere churn out huge amounts of information daily, and without some common, agreed-upon ideas about who owns this data, how private it stays, or how it should be ethically used, everything can get pretty messy. Without an internationally accepted set of guidelines, farmers might end up caught in a web of mixed rules, while large agritech companies could take advantage where protections are weak. Groups like the FAO or International Telecommunication Union (ITU) could help smooth out these differences, setting up standards that both respect those working the land and spark innovation by bridging gaps between different systems (Assimakopoulos et al., 2025).

Consider cyber threats—these do not check passports. A breach in one country's agricultural supply chain might easily send shock waves through food markets around the globe. It is a reminder that digital dangers ignore borders completely. Countries need to pass along early warnings on possible threats, agree on some basic, shared security measures, and join forces to build a tougher shield for smart farming tools. When nations mix their experience and even set up rapid-response backups for cyber mishaps, they are in a better spot to fend off attacks that ripple out unpredictably.

Trade is riding a similar wave with blockchain technology. Blockchain promises to make tracking food—from farms to tables—more transparent. But if there is no shared legal recognition for digital records and smart contracts, the promise of blockchain might fall flat. To really make it work, governments need to get together and align on both legal details and technical standards so that certifications or transaction records hold true no matter where they go. Bodies like the WTO might help drive these conversations, even if the conversation sometimes meanders a bit (Fuentes-Peñailillo et al., 2024).

When research centres, universities, and private companies share ideas, they can pool resources, trim down duplicate work, and develop tech that suits a range of farming realities—especially for places that are not flush with cash. Such collaborative efforts can lead to inventive AI tools, hardier crop varieties, and climate-smart techniques that adapt to different needs. Generally speaking, sharing expertise not only propels innovation forward but also helps ensure that the benefits trickle down to every corner of the globe. Building skills and spreading know-how are essential. In several regions—notably across many Global South nations—there simply is not yet enough technical know-how, digital infrastructure, or modern policy framework to really launch smart agriculture. Here, by offering funds, training, and some practical technical advice, international partnerships can boost local abilities. This sharing of skills, albeit sometimes a bit uneven, lays the groundwork for a future where digital farming becomes both robust and accessible, creating a more balanced global food system. Digital agriculture is quickly emerging as a practical solution that not only boosts food security in areas at risk but also helps make the global farming system stronger by making every nation more prepared for future challenges. It is not just about new technology; it is about ensuring that even the most vulnerable regions gain extra support, while the overall network of agriculture benefits too.

8. Case Studies

One example is IBM's Food Trust blockchain platform. Big names like Walmart and Nestlé have jumped on board to record every little detail from farm to shelf. In a twist that is almost too neat, every stakeholder—be it the farmer or a retailer—logs data on harvesting, how produce is handled, or even transportation details. This secure, nearly unhackable system dramatically cuts down the tracing time for a potentially dangerous product from long, stressful days to just seconds. Generally speaking, this kind of digital record-keeping forces us to think about how policies must step up, setting rules for data-sharing and legally recognizing these records. It is like technology and policy are dancing together in a sometimes clumsy but hopeful duet (Sristy, 2021).

Then there is Microsoft's FarmBeats project, a venture that is not afraid to get its hands dirty on small and medium farms. With a cocktail of low-cost sensors, drones, and using the idle TV frequencies (commonly known as TV white space networks), FarmBeats offers real-time insights into soil moisture, temperature, and overall crop health. This data helps farmers make choices on irrigation, fertilizer use, and pest control—ideas that sound high-tech, yet are tailored for farms where internet access is not always a given. Of course, if rural broadband is not upgraded through public support, even the sharpest tech risks gathering dust. It is a clear signal that sometimes innovation needs a little hand-holding from policy and community efforts (Microsoft, n.d.).

A decade-old, but still striking, example comes from India's e-Choupal initiative. Spearheaded by ITC Limited, this project flipped the script by putting internet-connected kiosks right in the heart of rural areas. Operated by local farmers known as Sanchalaks, these kiosks quietly deliver market prices, weather updates, and best farming practices directly to the producers. This setup slips past the traditional middleman and helps boost incomes—even though it might sometimes feel a bit rough around the edges. The initiative also benefited from government programmes aimed at improving digital literacy and infrastructure in the villages, proving that when tech meets grassroots support, things can really change (Council on Energy, Environment and Water, n. d.).

The African Union's Digital Transformation Strategy for Africa (2020–2030) brings a more international vibe into play. Although the overall scheme touches on many areas, digital agriculture is a key pillar, fostering shared digital frameworks and common rules for data governance across countries. Pilot projects, such as AI-driven pest detection apps in East Africa, are already stepping in to help farmers predict and manage locust swarms. These initiatives, in most cases, remind us that technology must be tailored to local needs, with cross-border cooperation playing a crucial role (Schuman Associates, 2020).

These varied stories—each a little disjointed and human in its execution—show that the promise of smart agriculture hinges on a delicate blend of innovation, policy tweaks, and real community engagement. The journey might be a bit bumpy and riddled with small inconsistencies, but it certainly points towards a future where technology and tradition waltz together in surprising, yet hopeful, ways. New challenges—including cybersecurity risks and algorithmic bias—are beginning to surface in the fast-evolving world of smart farming.

9. Future Perspectives

Smart agriculture is taking off in ways we never imagined. AI, blockchain, and other shiny tech are pushing farming into a new era. The whole global food system could get a serious makeover as digital ideas speed up, making farms more efficient, tough, and earth-friendly. But, you know, this digital dream will not just fall into place on its own—it needs smart rules, tech that everyone can use, and a genuine caring for ethics and the natural world.

Think about it: soon, farming might feel less like hard, old-school work and more as if tech and nature were teaming up in unexpected ways. AI and machine learning, for example, are set to slip right into daily farm life. Picture systems that not only recall past harvests but also pull in live weather updates, satellite photos, and even market vibes to guide decisions on planting or watering. These tools might help farmers decide when to sow seeds, water fields, or tackle pests—almost like having a real-time buddy on the ground. Machines could even work together in what seems like a spontaneous dance to adjust for sudden weather or soil changes. Still, if this high-tech farm future is ever to really take off, those tools need to be within reach for the little family farms too—not just the sprawling agribusiness operations—so no one gets left out in this digital rush.

Within the agri-food sector, blockchain technology is rapidly emerging as a transformative mechanism for supply chain management. Heightened concerns regarding food safety and verifiable provenance have catalysed interest in blockchain's capacity for immutable record-keeping. The integration of QR codes linked to blockchain databases can afford consumers unprecedented transparency into a product's lifecycle, including its origin, production methodologies, and a provisional assessment of its environmental impact. Concurrently, the employment of smart contracts holds the potential to automate processes such as payment protocols and insurance claims, contingent upon real-time farm data acquisition. Achieving the comprehensive potential of this system, however, demands the formulation of harmonized legal frameworks and the establishment of interoperable data standards that transcend international jurisdictions.

Novel paradigms in agricultural finance, particularly within the decentralized finance (DeFi) sector and digital lending platforms, are concurrently gaining traction. Peer-to-peer lending platforms, crowdfunding ventures, and microinsurance schemes offer farmers supplementary channels for accessing capital, bypassing traditional financial institutions. This is especially relevant for farmers situated in geographically isolated areas, potentially facilitating more equitable and expedited access to essential funding. Regulatory oversight by governmental and international bodies is imperative to mitigate risks associated with fraud, to safeguard data security, and to ameliorate market volatility, thereby ensuring the protection of vulnerable agricultural producers. More often than not, the convergence of technology and finance proffers the prospect of a more inclusive financial ecosystem, predicated on the adoption of judicious regulatory mechanisms.

Contemporary agricultural practices increasingly prioritize sustainability and responsible environmental stewardship. The imperative to augment productivity must be judiciously balanced with the concomitant need to preserve ecological integrity. Advanced sensor technologies and AI algorithms can optimize resource utilization, minimizing water consumption, curtailing chemical inputs, and mitigating greenhouse gas emissions. Blockchain technology could also facilitate the validation of carbon credits derived from regenerative agricultural methodologies. However, translating these technological advancements into demonstrable environmental benefits necessitates the implementation of well-articulated policies that effectively integrate technological innovation with ecological considerations, thereby ensuring the synergistic advancement of agricultural output and environmental sustainability.

International collaboration is critically essential for addressing complex global challenges in the agricultural sector. Climate change, pandemics, and geopolitical instability underscore the necessity for robust cross-border cooperation. The exchange of agricultural data, coordinated initiatives to combat crop diseases, and collaborative investments in rural technology have the potential to transform extant challenges into shared accomplishments. International organizations should assume a leadership role in establishing ethical guidelines for the application of AI, blockchain, and related digital technologies in agriculture, while simultaneously maintaining a steadfast focus on fairness, equity, and human-centric considerations. The future trajectory of digital agriculture hinges on prioritizing education and capacity building. As technology continues its exponential evolution, farmers require continuous training to effectively harness the potential of new tools and methodologies. Initiatives encompassing digital literacy programmes, informal knowledge-sharing networks, and youth engagement programmes are indispensable for adequately preparing the next cohort of agricultural professionals. Continuous learning and skill development remain indispensable for ensuring the effective adaptation of the agricultural sector to a rapidly evolving technological landscape.

10. Conclusion

The intersection of AI and blockchain within agriculture holds considerable promise. The emerging landscape of digitally integrated farms ostensibly enhances productivity and fortifies food supply chains; nonetheless, these advancements also raise critical issues pertaining to data security, ethical implications, and the necessity for adaptive regulatory mechanisms. Current policies suggest the need for innovative strategies to safeguard farmers' rights, uphold data privacy, and ensure equitable access to technology. Progress could be accelerated through enhanced public–private collaborations, international alliances, and flexible policymaking. It seems that such partnerships can generate economic advantages alongside broader social benefits. Moreover, increased investment in local educational resources, skills training, and rural infrastructure is likely required to fully integrate farmers into the digital agricultural sphere. Securing agriculture's digital transformation demands a holistic strategy that extends beyond merely deploying technology.

References

Allioui, H. and Mourdi, Y. (2023). Exploring the full potentials of IoT for better financial growth and stability: A comprehensive survey. *Sensors* 23(19): 8015.

Anoop, V.S., Adarsh, S. and Asharaf, S. (2022). Artificial Intelligence and the blockchain in smart agriculture: Emergence, opportunities, and challenges. pp. 43–55. *In*: Kose, U., Prasath, V.B., Mondal, M., Podder, P. and Bharati, S. (eds.). *Artificial Intelligence and Smart Agriculture Technology*. Auerbach Publications.

Assimakopoulos, F., Vassilakis, C., Margaris, D., Kotis, K. and Spiliotopoulos, D. (2025). AI and related technologies in the fields of smart agriculture: A review. *Information* 16(2): 100.

Choudhary, V., Guha, P., Pau, G. and Mishra, S. (2025). An overview of smart agriculture using Internet of Things (IoT) and web services. *Environmental and Sustainability Indicators* 26: 100607.

Council on Energy, Environment and Water. (n. d.). E-Choupal Project Framework for India's Sustainable Agriculture Initiatives. Available at https://www.ceew.in/sustainable-agriculture-initiatives/e-choupal-initiative-case-study (accessed on 26 September 2025).

Demestichas, K., Peppes, N. and Alexakis, T. (2020). Survey on security threats in agricultural IoT and smart farming. *Sensors* 20(22): 6458.

Dewitte, S., Cornelis, J.P., Müller, R. and Munteanu, A. (2021). Artificial intelligence revolutionises weather forecast, climate monitoring and decadal prediction. *Remote Sensing* 13(16): 3209.

Dhanaraju, M., Chenniappan, P., Ramalingam, K., Pazhanivelan, S. and Kaliaperumal, R. (2022). Smart farming: Internet of Things (IoT)-based sustainable agriculture. *Agriculture* 12(10): 1745.

Fuentes-Peñailillo, F., Gutter, K., Vega, R. and Silva, G.C. (2024). Transformative technologies in digital agriculture: Leveraging internet of things, remote sensing, and artificial intelligence for smart crop management. *Journal of Sensor and Actuator Networks* 13(4): 39.

Gangwani, N. (2024) AI-driven precision agriculture: Optimizing crop yield and resource efficiency. *International Journal for Multidisciplinary Research* 6(6).

Habib, G., Sharma, S., Ibrahim, S., Ahmad, I., Qureshi, S. and Ishfaq, M. (2022). Blockchain technology: Benefits, challenges, applications, and integration of blockchain technology with cloud computing. *Future Internet* 14(11): 341.

Holzinger, A., Saranti, A., Angerschmid, A., Retzlaff, C.O., Gronauer, A., Pejakovic, V., Medel-Jimenez, F., Krexner, T., Gollob, C. and Stampfer, K. (2022). Digital transformation in smart farm and forest operations needs human-centered AI: Challenges and future directions. *Sensors* 22(8): 3043.

John, S. and Arul Leena Rose, P.J. (2024). Smart farming and precision agriculture and its need in today's world. pp. 19–44. *In*: Balasubramanian, S., Natarajan, G. and Chelliah, P.R. (eds.). *Intelligent Robots and Drones for Precision Agriculture. Signals and Communication Technology*. Springer, Cham.

Kapoor, S.K., Agarwal, P. and Revathi, R. (2024). Addressing cybersecurity and privacy concerns in agricultural IoT systems and data-sharing practices for improved security. *African Journal of Biological Sciences* 6(9).

Kaur, R., Ali, A. and Faisal, M. (2022). Smart contracts: The self-executing contracts. pp. 35–49. *In*: Chakraborty, R., Ghosh, A., Balas, V.E. and Elngar, A.A. (eds.). *Blockchain: Principals and Application in IoT*. CRC Press.

Khan, A., Malebary, S.J., Dang, L.M., Binzagr, F., Song, H.K. and Moon, H. (2024). AI-enabled crop management framework for pest detection using visual sensor data. *Plants* 13(5): 653.

Khan, N., Ray, R.L., Sargani, G.R., Ihtisham, M., Khayyam, M. and Ismail, S. (2021). Current progress and future prospects of agriculture technology: Gateway to sustainable agriculture. *Sustainability* 13(9): 4883.

Khan, S., Pathania, N. and Kumar, N. (2025). Digital agriculture: transforming modern farming with Next-Gen technologies: A review. *International Journal of Creative Research Thoughts* 13(4): i119–i125.

Klein, J. (2024). Driving automation on the farm: self-driving tractors look to fill agriculture's labor shortage. *Agriculture Dive*. Available at https://www.agriculturedive.com/news/autonomous-tractors-driverless-vehicles-deere-agtonomy-ai-farming-labor/730007/ (accessed on 26 September 2025).

Lakhiar, I.A., Yan, H., Zhang, C., Wang, G., He, B., Hao, B., Han, Y., Wang, B., Bao, R., Syed, T.N., Chauhdary, J.N. and Rakibuzzaman, M. (2024). A review of precision irrigation water-saving technology under changing climate for enhancing water use efficiency, crop yield, and environmental footprints. *Agriculture* 14(7): 1141.

Mangeni, B. (2019). The role of Public-Private Partnerships (PPPs) in ensuring technology access for farmers in sub-saharan Africa. *African Journal of Food, Agriculture, Nutrition and Development* 19(1): 14137–14155.

Maraveas, C., Rajarajan, M. and Arvanitis, K.G. (2024). Cybersecurity threats and mitigation measures in agriculture 4.0 and 5.0. *Smart Agricultural Technology* 9: 100616.

Microsoft. (n.d.). FarmBeats democratizing AI for farmers around the world. Available at https://www.microsoft.com/en-us/garage/wall-of-fame/farmbeats/#:~:text=FarmBeats%20enables%20data%2Ddriven%20farming,the%20food%20yield%20of%20farms (accessed on 26 September 2025).

Moore, V. (2025). The Future is Now—How Technology is Revolutionising Agriculture. *Medium*. https://medium.com/@victoria_moore/the-future-is-now-how-technology-is-revolutionising-agriculture-ac4b8e9f0a74 (accessed on 26 September 2025).

Mutlutürk, M., Wynn, M. and Metin, B. (2024). Phishing and the human factor: Insights from a bibliometric analysis. *Information* 15(10): 643.

Ponnusamy, K. (2013). Impact of public private partnership in agriculture: A review. *Indian Journal of Agricultural Science* 83(8): 803–808.

Rane, J., Kaya, O., Mallick, S.K. and Rane, N.L. (2024). Smart farming using artificial intelligence, machine learning, deep learning, and ChatGPT: Applications, opportunities, challenges, and future directions. In *Generative Artificial Intelligence in Agriculture, Education, and Business*, 218–272. Deep Science Publishing.

Ranjan, J. and Kaushik, P. (2022). Here's how india can unlock the power of agricultural technology through private public partnerships. *World Economic Forum*. Available at https://www.weforum.org/stories/2022/03/unlock-the-power-of-agricultural-technology-through-private-public-partnerships/ (accessed on 26 September 2025).

Schuman Associates. (2020). The African Union's Digital Transformation Strategy. Available at https://www.schumanassociates.com/newsroom/the-african-union-s-digital-transformation-strategy (accessed on 26 September 2025).

Sen, L.T.H., Phuong, L.T.H., Chou, P., Dacuyan, F.B., Nyberg, Y. and Wetterlind, J. (2025). The opportunities and barriers in developing interactive digital extension services for smallholder farmers as a pathway to sustainable agriculture: A systematic review. *Sustainability* 17(7): 3007.

Sims, B. and Kienzle, J. (2017). Sustainable agricultural mechanization for smallholders: What is it and how can we implement it? *Agriculture* 7(6): 50.

Soma, T. and Nuckchady, B. (2021). Communicating the benefits and risks of digital agriculture technologies: Perspectives on the future of digital agricultural education and training. *Frontier in Communication* 6: 762201.

Sristy, A. (2021). Blockchain in the Food Supply Chain—What Does the Future Look Like? *Walmart Global Tech*. Available at https://tech.walmart.com/content/walmart-global-tech/en_us/blog/post/blockchain-in-the-food-supply-chain.html (accessed on 26 September 2025).

Xiong, H., Dalhaus, T., Wang, P. and Huang, J. (2020). Blockchain technology for agriculture: Applications and rationale. *Frontiers in Blockchain* 3: 7.

Chapter 10

AI-Powered Crop Disease Prediction with Enhanced Data Privacy

Kothai, G.,[1,*] *Sivakarthick, B.*[2] and *Vignesh, K.*[2]

Crop diseases, driven by climate change, global trade, and intensive farming practices, pose a significant threat to agricultural yields and global food security. Effective forecasting is crucial for enabling early interventions, ensuring sustainable farming practices, and safeguarding global food systems. Traditional methods of disease detection, such as visual inspections and laboratory diagnostics, are often unreliable, costly, and slow, making timely management challenging for farmers. In contrast, artificial intelligence (AI) offers a transformative solution. By leveraging technologies like machine learning, computer vision, and predictive analytics, AI enables early and accurate detection of crop diseases, optimizes resource utilization, reduces losses, and advances sustainable agricultural practices. However, AI success in agriculture requires sensitive data: geospatial, soil, and crop health metrics. It creates huge privacy issues. Inappropriate or unauthorized use of the data will decrease

[1] Department of Computational Intelligence, School of Computing, SRM Institute of Science and Technology, Tamil Nadu, India.
[2] Department of Computer Science and Engineering (Artificial Intelligence and Machine Learning), KPR Institute of Engineering and Technology, Tamil Nadu, India.
* Corresponding author: emailtokothaiganesan@gmail.com

DOI: 10.1201/9781003670568-10

the level of trust and will limit the adoption of AI. To combat these issues, new privacy-preserving techniques, such as federated learning, differential privacy, and blockchain technology, protect data security. These approaches make farmers feel empowered, accountable, and ensure that AI is used ethically in agriculture. This chapter discusses the prospect of AI for transforming crop disease prediction while focusing on the urgent need for advanced privacy-preserving solutions to create sustainable, ethical, and secure agricultural systems.

1. Introduction

Agriculture has always been the fulcrum of human survival and development of the economy. The global population is projected to reach around 9.7 to 9.8 billion by middle of this century (2050). At the same time, the agricultural sector faces many compound challenges of which perhaps the worst is the continuous emergence and re-emergence of crop diseases. Crop diseases that originate from fungi, bacteria, viruses, nematodes, and other pathogens can wipe out entire fields, diminish food quality, and endanger the very livelihood of farmers. These diseases have ceased to be localized but are now quite rightly becoming global terrors, thanks to the interconnectedness of food systems today. Several factors have merged over the years, making crop diseases spread and impact faster, thus tending to be more frequent, more severe, and even less predictable than in the past (Gupta et al., 2024).

1.1 Climate Change and Disease Proliferation

One of the leading factors for increasing crop disease prevalence is climate change. Global warming, erratic rainfall, prolonged dry spells, and changing humidity enhance the breeding environments of both pests and pathogens. For example, an increase in temperature has permitted certain fungal pathoses to survive in previously inhospitable regions, with excessive moisture causing the proliferation of pathogens with high virulence. Climate change disrupts the delicate balance in an ecosystem, hence allowing new disease vectors to emerge and those that already existed to spread into different territories. In addition, climatic stress impedes the natural defence mechanisms of plants and increases their susceptibility to infections. Hence, seasonal or localized diseases may become common due to changing climatic conditions (Gupta et al., 2024).

1.2 Impacts of Globalization and Rapid Disease Transmission

With the establishment of global trade, agriculture saw a transformation in the exchange of seeds, plants, and foods across continents. The downside of globalization is the spread of plant diseases. Contaminated plant material, soil, or package can potentially introduce foreign pathogens into a new ecosystem that may prove disastrous due to a lack of natural resistance in the local crops. A typical example is the case with Phytophthora infestans that caused the Irish potato famine in 1845. It was brought to Europe from the Americas, mostly unintentionally. Today we may have regulations of international trade meant to minimize such risks, but with the volume of global agricultural transactions, such risk prevention becomes almost impossible. Thereby, for their purposes, active surveillance and identified rapid response for limited impacts have become relevant nowadays (al Bakri et al., 2024).

1.3 Intensive Farming and Monoculture Practices

Presently, agriculture is geared towards intensive farming and monoculture—the use of huge brown fields containing a single variety of crop for maximum yield and easy management. This probably sounds okay for the short term; however, in the long run, intense farming and monoculture provide a favourable environment for the rapid spread of diseases. The moment a pathogen enters a monoculture field, it spreads with lightening speeds and uncontrollably due to the absence of genetic diversity and natural resistance. Creating strains resistant to these chemicals through the overuse of chemical pesticides and fungicides is much like antibiotics creating resistant bacteria of human concern. Resistance evolves as pathogens find alternative means of overcoming treatment, making the once valid control measure old and ineffective (Onteddu et al., 2025).

Figure 10.1 shows per capita production and yield losses (%) of five major crops—wheat, rice, maize, potato, and soybean—in different world regions. Each bar indicates the crop performance in terms of productivity and susceptibility to yield loss. The map in the figure shows the overall geographic regions analysed. Losses, particularly in rice, are notably higher in areas such as Sub-Saharan Africa and Southeast Asia. This indicates a need to improve disease forecast and management systems in vulnerable areas.

1.4 Socioeconomic and Food Security Implications

The effects of crop diseases extend far beyond the farm gates. According to the Food and Agriculture Organization (FAO), plant diseases cause

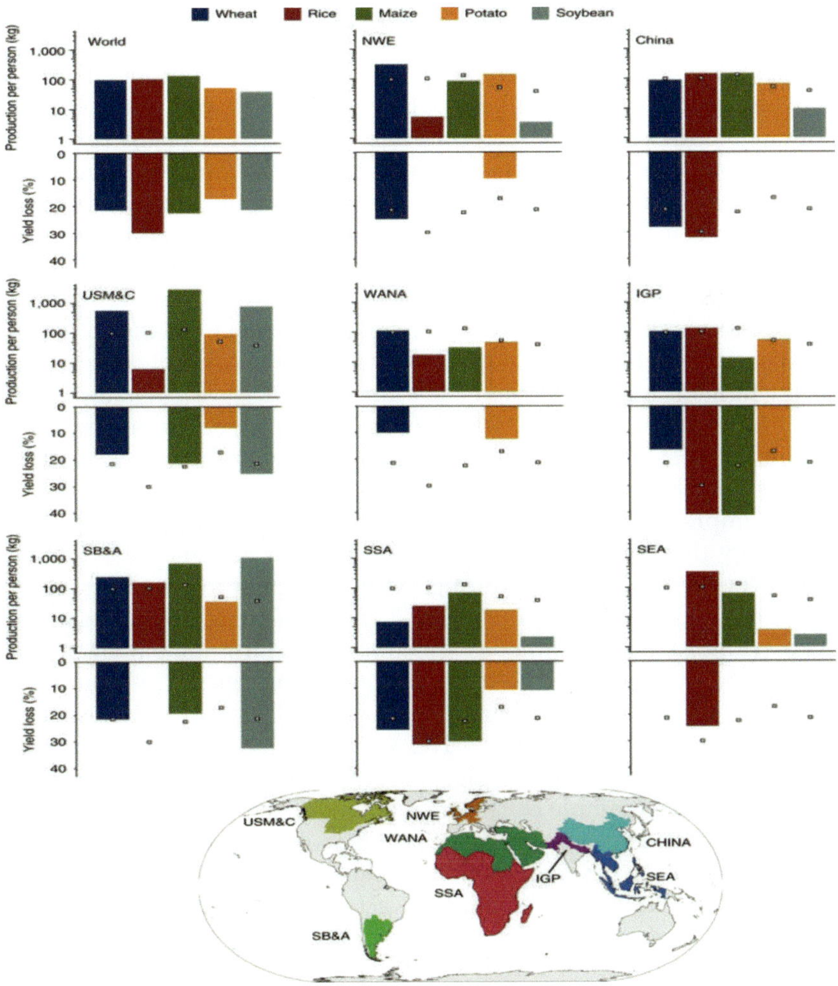

Figure 10.1: The global burden of pathogens and pests on major food crops (Savary et al. 2019).

more than $220 billion in damage to the world economy every year. For smallholder farmers in poorer countries, a single outbreak could mean the difference between subsistence farming and starvation. The income loss leads to food-price hikes, reliance on imported foods, and increased food insecurity. With ever-increasing pressure to sustainably feed the world, it is clear that disease-control strategies adopted until now have fallen short. Agriculture must advance through modern technology: effective, scalable, sustainable, and secure detection and management of crop diseases (Agrawal and Arafat, 2024).

2. Traditional Agricultural Approaches

Agricultural practices throughout the ages have depended upon conventional techniques of crop disease diagnosis and management. Although these practices were based on ages of personal experience and custom, they are now increasingly put to test due to the modern challenges of large-scale farming, altering climate conditions, and the increasing complication of crop diseases. Visual inspection has been the mainstay for quite a long time. Farmers tend to rely on their ability to recognize signs such as wilting, yellowing leaves, and the unusual spots, and sometimes the presence of pests and mould. Accessibility and inexpensiveness make this method very subjective—severely depending on the farmers' experiences and cognizance and alertness. In many cases, plant diseases are already reaching an advanced development stage before visible symptoms appear, hence delaying intervention and leading to considerable yield losses (Ferris, 2017).

To improve the accuracy of their diagnosis, some farmers consider laboratory diagnostics whereby infected samples are analysed through microscopic examination, culturing, or by molecular techniques such as Polymerase Chain Reaction (PCR) and Enzyme-Linked Immunosorbent Assay (ELISA). Such techniques scientifically confirm the pathogen and enable the pursuance of targeted treatment strategies. Unfortunately, they do come with certain demerits. Most often, laboratory analysis will take long and will be too expensive, as well as not readily available to farmers in some far or most under-resourced areas, with a critical period elapsing between sample collection and diagnosis especially when faced with very fast infectious pathogens. Their broad extent of chemical intervention, e.g., pesticide and fungicide use, results from all these factors. These treatments sometimes act as preventive or controlling measures for disease outbreaks, if applied early. Over-application, however, gives rise to other concerns: the emergence of pesticide-resistant strains, environmental pollution, and health risk to humans and animals (Dembani et al., 2025).

Another age-old pillar in crop disease management is the agricultural extension service wherein specialists/webinars guide farmers on the ground. These experts share knowledge, best practices, and sometimes act as early warning systems of disease outbreaks in the region. The coverage extent of this type of service is, however, very limited—especially in areas with a large number of farmers relative to few trained personnel. The visits are infrequent, and the recommendations might not always go with the real-time dynamics of a fast-spreading disease or vulnerability to rapidly changing environmental conditions (Ferrag et al., 2020).

Figure 10.2: Traditional vs modern farming practices.

There are two farming techniques being contrasted in Figure 10.2. The traditional methods appear on the left-hand side; workers pick the crops by hand, highlighting the fact that conventional agriculture is labour-intensive. The right side presents modern mechanized farming activities with several tractors working in tandem over a massive field, demonstrating a shift towards automation and efficiency. In essence, the comparison highlights technological transformation of agriculture that is opening pathways to smarter, artificial intelligence (AI)-powered farming solutions.

Traditional ecological knowledge has contributed a great deal to the way people farm in many parts of the world, especially indigenous and rural communities. Practices such as crop rotation, intercropping, and natural plant-based pesticides like neem or garlic have underlined the importance of indigenous knowledge. Such methods have generally been environmentally friendly and culturally viable, hence sustainable in the long run. However, they lack the necessary scientific rigor and scalability to tackle today's agricultural problems, more so when newer or more aggressive strains of a disease arise. Despite its immense contributions, traditional agriculture is becoming increasingly unable to meet the modern requirements of agriculturalism. Today, the global level of trade and climatic volatility require active and finer methodologies to track-out emerging situations. Conventional methods will not therefore provide the real-time information, prediction support, or massive coordination necessary in today's global agricultural arena. Traditional approaches, certainly still useful and relevant, must therefore be combined with modern science and technology, mainly AI, to combat the challenges associated with the prediction and management of crop diseases (Agrawal and Arafat, 2024).

3. The Role of AI in Crop Disease Prediction

3.1 A Paradigm Shift in Agricultural Practices

Artificial intelligence has been a radical departure from the old ways of agricultural intervention in response to crop health issues, mainly being different from the most reactive techniques in conservative agriculture. AI involves a data-based proactivity of predicting and managing diseases instead of waiting for the most reactive techniques in conventional agriculture. As agricultural data from satellite images, weather patterns, soil moisture, and crop images become increasingly available, AI systems will be able to detect patterns invisible to the human eye and thus warn the farmer well in advance before an outbreak of disease can wreak havoc. There is thus a significant paradigm shift in crop management, which has moved the focus away from treatment to prevention and made anticipating problems much more important than just responding (Gupta et al., 2024).

3.2 Machine Learning and Predictive Analytics

Artificial intelligence is a major part of machine learning—the part of AI that enables every system to learn from data and change its model due to learning over time without being explicitly programmed application in agriculture. For example, training datasets for crop disease prediction may require very extensive collections of images of crops in healthy and diseased states, past years' weather reports, yields data, and actual environmental conditions. Such a model could then be trained with this data to detect minute variations or trends that show onset of disease at its most incipient stage. At the next level comes predictive analytics, the progenitor of modelling, giving models that will quantify the odds of a disease according to the present state–past state combination. This is also helpful in letting farmers actually take proactive decision-making approaches and only apply treatment upon actual need, saving costs and minimizing damage to the environment (Elbasi et al., 2024).

In Figure 10.3, the step-by-step pipeline of identifying diseases in corn leaves using AI is presented, beginning with the capture of the image of the affected leaf, followed by background removal and segmentation of healthy and diseased areas. The segmented image is processed for analysis and features such as colour, texture, and shape. These features come into play during classification with machine learning or deep learning models. While machine learning requires that features need to be extracted manually, deep learning performs extraction and classification simultaneously, which enhances accuracy and provides automation in the detection of diseases.

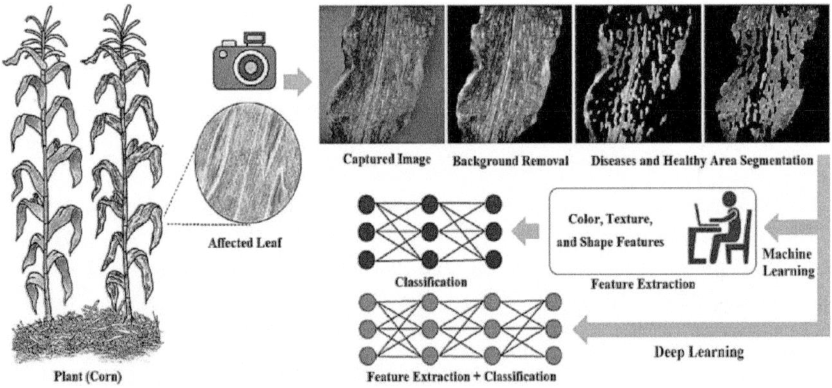

Figure 10.3: Steps for diagnosis and classification of plant leaf diseases (Javidan et al. 2024).

3.3 *The Power of Computer Vision in Plant Pathology*

Computer vision is seen as one of the most potential applications of AI in this field. Deep learning models are used particularly in the case of Convolutional Neural Networks (CNNs), which use AI to run analyses in high precision on images of crops taken by mobile, aerial, or satellite imagery from the camera. These systems notice changes on plants that include discoloration of leaves, deformities on leaves, or fungal spots which sometimes are too subtle for the human eye to detect or are often misconstrued. AI is also developing new mobile applications for even smaller farmers to photograph their plants and provide diagnosis and quick recommendations. This will broaden access to expert-level diagnostics and improve speed and scale disease management (al Bakri et al., 2024).

3.4 *Integration with Internet of Things (IoT)*

Integration is in some scenarios where AI-installed Internet of Things (IoT) devices are scattered all over the farm. The sensors will thus keep monitoring the soil pH, temperature, humidity, and light exposure continuously. Hence, these data can easily be assimilated with an AI model to give real-time information to AI systems. This integration, then, continuously feeds into AI systems that are then able to detect and warn farmers about diseases that are likely to affect the crops. The union of IoT and AI demonstrates an intelligent agricultural environment where early detection is not only possible but also scaled and adaptable with varying climatic and geographical parameters.

With the development and establishment of an AI system linked with smart IoT farming, farm-level AI will operate through a sensory network deployed in the farm premises. Such a sensor would, throughout its existence, monitor soil pH, temperature, humidity, and light exposure parameters over time and feed all this information, in real-time, into the AI model. Such an integration keeps providing data to AI systems that are designed to continuously receive sample data from IoT devices and process it to predict the environmental conditions favourable for the establishment of some diseases and issue warnings to farmers for action. The combination of IoT and AI is indeed forming a smart agricultural ecosystem that enables early detection of disease, and it is a model that is scalable and adaptable to varying climatic and geographical factors (Ferrag et al., 2020).

3.5 Maximizing Productivity and Reducing Waste

Sustaining and eventually achieving food security is the most important advantage of crop disease prediction by AI. Through early and accurate detection, treatment can be focused only on affected areas, thereby saving chemicals and maintaining beneficial organisms. Moreover, healthier crops yield higher produce, have fewer losses, and use water and fertilizers more efficiently. In those areas where farming is the major source of income and food, AI becomes not only a tool of modernity but also the lifeline for economic resilience and nutritional well-being.

3.6 Overcoming Barriers and Future Prospects

Though it is one of the most promising new technologies on the scene today, several constraints are preventing AI from being effectively adopted in agriculture. These include data quality and availability, which are primary concerns in certain regions of the world. Furthermore, the costs of procuring AI technologies and training farmers pose a high buy-in for these services. Ethical issues surrounding data ownership and transparency in AI decision-making should also be highlighted. Hope prevails, though. With new iterations of affordable technology, open-source models, and concerted efforts by governments and the private sector, AI now stands an even greater chance of becoming a true friend in combating crop diseases and thereby aiding in the realization of a resilient and intelligent agricultural future (Dembani et al., 2025).

4. Understanding the Data: What Information is Collected from Farms

4.1 The Foundation of AI in Agriculture

At the heart of any AI system, data are abundant, varied, and dynamic. Data collection in agriculture has gone beyond being a mere support activity; it is now a major pillar for smart decision-making. Today, farms are becoming increasingly digitized, with various sensors, devices, and tools capturing data continuously in many disparate forms. Thus, this huge pool of information stands as raw material for machine learning algorithms to learn how crops behave, decipher early symptoms of diseases, and give precise recommendations on the diseases affecting crops. Without accurate real-time contextual data, AI models become meaningless: thus, data collection becomes very crucial for AI-based farming (Onteddu et al., 2025).

4.2 *Geospatial and Climate Data*

Geospatial data collected from all the farms includes not only the physical and geographical features of the land but also satellite images, Unmanned Aerial Vehicle (UAV) surveys, topographic maps, and GPS-based coordinates that define field boundaries and capture variability across zones. When combining such information with climatic data—temperature, humidity, rainfall, and wind speed—it becomes easier to predict farm disease risks as they relate to environmental conditions. Some diseases of crops are induced or intensified in particular weather conditions; therefore, AI systems can forecast inhibited developments and recommend timely interventions (Agrawal and Arafat, 2024).

4.3 *Soil and Nutrient Profile Data*

This covers the understanding of the kind of soil in which crops grow. Continuous monitoring conducted within the field through soil sensors can measure critical soil parameters such as pH, moisture content, temperature, salinity, and concentrations of key nutrients like nitrogen, phosphorus, and potassium. The data on fine-grained soil profiling serve as important inputs in understanding the plant growth environment and its stress factors that predispose crops to diseases. Thus, AI models leverage such data to correlate soil conditions with diseases incidence, enabling farmers to take timely action with regards to irrigation, fertilization, or soil treatments to keep their crops in good health (Ferrag et al., 2020).

4.4 *Crop Health and Visual Data*

Today, at long last, visual data is becoming one of the most effective tools for the detection of diseases in field crops. Digital imaging devices have advanced so far that they can actually capture high-resolution images with the use of a drone, tractor, or even smartphone. The images are then analysed to identify early symptoms such as leaf spotting, discolouration,

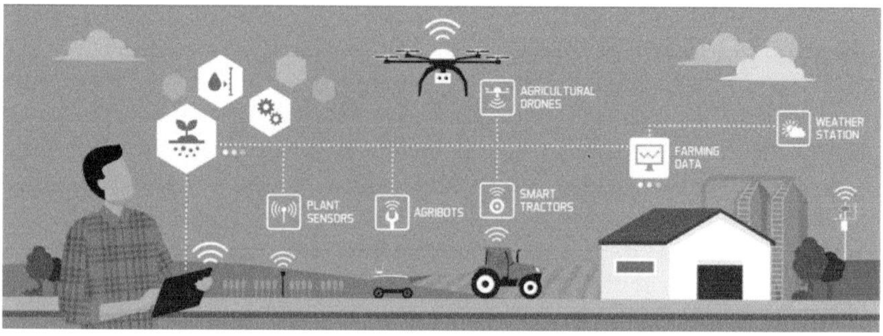

Figure 10.4: Smart farming with IoT and AI integration.

wilting, or abnormality in growth. When aggregated over several thousands of such images over time and geography, it becomes possible for AI models to learn how to classify diseases with great accuracy and even differentiate among similar-looking conditions. This kind of data bridges the gap between visible symptoms and unseen hazards, thus providing real-time status updates for farmers' crops (al Bakri et al., 2024).

Smart farming has evolved a long way using IoT and AI, as shown in Figure 10.4. Technologies such as agricultural drones, plant sensors, weather stations, smart tractors, and agribots can be put into a system for the collection and analysis of farming data. In real time, the farmer is observed using a tablet to control and monitor the system. This smart farming ecosystem can boost productivity, facilitate precision agriculture, and provide data-based decision-making for sustainable and efficient agricultural practices.

4.5 Farm Management and Operational Data

Information pertaining to the day-to-day running of the farm also has a significant role in AI-driven predictive systems. Such information includes parameters such as the time when planting took place, when irrigation was undertaken, the application of pesticides and fertilizers in the past, crop rotation cycles, and records of what was harvested. The combined effect of such datasets with disease reports and environmental conditions would enable AI systems to process cause–effect relations and optimize future decisions. For instance, certain pesticides might be associated with resistance build-up in pathogens while specific methods of irrigation might create grossly high humidity, which favours fungal diseases. Knowledge of these operational intricacies allows AI to make specific and practicable recommendations (Elbasi et al., 2024).

4.6 Sensor and IoT Data Streams in Real Time

Because of the mounting integration of IoT in modern farming, real-time data streams have become a game changer. Sensors scattered around the field keep numbers rolling in every second and feed the AI systems with the most recent environmental and biological indicators, making possible dynamic prediction and quick response mechanisms. With this continuous stream of data, a spike in humidity triggering a sharp fall of soil temperature would provide both indicators of potential disease risk. Following such an event, the AI system can issue alerts and recommend specific targeted action before visible damage takes place. Such real-time responsiveness is what counts as the actual measure by which AI differs from traditional farming methods (Onteddu et al., 2025).

4.7 Data Interoperability and Aggregation

For AI to function correctly, data from sources such as satellites, drones, sensors, and even the farmers' data must be aggregated and made interoperable—unification of data from distinct sources in such a manner that they can be standardized, mixed, and/or otherwise processed meaningfully. Current data integration platforms leverage cloud computing, Application Programming Interfaces (APIs), and data lakes to house everything in one great view of the farm. As a result, when added to a dataset later, the complete collection sets up an environment for training AI algorithms, endowing them with multidimensional inputs for accuracy and robustness (Ferris, 2017).

5. Data Privacy Concerns in Agricultural AI

5.1 The Rising Importance of Data in Agriculture

New data ecosystems are emerging with the advent of digitization in farming. All large datasets are collected, organized, and processed to optimize nearly every aspect of agricultural production—from soil health to crop conditions and from climatic parameters to farm operations. AI systems depend on this data to predict disease, increase yields, and diminish farm management burdens. The rise in fear for data sovereignty is another development accompanying the digital transformation. Farmers and agricultural stakeholders are becoming fully aware not only of their reliance on digital tools but also of how those tools collect, manage, and misuse their data (Gupta et al., 2024).

5.2 The Importance of Privacy to Farmers

For most farmers, their data pertains to their livelihood. From studies of land fertility, crop history, production levels, and episodes of pest infestation, all these are sensitive bits of information that could play a role in market decisions, insurance premiums, or land valuations. Whenever such data is misused or exposed, it could endanger the farmer's financial state or lead to an unfair competition situation. Above all, many smallholder and independent farmers work on trust, whereby any breach of privacy could trigger a substantial resistance to the adoption of technological solutions. Thus, data privacy is a socio-economic issue of paramount importance, one affecting the trust of the farmer's engagement in AI-based systems (Dembani et al., 2025).

5.3 The Threat of Unauthorized Access and Data Exploitation

There can be dangerous consequences from the unauthorized access of agricultural data. The collected data can fall into the hands of unscrupulous or fraudulent elements that can possibly commercialize or distort it in a manner that would alter market pricing. The fear of such situations arises when the tech or agribusiness companies pool data from farmers across regions to forecast commodity trends, giving them an advantage. In such situations, farmers could be the contributors of this data without receiving any benefits or compensations. In another possible scenario, hackers can target agricultural data and, in the process, disrupt the supply chain, thereby threating food security (Ferrag et al., 2020).

5.4 Regulatory Gaps and their Impact

Another major challenge to securing agricultural data comes from the lack of adequate regulatory frameworks directly addressing the subject. Agriculture, unlike sectors such as finance or healthcare where robust data protection laws are in operation, lags behind in these matters. This gap in regulation puts the farmers in a vulnerable position, facing the absence of any clear law regulating who owns the data generated or how that data can be shared and under what conditions that data should be anonymized. Most of the time, this means that farmers are forced to sign vaguely written contracts with service providers in the absence of clear policies, thus actually retaining little to no control over their data (Ferris, 2017).

5.5 Ethical Concerns in Data Handling

In this exploration of data privacy, an ethical dimension emerges and extends beyond matters of legality. The data on which the AI models are trained stem from the labour and experience of farmers; nevertheless, the benefits from AI systems may not always be evenly distributed. The clamour becomes louder when the data are obtained without transparency, used to train an AI system in secrecy, and released into a market with little or no sharing of the value derived with the initial contributors. In another scenario, farmers, especially in areas with low digital literacy, may not be able to differentiate between the pros and cons of sharing their data and may, therefore, be vulnerable to exploitation. Ethical data practices must underpin the legitimacy of all systems in a manner that respects the rights and dignity of stakeholders at all levels (al Bakri et al., 2024).

5.6 *The Potential for Surveillance and Behavioural Tracking*

As digital monitoring becomes increasingly refined, there emerges a thin line, indeed, between insights that can help and insight surveillance that could invade. Sensors, drones, and satellite imaging are always following and behaviourally tracking farmers' activities, whereby their choices, routines, and practices are under constant analysis. Such assessments might increase productivity but present glaring privacy issues. In some cases, farmers may feel that they are being watched or scrutinized for their farming practices, which can prompt discomfort and reduce autonomy. Thus, for the real acceptance of AI-based solutions, boundaries must be defined and enforced to protect individual and corporate freedom (Elbasi et al., 2024).

5.7 *Development of Consent and Transparency Culture*

Consent and transparency can resolve privacy dilemmas. Farmers must know what data is collected, why it is needed, how it will be used, and who will access the data. Informed consent should be the main principle and supported by a user-friendly interface and clear documentation. Transparency builds the farmers' trust, which paves the way for AI to be introduced successfully in agricultural systems. If none exist, suspicion will thrive, stopping innovation and crippling collaboration in data-based agriculture (Onteddu et al., 2025).

6. Enhanced Privacy Techniques for Farmers' Data

New changes persistently accuse AI of changing the agricultural world, as the accuracy of predictions and timely recommendations are dependent on farm data. The possible rise in data collection—providing everything from soil health parameters to drone-acquired crop imagery—raises genuine privacy questions for farmers and farm cooperatives alike. Agricultural data in unauthorized hands can not only hurt individual livelihoods but also reap changes in market behaviour and regional competitiveness. In order to overcome such experiences while still being able to benefit from the use of AI, researchers and technologists are developing novel privacy-preserving methods that aim to protect farmers' sensitive information without impeding the advancement of technology.

6.1 Data Locality in Federated Learning

By far, one of the state-of-the-art approaches claiming to safeguard agricultural data privacy is federated learning. While conventional AI systems operate in a centralized manner in order to train their models, federated learning allows data to essentially stay where it is rather than centralize it. Here, AI models are sent to farmers' devices or local data hubs, where they learn from data on-site. Only model updates or summarized parameters, instead of raw data, are sent back to the central system after the AI model is trained. This allows for multiple farms to collaborate in improving an AI model for disease identification or yield prediction without ever having sensitive data leave their premises. This is very much in the favour of smallholder farmers so that they can benefit from collective intelligence while still controlling private farm data.

6.2 Safeguarding Identities with Differential Privacy

While federated learning protects data from being transferred, differential privacy allows sharing data or model outputs in such a way that no individual detail about a particular farm or about a farmer is revealed. This is realized through the mathematical injection of controlled, managed "noise" into datasets or AI responses, where the noise clouds individual records but preserves the overall accuracy. In the application of agriculture, this kind of technique could allow a policymaker or an agronomist to receive information on a healthy crop across a given location without being able to determine disease attacks on the individual farms. This ends up creating a very meaningful protective layer, especially in sensitive cases where a disclosure would impact prices in the market or stigmatize particular communities of farmers.

6.3 Blockchain for Transparent, Farmer-Controlled Data Sharing

Another essential technology for protecting sounds in the digital information of farmers is blockchain. It is a decentralized, irrefutable ledger that registers transactions or exchanges of data in a secure and virus-free manner. Blockchain technology has its application in agricultural AI systems where it records access, modification, and sharing of data using a complete transparency levelled system in which it is intimately known

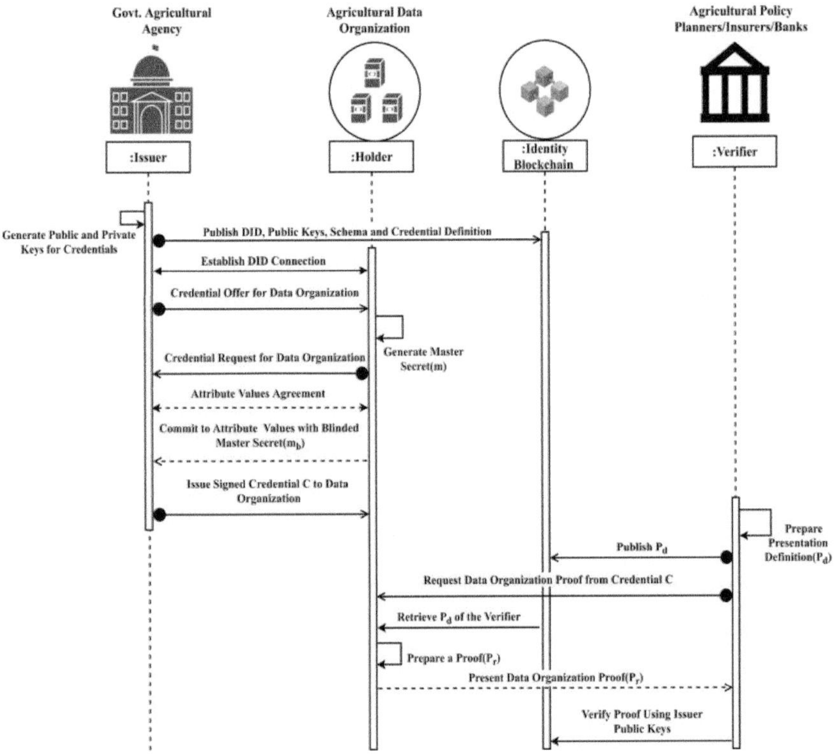

Figure 10.5: Blockchain-based agricultural credential verification system (Manoj et al., 2025).

how farmers' data is being accessed. In the same way, intelligent contracts can be automated, self-executing agreements constructed on a blockchain network, and allowing farmers to specify in detail who can access their information and on what grounds. For instance, a farmer might create a smart contract for sharing the data with a university for a research project but deny it for commercial purposes without any manual intervention.

The flowchart as shown in Figure 10.5 describes the process in agriculture for secure credential issuance and verification through blockchain technology. The process involves four main parties: the government agricultural agency, which acts as the issuer; the agricultural data organization acting in the capacity of the holder; an identity blockchain; and a verifier such as banks or policy planners. The process includes the generation of keys, publication of schemas, opening of connections, issuing credentials with blinded secrets, and, finally, the verification of the data with cryptographic proofs. The blockchain secures data integrity, privacy, and trust within the agricultural ecosystem.

6.4 Secure Multi-Party Computation: Collaborative Analysis without Data Exposure

Secure multi-party computation (SMPC) enables several farms or organizations to work together in building robust AI models; e.g., forecasting disease across a larger geography. It allows all parties to run computations based on their private data locally and then share encrypted, anonymized output for collective analysis. No raw data at any time is revealed to other participants, making it possible to carry out a meaningful joint analysis while safeguarding privacy. In agriculture, SMPC will benefit emerging collaborative partnerships among farms, agricultural extension agencies, and technology providers with no requirement to trust one another or expose their data to the centralized authority.

6.5 Shaping the Future with Privacy-Centric Agricultural AI

Equipped with these new additional privacy-preserving technologies—federated learning, differential privacy, blockchain, and SMPC—agriculture can then pave its way into the digital world wherein farmers are always in control of their data. These prevent unauthorized usage and instil confidence in the AI tools, thus promoting their wider adoption and data-sharing cooperation. Data privacy should therefore be designed into AI-enabled systems to protect farmers' rights while fostering sustainable, ethical, and technologically advanced systems of agriculture (van der Burg et al., 2021).

7. AI Anchored in Security and Trust

The prospective use of AI in modern agricultural systems is seen as a revolution concerning productivity, sustainability, and pest/disease management. However, technological advancement in agriculture can only be fully realized with the buy-in of the farming community and stakeholders connected to agriculture. In this instance, trust becomes the central tenet of the adoption process, i.e., trusting the technology, the institutions that use it, and in the handling of sensitive farm data. Without this trust being established, even the most advanced AI solutions would risk being rejected or underused. It is here that secure AI systems come in, by enhancing that trust through transparency, fairness, and accountability, and respecting data privacy in agricultural applications.

7.1 The Role of Data Security in Trust Formation

It is fair to say that, for farmers and cooperatives, the decision to adopt any AI-based tool is related to the trust that their data—be it personal, environmental, or operational—will be handled properly. As such, with significant value now being attached to agricultural datasets in terms of both commerce and strategy, one cannot blame farmers for fearing unauthorized access, data breaches, or exploitation of their data. Secure AI systems address this by building strong security protocols, encryption, and controlled access into the AI system. Farmers' trust in those digital platforms grows stronger when they know that their data will be safeguarded—whether in local storage, while being processed by AI models, and during sharing for research.

7.2 *Transparency in AI Decision-Making*

Transparency of AI decision-making processes is another area of utmost importance for building trust. In fact, many AI models that are driven by some complex neural networks would often be considered "black-box" types, making it quite nearly impossible to interpret how certain recommendations or predictions were asserted. Such decisions in agriculture are, however, determined on the basis of AI inputs which have effects on the farmers' livelihoods; thus, systems employing AI ought to present insightful and explainable findings. Secure AI solutions actually incorporate explainable AI (XAI) technologies that harness intelligent actions from transformed model outputs that clarify the information to be utilized by farmers. When AI models make predictions about crop disease, or suggest allocating resources to some controlled regions, farmers are far more willing to trust and act upon them when they have more understandable explanations or justifications behind them (Zhang et al., 2020).

7.3 *Ethical Data Governance and Fair Usage Policies*

Another factor determining trust in AI systems is how appropriate data governing policies are developed, implemented, and enforced in agri-ecosystems. Ethically, secure AI systems must go beyond the technical aspect to provide ethical data stewardship frameworks which give standards on who owns farm data, how it will be used, and under what fronts it can be shared. Farmers are assured that they have control over their data by establishing clear, transparent agreements on data ownership and fair usage policies. Such AI systems always come with consent management capabilities whereby farmers can give or withhold their consent for data sharing, and change this decision anytime. That is, in essence, building farmers up as active, worthy participants in the digital agricultural value chain rather than as passive data suppliers.

7.4 Collaboration between Technology Providers and Agricultural Communities

The successful long-term application of AI in agriculture depends upon the interplay of open and collaborative relationships among technology providers, researchers, government agencies, and farming communities. Secure AI systems nurture such collaborations by enabling farmers to raise concerns, offer suggestions, and track the use of their data over a period of time. Such participatory models create mutual respect and foster an environment whereby farmers are seen as empowered rather than exploited. Farmers' trust is then achieved when AI tools are truly developed with end-users in mind and greatly respect the rights and interests of farmers.

7.5 Building a Sustainable and Trustworthy Agricultural Future

The ultimate acceptance of AI in agriculture hinges not just on the technical side, but also on the social and ethical infrastructure that surrounds its deployment. In this way, secure AI systems—designed with built-in privacy protections, transparent operations, and participatory governance—are a solid start towards a trustworthy digital farming landscape. These technologies help to create a bridge connecting innovation with human values, thereby allowing farmers and stakeholders to maintain confidence in the systems that support them. Going beyond privacy and security, the agricultural applications of AI can thus become a potent and inclusive engine towards sustainable food production and rural empowerment (Bronson and Knezevic, 2016).

8. Case Studies: Successful Applications of AI in Crop Health

Artificial intelligence holds great potential to transform the farming domain, and the practical AI applications are on the rise. These AI solutions across the globe are being used to diagnose plant diseases, predict pest outbreaks, optimize irrigation schedules, and sustain farm productivity. Such implementations in real life not only highlight AI's capacity to enhance crop health, but they also demonstrate how the farmer benefits from improvements in yield, input efficiency, and sustainable land management. This section describes a few significant case studies of successful AI implementation to remedy crop health problems (van der Burg et al., 2021).

8.1 AI-Powered Disease Detection in Cassava Crops

In East Africa, a case of AI assisting in plant health management was one of the most validated ones, wherein researchers from the International Institute of Tropical Agriculture (IITA) and Pennsylvania State University developed a mobile application called Nuru. The computer vision–based application diagnoses diseases of cassava plants, an important food crop for millions in the region. Farmers can use a smartphone to take a picture of a cassava leaf to obtain immediate feedback on whether the plant exhibits symptoms of potentially damaging diseases such as Cassava Mosaic Disease or Cassava Brown Streak Disease. Field trials in Tanzania and Kenya showed that Nuru's disease detection accuracy reached up to 98% for certain conditions, significantly outperforming human visual inspections (Ramcharan et al., 2019). The tool empowers farmers with early detection capabilities, enabling timely interventions such as removing infected plants or applying targeted treatments, thus reducing crop losses and improving food security in vulnerable communities (Ramcharan et al., 2019).

8.2 Predictive Pest Monitoring in Cotton Farming

The AI-enabled pest monitoring platforms have been widely used in India to combat the pests that threaten cotton yields. CropIn, an agritech company, developed an AI-based platform that predicts pest outbreaks, mainly due to the pink bollworm, an important pest of cotton, using satellite images, ground sensor data, and weather forecasts. The AI system investigates environmental conditions and historical pest behaviour, and then advises farmers through predictive alerts and management suggestions. Pilot projects in Gujarat and Maharashtra showed a 20–30% reduction in pesticide application, with 12% and 15% improvement in yield (CropIn, 2021). This has simultaneously reduced excess chemical usage and crop losses and established environmentally sustainable pest management (CropIn, 2021).

8.3 AI-based Rice Yield and Disease Forecasting in Japan

The AI applications in rice yield forecast and disease risk assessment have been put to use in Japan. The National Agriculture and Food Research Organization (NARO) has employed AI models that integrate long-term climatic, soil, and cultivation data to predict the likelihood of disease occurrences such as rice blast disease. These models have been integrated with field sensors and drone-captured imagery to generate dynamic and region-specific forecasts. The pilot project results from

Yamagata and Ibaraki prefectures showed that AI-assisted advisory services improved disease-management decision-making by 25% and optimized the pesticide application schedule, resulting in a measured 10% increase in harvested yield over two cropping seasons (National Agriculture and Food Research Organization, 2020).

8.4 Computer Vision in Vineyard Disease Monitoring

Computer vision has been used for the early detection of viticulture diseases. The startup AgroSmart Solutions from Spain enabled the monitoring of vineyards with AI drones powered with multispectral cameras to identify early signs of fungal diseases such as powdery mildew and downy mildew. AI systems examine colour, leaf texture, and temperature fluctuation influences on drone images, delivering early alerts that allow vineyard managers to target fungicide applications instead of blanket spraying. In La Rioja and Catalonia wine regions, trials have reduced chemical applications by 30% with reduction in harvest loss related to a disease being up to 40% less than the traditional techniques (AgroSmart Solutions, 2022).

8.5 AI-driven Wheat Rust Surveillance in Ethiopia

The Ethiopian Institute of Agricultural Research (EIAR) partnered with CIMMYT and the University of Cambridge and piloted an AI-driven surveillance system against wheat rust diseases. The AI platform quickly detects the occurrence of rust infections and creates a national map of their spread using smartphone photographs uploaded by farmers and extension agents. Such early warning notifications then prompt the regional authorities to carry out control measures on time using fungicides and the planting of rust-resistant wheat varieties. According to project evaluation done in 2021, these interventions protected over 200,000 ha of wheat fields from adverse and severe rust infections, guaranteeing millions against uncertainty in food security (CIMMYT, 2021).

9. Future Trends: Integrating AI and Privacy in Agriculture

The future of agriculture is inexorably bound up with advances in AI and data security. Digital technologies, which are currently rapidly changing farming systems, present a critical challenge to agriculture: balancing new innovations with adequate protection of sensitive farm-level data. The next generation of AI-powered tools shall deliver meaningful insight into crop health, yield forecasting, and disease risk; however, again, these advances can gain significance only when privacy issues are satisfactorily resolved. With this in mind, some researchers, developers, or policymakers are exploring new privacy-preserving technologies that interface seamlessly with AI systems for the benefit of farmers, who get to retain ownership and control of their data while accessing collective intelligence.

9.1 Emergence of Federated Learning and Edge AI

Another vital development in that regard is the use of decentralized AI models under the umbrella of federated learning and edge AI systems. Traditionally, farming data such as soil health measurements, pest sightings, and weather records have been sent out to centralized cloud servers for processing. This has aided in training AI systems but also raised serious concerns about data misuse and claims to ownership, not to mention the exposure to security threats. In federated learning, AI models can be trained locally on a farm, essentially teaching the model from various sources while keeping the sensitive data on site by not transferring it out from the farm. Edge AI processes data on site through local edge devices, sensors, and drones. In this manner, real-time identification of plant diseases or environmental changes by AI systems reduces latency as it does not rely on external data centres. Such systems enhance privacy by limiting exposure to data, ensuring sensitive information remains in the farm's perimeter while contributing to larger AI advancements.

9.2 Integration of Blockchain for Data Ownership and Security

One of the most virtuous actions towards the control of personal privacy in agriculture is bringing to life the concept of blockchain technology. Each data-collecting activity—from crop imagery to disease predictions—is thus put into a decentralized ledger system that records it securely, stamps when it was created, and makes sure it is tamper-proof. With such technology, farmers can manage how and when their data is shared or accessed or used. Smart contracts can be incorporated into such a blockchain system, providing for automated agreements between farmers and agritech providers, specifying the terms under which access and usage of the data could occur. Thus, farmers will benefit from the recognition of their rights, while building a platform for transparent, trust-based exchanges of data and setting a new benchmark in ethical data management in digital agriculture.

9.3 Advancements in Differential Privacy

As AI models increasingly rely on large datasets aggregated from multiple farms and regions, there arises the challenge of protecting individual identities, while still allowing meaningful data analysis. Differential privacy is an emerging technique designed to remedy this situation. The addition of controlled statistical noise to the datasets ensures that while data related to individual farms cannot be traced or pinpointed, the properties necessary for AI-informed understanding can be retained. The differential privacy standard is expected to be incorporated into future agricultural decision support systems, disease surveillance platforms, and yield forecasting tools so that inferences at the regional or national level can be made by governments, cooperatives, and researchers without jeopardizing individual farmers' privacy. These methods will go a long way towards boosting participation in AI ventures, especially where fears of data misuse are common and impede digital adoption.

9.4 Growth of Secure Multi-Party Computation

One of the more encouraging developments in privacy-preserving AI is SMPC. This mechanism allows different narrations to work together in the training or analysis of an AI model based on their joint data without actually sharing their true datasets amongst each other. This, in agriculture, stands to address several monumental and genuine threats to common agricultural phenomena like pest outbreaks, disease epidemics, and weather irregularities occurring to many farms together.

The SMPC guarantees the collective strength of their data in favour of farmers and agricultural organizations, while at the same time strictly protecting the privacy of every contributor. The advancement of this technology could also facilitate regional disease prediction networks or collaborative soil health monitoring systems that rely on data-driven decisions made by secure and confidential computation. With the scaling of AI applications in agriculture, SMPC provides a collaborative environment while respecting individual data borders.

9.5 AI Governance Frameworks and Farmer-Centric Data Policies

Apart from these technical innovations, future trends will witness the development of AI governance frameworks and farmer-centric data rights policies. A clear landscape regarding data ownership, consent, access, and transparency in usage becomes extremely necessary as AI tools gain popularity in modern farming schemes. Collaborations among policymakers, agricultural associations, and the technical developer fraternity will develop ethical strands that protect farmer autonomy against exploitative practices. The future of digital agriculture will likely see the widespread adoption of standardized data privacy protocols, including informed consent procedures, transparent data use declarations, and independent data audit mechanisms. Such frameworks will not only serve the ethical use of AI but also help build trust in the long term among farmers that they can safely engage in data-sharing initiatives that advance agricultural sustainability (Kamilaris and Prenafeta-Boldú, 2018).

10. Conclusion

The future of agriculture will be defined by intelligent technology and responsible data management. While more and more AI will be critical to predicting crop diseases, optimizing yields, and ensuring sustainable farming methods, it is equally essential to protect the privacy and autonomy of farmers whose data is fed into those systems. Such modern privacy-preserving techniques would include federated learning, differential privacy, and blockchain, all intended to provide the agricultural sector a safe environment in which innovation and ethics coexist. A sustainable and secure agricultural future will owe much to technological innovation, but even more to inclusive policies, transparent data governance, and trust-building initiatives that empower farmers as active participants in the digital transformation. In this balanced approach, AI can become a significant contributor to the world's food security while respecting individual rights as well as keeping agricultural information confidential.

References

Agrawal, J. and Arafat, M.Y. (2024). Transforming farming: A review of AI-powered UAV technologies in precision agriculture. *Drones* 8(11): 664.

AgroSmart Solutions. (2022). AI in Vineyard Disease Management. Available at https://doi.org/10.1016/j.procs.2024.06.049.

al Bakri, K.Z.S., Al Flaiti, M.K.S., Al-Balushi, S.A.S. and Poorngalingam, J. (2024). Revolutionizing agriculture: Harnessing the power of artificial intelligence for sustainable farming practices.

Bronson, K. and Knezevic, I. (2016). Big data in food and agriculture. *Big Data & Society* 3(1): 2053951716648174.

CIMMYT. (2021). AI-Powered Wheat Rust Mapping in Ethiopia. Available at https://www.cimmyt.org/.

Clare Allen-Sader, William Thurston, Marcel Meyer, Elias Nure, Netsanet Bacha, Yoseph Alemayehu, Richard O.J.H Stutt, Daniel Safka, Andrew P. Craig, Eshetu Derso, Laura E. Burgin, Sarah C. Millington, Matthew C. Hort, David P. Hodson and Christopher A. Gilligan. (2019). An early warning system to predict and mitigate wheat rust diseases in Ethiopia. *Environ. Res. Lett.* 14: 115004.

CropIn. (2021). AI-Driven Crop Monitoring Solutions. Available at https://www.cropin.com/.

Dembani, R., Karvelas, I., Akbar, N.A., Rizou, S., Tegolo, D. and Fountas, S. (2025). Agricultural data privacy and federated learning: A review of challenges and opportunities. *Computers and Electronics in Agriculture* 232: 110048.

Elbasi, E., Mostafa, N., Zaki, C., AlArnaout, Z., Topcu, A.E. and Saker, L. (2024). Optimizing agricultural data analysis techniques through AI-powered decision-making processes. *Applied Sciences* 14(17): 8018.

Ferrag, M.A., Shu, L., Yang, X., Derhab, A. and Maglaras, L. (2020). Security and privacy for green IoT-based agriculture: Review, blockchain solutions, and challenges. *IEEE Access* 8: 32031–32053.

Ferris, J.L. (2017). Data privacy and protection in the agriculture industry: Is federal regulation necessary? *Minnesota Journal of Law, Science & Technology* 18: 309.

Gupta, D.K., Pagani, A., Zamboni, P. and Singh, A.K. (2024). AI-powered revolution in plant sciences: Advancements, applications, and challenges for sustainable agriculture and food security. *Exploration of Foods and Foodomics* 2: 443–459.

Javidan, S.M., Banakar, A., Rahnama, K., Vakilian, K.A. and Ampatzidis, Y. (2024). Feature engineering to identify plant diseases using image processing and artificial intelligence: A comprehensive review. *Smart Agricultural Technology* 8: 100480.

Kamilaris, A. and Prenafeta-Boldú, F.X. (2018). Deep learning in agriculture: A survey. *Computers and Electronics in Agriculture* 147: 70–90.

Khan, A., Malebary, S.J., Dang, L.M., Binzagr, F., Song, H.-K. and Moon, H. (2024). AI-enabled crop management framework for pest detection using visual sensor data. *Plants* 13(5): 653. https://doi.org/10.3390/plants13050653.

Kim, Y., Roh, J.-H. and Kim, H.Y. (2018). Early forecasting of rice blast disease using long short-term memory recurrent neural networks. *Sustainability* 10(1): 34. https://doi.org/10.3390/su10010034.

Manoj, T., Makkithaya, K. and Narendra, V.A. (2025). Blockchain-assisted trusted federated learning for smart agriculture. *SN Computer Science* 6: 221.

National Agriculture and Food Research Organization (NARO). (2020). Smart Agriculture Initiative. Available at https://www.naro.go.jp/.

Onteddu, A.R., Kundavaram, R.R., Kamisetty, A., Gummadi, J.C.S. and Manikyala, A. (2025). Enhancing agricultural efficiency with robotics and AI-powered autonomous farming systems. *Malaysian Journal of Medical and Biological Research* 12(1): 7–22.

Ramcharan, A., Baranowski, K., McCloskey, P., Ahmed, B., Legg, J. and Hughes, D.P. (2019). Deep learning for image-based cassava disease detection. *Frontiers in Plant Science* 10: 272.

Savary, S., Willocquet, L., Pethybridge, S., Esker, P., McRoberts, N. and Nelson, A. (2019). The global burden of pathogens and pests on major food crops. *Nature Ecology & Evolution* 3: 430–439.

van der Burg, S., Boessenkool, L. and Polman, C.R. (2021). The role of data governance in agri-food innovation. *Frontiers in Sustainable Food Systems* 5: 578482.

Zhang, Y. et al. (2020). Explainable Artificial Intelligence (XAI): Concepts, taxonomies, opportunities and challenges toward responsible AI. *Information Fusion* 67: 44–73.

Chapter 11

Artificial Intelligence in Cyber Threat and Malware Detection for IoT-enabled Smart Agriculture System

A Comprehensive Review

Santosh K. Smmarwar,[1,*] *Rahul Priyadarshi*,[1]
Sushil Bahadur Pankaj,[1] *Pratik Angaitkar*[2] and *Subodh Mishra*[3]

The technological development in smart agriculture through Internet of Things (IoT) devices has increased production and reduced operational costs. Integrating IoT devices in agriculture has revolutionized farming practices, enabling monitoring of environmental conditions, livestock health, crop growth, and machinery performance. However, these advancements have introduced cybersecurity vulnerabilities, making IoT-enabled smart agricultural devices susceptible to various threats. Although many methods have been proposed to detect cyber threats in IoT devices, most techniques cannot find new malware variants. Therefore,

[1] Centre of Internet of Things, Department of Computer Science and Engineering, Siksha 'O' Anusandhan (Deemed to be University), Odisha, India.
[2] Department of Artificial Intelligence & Data Science, P.R. Pote Patil College of Engineering & Management, Maharashtra, India.
[3] Department of SCSET, Bennett University, Uttar Pradesh, India.
* Corresponding author: santoshsamarwar@soa.ac.in

DOI: 10.1201/9781003670568-11

artificial intelligence (AI)–empowered cybersecurity systems are emerging as a crucial solution for detecting and mitigating these risks. This chapter thoroughly explores how AI enhances cybersecurity for IoT-enabled smart agriculture and helps identify emerging threat landscapes, such as vulnerabilities, data risks, unauthorized access, and supply chain attacks. The key AI techniques used in smart agriculture are deep learning (DL), machine learning (ML), natural language processing (NLP), reinforcement learning (RL), and federated learning (FL) for cyber-attack detection. This chapter also presents applications of AI in smart agriculture for different kinds of malicious attack detection for improving operational efficiency and discusses future challenges and directions.

1. Introduction

The rapid advancement of artificial intelligence (AI) has revolutionized various industries, with agriculture being no exception. Modern farming practices, often referred to as smart or precision agriculture, leverage innovative tools like AI and Internet of Things (IoT) to boost crop yields and tackle worldwide issues like food scarcity and ecological preservation. As the global population expands, placing greater demands on limited resources to meet food needs while maintaining sustainability, conventional agricultural techniques are proving inadequate. The United Nations Food and Agriculture Organization (FAO) estimates that global food output needs to rise by more than 70% by 2050 to meet the demands of an expanding population. Meanwhile, the smart agriculture industry, powered by IoT technology, is expected to exceed $15.3 billion in value by 2025 (Kumar et al., 2021). AI empowers farmers with data-centric insights, helping minimize waste and optimize harvests. The widespread adoption of IoT in agriculture has modernized traditional methods by facilitating real-time tracking, precision farming, and effective resource allocation. IoT tools, including sensors, drones, and automated equipment, are instrumental in gathering and relaying data to improve efficiency, cut expenses, and reduce ecological harm. However, this shift towards digitization also makes farming systems vulnerable to cyber risks such as data leaks, unauthorized intrusions, and malicious software, which can hinder operations and expose confidential data (Kumar et al., 2021). AI has become a crucial tool in countering these cybersecurity threats. Using sophisticated machine learning (ML) models, pattern analysis, and anomaly detection, AI improves the capacity to recognize, forecast, and neutralize cyber-attacks in IoT-based agricultural networks. AI-powered security systems can process large datasets instantly, spot irregularities, and take pre-emptive action against possible breaches, ensuring the stability and protection of IoT infrastructure in farming (Kumar et al., 2024).

This chapter investigates AI's role in enhancing cyber threat detection for IoT-supported smart agriculture. It discusses the security risks associated with IoT in farming, underscores the significance of AI-driven threat identification methods, and evaluates their efficiency in protecting these vital systems. With agriculture increasingly relying on IoT, embedding AI into cybersecurity strategies is imperative to promote secure and sustainable advancements in farming.

1.1 Motivation and Contribution

While IoT-based smart agriculture systems enhance efficiency through internet connectivity, they also become prime targets for malware attacks. Detecting these threats, especially new, evolving malware, poses a significant security challenge. This research presents an advanced malware detection framework tailored for smart agriculture IoT as mentioned in Figure 11.1, ensuring high accuracy in identifying known and unknown malicious intrusions.

The main contribution of this chapter can be explained as follows:

I. This chapter presents a detailed exploration of how AI enhances cybersecurity for Ag-IoT systems and different kinds of potential cyber threats landscapes to IoT-enabled smart agriculture systems.

II. It discusses the various challenges for AI in detecting cyber threats in IoT-based smart agriculture systems and key AI models for cyber threat and malware attack detection.

III. It discusses the applications, challenges, and future trends of AI techniques for IoT-based cyber threat detection.

2. Related Work

Adoption of IoT devices in smart agriculture has introduced new vulnerabilities to malware attacks, prompting significant research into ML-based detection systems. Early studies primarily relied on signature-based methods, but these proved ineffective against evolving threats. This gap highlights the need for adaptive, ML solutions tailored to the unique constraints of smart agriculture systems. This section discusses foundational concepts of existing work used for constructing malware and intrusion detection for IoT-based smart agriculture network systems, associated threats, ML, and deep learning (DL) techniques for identifying malicious activity and intrusions.

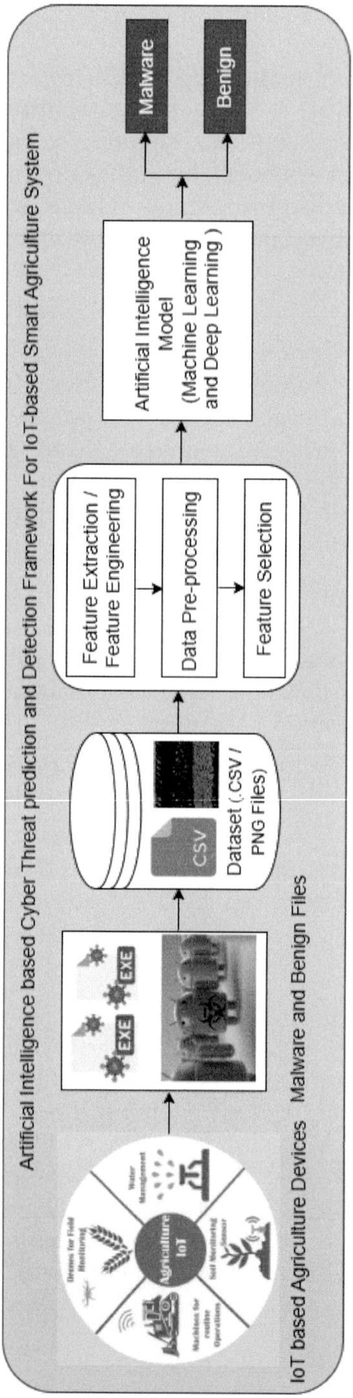

Figure 11.1: An overview of AI-based cyber threat prediction and detection framework.

Thilakarathne et al. (2025) propose a Cyber Threat Intelligence (CTI) platform designed to assess and mitigate cybersecurity risks in smart agriculture (AgriTech) systems.

Ferreira et al. (2025) introduce the Farm-Flow Dataset, a novel benchmark dataset designed to improve intrusion detection systems (IDS) for smart agriculture. It addresses the lack of realistic network traffic data in agricultural IoT environments, enabling better threat detection in farming-related networks.

Kumar et al. (Kumar et al., 2022a) developed Privacy-Encoding-Based Federated Learning (PEFL), an innovative model that addresses data privacy concerns in federated learning (FL) systems for precision agriculture without compromising predictive performance. Their approach integrates a dual mechanism of data perturbation techniques with an LSTM-autoencoder structure to preserve data confidentiality during distributed model training. The architecture utilizes a federated Gated Recurrent Unit (GRU) neural network (FedGRU) to process encoded agricultural IoT data for anomaly detection. Benchmark tests conducted on the ToN-IoT dataset reveal superior threat detection capabilities compared to both conventional FL systems and centralized ML models, particularly in maintaining classification accuracy despite data obfuscation.

Zhou et al. (2025) propose CBCTL-IDS, an advanced intrusion detection system designed to secure IoT-based smart agriculture. It combines cross-domain transfer learning with a novel Black Kite Algorithm (BKA) for optimization, addressing data scarcity and evolving cyber threats in agricultural IoT systems.

Rudrakar and Rughani (2023) comprehensively analyse IoT-based agriculture. They examine the layered architecture of IoT systems, highlighting vulnerabilities in connectivity, data transmission, and edge or cloud processing. They investigate prevalent attacks, such as device tampering and Distributed Denial of Service (DDoS) attacks, and evaluate countermeasures, including encryption, intrusion detection, and blockchain-based solutions. Additionally, the research explores forensic methodologies for post-attack analysis in Ag-IoT environments, addressing evidence collection, log analysis, and incident response.

Wajahat et al. (2024) present GuardDroid, a transparent and lightweight malware detection framework designed to secure Android-based IoT devices. The system operates with minimal overhead, leveraging real-time behavioural analysis and heuristic monitoring to identify malicious activities without requiring user intervention or device modifications. By integrating kernel-level event tracking and anomaly detection, GuardDroid effectively detects both known and zero-day malware while maintaining low computational costs. Experimental results demonstrate a high detection accuracy of 98.5% with negligible performance impact, making it suitable for resource-constrained IoT environments.

Aljuhani et al. (2023) propose a fog intelligence–based architectural framework to enhance security and efficiency in smart villages, addressing the limitations of centralized cloud computing in rural environments. By leveraging distributed fog nodes, the framework reduces latency, improves real-time decision-making, and ensures data privacy for critical applications like precision agriculture, healthcare, and energy management.

Campoverde-Molina and Luján-Mora (2025) emphasize the need for organizational investments in cybersecurity infrastructure, employee training, and threat response protocols. By synthesizing existing research, this review identifies current trends, knowledge gaps, and practical solutions for securing smart agriculture systems. Tailored for researchers, farmers, and agribusinesses, the findings provide actionable insights for adopting frameworks, models, and technologies to mitigate cyber threats in agricultural environments.

3. Different Types of Potential Cyber Threats to IoT-enabled Smart Agriculture

The IoT devices in smart agriculture are integral to precision farming, real-time monitoring, and automation, but their widespread adoption also introduces significant cybersecurity risks. These systems face many cyber threats due to their reliance on interconnected devices, wireless communication, and cloud-based platforms. There are potential cyber threats specific to IoT devices in smart agriculture (Bui et al., 2024):

- *Unauthorized Access*: Attackers may gain unauthorized access to IoT devices, sensors, or networks, allowing them to steal sensitive data, manipulate systems, or disrupt operations. Weak authentication mechanisms (Madan et al., 2022) and insecure default configurations often make these systems vulnerable (Kumar et al., 2021).
- *Data Breaches*: Sensitive agricultural data, such as crop conditions, yield predictions, and resource usage, can be intercepted during transmission or extracted from storage systems. These breaches can lead to financial losses, compromised privacy, or competitive disadvantages (Carvalho et al., 2025).
- *Malware and Ransomware Attack*: Malicious software, such as viruses, worms, or ransomware, can infect IoT devices or servers, causing data loss, operational disruptions, or unauthorized data encryption. Ransomware attacks may demand payment to restore access to critical systems or data (Ramesh and Menen, 2020).

- *Device Exploitation*: This explains two types of exploitation. The first is the Unsecured Endpoints, like IoT devices with weak or default security settings, which can be exploited for unauthorized access, and the other is Outdated Firmware. Many IoT devices operate on outdated firmware, leaving vulnerabilities open to exploitation (Srivastava et al., 2019).
- *Data Interception*: Unencrypted communication and data transmitted between IoT devices and central systems can be intercepted by attackers, if not encrypted, exposing sensitive information (Thilakarathne et al., 2025).
- *Wireless Network Sniffing*: Attackers can use network sniffing tools to intercept data from IoT devices communicating over insecure wireless networks (Yang et al., 2021).
- *Denial of Service (DoS) Attacks (Network Overloading)*: In this, attackers can flood IoT devices with requests, causing them to become unresponsive and disrupting agricultural operations. Limited computational and energy resources in IoT devices make them particularly susceptible to resource-exhausting DoS attacks (Swarna Priya et al., 2020).
- *Device Hijacking*: Attackers can hijack IoT devices such as drones, automated machinery, or irrigation systems, disrupting their intended operations.
- *Botnet Creation*: Hijacked IoT devices may be conscripted into botnets to launch larger-scale attacks, such as DDoS (Kumar et al., 2022b).
- *Sensor Manipulation (Data Tampering)*: Manipulating sensor readings (e.g., soil moisture, temperature) can lead to incorrect decisions, such as overwatering or under-fertilizing crops (Kumar et al., 2021b).
- *Intercepted Communication*: Attackers can intercept and change data between IoT devices and their controlling systems, compromising data integrity and system functionality (Swarna Priya et al., 2020).
- *Ransomware Attacks (Device Lockdown)*: IoT devices may be targeted by ransomware, encrypting their functionality until a ransom is paid. Attackers can encrypt critical data collected by IoT devices, disrupting operations and demanding payment for its release (Singh and Singh, 2021).
- *Spoofing Attacks (Impersonation)*: An attacker can impersonate legitimate IoT devices to inject malicious data or gain unauthorized access to the system. Spoofed devices can mislead systems into trusting and communicating with malicious entities (Kumar et al., 2022b).

4. Challenges for AI in Detecting Cyber Threats

While AI offers promising capabilities in detecting and mitigating cyber risk in IoT-based smart agriculture devices, several issues and challenges can hinder its effectiveness. These challenges stem from the complexity of IoT environments and the limitations of AI models. The key issues and challenges are:

- *Diversity of IoT Devices and Systems (Heterogeneity)*: IoT devices in agriculture come from various manufacturers with different protocols, architectures, and capabilities, making it complex to create a unified AI-based detection system (Madan et al., 2022).
- *Data Quality and Availability (Incomplete Data)*: IoT devices may not consistently generate or transmit data due to connectivity issues or device failures, leading to incomplete datasets for AI analysis (Schmitt, 2023).
- *Noisy Data and Insufficient Labelled Data*: Sensor readings may contain noise or inaccuracies, complicating the process of distinguishing between legitimate anomalies and cyber threats. AI models, especially those based on supervised learning, require labelled datasets for training. Collecting high-quality labelled data specific to cyber threats in smart agriculture is challenging (Bhardwaj et al., 2024).
- *Dynamic Nature of Cyber Threats (Evolving Threats)*: Cyber attackers constantly develop new methods to bypass detection, requiring AI models to adapt quickly to unknown and sophisticated threats (Kumar et al., 2025).
- *Zero-Day Vulnerabilities*: AI models may struggle to detect attacks that exploit previously unknown vulnerabilities due to a lack of training data for such scenarios (Kumar and Subbiah, 2022).
- *Real-Time Processing Requirements (Latency Issues)*: AI systems need to process vast amount of IoT data in real time to detect threats promptly, which can be challenging given the constraints of IoT networks (Ahluwalia and Mittal, 2021).
- *Scalability*: Ensuring that AI systems can handle the increased data flow without performance degradation becomes difficult (Dey et al., 2023a).
- *Interpretability and Explainability*: Many AI models, especially DL algorithms, operate as "black boxes", making it difficult for users to understand how decisions are made. Providing clear and actionable insights from AI-detected threats is essential for effective incident response, which is not always straightforward (Kumaret al., 2024).

5. Mitigation Strategies for Challenges in AI-driven Cyber Threat Detection for IoT-enabled Smart Agriculture Systems

The deployment of AI for cyber threat detection in IoT-based smart agriculture presents unique challenges, but innovative solutions are emerging to address these limitations. One major hurdle is posed by the resource constraints of agricultural IoT devices, which often have limited processing power and energy capacity. This can be mitigated through lightweight AI models like TinyML and model quantization, which reduce computational demands while maintaining detection accuracy. Additionally, edge-fog computing architectures can distribute processing tasks, allowing simpler devices to offload complex analysis to nearby fog nodes. Another critical challenge is the lack of labelled attack data specific to agricultural IoT systems. To overcome this, synthetic data generation techniques such as Generative Adversarial Networks (GANs) and SMOTE can artificially expand training datasets. At the same time, FL enables collaborative model training across multiple farms without compromising data privacy. Transfer learning from related IoT domains (e.g., industrial IoT) can compensate for data scarcity by leveraging pre-trained models. The dynamic nature of cyber threats, including zero-day attacks, requires adaptive detection mechanisms. Unsupervised learning approaches like autoencoders and isolation forests excel at identifying anomalous behaviour without prior knowledge of attack signatures. These systems can continuously evolve to counter emerging threats when combined with real-time threat intelligence feeds and reinforcement learning (RL)–based adaptive defences.

The diversity of IoT devices in smart agriculture complicates threat detection. Protocol-agnostic AI models, particularly graph neural networks, can analyse network traffic patterns across diverse devices, while middleware solutions help standardize data formats for consistent processing. Digital twin technology offers another promising solution, which is simulating attacks in virtual replicas of farm networks to improve detection strategies. To reduce false positives and alert fatigue, explainable AI (XAI) techniques provide transparency in threat classifications, helping security teams prioritize genuine risks. Ensemble learning methods, such as soft voting classifiers, aggregate predictions from multiple AI models to enhance reliability, while adaptive thresholding mechanisms dynamically adjust sensitivity based on contextual risk factors.

Finally, adversarial attacks targeting AI models themselves pose a growing threat. Defensive strategies like adversarial training and defensive distillation enhance model robustness against evasion techniques, while runtime integrity checks detect attempts to manipulate AI systems. Looking ahead, integrating blockchain-based secure logging and autonomous response mechanisms will further strengthen the resilience of smart agriculture systems. By combining these solutions, AI-driven cybersecurity can effectively protect IoT-enabled agriculture from evolving threats while operating within the unique constraints of farm environments.

6. AI Models for Cyber Threat and Malware Attack Detection

Modern smart farming systems utilizing IoT technologies increasingly rely on ML approaches to detect and neutralize cybersecurity threats. These AI-driven methods effectively address vulnerabilities including unauthorized data access, compromised agricultural sensors, and infrastructure breaches. The primary AI methodologies employed for security monitoring in agricultural IoT networks include:

(a) *Machine Learning*: The ML models analyse vast datasets to detect patterns and anomalies indicative of cyber threats or malware. There are three types of learning used for classification. The first one is supervised learning, which is used for classification tasks such as identifying malicious vs benign files. It requires labelled datasets with examples of threats and normal activity. Examples: Decision Trees, Random Forest, Support Vector Machines (SVMs). Another type is unsupervised learning that detects unknown threats or anomalies without prior labelling. It is suitable for discovering new malware or zero-day attacks. Examples are K-Means, Clustering, Principal Component Analysis (PCA), and Autoencoders. The third type is RL. In this model, we learn by interacting with the environment to develop optimal defence strategies. It is used for automated response systems in cybersecurity. Examples of this include Q-Learning and Deep Q-Network (DQN).

(b) *Deep Learning*: DL has emerged as a powerful tool for malware and cyber threat detection in IT-based smart agriculture systems, leveraging its ability to analyse complex, high-dimensional data from IoT devices, networks, and cloud platforms. Unlike traditional ML, DL models such as Convolutional Neural Networks (CNNs) (Kim et al., 2018), Recurrent Neural Networks (RNNs), and Transformer-based architectures can automatically extract intricate patterns from raw data, making them highly effective against evolving cyber threats. In smart agriculture, where IoT sensors, drones, and automated irrigation systems generate vast amounts of operational data, DL excels at detecting anomalies, malware intrusions, and adversarial attacks that could disrupt farm operations (Ahmad and Alsmadi, 2021). For instance, CNNs can analyse network traffic logs or firmware images to identify malicious code. In contrast, RNNs and Long Short-Term Memory (LSTM) networks are ideal for detecting sequential anomalies in time-series data, such as unexpected sensor behaviour indicating a cyber-attack. Autoencoders, an unsupervised DL technique, can flag deviations from normal system operations, helping identify zero-day exploits or data poisoning attempts in precision agriculture AI models. Additionally, Transformer models, like BERT adapted for cybersecurity, can process large-scale log files to uncover sophisticated multi-stage attacks (Yu et al., 2021; Dey et al., 2023b). By integrating DL into smart agriculture cybersecurity frameworks, farms can achieve real-time threat detection, reduce false positives, and adapt to emerging attack vectors, ensuring the integrity and reliability of automated agricultural systems. However, challenges such as computational resource demands and the need for large, labelled datasets must be addressed to deploy these solutions effectively in resource-constrained farming environments (Kumar et al., 2025).

(c) *Natural Language Processing (NLP)*: It plays a crucial role in cyber threat detection within IT-based smart agriculture systems by analysing unstructured textual data to identify malicious activities (Yang et al., 2024). Cyber threats often manifest in log files, network traffic reports, threat intelligence feeds, and even phishing emails, all of which contain valuable linguistic patterns that NLP can decode. By leveraging ML models like transformer-based architectures (BERT, RNNs) and named entity recognition (NER) systems, NLP can automatically detect suspicious commands, malicious IP addresses, or anomalous communication patterns in agricultural IoT networks (Garg and Baliyan, 2022; Rey et al., 2022). For example, NLP techniques can parse server logs to identify SQL injection attempts or analyse email content to flag phishing scams targeting farm management personnel. Additionally, sentiment analysis and topic modelling can help uncover social engineering attacks disguised as legitimate communications (Biswas et al., 2024). In smart agriculture, where vast amounts of operational data are generated by sensors, drones, and automated systems, NLP enhances threat detection by converting raw text into actionable insights, enabling real-time alerts for potential breaches. However, challenges such as multilingual cyber threats, adversarial text manipulations, and the need for domain-specific training data must be addressed to maximize

NLP's effectiveness in securing agricultural IoT ecosystems (Usman et al., 2021). Threat Intelligence Mining uses AI and leverages threat intelligence data to predict and mitigate threats. Knowledge Graphs employed by AI builds connections between indicators of compromise (IoCs) to identify threat actors. Clustering and Classification group threat indicators into known threat categories for rapid response (Martín et al., 2019).

7. Applications of AI Techniques for IoT-based Cyber Threat Detection

Artificial intelligence techniques are revolutionizing IoT-based cyber threat detection by proactively identifying intrusions, malware, and sophisticated attacks in smart agriculture. This enables intelligent, real-time analysis of vast network data to identify and neutralize emerging security risks.

- *Intrusion Detection Systems*: IDS serve as essential security components in agricultural IoT networks, providing real-time surveillance of data flows, equipment operations, and system activities to detect and prevent cyber incidents. As smart farming grows more dependent on connected technologies, including environmental sensors, autonomous field equipment, and precision irrigation controllers, these systems become exposed to security risks ranging from credential theft to equipment takeover. Modern agricultural IDS implementations combine two complementary approaches: pattern-matching for established threat signatures (like ransomware or botnet attacks) and behavioural analysis to spot abnormal events such as irregular moisture sensor readings or a typical access patterns to control systems. ML-enhanced IDS can analyse vast streams of IoT-generated data in real time, using algorithms like Random Forest or Neural Networks to detect zero-day exploits and sophisticated intrusions (Kumar et al., 2021a). For instance, an IDS might flag a sudden spike in data requests from a single device as a potential brute-force attack or detect manipulated sensor readings indicating a man-in-the-middle attack. Additionally, hybrid IDS approaches combine network-based monitoring (e.g., inspecting MQTT/CoAP protocols) with host-based detection (e.g., verifying firmware integrity on edge devices) to provide comprehensive protection (Kumar et al., 2022a). By integrating IDS with blockchain for tamper-proof logging or with FL for distributed threat analysis, smart agriculture systems can enhance resilience against evolving cyber threats while minimizing false positives. However, challenges remain, including the limited computational power of IoT devices and the requirement for adaptive models that change with new attack vectors in precision farming environments (Kumar et al., 2022b).

- *Malware Classification*: AI has become indispensable in malware analysis for IoT-based smart agriculture systems, offering advanced techniques to detect, classify, and mitigate evolving cyber threats targeting connected devices. Studies reveal that IoT agriculture networks, which rely on sensors, drones, and automated irrigation systems, are increasingly vulnerable to malware attacks such as botnets (e.g., Mirai), ransomware, and firmware exploits (Kumar et al., 2021a). AI-driven approaches, particularly ML and DL, enhance malware detection by analysing behavioural patterns, network traffic anomalies, and code structures (Dib et al., 2021). Similarly, DL-based solutions have effectively detected zero-day malware by analysing binary code and Application Programming Interface (API) call sequences. In smart agriculture, AI models can flag suspicious activities like abnormal sensor data transmissions, a sign of data poisoning, or unauthorized access attempts to farm management systems. As per Kumar et al. (2022b), FL is a decentralized AI approach that improves malware detection across distributed agricultural IoT devices while preserving data privacy. Additionally, AI-powered sandboxing techniques dynamically analyse malware behaviour in isolated environments, mitigating risks like ransomware attacks on automated irrigation controllers (Namavar et al., 2020).
- *Zero-Day Attack Mitigation*: AI has become a transformative force in combating zero-day cyber threats within smart agriculture systems, offering proactive protection against previously unknown vulnerabilities. Using ML and DL techniques, AI systems can analyse behavioural patterns, network anomalies, and operational activities in real time, unlike traditional signature-based detection methods. Unsupervised learning algorithms like isolation forests and one-class SVMs enable the detection of subtle operational deviations that may indicate zero-day attacks, even without prior knowledge of specific threat signatures. DL architectures, particularly LSTM networks and transformer models, excel at identifying temporal anomalies in IoT device communications and predicting potential attack vectors before they cause damage. These systems are further enhanced by RL, which allows for adaptive responses that automatically update security protocols as threats evolve. In agricultural environments where IoT sensors and automated equipment are prime targets, AI-powered solutions can effectively identify suspicious activities such as abnormal irrigation commands or unauthorized firmware

updates, triggering immediate defensive measures. Recent studies show AI-driven approaches can reduce zero-day attack detection times by up to 80% while maintaining low false-positive rates, making them essential for safeguarding critical agricultural infrastructure against emerging cyber threats. The technology's ability to continuously learn from operational data and adapt to new attack patterns provides a significant advantage over conventional security systems in protecting distributed agricultural networks (Muzaffar et al., 2022).

8. Conclusion and Future Scope

Artificial intelligence has transformed cybersecurity in smart agriculture by providing dynamic, adaptive solutions for detecting sophisticated cyber threats and malware. These AI-powered systems enable organizations to proactively protect their digital infrastructure through continuous learning and real-time threat analysis. Within agricultural IoT ecosystems, the growing sophistication of cyber-attacks targeting connected devices necessitates comprehensive security strategies incorporating multi-factor authentication, continuous software patching, end-to-end encryption, physical security controls, and AI-driven monitoring systems. Beyond security applications, AI-driven IoT solutions are revolutionizing farming practices by optimizing resource allocation, enhancing predictive analytics, and improving operational efficiency. Farmers leveraging these technologies gain data-driven insights for better crop and livestock management while supporting sustainable food production to meet global demands. Current research opportunities include developing specialized AI algorithms for anticipating novel agricultural cyber threats and investigating blockchain integration to create tamper-proof security frameworks for farm data. These advancements will further strengthen the resilience of smart agriculture systems against emerging digital risks while maximizing agricultural productivity through technological innovation.

References

Ahluwalia, P. and Mittal, N. (2021). Internet of Things concept and its applications. pp. 7–36. *In*: Gupta, D., Hugo C. de Albuquerque, V., Khanna, A. and Mehta, P.L. (eds.). *Smart Sensors for Industrial Internet of Things*. Springer, Cham.

Ahmad, R. and Alsmadi, I. (2021). Machine learning approaches to IoT security: A systematic literature review [Formula presented]. *Internet of Things (Netherlands)* 14: 100365.

Aljuhani, A., Kumar, P., Islam, A.K.M.N., Kumar, R. and Jolfaei, A. (2023). Fog intelligence for secure smart villages: Architecture and future challenges. *IEEE Consumer Electronics Magazine* 12(5): 12–21.

Bhardwaj, S., Li, A.S., Dave, M. and Bertino, E. (2024). Overcoming the lack of labeled data: Training malware detection models using adversarial domain adaptation. *Computers and Security* 140: 103769.

Biswas, B., Mukhopadhyay, A., Kumar, A. and Delen, D. (2024). A hybrid framework using Explainable AI (XAI) in cyber-risk management for defence and recovery against phishing attacks. *Decision Support Systems* 177: 114102.

Bui, H.T., Aboutorab, H., Mahboubi, A., Gao, Y., Sultan, N.H., Chauhan, A., Parvez, M.Z., Bewong, M., Islam, R., Islam, Z., Camtepe, S.A., Gauravaram, P., Singh, D., Ali Babar, M. and Yan, S. (2024). Agriculture 4.0 and beyond: Evaluating cyber threat intelligence sources and techniques in smart farming ecosystems. *Computers and Security* 140: 103754.

Campoverde-Molina, M. and Luján-Mora, S. (2025). Cybersecurity in smart agriculture: A systematic literature review. *Computers and Security* 150: 104284.

Carvalho, N., Adão, T., Morais, R., Costa, A.R. and Peres, E. (2025). Cybersecurity in precision agriculture: A short review and a practical status assessment over mySense IoT-based platform. *Procedia Computer Science* 256: 255–266.

Dey, A.K., Gupta, G.P. and Sahu, S.P. (2023a). A metaheuristic-based ensemble feature selection framework for cyber threat detection in IoT-enabled networks. *Decision Analytics Journal* 7(March): 100206.

Dey, A.K., Gupta, G.P. and Sahu, S.P. (2023b). A metaheuristic-based ensemble feature selection framework for cyber threat detection in IoT-enabled networks. *Decision Analytics Journal* 7(January): 100206.

Dib, M., Torabi, S., Bou-Harb, E. and Assi, C. (2021). A multi-dimensional deep learning framework for IoT malware classification and family attribution. *IEEE Transactions on Network and Service Management* 18(2): 1165–1177.

Ferreira, R., Bispo, I., Rabadão, C., Santos, L. and Costa, R.L. de C. (2025). Farm-flow dataset: Intrusion detection in smart agriculture based on network flows. *Computers and Electrical Engineering* 121: 109892.

Garg, S. and Baliyan, N. (2022). M2VMapper: Malware-to-Vulnerability mapping for android using text processing. *Expert Systems with Applications* 191: 116360.

Kim, C.H., Kabanga, E.K. and Kang, S.J. (2018). Classifying malware using convolutional gated neural network. *International Conference on Advanced Communication Technology, ICACT, 2018-February*, 40–44.

Kumar, M., Kavita, Verma, S., Kumar, A., Ijaz, M.F. and Rawat, D.B. (2022). ANAF-IoMT: A novel architectural framework for IoMT-enabled smart healthcare system by enhancing security based on RECC-VC. *IEEE Transactions on Industrial Informatics* 18(12): 8936–8943.

Kumar, P., Gupta, G.P. and Tripathi, R. (2021a). TP2SF: A trustworthy privacy-preserving secured framework for sustainable smart cities by leveraging blockchain and machine learning. *Journal of Systems Architecture* 115: 101954.

Kumar, P., Gupta, G.P. and Tripathi, R. (2021b). An ensemble learning and fog-cloud architecture-driven cyber-attack detection framework for IoMT networks. *Computer Communications* 166: 110–124.

Kumar, P., Gupta, G.P. and Tripathi, R. (2022a). PEFL: Deep privacy-encoding-based federated learning framework for smart agriculture. *IEEE Micro* 42(1): 33–40.

Kumar, P., Gupta, G.P. and Tripathi, R. (2022b). PEFL: Deep privacy-encoding-based federated learning framework for smart agriculture. *IEEE Micro* 42(1), 33–40.

Kumar, P., Javeed, D., Islam, A.K.M.N. and Luo, X. (Robert). (2025). DeepSecure: A computational design science approach for interpretable threat hunting in cybersecurity decision making. *Decision Support Systems* 188: 114351.

Kumar, P., Javeed, D., Kumar, R. and Islam, A.K.M.N. (2024). Blockchain and Explainable AI for enhanced decision making in cyber threat detection. *Software - Practice and Experience* 54(8): 1337–1360.

Kumar, P., Kumar, R., Aloqaily, M. and Islam, A.K.M.N. (2024). Explainable AI and blockchain for metaverse: A security and privacy perspective. *IEEE Consumer Electronics Magazine* 13(3): 90–97.

Kumar, P., Kumar, R., Srivastava, G., Gupta, G.P., Tripathi, R., Gadekallu, T.R. and Xiong, N.N. (2021). PPSF: A privacy-preserving and secure framework using blockchain-based machine-learning for IoT-driven smart cities. *IEEE Transactions on Network Science and Engineering* 8(3): 2326–2341.

Kumar, R., Kumar, P., Tripathi, R., Gupta, G.P., Gadekallu, T.R. and Srivastava, G. (2021). SP2F: A secured privacy-preserving framework for smart agricultural unmanned aerial vehicles. *Computer Networks* 187: 107819.

Kumar, R., Kumar, P., Tripathi, R., Gupta, G.P., Islam, A.K.M.N. and Shorfuzzaman, M. (2022). Permissioned blockchain and deep-learning for secure and efficient data sharing in industrial healthcare systems. *IEEE Transactions on Industrial Informatics* 18(11): 8065–8073.

Kumar, R. and Subbiah, G. (2022). Zero-day malware detection and effective malware analysis using shapley ensemble boosting and bagging approach. *Sensors* 22(7): 2798.

Madan, S., Sofat, S. and Bansal, D. (2022). Tools and techniques for collection and analysis of internet-of-things malware: a systematic state-of-art review. *Journal of King Saud University - Computer and Information Sciences* 34(10): 9867–9888.

Martín, A., Lara-Cabrera, R. and Camacho, D. (2019). Android malware detection through hybrid features fusion and ensemble classifiers: The AndroPyTool framework and the OmniDroid dataset. *Information Fusion* 52: 128–142.

Muzaffar, A., Ragab Hassen, H., Lones, M.A. and Zantout, H. (2022). An in-depth review of machine learning based android malware detection. *Computers and Security* 121: 102833.

Namavar Jahromi, A., Hashemi, S., Dehghantanha, A., Choo, K.K.R., Karimipour, H., Newton, D.E. and Parizi, R.M. (2020). An improved two-hidden-layer extreme learning machine for malware hunting. *Computers and Security* 89: 101655.

Ramesh, G. and Menen, A. (2020). Automated dynamic approach for detecting ransomware using finite-state machine. *Decision Support Systems* 138: 113400.

Rey, V., Miguel, P., Sánchez, S., Huertas, A. and Bovet, G. (2022). Federated learning for malware detection in IoT devices. *Computer Networks* 204: 108693.

Rudrakar, S. and Rughani, P. (2023). IoT based Agriculture (Ag-IoT): A detailed study on architecture, security and forensics. *Information Processing in Agriculture* 11: 524–541.

Schmitt, M. (2023). Securing the digital world: protecting smart infrastructures and digital industries with Artificial Intelligence (AI)-enabled malware and intrusion detection. *Journal of Industrial Information Integration* 36: 100520.

Singh, J. and Singh, J. (2021). A survey on machine learning-based malware detection in executable files. *Journal of Systems Architecture* 112: 101861.

Srivastava, P., Peng, H., Li, J., Okhravi, H., Shrobe, H. and Payer, M. (2019). FirmFuzz: automated IoT firmware introspection and analysis. *IoT S and P 2019 - Proceedings of the 2nd International ACM Workshop on Security and Privacy for the Internet-of-Things*, 15–21.

Swarna Priya, R.M., Maddikunta, P.K.R., Parimala, M., Koppu, S., Gadekallu, T.R., Chowdhary, C.L. and Alazab, M. (2020). An effective feature engineering for DNN using hybrid PCA-GWO for intrusion detection in IoMT architecture. *Computer Communications* 160: 139–149.

Thilakarathne, N.N., Bakar, M.S.A., Abas, P.E. and Yassin, H. (2025). A novel cyber threat intelligence platform for evaluating the risk associated with smart agriculture. *Scientific Reports* 15(1): 3904.

Usman, N., Usman, S., Khan, F., Jan, M.A., Sajid, A., Alazab, M. and Watters, P. (2021). Intelligent dynamic malware detection using machine learning in IP reputation for forensics data analytics. *Future Generation Computer Systems* 118: 124–141.

Wajahat, A., He, J., Zhu, N., Mahmood, T., Nazir, A., Ullah, F., Qureshi, S. and Dev, S. (2024). Securing android IoT devices with GuardDroid transparent and lightweight malware detection. *Ain Shams Engineering Journal* 15(5): 102642.

Yang, H., Wang, Y., Zhang, L., Cheng, X. and Hu, Z. (2024). A novel android malware detection method with API semantics extraction. *Computers and Security* 137: 103651.

Yang, X., Shu, L., Chen, J., Ferrag, M.A., Wu, J., Nurellari, E. and Huang, K. (2021). A survey on smart agriculture: Development modes, technologies, and security and privacy challenges. *IEEE/CAA Journal of Automatica Sinica* 8(2): 273–302.

Yu, K., Tan, L., Mumtaz, S., Al-Rubaye, S., Al-Dulaimi, A., Bashir, A.K. and Khan, F.A. (2021). Securing critical infrastructures: deep-learning-based threat detection in IIoT. *IEEE Communications Magazine* 59(10): 76–82.

Zhou, H., Zou, H., Zhou, P., Shen, Y., Li, D. and Li, W. (2025). CBCTL-IDS: A transfer learning-based intrusion detection system optimized with the black kite algorithm for IoT-enabled smart agriculture. *IEEE Access* 13: 46601–46615.

Chapter 12

Enhancing Security and Privacy in Smart Agriculture

Integrating Blockchain and Artificial Intelligence

Manabhanjan Sahu

Purpose: This research investigates ways blockchain together with artificial intelligence (AI) technology tackles security and privacy problems which exist in Internet of Things (IoT)-based smart agriculture systems.

Design/Methodology/Approach: A scientific review of 92 peer-reviewed publications from 2015 to 2025 was performed according to PRISMA 2020 standards. The research studied blockchain and AI mechanisms independently and jointly in their role of protecting agricultural IoT data ecosystems.

Findings: Party blockchain technology provides agricultural security through three key features including unmodifiable data properties and decentralized management of system identity and complete supply chain visibility. AI supports real-time threat

School of Pharmacy and Technology Management, SVKM's Narsee Monjee Institute of Management Studies (Deemed to be University), Maharashtra, India.
Emails: Sahumana2016@gmail.com, Manabhanjan.sahu@nmims.edu

DOI: 10.1201/9781003670568-12

detection, anomaly analysis, and predictive decision-making. A four-layer security framework and proof-of-concept architecture were proposed which integrates IoT sensors with AI analytics then uses blockchain verification and contains user interaction interfaces. The practical implementation of these technologies encounters obstacles because of high energy needs and expensive computations together with difficulties in system interoperability. Less than two out of twelve published studies featured actual field executions.

Practical Implications: The paper establishes a comprehensive guide that helps researchers and policy makers and aggrotech developers create secure scalable digital farming systems which preserve user privacy. The authors specify using minimal AI and blockchain resources alongside field-based experimentation and standardizing secured networks for agricultural Internet of Things systems.

Originality/Value: The investigation serves as a pioneering examination which gathers all available literature about blockchain and AI collaboration in smart agriculture regarding security and privacy aspects. The paper presents a unified model together with research areas that upcoming studies need to explore.

1. Introduction

Digital transformation affects the agricultural sector because new digital technologies have redefined farming into a system that relies on data collection and automation. Networked devices and intelligent systems under precision agriculture applications provide enhanced production, sustainability and tracking capabilities (Soussi et al., 2024). The digital revolution creates essential problems for smart farm security which includes the protection of data generated and distributed through Internet of Things (IoT)-enabled farm systems.

Real-time environmental monitoring of conditions together with crop health check-ups and operational process evaluation becomes possible because of the increased use of IoT sensors and drones and automated machinery (Ashraf et al., 2023). Systems that operate in low-resource areas along with weak security features become highly exposed to threats which include data breaches and unauthorized access as well as system manipulation. Data protection protocols standards along with low cybersecurity awareness of end-users in smallholder and rural areas make these risks even more severe (Tapia and Avila-Pesantez, 2021).

The solution to these vulnerabilities appears through blockchain and artificial intelligence (AI) technology integration. The blockchain system maintains data trustworthiness and enables distributed network access control but also supports full chain visibility because it uses an immutable record system (Strang and Sun, 2017). Through real-time threat analysis, AI establishes dynamic security capabilities that use anomaly detection and predictive systems for threat mitigation (Tapia and Avila-Pesantez, 2021). These two elements create a dual field architecture that integrates secure data infrastructure protection with adaptive risk detection and mitigation capabilities.

The adoption of blockchain-AI integration in agricultural settings occurs at limited rates despite their proved compatibility. The widespread adoption of blockchain-AI integration in agriculture remains limited because of energy-consuming blockchain consensus protocols and demanding AI calculations as well as challenges with device and platform interoperability. Very few empirical studies have been conducted to confirm the validity of these technologies when used in real agricultural settings (Kose et al., 2022).

The research fills these gaps through a systematic literature review (SLR) which analyses peer-reviewed publications alongside grey literature produced between 2015 and 2025. This chapter accomplishes three main goals: it investigates blockchain and AI roles when implemented separately or in combination for smart agriculture security; it details technology limitations that affect implementation; and it develops a conceptual model for secure agricultural ecosystems.

The study brings insights into agricultural cybersecurity research by presenting contemporary knowledge and future prospects within the domain. The target audience is policymakers and agrotech innovators as well as researchers who need this guideline to build upcoming resilient smart farming systems.

2. Background and Theoretical Foundations

The agricultural integration of digital technologies has changed food production history through fundamental transformation of farming systems operations. Smart agriculture emerges through technological integration of IoT, blockchain and AI to establish this framework (Awan et al., 2020). The chapter investigates digital agriculture's historical transformation path before evaluating security issues facing agriculture in the current era. The essay shows how blockchain and AI work as technical solutions to defend against these risks while establishing strong digital farming systems.

2.1 *Blockchain and Smart Agriculture*

The implementation of blockchain technology solves various privacy and security issues which smart agriculture presents. The invention of blockchain to support cryptocurrencies has developed into a general-purpose system which upholds distributed data integrity through transparency and trust-based operations (Qadri et al., 2024). Its agricultural utilization stems from its ability to deliver tamper-proof distributed event records that multiple stakeholders can securely access. When used in smart agriculture, there are several primary advantages of blockchain technology.

First, data integrity deals with every block of data inserted into a blockchain system which becomes permanently stable because all participants within the network need to endorse any modification attempt. Agriculture benefits extensively from this technology since validation of sensor data and transaction processes along with proof of origin needs to be absolutely reliable. Blockchain technology provides agricultural sectors with data accuracy which remains impervious to fraud attempts (Senthilkumar, 2020).

Second, under decentralized access control, the blockchain platform enables smart contracts to establish distinct permissions for user access within their system. Crop treatment schedules can be modified only by approved agronomists through the system yet farmers can observe analytics from the system without affecting the original data. The decentralized system requires no central authority; therefore, it prevents failures that affect a single source (Manoj et al., 2024).

Third, under traceability, the blockchain experts can track every step throughout the entire agricultural supply chain without limitations. Both seeding operations and soil treatments and each production step through harvesting and storage and distribution activities may be recorded permanently on the blockchain system. The implementation of transparent systems through blockchain markers offers necessary verification capabilities for organic certification alongside compliance oversight and prompt handling of product recalls (Mohamad et al., 2022).

Finally, blockchain operates as a trust foundation by creating fail-proof transaction records which remain secure within a shared database accessible to the permitted user base.

2.2 *Artificial Intelligence and Smart Agriculture*

Blockchain establishes authentic and pristine agricultural data, yet it does not provide analysis or interpretation services. AI functions as an additional platform to support operations because of its capabilities. The combination of AI technology allows users to transform enormous IoT device datasets into practical knowledge during analysis. The combination of autonomous decision-making capability and pattern learning ability makes AI a fundamental tool which secures while optimizing smart agricultural management procedures (Alzahrani et al., 2025).

Artificial intelligence has three main roles for agricultural cybersecurity operations.

First, the system operates by deploying AI algorithms for persistent threat detection through data anomaly analysis. Unusual temperature readings detected by sensors will trigger AI to activate automated containment procedures which mark the event as a potential attack (Catalano et al., 2022). Second, AI systems perform anomaly analysis by identifying operational abnormalities beyond evident security issues. Mild adjustments in irrigation patterns could point to a malfunctioning valve during a cyber intrusion that has just begun. AI enables the detection of anomalies in time which consequently helps stop failures from spreading further (Rusev et al., 2024). Third, AI technology demonstrates particular excellence in the capability to develop future predictions through the analysis of past information. Predominant agricultural applications enable the forecast of looming pest problems as well as equipment problems and weather conditions requiring observation (Noor et al., 2024). The combination of blockchain-secured data with predictive models results in improved reliability through which farmers obtain advance warning systems along with response strategies. AI systems achieve three essential capabilities including detecting fraudulent patterns and optimally managing supply chain logistics and helping policy creators through large data aggregation and simulation.

3. Research Design and PRISMA Protocol

The research design of this study uses the SLR method to analyse blockchain and AI technologies that tackle security and privacy issues in smart agriculture. The methodological process follows PRISMA 2020 framework alongside Kitchenham's methodology to ensure robustness and open transparency and reproducibility of results. An analysis of 92 research documents between 2015 and 2025 included peer-reviewed studies with grey literature sources through three-stage thematic coding. Table 12.1 demonstrates the logical connection between research questions (RQs) with linked analytical dimensions and methodological activities.

The SLR protocol demanded researchers to define search queries before selecting specific criteria for screening and conducting qualitative

Table 12.1: Mapping of research questions to methods and analysis dimensions.

Research Question (RQ)	Methodological Activity	Analytical Dimension
RQ1: How does blockchain technology contribute to enhancing security and privacy in smart agriculture?	Literature search and content coding	Blockchain functionalities (immutability, access control, traceability)
RQ2: What are the roles of AI in mitigating threats and improving decision-making in agricultural IoT systems?	Thematic extraction from selected studies	AI techniques (anomaly detection, predictive modelling, adaptive learning)
RQ3: What are the critical barriers to the adoption of blockchain and AI integration in smart agricultural environments?	Comparative analysis and synthesis of empirical studies	Adoption challenges (scalability, energy demands, interoperability)
RQ4: What frameworks or models have been proposed, and where do gaps exist for real-world implementation?	Synthesis of conceptual and applied frameworks	Evaluation of integration architectures and validation gaps

thematic synthesis. Research articles were collected from Scopus and IEEE Xplore as well as Web of Science, ScienceDirect, SpringerLink, and ACM Digital Library between 2015 and 2025.

The review incorporated information from grey literature sources including white papers, policy briefs, and technical reports for capturing modern practical insights. The implementation of two-source approaches successfully expanded understanding about blockchain and AI application within agricultural cybersecurity.

The subsequent parts of the research utilize this methodology to display thematic analysis findings and interpret technology integration alongside proposing an empirical and theory-based conceptual framework.

The PRISMA framework given in Figure 12.1 shows the systematic approach for the literature review which integrates blockchain and AI to boost security features and privacy aspects in smart agriculture applications. Academic publishers recognize this framework as per PRISMA 2020 guidelines, which make it ready for journal publication.

4. Results and Analysis

The synthesized outcomes from 92 peer-reviewed and grey literature sources form this section. The research findings present three primary subtopics:

(i) blockchain security

(ii) enhancements for agriculture

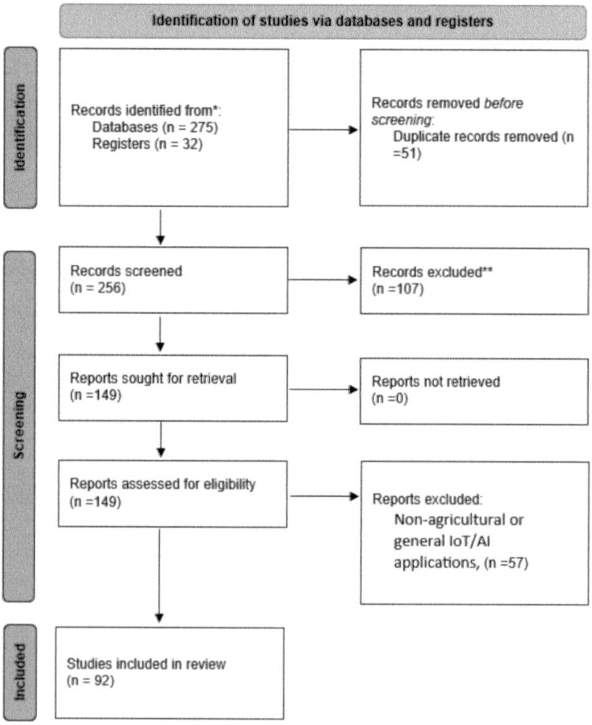

Figure 12.1: PRISMA flow diagram summary (literature selection process).

(iii) and AI threats detection together with decision-making frameworks and joint implementations of the two systems.

The analysis shows that blockchain together with AI possesses separate and beneficial capabilities that can strongly boost the security and privacy measures for smart agricultural systems through effective integration.

4.1 Keyword and Trend Analysis

The SLR consisted of an analysis phase which determined frequent keywords in chosen research studies. Table 12.2 presents information about the prevailing technological areas, conceptual aspects, and thematic elements that researchers focus on when discussing secure smart agriculture through keyword frequency analysis.

The keyword analysis demonstrated that the domain is highly focused through repeated usage of core terms that include "agriculture" and "smart agriculture". Technical terms "blockchain technology" and "machine learning" appeared to lead the field because they converge as

Table 12.2: Summary of keyword occurrences in literature.

Keyword	Occurrences
Agriculture	120
Smart Agriculture	42
Blockchain Technology	28
Machine Learning	35
Data Integrity	18

researchers develop agricultural innovations. Scholarly concern regarding agricultural data reliability as well as security technology effects on sustainable development is evident through regular occurrences of "data integrity" and "food security" in research publications.

The prevalence of these keywords also signals an interdisciplinary convergence. For instance, the pairing of "data integrity" with "blockchain" highlights how trust mechanisms are being embedded into digital agriculture, while the co-occurrence of "machine learning" and "smart farming" reflects the application of advanced analytics in real-time agricultural decision-making. Beyond frequency, qualitative patterns reveal an expanding research trajectory—from early conceptual discussions to prototype development, and in some cases, pilot implementations in resource-constrained farming environments.

4.2 The Role of Blockchain in Agricultural Security

Blockchain represents a widely evaluated transformative technology which advances trust alongside accountability and data assurance within smart agriculture operations. Agricultural IoT systems gain their foundational features from blockchain technology through these three enabled capabilities: Immutability, Smart contract and Traceability (Table 12.3).

Table 12.3: Blockchain contributions to agricultural security.

Blockchain Feature	Agricultural Benefit
Immutability	Ensures that data (e.g., sensor readings, transaction logs) remains tamper-proof, preserving accuracy for audits, compliance, and farm management records.
Smart Contracts	Automate access permissions and workflow triggers, enabling decentralized enforcement of rules (e.g., who can access field data or update inventory logs).
Traceability	Enhances supply chain visibility by recording each stage of the crop cycle—from planting to processing—enabling verifiable food safety, certification, and quality assurance.

Immutability or the ability to prevent any unauthorized changes in data remains essential for agricultural systems which rely on authentic information. Sensors capture real-time agricultural data through measurements of soil moisture besides crop health conditions and livestock tracking information for situational awareness (Gupta et al., 2024). Blockchains guarantee absolute data immutability via network consensus because users need total agreement to change recorded data. The tamper-evident properties of blockchain systems help stop the modification of essential agricultural records before or after they are recorded. Because blockchain records remain permanently unchangeable, all stakeholders who share the same datasets feel secure and maintain strong accountability towards one another (Dargaoui et al., 2024).

Smart contracts, which are the other critical blockchain functionality, facilitate the automation of processes based on data as well as controlling access. These scripts that are executed automatically are programmed to execute in reaction to certain data conditions, and are thus optimizing the agriculture processes (Dos Santos et al., 2021; Voutos et al., 2019). For example, a smart contract could execute an automatically triggered pesticide application procedure only if a pre-defined level of pest infestation was reached and validated through sensor inputs. This would mean (for now, anyway) that human monitoring could be cut back quite a bit, with the upside being that pesticide application would be done in a "timely manner, with precision, and in a way that's compliant with safety regulations" ((Ishengoma, 2024)). In addition to these applications for smart contracts, there is also the matter of rights of access. Smart contracts can define "who can see what" among the various stakeholders in a given agricultural situation. And they can do that quite securely (Ishengoma, 2024).

Traceability is a critical aspect of modern agriculture, particularly for global food chains demanding transparency in certification, compliance, and consumer trust. The modern agricultural system increasingly hinges on being able to demonstrate trustworthiness—particularly for the global food chains that demand complete transparency when it comes to certification and compliance with regulations and standards, as well as to the consumers who want to know what they are really buying (Ishengoma, 2024).

4.3 AI Contributions to Threat Detection and Decision Support

Complementing the blockchain's static security is AI, which makes dynamic, adaptive intelligence possible in agriculture. The studies treat AI as key to real-time threat detection, adaptable predictive analytics, and ongoing system optimization (Alahmadi et al., 2022). These features manage the inescapable temporal and environmental uncertainties of agriculture to facilitate anticipatory risk management and adaptive decision-making (see also Table 12.4).

Identifying normal and abnormal behaviour of the elements selected for the agronomics domain is the first step towards the application of AI in agriculture (Romanova and Levina, 2020). Features selected for the farming domain, where smart agriculture is heavily based on the use of various forms of sensors, form the basis for AI to serve as the brain of smart agriculture—doing real-time analysis that sorts out the different types of performances of different parts of the equation (the smart IoT sensors, the actuators, the crops, the environment, and the robotic systems that move between the parts of the farm). However, anomaly detection is really understood only in terms of what types of features are used to do the detection and how they performed in smart agriculture (Chukkapalli et al., 2021).

The most vital contribution of AI to agriculture is in predictive modelling. It studies the patterns in the huge amounts of environmental and operational data being collected and forecasts a variety of risks that cannot otherwise be foreseen (Murali et al., 2022). That includes the kinds of problems, like pest infestations and crop diseases, that are routinely too unpredictable to make plans for. And it is not just pests and plants that can be predicted; predictive modelling can also forecast when machinery is going to break down (Ashraf et al., 2023).

Optimization in machine learning makes the AI systems that use it far more useful than static, rule-based systems. Unlike rule-based systems that require reprogramming to remain relevant, AI systems that use machine learning can get better and better at what they do by learning from new inputs and using those inputs to hone their existing algorithms (Kethineni and Gera, 2023). They do this all day, every day, and in a kind of system that almost guarantees improvements, farming can be one of the optimized engines of IoT.

Table 12.4: AI contributions to threat detection and decision support.

AI Technique	**Application in Smart Farming**
Anomaly Detection	Identifies irregular system behaviour, such as cyber threats targeting irrigation systems or drones (Catalano et al., 2022)
Predictive Analytics	Anticipates events such as pest outbreaks, disease progression, or equipment malfunction, enabling pre-emptive responses (Krishnan et al., 2023)
Machine Learning	Supports adaptive models that refine themselves based on environmental data to improve crop disease detection and resource allocation (Raj et al., 2025)

These AI features combined give smart agrotech systems the ability to self-monitor, to forecast, to anticipate. They can do all that (and more) in real time. They can (and do) act on what they sense without always waiting for humans to tell them what to do first. And when they do act, the measures they take can be logged in such a way that makes it almost foolish to try and move away from secure, compliant, and data-driven agricultural operations (Padiya et al., 2023).

5. Proposed Integrated Architecture: Conceptual and Proof-of-Concept Frameworks for Secure Smart Agriculture

The increasing digitization of farming has rendered the industry more dependent on networked devices, process automation based on data, and smart automation. But with this progress comes an accompanying increase in cyber-physical vulnerabilities spanning from data tampering and unauthorized access to disruption of operations (Wang et al., 2025). In order to meet these new threats, this research suggests a new four-layered security model that brings together the complementary strengths of IoT, AI, blockchain technology, and human-centred interfaces. In contrast to previous models that address each of these technologies separately, this architecture prioritizes adaptive intelligence and verifiable trust as central design principles and ensures both resilience and transparency in agricultural cyber-infrastructures (Kansal et al., 2021).

Table 12.5 shows the layered structure behind the suggested proof-of-concept for secure smart agriculture, combining IoT sensors, AI analytics, blockchain technology, and stakeholder interfaces. Each layer is structured to perform a particular role in the system, together supporting real-time data acquisition, secure processing, immutable record-keeping, and user interaction. The architecture illustrates the feasibility and scalability of the model for implementation in precision agriculture environments.

This schematic diagram is a proof-of-concept structure for a secure, data-oriented smart agriculture system that combines IoT, AI, and blockchain technologies. The system aims to tackle security, transparency, and efficiency in agricultural processes by means of a layered structure.

5.1 Proposed Proof-of-Concept Architecture for Secure Smart Agriculture Using IoT, AI, and Blockchain

This proof-of-concept demonstrates a workable design for next-gen, intelligent, smart agriculture systems that are secure, transparent, and smart technologies. The layered structure does not just enable modular development and testing; it also serves as a template for possible future "scale up and deployment" scenarios (Chukkapalli et al., 2020).

Table 12.5: Layered architecture for secure smart agriculture – Proof-of-concept overview.

Layer	Components	Functions	Proof-of-Concept Contribution
1. Data Acquisition Layer (IoT Sensors)	Soil moisture sensors, drones, weather stations, camera traps	Captures real-time environmental and operational data such as soil health, climate conditions, crop growth, and intrusions	Validates the capability to collect distributed, diverse agricultural data streams
2. Integrity Layer (Blockchain Ledger)	Blockchain nodes (e.g., Ethereum/ Hyperledger), smart contracts	Ensures data immutability, provenance, and secure access via cryptographic hashing and decentralized ledgers	Demonstrates secure and transparent data management to prevent tampering and unauthorized access
3. Processing Layer (AI Analytics Engine)	Machine learning models, neural networks, edge AI processors	Performs data filtering, pattern recognition, threat detection, and yield forecasting	Shows the feasibility of real-time analytics and autonomous decision support
4. Interaction Layer (Stakeholder Interfaces)	Mobile apps, web dashboards, data visualization tools	Allows end-users (farmers, regulators, suppliers) to access actionable insights, monitor Key Performance Indicators, and make informed decisions	Confirms multi-user interface operability and utility for decision-making
5. Cross-Layer Flow	Encrypted communication protocols, Application Programming Interfaces	Secures unidirectional or authenticated bidirectional data transmission across layers	Ensures integrity, availability, and controlled access throughout the system

This architecture design presents a smart agriculture system that is safe, data-driven, and synergistically interwoven with IoT, sensors, AI, and blockchain technology. The system increases transparency, integrity, and operational efficiency (Anand, 2022). It consists of five connected layers with safe data flows, and performs five main functions.

This conceptual model serves as a proof of concept that the next generation of intelligent agriculture systems can function as intended and be secure and transparent, and uses blockchain technology. This architecture design presents a smart agriculture system that is safe, data-driven, and synergistically interwoven with IoT, sensors, AI, and blockchain technology. The system increases transparency, integrity, and operational efficiency (Anand, 2022). It consists of five connected layers with safe data flows, and performs five main functions (Figure 12.2).

The Data Acquisition Layer of IoT devices encompasses everything from drones to soil moisture sensors. It is a collection of devices that

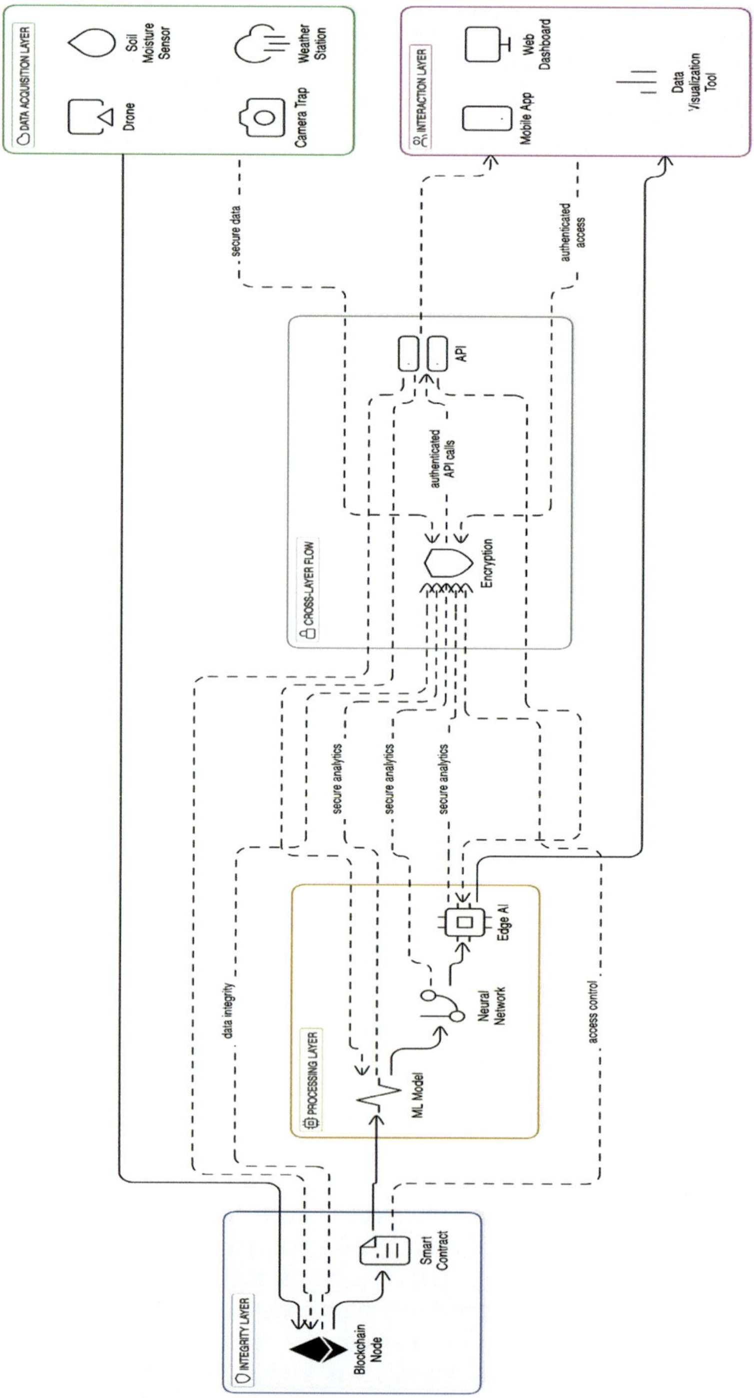

Figure 12.2: Proof-of-Concept architecture for secure smart agriculture using IoT, AI, and blockchain.

assemble a network capturing nearly instantaneous and diverse environmental data; everything from soil humidity and atmospheric conditions to pest movement. These devices are the first layer of the assemblage that is IoT (Suma and Madhumathy, 2019; Zhiqiang et al., 2019).

The Integrity Layer, built on blockchain technology, guarantees that all incoming sensor data is hashed, time-stamped, and written to a decentralized, secure ledger. It uses smart contracts to make the data immutable (Senthilkumar, 2020). If the data were not trustworthy, say a person hacked a sensor or altered it in some way, then the data retrieved from the Integrity Layer would indicate that something was amiss. The layer is important in securing the provenance of the data we access (Ranaveer et al., 2025).

The core of this elaborate data management system is the Processing Layer. It performs real-time analysis and interpretation of the tremendous amount of data collected (Zhiqiang et al., 2019). Yet, it is not only advanced machine learning models and state-of-the-art neural networks that do the heavy lifting of actual data crunching (Keppmann et al., 2017). At the same time, edge AI technologies also carry out significant computing tasks that help transform the appearance of the input data to something that has smarts, in other words, actionable intelligence that can be put to use. This layer does all the predictive analytics that happens (Liu et al., 2024).

The key applications here perform functions related to (i) yield forecasting; (ii) detecting anomalies, including the breakout of diseases; and (iii) optimizing the utilization of resources, including what is likely to be a schedule for irrigating. Integrating edge AI layers in the Processing layer enhances performance. It does that by principally enabling near-source intelligence (NSI) (Wang et al., 2025).

The Cross-Layer Flow module guarantees that communication among the different architectural layers of the system is secure and authenticated. It does this by employing robust encryption protocols that were specifically formulated to ensure the confidentiality of the data that flows "up" and "down" between the layers and to prevent any unauthorized access to "sensitive" information which is, in this case, the communication itself (Shakeel et al., 2023).

For both the encryption and decryption processes, the well-known confidentiality, integrity, availability (CIA) model of basic cybersecurity is followed (Senthilkumar, 2020). Mobile apps, web-based dashboards, and data visualization platforms all interface conveniently with the system's analytics. They are called the Interaction Layer for a reason. The Interaction Layer makes it easy for the system's different kinds of stakeholders—farmers, agronomists, supply chain members, and policymakers—to engage with the system and make decisions based on its outputs (Keppmann et al., 2017).

6. Discussion and Implications

The fusion of blockchain and AI in smart agriculture is a revolutionary change not only in the technology infrastructure of agricultural systems but also in the way trust, decision-making, and data management are understood and implemented in the digital era. This discussion takes the analysis beyond descriptive presentation of results and moves in the direction of a more substantial and critical examination of the theoretical basis, technological design needs, and practical avenues of implementation. The subsequent sub-sections detail these implications (Mukhtar et al., 2025).

6.1 *Practical Implications*

Though the technological potential of blockchain and AI is intriguing, their effective use in agriculture is dependent on practical interventions that address the gap between conceptual models and ground-level realities. These interventions need to be co-developed by policymakers, industry captains, researchers, and the farming community (Wang and Zhang, 2023).

Among the most pressing requirements is financing and rolling out region-based pilot schemes (Wang and Zhang, 2023). The literature review finds that there is a lack of empirical studies to prove the combined use of blockchain and AI in actual farm environments (Albaaji and Chandra, 2024). Lacking field tests, it is challenging to assess system resilience, user convenience, and environmental effects. Governments, international development agencies, and private sector players need to invest in multi-location demonstration projects that experiment with integrated solutions across agro-climatic zones, farm sizes, and socio-economic environments (Chourey et al., 2023). These pilots can also refine frameworks, locate bottlenecks, and enhance local capacities.

A second applied imperative is establishing agricultural cybersecurity standards specific to the industry's needs and limitations. Existing cybersecurity protocols are largely derived from industrial or financial networks, which have very dissimilar parameters (Ashraf et al., 2023). Farming needs sector-specific procedures that address intermittent connectivity, legacy systems, and human-computer interface obstacles. These standards need to be collaboratively developed with stakeholders, incorporating both global best practices and local operational conditions (Neethirajan, 2025).

Third, ensuring the permanence of digital security arrangements in agriculture necessitates an increase in the digital security literacy of farmers and stakeholders in rural regions (Huang, 2023). The question of technology adoption is not so much about infrastructure as it is about user trust and knowledge. Given this, unfamiliarity and distrust may make the adoption of technology less likely. More importantly, if potential users adopt greater digital security literacy, they might also work to ensure that the systems are reliable enough for them to feel comfortable using all the data they collect (Pasupuleti, 2025).

Finally, it is essential to regard the integration of blockchain and AI as a kind of social and technical change, not simply a technical change. These new technologies are affecting power relationships, data ownership, and knowledge distribution throughout the agricultural value chain (Gupta et al., 2024). If we want to translate the promise of these new systems into a reality that benefits everyone, we must couple practical implementation plans with governance models that ensure equal access, accountability, and benefit-sharing among all stakeholders (Wei et al., 2024).

7. Conclusion

Smart agriculture's fast development now reshapes contemporary agriculture through networked digital technologies that produce precise automated operations. The rapid technological progress in smart agriculture introduces vital security and privacy risks as well as ethical considerations stemming from privacy infringements in a cyber-threatened digital landscape. A systematic review examines how blockchain and AI work together to solve smart agriculture problems. Through a PRISMA methodology we evaluated 1,032 articles which were published between 2015 and 2025, resulting in the selection of 92 high-quality studies for comprehensive examination. The results show that blockchain technology delivers transparent operations with immutable data features and distributed trust systems alongside AI capabilities which deliver resourceful decision support and analytic tools for anomaly finding and predictive forecasting. Both blockchain and AI create a powerful unified system that helps businesses maintain privacy and security through secure data sharing, real-time threat alerts, and asset tracking. This chapter presented both a classification of existing implementations alongside an identification of research voids followed by a conceptual blueprint for deploying smart agricultural systems with security and privacy safeguards. The chapter established both practical usage recommendations and future research guidelines which stakeholders can use to adopt emerging technologies properly and effectively.

References

Alahmadi, A.N., Rehman, S.U., Alhazmi, H.S., Glynn, D.G., Shoaib, H. and Solé, P. (2022). Cyber-security threats and side-channel attacks for digital agriculture. *Sensors* 22(9): 3520.

Albaaji, G.F. and Chandra, S.S.V. (2024). Blockchain technology in agriculture: Digitizing the Iraqi agricultural environment. *Environment, Development and Sustainability* 27: 17741–17752.

Alzahrani, F., Hasanin, T. and Jambi, S. (2025). Smart agriculture prediction using IoT in Al-bahah province. *Cuestiones de Fisioterapia* 54(4): 5700–5721.

Ashraf, S.N., Manickam, S., Zia, S.S., Abro, A.A., Obaidat, M., Uddin, M., Abdelhaq, M. and Alsaqour, R. (2023). IoT empowered smart cybersecurity framework for intrusion detection in internet of drones. *Scientific Reports* 13(1): 18422.

Awan, K.A., Din, I.U., Almogren, A. and Almajed, H. (2020). Agritrust—A trust management approach for smart agriculture in cloud-based internet of agriculture things. *Sensors (Switzerland)* 20(21): 1–21.

Catalano, C., Paiano, L., Calabrese, F., Cataldo, M., Mancarella, L. and Tommasi, F. (2022). Anomaly detection in smart agriculture systems. *Computers in Industry* 143: 103750.

Chourey, P., Singh, N.J., Soni, K. and Agarwal, R. (2023). IoT-enabled sensor node for environmental monitoring. *Lecture Notes in Electrical Engineering* 906: 353–362.

Chukkapalli, S.S.L., Piplai, A., Mittal, S., Gupta, M. and Joshi, A. (2020). A smart-farming ontology for attribute based access control. *Proceedings—2020 IEEE 6th Intl Conference on Big Data Security on Cloud, BigDataSecurity 2020, 2020 IEEE Intl Conference on High Performance and Smart Computing, HPSC 2020 and 2020 IEEE Intl Conference on Intelligent Data and Security,* IDS 2020, 29–34.

Chukkapalli, S.S.L., Ranade, P., Mittal, S. and Joshi, A. (2021). A privacy preserving anomaly detection framework for cooperative smart farming ecosystem. *Proceedings—2021 3rd IEEE International Conference on Trust, Privacy and Security in Intelligent Systems and Applications,* TPS-ISA 2021, 340–347.

Dargaoui, S., Azrour, M., El Allaoui, A., Guezzaz, A., Benkirane, S., Alabdulatif, A. and Amounas, F. (2024). Internet-of-Things-enabled smart agriculture: Security enhancement approaches. *2024 4th International Conference on Innovative Research in Applied Science, Engineering and Technology, IRASET 2024,* 1–5.

Dos Santos, R.B., Torrisi, N.M. and Pantoni, R.P. (2021). Third party certification of agri-food supply chain using smart contracts and blockchain tokens. *Sensors* 21(16): 5307.

Anand G., M., Reddy, S., S., Venkat Sai, T., Charan, M., Mohan, A.L., Dharmendra, T., Sarath, P. and Karthikeyan, R. (2022). Smarticulture: Novel farming technique to achieve automation in farming and higher crop yield with aid of artificial intelligence. *International Journal for Research in Applied Science and Engineering Technology* 10(6): 1198–1201.

Gupta, S., Kuntoji, A. and Singh, S. (2024). Data security and privacy in IoT-enabled agriculture. pp. 289–318. *In*: Gupta, S., Hasan, W., Singh, S., Kumar, D., Ansari, M.J. and Nisar, S. (eds.). *Agriculture 4.0*. CRC Press.

Huang, K. (2023). Chain security: Nodes, algorithm, and network. pp. 31–60. *In*: Huang, K., Budorin, D., Tan, L.J., Ma, W. and Zhang, Z.W. (eds.). *A Comprehensive Guide for Web3 Security. Future of Business and Finance*. Springer, Cham.

Ishengoma, F. (2024). Smart contracts for efficient resource allocation and management in hyperautomated agricultural information systems. pp. 15–25. *In*: Singh, S., Sood, V., Srivastav, A.L. and Ampatzidis, Y. (eds.). *Hyperautomation in Precision Agriculture: Advancements and Opportunities for Sustainable Farming*. Academic Press.

Kansal, N., Bhushan, B. and Sharma, S. (2021). Architecture, security vulnerabilities, and the proposed countermeasures in Agriculture-Internet-of-Things (AIoT) systems. *Studies in Big Data* 99: 329–353.

Keppmann, F.L., Maleshkova, M. and Harth, A. (2017). Adaptable interfaces, interactions, and processing for linked data platform components. *ACM International Conference Proceeding Series, 2017-September*, 41–48.

Kethineni, K. and Gera, P. (2023). Iot-based privacy-preserving anomaly detection model for smart agriculture. *Systems* 11(6): 304.

Kose, U., Prasath, V.B.S., Mondal, M.R.H., Podder, P. and Bharati, S. (2022). *Artificial Intelligence and Smart Agriculture Technology*. Auerbach Publications.

Krishnan, S., Anand, A.J., Prasanth, N., Goundar, S. and Ananth, C. (2023). *Predictive Analytics in Smart Agriculture*. CRC Press.

Liu, B., Guo, T., Luo, B., Cui, Z. and Yang, J. (2024). Cross-attention regression flow for defect detection. *IEEE Transactions on Image Processing* 33: 5183–5193.

Manoj, T., Makkithaya, K., Narendra, V.G. and Vijaya Murari, T. (2024). Blockchain oracles for decentralized agricultural insurance using trusted IoT data. *Frontiers in Blockchain* 7.

Mohamad, U.H., King, D.W.Y., Riza, M.A. bin and Ahmad, M.N. (2022). Emerging crop traceability systems in smart farming: A review. In *Proceedings of the International Conference on Computer, Information Technology and Intelligent Computing (CITIC 2022)*, 182–194. Atlantis Press.

Mukhtar, S., Bhat, J.A., Chesti, M.H., Ganie, M.A., Renuka, Mansoor, T. and Dolker, T. (2025). AI and smart technologies for smart agriculture environment. pp. 67–87. *In*: Jadhav, D.A., Khaple, S., Wable, P.S. and Chendake, A.D. (eds.). *Integrated Land and Water Resource Management for Sustainable Agriculture,* Volume 2. Springer, Singapore.

Murali, N., Kumar, A.S., Karunamurthy, A., Suseendra, R. and Manikandan, S. (2022). Intelligent outlier detection for smart farming application using deep neural network. *2022 IEEE 2nd International Conference on Mobile Networks and Wireless Communications, ICMNWC 2022*, 1–5.

Neethirajan, S. (2025). Safeguarding digital livestock farming—A comprehensive cybersecurity roadmap for dairy and poultry industries. *Frontiers in Big Data* 8.

Noor, M., Sithungu, S. and Lebea, K. (2024). An anomaly detection framework for IIoT-based smart farming systems. In *Intelligent Computing. SAI 2024. Lecture Notes in Networks and Systems*, Volume 1019, 396–409. Springer, Cham.

Padiya, S.D., Raut, A., Mittal, B., Patel, M. and Polshettiwar, V. (2023). Machine learning and IoT applications in agriculture. *International Journal of Advanced Research in Science, Communication and Technology* 3(6): 287–293.

Pasupuleti, M.K. (2025). Quantum AI for food security and sustainable agriculture. *Food Security and Sustainable Agriculture with Quantum AI,* 101–110. National Education Services.

Qadri, S., Malik, J.A., Shah, H., Raza, M.A., alsanoosy, T. and Saleem, M. (2024). Innovating with quantum computing approaches in block-chain for enhanced security and data privacy in agricultural IoT systems. pp. 339–370. *In*: Sumithra, M.G., Sathyamoorthy, M., Manikandan, M., Dhanaraj, R.K. and Ouaissa, M. (eds.). *Computational Intelligence in Internet of Agricultural Things. Studies in Computational Intelligence,* Volume 1170. Springer, Cham.

Raj, G., Unhelker, B. and Choudhary, A. (eds.). (2025). *Advances in Artificial Intelligence and Machine Learning*. Springer Nature.

Ranaveer, I., Rao, K.S., Renuka, K., Pachimatla, D., Kilari, R. and Ranitha, I.B. (2025). Exploring decentralized ledger technology to ensure the integrity and origin of visual data using ML algorithms. pp. 429–440. *In*: Gunjan, V.K. and Zurada, J.M. (eds.). *Proceedings of 5th International Conference on Recent Trends in Machine Learning, IoT, Smart Cities and Applications. ICMISC 2024. Lecture Notes in Networks and Systems,* Volume 1182. Springer, Singapore.

Romanova, Y.A. and Levina, E.V. (2020). Agriculture 4.0—A project of the future or a platform for responding to major challenges and threats to national security. *Market Economy Problems* 3: 84–94.

Rusev, M., Rusev, D., Tabakova-Komsalova, V. and Doukovska, L. (2024). Anomaly identification in a smart farming platform. *2024 IEEE 12th International Conference on Intelligent Systems (IS)*, 1–6.

Senthilkumar, D. (2020). Data confidentiality, integrity, and authentication. In *Research Anthology on Blockchain Technology in Business, Healthcare, Education, and Government, ed. Information Resources Management Association*, 459–487. IGI Global Scientific Publishing.

Shakeel, M., Krishnammal, P.M., Vekariya, V., Akram, S.V., Kumar, P.P. and Kapila, D. (2023). The design and implementation of a double layered security network with an authentication system through block chain technology. *2023 3rd International Conference on Advance Computing and Innovative Technologies in Engineering, ICACITE 2023*, 1469–1474.

Soussi, A., Zero, E., Sacile, R., Trinchero, D. and Fossa, M. (2024). Smart sensors and smart data for precision agriculture: A review. *Sensors* 24(8): 2647.

Strang, K.D. and Sun, Z. (2017). Big data paradigm: What is the status of privacy and security? *Annals of Data Science* 4(1): 1–17.

Suma, M.R. and Madhumathy, P. (2019). Acquisition and mining of agricultural data using ubiquitous sensors with internet of things. pp. 249–261. *In*: Smys, S., Bestak, R., Chen, J.Z. and Kotuliak, I. (eds.). *International Conference on Computer Networks and Communication Technologies. Lecture Notes on Data Engineering and Communications Technologies*, Volume 15. Springer, Singapore.

Tapia, J.Y. and Avila-Pesantez, D. (2021). Blockchain and IoT-challenges and its role in security: A brief overview. *2021 IEEE URUCON*, 504–507.

Voutos, Y., Drakopoulos, G. and Mylonas, P. (2019). Smart agriculture: An open field for smart contracts. *2019 4th South-East Europe Design Automation, Computer Engineering, Computer Networks and Social Media Conference, SEEDA-CECNSM 2019*, 1–6.

Wang, B.H. and Zhang, K.J. (2023). Impact of green digital finance on green economic recovery and green agricultural development: Implications for green environment. *Environmental Science and Pollution Research* 30(49): 107611–107623.

Wang, X., Seng Kai Kho, A., Liu, J., Mao, T., Gilchrist, M.D. and Zhang, N. (2025). Mechanistic modelling of coupled UV energy penetration and resin flow dynamics in digital light processing (DLP)-based microfluidic chip printing. *Micromachines* 16(2): 115.

Wang, X., Wu, Q., Zeng, H., Yang, X., Cui, H., Yi, X., Piran, Md. J., Luo, M. and Que, Y. (2025). Blockchain-empowered H-CPS architecture for smart agriculture. *Advanced Science* 12(27).

Wei, Z., Li, R., Jiang, K., Luo, Q., Sun, Z., Han, T., Bi, Z. and Wang, Y. (2024). PCS-ADS: Privacy computing system for agricultural data security. pp. 278–283. *In*: Zhang, W., Yue, Y. and Ogiela, M. (eds.). *Proceedings of the 2024 8th International Conference on Control Engineering and Artificial Intelligence*. Association for Computing Machinery.

Zhiqiang, Z., Quan, C.W., Xiaoming, D. and Ashok, P.V. (2019). Smart factory of Industry 4.0: Connection infrastructure, data acquisition, data processing, and applications. In *ASME 2019 14th International Manufacturing Science and Engineering Conference*, Volume 1. ASME.

Chapter 13

Advances in AI and Machine Learning for Risk Assessment in Agricultural Cybersecurity

A Systematic Review

Rahul Priyadarshi,[1,*] *Santosh K. Smmarwar*,[1] *Sibun Parida*,[1] *Pratik Angaitkar*[2] and *Subodh Mishra*[3]

Agricultural data security is critical as Internet of Things (IoT)-based smart farming systems generate vast amounts of sensitive information. This survey examines recent advancements in artificial intelligence (AI) and machine learning for risk assessment and threat detection in agricultural cybersecurity. We explore various machine learning models, including supervised, unsupervised, and reinforcement learning techniques, highlighting their applications in detecting cyber threats and assessing security risks. Additionally, we compare different datasets, evaluation metrics, and frameworks used in this domain. The chapter concludes with key insights into the limitations of current methodologies and suggests future research directions for strengthening cybersecurity in smart agriculture.

[1] Institute of Technical Education and Research, Siksha 'O' Anusandhan (Deemed to be University), Odisha, India.
[2] Department of Artificial Intelligence & Data Science, P.R. Pote Patil College of Engineering & Management, Maharashtra, India.
[3] Department of SCSET, Bennett University, Uttar Pradesh, India.
* Corresponding author: rahulpriyadarshi@soa.ac.in

DOI: 10.1201/9781003670568-13

1. Introduction

The agricultural sector is undergoing a remarkable digital transformation through the adoption of smart farming technologies. These technologies continuously generate real-time, high-volume agricultural data, facilitating data-driven decision-making throughout the supply chain, from crop monitoring and pest control to harvesting and logistics. This paradigm shift, often referred to as Agriculture 4.0, relies heavily on cyber-physical systems and interconnected infrastructures. However, while these advancements offer increased efficiency, productivity, and sustainability, they also introduce significant cybersecurity challenges. The growing reliance on digital infrastructure makes agricultural systems vulnerable to a wide array of cyber threats, including data breaches, ransomware, spoofing, and denial-of-service (DoS) attacks, which can disrupt critical operations, compromise sensitive information, and pose risks to food security (Ali et al., 2024).

The importance of cybersecurity in agriculture is underscored by the expanding attack surface introduced by distributed and remotely located Internet of Things (IoT)–based infrastructures. Many agricultural operations are resource-constrained and operate in isolated environments, making them especially prone to undetected and prolonged cyber intrusions. Furthermore, geopolitical motives or economic sabotage could also make agricultural systems attractive targets for adversaries. These vulnerabilities call for robust and context-aware cybersecurity strategies that go beyond traditional rule-based mechanisms, which often fall short in addressing the dynamic and evolving nature of cyber threats (Adewusi et al., 2022a).

In this context, artificial intelligence (AI) and machine learning (ML) have emerged as promising tools for proactive cybersecurity risk assessment in agriculture. ML algorithms are capable of identifying anomalies, predicting security breaches, and adapting to new threat patterns through data-driven insights. By leveraging supervised, unsupervised, and reinforcement learning (RL) approaches, these models can handle the complexity and scale of heterogeneous data generated by smart agricultural systems. Additionally, AI-powered frameworks can automate threat detection and response, making cybersecurity more scalable and efficient. RL techniques further enhance this potential by enabling systems to learn optimal defence strategies based on real-time interactions and feedback. Integrating AI and ML into agricultural cybersecurity infrastructure is thus essential for developing resilient, intelligent, and adaptive defences capable of protecting modern farming systems from emerging cyber risks (Kulkarni et al., 2024).

1.1 *Objectives and Scope*

This chapter presents a systematic review of recent advancements in AI and ML approaches for risk assessment and threat detection in agricultural cybersecurity. The key objectives of the chapter are:

- To analyse the state-of-the-art ML models used for detecting cyber threats in smart agriculture.
- To compare supervised, unsupervised, and RL methods applied in the domain.
- To review commonly used datasets, evaluation metrics, and experimental frameworks.
- To highlight limitations of existing techniques and suggest directions for future research.

The scope of this chapter encompasses a comprehensive review of peer-reviewed literature, practical applications, and challenges in deploying AI/ML solutions for cybersecurity in agricultural environments. The insights presented here aim to aid researchers, practitioners, and policymakers in developing secure, intelligent, and scalable smart farming systems.

2. Agricultural Cybersecurity: An Overview

The integration of digital technologies in agriculture has significantly enhanced productivity, precision, and sustainability. However, this digital transformation, often termed as Agriculture 4.0, also introduces a range of cybersecurity concerns due to the interconnected nature of modern farming infrastructures. Agricultural cybersecurity refers to the protection of digital assets, data, and infrastructure within agricultural systems from cyber threats that may lead to operational, financial, or environmental damage (Elbasi et al., 2022).

2.1 *Definition and Scope of Agricultural Cybersecurity*

Agricultural cybersecurity encompasses the strategies, practices, and technologies used to safeguard digital components of the agricultural ecosystem, including IoT devices, cloud platforms, communication networks, and data analytics systems. The scope of agricultural cybersecurity extends beyond farm-level protection; it includes supply chain security, data integrity, privacy of stakeholders, and the resilience of national food systems against cyber-attacks. Given the increasing reliance on sensors, drones, GPS technologies, and wireless communication, cybersecurity has become a critical pillar in ensuring the reliability and sustainability of smart farming operations (Ferrag et al., 2021).

2.2 *Typical Threats in Smart Farming Environments*

Smart farming environments are susceptible to a variety of cyber threats due to their heterogeneous and distributed nature. The common threats include:

- Data breaches resulting in unauthorized access to sensitive agricultural data such as yield statistics, proprietary farming methods, or location data.
- Denial-of-Service (DoS) attacks, which disrupt services such as automated irrigation or drone-based monitoring.
- Spoofing and man-in-the-middle attacks, where attackers manipulate communication between devices.
- Ransomware attacks, where critical farming infrastructure is locked in exchange for ransom payments.
- Firmware and software vulnerabilities, especially in devices that are infrequently updated or lack robust security protocols.

These threats not only compromise the confidentiality, integrity, and availability of data but also threaten operational continuity and stakeholder trust (Adewusi et al., 2022b).

2.3 *Role of IoT Devices and Data Vulnerabilities*

The IoT devices form the backbone of smart agriculture by providing continuous real-time monitoring and control capabilities. However, their proliferation also introduces numerous security risks. Many of these devices operate with limited computational resources, making it challenging to implement standard encryption and authentication mechanisms. Additionally, inconsistent firmware updates, lack of security-by-design principles, and insecure communication channels can expose the entire network to exploitation. The data generated by these devices is often transmitted to centralized platforms or cloud services, further increasing the risk of interception, manipulation, or unauthorized access. These vulnerabilities necessitate the development of intelligent, lightweight, and adaptive security mechanisms to protect data confidentiality and system integrity across the agricultural IoT ecosystem (Kang, 2023).

2.4 Case Examples of Cyber Incidents in Agriculture

While agricultural cybersecurity remains an emerging discipline, several real-world incidents highlight its growing importance:

- In 2021, a ransomware attack on a major grain cooperative in the US disrupted grain processing and storage operations, affecting food supply chains.
- Attackers have exploited GPS spoofing techniques to mislead autonomous tractors and drones, resulting in operational inefficiencies.
- Researchers have demonstrated vulnerabilities in smart irrigation systems, where unauthorized access could lead to water misuse or sabotage.
- In another reported case, malware infections in greenhouse control systems resulted in crop damage due to temperature regulation failures.

These examples underline the urgent need for resilient cybersecurity frameworks tailored to agricultural environments. Figure 13.1 depicts interconnected IoT devices such as drones, sensors, and autonomous tractors transmitting data within a digitally secured environment, symbolizing the intersection of agriculture, technology, and cyber defence. This visual emphasizes the importance of securing smart farming infrastructures against evolving cyber threats. A comprehensive understanding of threat vectors, vulnerabilities, and attack consequences

Figure 13.1: Smart farm under cyber shield.

4.3 *Behaviour-based Threat Models*

Behaviour-based models analyse user or device activity over time to build dynamic profiles and detect deviations that suggest potential threats. These models often use time-series data, Markov models, or recurrent neural networks (RNNs).

A simple behaviour-based threat score can be computed using a Markov Chain, where the probability of transitioning from state s_i to state s_j is given by:

$$P_{ij} = \frac{N_{ij}}{\Sigma_k N_{ik}}$$

where N_{ij} = number of transitions from s_i to s_j, $\Sigma_k N_{ik}$ = total transitions from s_i.

Unexpected transitions with low probabilities may indicate abnormal behaviour and trigger alerts. For example, if a soil sensor suddenly starts communicating with unauthorized servers, the model would assign a high threat score to that event.

5. Datasets, Evaluation Metrics, and Experimental Frameworks

To effectively design and evaluate ML models for cybersecurity in smart agriculture, the availability of appropriate datasets and evaluation frameworks is crucial. This section explores publicly available datasets used in agricultural cybersecurity, the key performance metrics adopted for assessing AI/ML models, and commonly used experimental setups for validating proposed techniques.

5.1 *Publicly Available Datasets*

The development and benchmarking of ML models for agricultural cybersecurity heavily depend on the availability of large, labelled datasets that closely mimic real-world smart farming environments. However, due to privacy concerns and the niche nature of agricultural IoT, domain-specific datasets are scarce. As a result, researchers often rely on generalized cybersecurity datasets to simulate agricultural scenarios. Notable among these are *NSL-KDD*, an improved version of the *KDD'99* dataset widely used for IDS evaluation; *CICIDS 2017*, which offers realistic network traffic flows with labelled attacks such as DDoS, brute force, and botnets; *UNSW-NB15*, which includes modern attack profiles with rich traffic features; and *TON_IoT*, which is particularly relevant due to its inclusion of telemetry data from IoT sensors and corresponding cyber-attack logs, making it ideal for emulating smart agriculture conditions. In the absence of sufficient domain-specific datasets, researchers frequently generate synthetic data through testbeds or simulation platforms like Cooja (for Contiki OS), GNS3, or Mininet to evaluate the performance of AI/ML-based cybersecurity models.

6. Comparative Analysis of Existing Approaches

This section provides a detailed comparative analysis of ML-based cybersecurity models applied in the agricultural domain. It highlights the advantages, limitations, and effectiveness of different AI/ML algorithms, based on various criteria such as accuracy, adaptability, scalability, and computational efficiency.

6.1 Supervised Learning Approaches

Supervised learning in agricultural cybersecurity leverages labelled datasets to train models that can classify activities as benign or malicious. This approach is valuable in identifying known threats within smart farming environments where IoT devices generate vast data streams. Common algorithms include Support Vector Machines (SVM), Random Forest (RF), Decision Trees (DT), and Artificial Neural Networks (ANNs). These models offer high accuracy when trained on clean and well-annotated data, with tree-based methods providing interpretability and SVMs excelling in high-dimensional environments. However, their effectiveness is constrained by the availability and quality of labelled data, making them less suitable for detecting zero-day or unknown attacks. Additionally, their performance may not generalize well across diverse and dynamic agricultural settings, where device heterogeneity and environmental variability are prevalent. Despite these challenges, supervised learning forms the foundation of many initial threat detection systems in smart farming and can be powerful when integrated with complementary methods. Table 13.1 and Figure 13.2 present the evaluation

Table 13.1: Performance comparison of supervised learning models in agricultural cybersecurity.

Model	Accuracy	Precision	Recall	F1 Score	Remarks
SVM	93%	0.91	0.92	0.91	Good generalization, needs tuning
RF	95%	0.94	0.93	0.93	Robust to overfitting
ANN	92%	0.90	0.91	0.90	Requires large training data

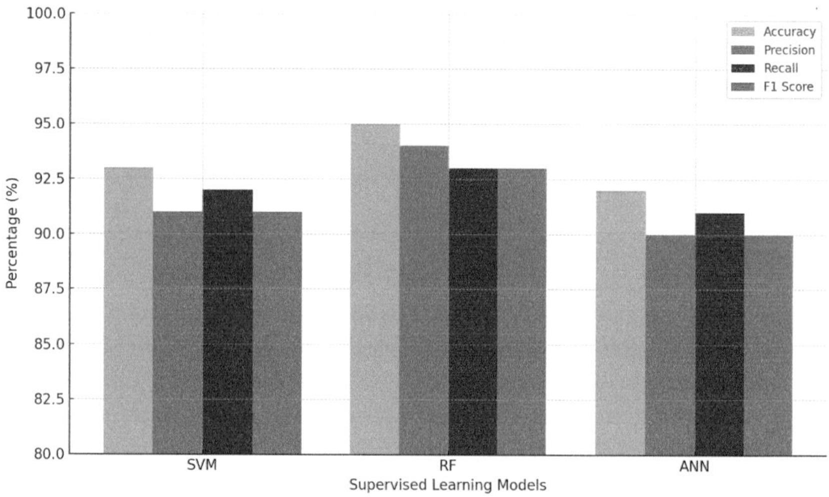

Figure 13.2: Performance comparison of supervised ML models in agricultural cybersecurity.

metrics accuracy, precision, recall, and F1-score for commonly used supervised learning algorithms such as SVM, RF, and ANN, along with qualitative remarks on their suitability.

6.2 *Unsupervised Learning Approaches*

They are capable of identifying zero-day and stealth attacks, thereby reducing reliance on pre-labelled datasets and enhancing the system's adaptability to evolving threats. However, their effectiveness is often influenced by the quality of input features, and they can struggle with noisy or high-dimensional data. Additionally, clustering results may be difficult to interpret in real time, which poses a challenge for practical deployment. A comparison of popular models shows that Autoencoders achieve a higher detection rate (88%) with fewer false positives and moderate interpretability and scalability, while K-Means and DBSCAN offer reasonable detection capabilities with varying trade-offs in scalability and interpretability. Table 13.2 highlights the effectiveness of unsupervised models like K-Means, Autoencoders, and DBSCAN in

Table 13.2: Evaluation of unsupervised learning models for threat detection.

Model	Detection Rate	False Positives	Interpretability	Scalability
K-Means	80%	Moderate	Low	High
Autoencoders	88%	Low	Moderate	High
DBSCAN	83%	Moderate	Moderate	Moderate

detecting unknown threats, assessing them based on detection rate, false positives, interpretability, and scalability.

6.3 RL Approaches

Reinforcement learning is emerging as a promising approach in agricultural cybersecurity due to its ability to provide adaptive, real-time defence mechanisms against evolving cyber threats. These methods can dynamically respond to cyber threats without explicit programming by learning from experience. The key strengths of RL lie in its adaptability, suitability for real-time decision-making, and reduced reliance on human intervention. However, RL approaches come with challenges like high computational demands, long training durations, and sensitivity to reward design. A comparative summary of key RL algorithms highlights their trade-offs in learning time, reward schemes, and application suitability in agricultural environments. Table 13.3 summarizes key characteristics of RL techniques such as Q-Learning, Deep Q-Network (DQN), and Actor-Critic, focusing on learning environment, time, reward structure, and use case examples in smart farming security.

In contrast, unsupervised learning does not depend on labelled data and is highly effective for identifying unknown or stealthy attacks, though it may suffer from noisy data and lower real-time applicability. RL stands out for its adaptability and real-time decision-making capabilities, learning optimal defence strategies through interaction with dynamic environments; however, its implementation is computationally intensive and still in early stages for smart agriculture applications. As summarized in Table 13.4, each learning type exhibits distinct trade-offs across criteria like scalability, interpretability, and real-time suitability. Therefore, the ideal cybersecurity solution in agriculture should be context-driven: lightweight supervised models for smaller farms, and hybrid or RL-based systems for large-scale smart farming. Future research should explore integrated frameworks that leverage the strengths of all three approaches

Table 13.3: Reinforcement learning algorithms and their application characteristics in agriculture.

RL Algorithm	Environment	Learning Time	Reward Type	Application Example
Q-Learning	Tabular	Fast	Fixed Reward Values	Node-level anomaly detection
DQN	Continuous	Slow	Dynamic	Intrusion Response System
Actor-Critic	Complex	Medium	Optimized policies	Automated threat mitigation

Table 13.4: Comparative summary of ML approaches in agricultural cybersecurity.

Criteria	Supervised Learning	Unsupervised Learning	Reinforcement Learning
Need for Labels	Yes	No	Yes (environment rewards)
Novel Threat Detection	Limited	High	High
Interpretability	High (e.g., RF, DT)	Medium	Low to Medium
Real-Time Suitability	Medium	Medium	High
Computational Cost	Low to Medium	Medium	High
Scalability	High	High	Medium

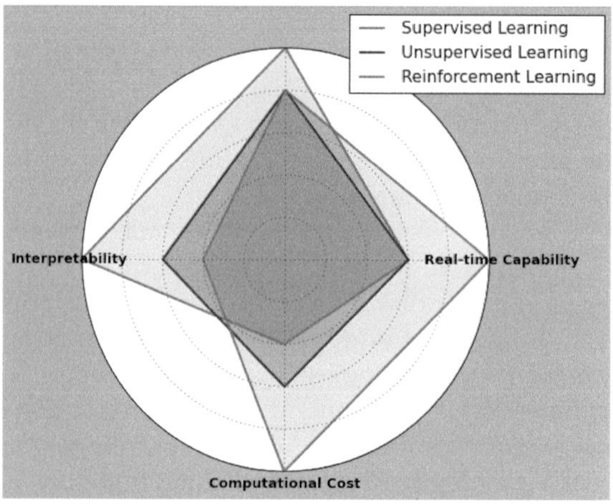

Figure 13.3: Performance comparison of supervised ML models in agricultural cybersecurity.

to develop intelligent, adaptive, and scalable agricultural cybersecurity architectures. Radar chart comparing supervised, unsupervised, and RL approaches in agricultural cybersecurity based on four key criteria: real-time capability, accuracy, interpretability, and computational cost. Figure 13.3 illustrates the trade-offs among different ML paradigms, highlighting the strengths of RL in adaptability and real-time response, while showcasing the interpretability and accuracy of supervised learning.

7. Applications and Case Studies

This section presents real-world applications, simulated scenarios, and pilot projects that demonstrate the effectiveness of AI/ML in enhancing agricultural cybersecurity.

7.1 Real-World Applications of AI in Agriculture Cybersecurity

Artificial intelligence has begun to penetrate the agricultural domain through a variety of cybersecurity use cases:

- *Secure Smart Irrigation Systems*: Smart irrigation platforms are often controlled via cloud-based applications or remote servers. AI algorithms, particularly anomaly detection models, are deployed to monitor sensor data (like soil moisture, humidity, or valve status) for unusual activity. These models can raise alerts if they detect manipulated data inputs or unauthorized control commands.
- *Drone and UAV Communication Security*: Unmanned aerial vehicles (UAVs) used in aerial mapping and pesticide spraying are increasingly integrated with AI to ensure secure and encrypted communication. AI models monitor for spoofing attacks or unauthorized data interception during drone operations.
- *Blockchain-AI Integration*: In supply chain tracking and crop lifecycle management, AI is used alongside blockchain technology to ensure the integrity and authenticity of agricultural data. AI algorithms verify transaction consistency and detect anomalies that might indicate tampering or fraud.

7.2 Simulated Scenarios Demonstrating Risk Assessment

Since real-time testing of cyber-attacks in live agricultural systems can be risky and impractical, simulation-based evaluation is commonly adopted. These simulations replicate threat scenarios and assess how AI models perform under cyber stress.

- Case 1: Smart Greenhouse Anomaly Detection

  A simulated attack is carried out by injecting false temperature readings into a greenhouse monitoring system. An autoencoder-based anomaly detection model is tested to identify the abnormal patterns. Results show that the model effectively detects the intrusion with a 92% detection rate and low false positives.

- Case 2: RL in Threat Response

  A simulation environment mimics various cyber-attacks (e.g., data injection, denial of service) on a smart farm network. A DQN is trained to respond optimally by isolating infected nodes and rerouting data. Over time, the model learns to minimize successful attacks and maintain system uptime.

- Case 3: IoT Device Hijacking Simulation

  A simulated scenario involves unauthorized access to field sensors used in a crop monitoring system. An SVM classifier, pre-trained on labelled data, is deployed to identify malicious commands. The model demonstrates over 90% accuracy in preventing unauthorized control.

These simulated environments validate the effectiveness of different AI models and help fine-tune algorithms before deployment in real farms.

7.3 Pilot Projects or Industry Use Cases

Several pilot projects and industry use cases have demonstrated the transformative role of AI in strengthening agricultural cybersecurity. The AgriSense EU Project leverages ML to detect anomalies in livestock behaviour and sensor data, offering early warnings against cyber threats. In the US, John Deere's smart tractors utilize AI to secure firmware updates and detect intrusions, ensuring operational integrity. IBM and Cisco, in collaboration with agri-tech startups, deploy edge AI models that process data locally, reducing cloud exposure and enhancing real-time threat detection. In Australia, the PACyberLab develops hybrid AI models for comprehensive threat assessment across precision farming systems. These initiatives collectively underscore AI's critical role in securing smart agriculture, highlighting the need for adaptive, layered defence strategies powered by supervised, unsupervised, and RL techniques.

8. Challenges and Limitations

While AI and ML (AI/ML) offer promising solutions for enhancing cybersecurity in agriculture, their implementation is not without significant challenges. This section outlines the core limitations, concerns, and technical barriers that currently hinder the full-scale deployment of AI-driven security frameworks in the agricultural domain.

8.1 Limitations in Current ML Models

Despite high accuracy and efficiency in experimental settings, current ML models exhibit several limitations when applied in real-world agricultural environments:

- *High Dependence on Quality Data*: Many ML algorithms, especially supervised ones, rely heavily on the availability of high-quality, labelled data. However, in agriculture, annotated cybersecurity datasets are scarce, making model training and validation difficult.

- *Lack of Contextual Understanding*: ML models often struggle with understanding the broader context of an agricultural event or cyber incident. For example, distinguishing between a malfunction and a cyber-attack can be difficult without domain-specific knowledge.
- *Model Overfitting*: Models trained on limited or homogeneous data may overfit to specific environments and perform poorly in diverse agricultural setups, such as varying climate zones or crop types.

8.2 Data Privacy and Ethical Concerns

The integration of AI in cybersecurity requires access to large volumes of operational and personal data, leading to significant privacy and ethical issues:

- *Sensitive Farmer Data*: AI systems often collect detailed data on land use, crop health, irrigation schedules, and financial transactions. Mishandling or unauthorized access to this data can compromise farmer privacy.
- *Consent and Ownership*: It is often unclear who owns the data collected by AI systems—the farmer, the platform provider, or the government. This ambiguity leads to ethical concerns about usage rights, especially in cross-border cloud-based services.
- *Bias and Discrimination*: ML models trained on biased data may reinforce inequalities. For instance, systems might prioritize cybersecurity in high-income regions or large farms, ignoring smallholder farmers in rural or underdeveloped areas.

8.3 Generalization and Model Robustness Issues

The AI systems developed in one agricultural context may not generalize well to others due to differences in infrastructure, crops, and environmental conditions:

- *Domain Shift*: A model trained on data from one geographic region or crop type might perform poorly when applied elsewhere due to domain variability (soil, temperature, pest patterns).
- *Adversarial Vulnerabilities*: Many AI models are susceptible to adversarial attacks, where small perturbations in the input can deceive the model. This is a critical risk in cybersecurity systems that must withstand intentional tampering.
- *Model Drift*: Over time, the characteristics of data and attacks evolve. Without periodic retraining, models become outdated and less effective in detecting new threats.

8.4 Interoperability of Security Frameworks

Agriculture involves a mix of devices, platforms, and stakeholders, making interoperability a significant concern:

- *Heterogeneous Devices*: Smart farms use sensors, UAVs, irrigation controllers, and tractors from various manufacturers. Ensuring that AI-driven cybersecurity solutions work seamlessly across this diverse ecosystem is challenging.
- *Lack of Standard Protocols*: There is no unified cybersecurity standard for smart agriculture systems. This lack of harmonization complicates the deployment and integration of ML-based security tools.
- *Integration with Legacy Systems*: Many farms still operate older or semi-automated systems. Integrating modern AI frameworks with these legacy infrastructures without disrupting operations is technically demanding.

The challenges facing AI/ML applications in agricultural cybersecurity are multifaceted. While technological progress is promising, real-world deployment requires overcoming significant barriers, including data limitations, privacy concerns, generalization issues, and infrastructure heterogeneity.

9. Conclusion

This study presented a comprehensive analysis of how ML models are transforming cybersecurity in the agricultural domain. Through the comparative evaluation of supervised, unsupervised, and RL approaches, we identified that each paradigm has unique strengths and limitations. Supervised models offer high accuracy when labelled data is available but struggle with unknown threats. Unsupervised methods excel in detecting anomalies without prior labels, while RL shows promise for real-time, adaptive defence mechanisms in dynamic environments. ML is no longer optional but a critical enabler of smart and secure agriculture. Its role extends beyond detection and response providing predictive insights, minimizing human intervention, and enhancing system autonomy. However, challenges remain, including data privacy concerns, generalization issues, and the interoperability of various security frameworks. Looking ahead, the development of robust, ethical, and scalable AI-driven security solutions in agriculture will demand multidisciplinary collaboration bridging gaps among data scientists, agronomists, cybersecurity professionals, and policymakers. Moreover, a globally coordinated effort is essential to build resilient food systems that are protected from the growing spectrum of cyber threats in the digital era.

References

Abdullahi, M., Baashar, Y., Alhussian, H., Alwadain, A., Aziz, N., Capretz, L.F. and Abdulkadir, S.J. (2022). Detecting cybersecurity attacks in internet of things using artificial intelligence methods: A systematic literature review. *Electronics* 11(2): 198.

Adewusi, A.O., Chiekezie, N.R. and Eyo-Udo, N.L. (2022a). Cybersecurity threats in agriculture supply chains: A comprehensive review. *World Journal of Advanced Research and Reviews* 15(3): 490–500.

Adewusi, A.O., Chiekezie, N.R. and Eyo-Udo, N.L. (2022b). The role of AI in enhancing cybersecurity for smart farms. *World Journal of Advanced Research and Reviews* 15(3): 501–512.

Aldhyani, T.H. and Alkahtani, H. (2023). Cyber security for detecting distributed denial of service attacks in Agriculture 4.0: Deep learning model. *Mathematics* 11(1): 233.

Ali, G., Mijwil, M.M., Buruga, B.A., Abotaleb, M. and Adamopoulos, I. (2024). A survey on artificial intelligence in cybersecurity for smart agriculture: State-of-the-art, cyber threats, artificial intelligence applications, and ethical concerns. *Mesopotamian Journal of Computer Science* 2024: 53–103.

Elbasi, E., Mostafa, N., AlArnaout, Z., Zreikat, A.I., Cina, E., Varghese, G. and Zaki, C. (2022). Artificial Intelligence technology in the agricultural sector: A systematic literature review. *IEEE Access* 11: 171–202.

Ferrag, M.A., Shu, L., Friha, O. and Yang, X. (2021). Cyber security intrusion detection for agriculture 4.0: Machine learning-based solutions, datasets, and future directions. *IEEE/CAA Journal of Automatica Sinica* 9(3): 407–436.

Kang, Y. (2023). Development of large-scale farming based on explainable machine learning for a sustainable rural economy: The case of cyber risk analysis to prevent costly data breaches. *Applied Artificial Intelligence* 37(1): 2223862.

Kulkarni, A., Wang, Y., Gopinath, M., Sobien, D., Rahman, A. and Batarseh, F.A. (2024). A review of cybersecurity incidents in the food and agriculture sector. *arXiv preprint arXiv:2403.08036*.

Kumar, S. and Faisal, M. (2024). Critical review of cybersecurity risks in precision agriculture. In *2024 Second International Conference Computational and Characterization Techniques in Engineering & Sciences (IC3TES)*, 1–7. IEEE.

Chapter 14

Applications of Blockchain and Cryptography for Secure Cloud Data Transmission in Agricultural IoT and Beyond

Abdhisuta Dash, Subham Kumar Sahoo,
Sugyan Kumar Mishra and *Sambit Kumar Mishra**

Agriculture, the foundation of human civilization, is undergoing dramatic transformation driven by the Internet of Things (IoT). IoT devices are enabling farmers to boost yields, reduce waste, and guarantee a safer and more sustainable food supply chain through everything from accurate crop health monitoring to resource optimization and improved food traceability. However, there are serious risks of illegal access, data manipulation, and privacy violations as data moves through cloud-based platforms. These weaknesses may result in poor decision-making, financial damage, and hazards to the safety of food. Blockchain technology is revolutionary because it offers a decentralized, secure foundation for protecting agricultural data. Together with more sophisticated cryptographic methods like homomorphic encryption and zero-knowledge proofs, it forms a strong framework for guaranteeing

SRM University-AP, Andhra Pradesh, India.
* Corresponding author: sambitkumar.m@srmap.edu.in

DOI: 10.1201/9781003670568-14

data security and privacy. This chapter explores how blockchain and cryptography might be combined to address these pressing problems, providing innovative solutions including safe data storage, decentralized sharing systems, and smart contracts that facilitate effective and transparent transactions. We offer a thorough examination of the most recent developments and enduring difficulties in agricultural data management by classifying blockchain applications and investigating fundamental components including consensus mechanisms and cryptography tools. We show how blockchain technology may transform agriculture, from enhancing the traceability of the food supply chain to resolving the issues of unreliable stakeholders. This chapter also emphasizes the broader potential of these technologies, showcasing their scalability to other domains and their capacity to drive innovation in sustainable resource management and data security.

1. Introduction

The Internet of Things (IoT) has rapidly advanced, resulting in revolutionary applications in a variety of fields. IoT-enabled solutions have greatly improved productivity, visibility, and decision-making, particularly in agriculture. In order to monitor environmental conditions, maximize resource usage, and guarantee effective decision-making, IoT systems in smart agriculture combine wireless sensors, automated control technologies, and real-time data processing. It has been demonstrated that this strategy supports accurate data gathering and real-time monitoring for increased productivity while also saving time and money (Ren et al., 2021).

1.1 IoT in Agriculture Overview

In order to improve farming sustainability and efficiency, smart agriculture integrates cutting-edge technologies like blockchain, IoT, cloud, and artificial intelligence (AI). Drones and other IoT devices, such as sensors, gather data on crop health, weather, and soil conditions in real time. Cloud is used to store the data in the server. AI algorithms are used to analyse this data in order to predict yields, optimize resource use, and automate processes like pest management and irrigation. Blockchain preserves data integrity and builds trust by ensuring safe and transparent data sharing across stakeholders. Smart agriculture promotes sustainable agricultural practices, reduces environmental impact, and increases productivity by facilitating precision farming and data-driven decision-making (Ahmed et al., 2024).

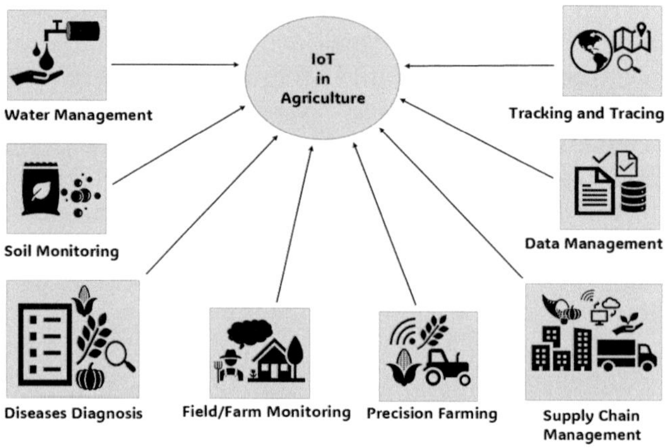

Figure 14.1: IoT in agriculture.

The use cases of IoT in precision farming are shown in Figure 14.1, which is adapted and modified from Vinueza-Naranjo et al. (2021). Smart farming, known as precision agriculture, uses data-driven insights from drones, IoT sensors, and other technology to deliver real-time information on weather patterns, crop health, and soil conditions. With the use of these insights, supply chain actors, farmers, and researchers can make well-informed decisions that improve sustainability and productivity (Kalimuthu and PrabuPelavendran, 2024). However, the safety and precision of agricultural operations may be jeopardized by hostile assaults such as altered data and system breaches, which are made more likely by the increasing interconnectedness of equipment (Ahmed et al., 2024).

1.2 Cloud-based Data Exchange Challenges and the Role of Cryptography and Blockchain

Although the aforementioned technologies work well for centralized management, traditional cloud-based data storage systems pose problems such as lack of transparency, single points of failure, and data manipulation. These issues highlight the need for robust, decentralized solutions capable of ensuring data security, traceability, and authenticity (Ahmed et al., 2024). With its distributed ledger features, blockchain technology offers a viable framework for overcoming these obstacles. Blockchain strengthens the robustness of IoT systems against cyber-attacks and promotes trust in data transactions by using features including transparent recording, tamper-proof storage, and secure data sharing (Ferrag et al., 2020).

Blockchain in precision agriculture enhances data integration and analysis across disparate platforms in addition to facilitating safe data sharing. This facilitates the deployment of automated decision-making systems for improved crop production and resource management as well as a more thorough understanding of agricultural ecosystems (Kalimuthu and PrabuPelavendran, 2024; Vangala et al., 2020). The combination of blockchain and IoT stands out as a crucial innovation for attaining sustainable and effective farming practices as agriculture continues to incorporate cutting-edge technologies (Vangala et al., 2020).

2. Blockchain Technology for Protecting Agricultural Data

Blockchain is used in agriculture for various applications, such as precision farming (Torky and Hassanein, 2020), livestock tracking and management (Iqbal and Butt, 2020), sustainable farming practices (Akella et al., 2023), agricultural insurance (Nguyen et al., 2019), food waste management (Jiang et al., 2023), farmer-to-consumer markets (Takale et al., 2024), pest disease control (Rahman et al., 2024), water management systems (Pincheira et al., 2021), fish farming, and aquaculture (Hang et al., 2020). These applications of blockchain technology in agriculture address critical data security, integrity, and transparency challenges. As a data-intensive industry, agriculture requires strong safeguards to protect sensitive data, such as supply chain records, crop data, soil conditions, and weather patterns. The decentralized and immutable characteristics of blockchain provide a safe foundation for data management, facilitating smooth and resistant transactions across different agricultural ecosystem stakeholders.

2.1 *Essential Blockchain Features for Secure Data Transfer*

Blockchain technology offers a suite of features that make it an ideal solution for secure and efficient data management (Rajasekaran et al., 2022; Nakamoto, 2009). Immutability guarantees that data cannot be changed or removed once it is stored on the blockchain, protecting data integrity and removing the possibility of manipulation (Gad et al., 2022; Bairagi and Bang, 2015; Murthy et al., 2020). Transparency promotes accountability and trust by enabling all parties to view a shared ledger with transparent and verifiable transactions (Murthy et al., 2020; Arulananth et al., 2021; Liu et al., 2023). Decentralization reduces single points of failure and distributes control throughout a network of nodes, doing away with the need for central authorities (Rajasekaran et al., 2022). Cryptographic techniques are used to achieve security by preventing unwanted access and protecting sensitive data (Liu et al., 2023). As the blockchain links and validates data blocks continuously, data integrity is maintained, guaranteeing correctness and consistency throughout time. Auditability enables seamless tracking and verification of transactions (Salah et al., 2019). It allows stakeholders to trace the history of any entry. Last, but not the least, consensus procedures that guarantee that all participants agree on the accuracy of the data build a strong and reliable system. These characteristics collectively make blockchain a game-changing solution for transparent and secure data ecosystems (Rajasekaran et al., 2022; Guo and Yu, 2022; Li et al., 2021). Figure 14.2 shows the different features of the blockchain that we discussed.

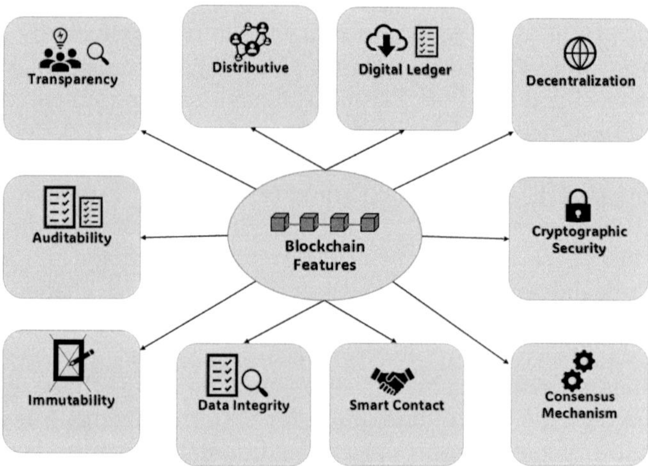

Figure 14.2: Features of blockchain.

2.2 *Agricultural Data Management and Strengthening Transparency in the Food Supply Chain*

The complexity of the global food supply chain is growing, which raises questions regarding sustainability, traceability, and transparency. Building trust with stakeholders and customers requires transparency, which makes sure that each stage of the supply chain is transparent and verifiable. By providing decentralized and immutable data storage, blockchain-enabled cloud computing improves transparency by enabling stakeholders to monitor items from their point of origin to the end user and receive real-time updates (Astill et al., 2019). By addressing issues like the 2013 European horse meat crisis, where dishonest tactics damaged customer confidence and brought attention to the need for dependable, impenetrable systems, this integration reduces information asymmetry (Astill et al., 2019).

Another crucial component of managing the food supply chain is traceability, especially when it comes to reducing the risks of contamination and foodborne illnesses. Modern supply chains are too complicated for traditional approaches, like Canada's "one-step back and one-step forward" regulation. By establishing a single, decentralized ledger that safely logs each transaction in the supply chain, blockchain-enabled cloud computing gets beyond these restrictions (Trienekens et al., 2012). In order to significantly improve response times during food safety emergencies, Walmart's blockchain testing for mangoes showed that time taken for tracking the origin of a tainted product may be cut down from days to seconds (Trienekens et al., 2012). Blockchain technologies improve accountability and efficiency in addressing traceability issues by guaranteeing that documents are easily available and impenetrable.

Blockchain-enabled cloud computing also has a revolutionary effect in sustainability, which includes social, economic, and environmental aspects. By combining these technologies, food waste is decreased, inefficiencies are reduced, and procedures are streamlined. Walmart has demonstrated how blockchain technology could potentially be used to streamline farm-to-fork processing times, guaranteeing fresh fruit reaches customers while lowering carbon footprints (Wognum et al., 2011). The real-time data that blockchain can provide also aids in locating supply chain operational inefficiencies, leading to enhancements that promote sustainability. Additionally, by isolating and removing just impacted batches during foodborne outbreaks, blockchain systems reduce economic losses and prevent broad waste and financial consequences (Wognum et al., 2011).

By tackling the major issues of sustainability, traceability, and transparency, blockchain-enabled cloud computing is completely changing the food supply chain. These technologies improve trust, guarantee accountability, and encourage sustainable practices by providing secure, decentralized, and real-time data solutions. Real-world applications, like Walmart's blockchain initiatives, demonstrate the transformative potential of blockchain integration. This makes blockchain a cornerstone for future food supply chain management (Astill et al., 2019; Trienekens et al., 2012; Wognum et al., 2011).

3. Enhanced Privacy Cryptographic Techniques

Advanced cryptographic algorithms have become essential enablers as the need for safe and private data processing increases across digital ecosystems, particularly in cloud, blockchain, and IoT-based infrastructures. These methods seek to provide privacy-preserving computations without sacrificing efficiency or confidence, in addition to protecting data during transmission and storage. The need for improved privacy is critical in the agricultural industry, as sensitive data including supply chain records, weather patterns, crop yields, and soil health metrics are being digitized and shared across decentralized platforms. These data-driven agricultural applications are crucially secured by enhanced privacy cryptographic techniques like homomorphic encryption, zero-knowledge proofs, and cryptographic mechanisms in blockchain systems, which guarantee that farmers, suppliers, and customers can communicate in a secure, transparent, and confidential environment.

3.1 Homomorphic Encryption Overview

A transformative cryptographic technique called homomorphic encryption (HE) enables calculations to be done directly on encrypted data (ciphertext) without the need to decrypt it. This guarantees the confidentiality of sensitive data during the computing process. When we perform a mathematical operation on the encrypted data (ciphertext) and then decrypt it, the result will be the same as if we performed the same operation on the original data (plaintext) before encrypting it. This ensures that the data remains accurate and confidential (Regueiro et al., 2021; Kumar et al., 2022; Geng et al., 2019).

Traditionally, encryption techniques depend on a reliable third party to perform calculations, necessitating data decryption and sometimes compromising confidentiality. On the other hand, HE makes it unnecessary to decrypt data while it is being computed, enabling other parties to process encrypted data without having access to the original values. The encryption key secures plaintext, while the decryption key enables access only for authorized parties, ensuring data privacy even during processing (Regueiro et al., 2021; Kumar et al., 2022; Geng et al., 2019).

Homomorphic encryption can be categorized into three main types based on the operations supported and their frequency:

(i) *Partially Homomorphic Encryption (PHE)*: A single mathematical operation, such addition or multiplication, can be applied to ciphertext indefinitely with PHE (Regueiro et al., 2021; Geng et al., 2019). El-Gamal, Paillier, and RSA encryption techniques are notable examples.

(ii) *Somewhat Homomorphic Encryption (SHE)*: A restricted amount of addition and multiplication operations are allowed by SHE before the ciphertext becomes unmanageable due to encryption noise. One important example in this category is Boneh–Goh–Nissim (BGN) encryption (Regueiro et al., 2021; Geng et al., 2019).

(iii) *Fully Homomorphic Encryption (FHE)*: It facilitates arbitrary calculations by permitting an infinite number of additions and multiplications on ciphertexts. Despite being extremely safe, FHE requires a lot of computation, which makes it difficult to use in practice (Regueiro et al., 2021; Geng et al., 2019).

Figure 14.3 shows the workflow of computation of data in an encrypted manner.

1. Plaintext Input by User: The user starts with the original data in plaintext form.
2. Encryption: This plaintext data is encrypted using a public key, resulting in encrypted data (ciphertext). The original data is now protected and unreadable to unauthorized parties.
3. Data Sent to Cloud or Server: The encrypted data is sent to an untrusted server or cloud where the computation needs to occur. The cloud receives and handles only the ciphertext, never the original data.
4. Computation on Encrypted Data: The cloud performs computations directly on the encrypted data using homomorphic operations. The result is an encrypted version of the final output (still ciphertext).
5. Encrypted Result Sent Back to User: The server returns the computed encrypted result to the user.
6. Decryption by User: The user decrypts the result using a private key, revealing the modified plaintext output.

Since Rivest et al., first conceptualized HE as "privacy homomorphism" in 1978 (Geng et al., 2019; Rivest et al., 1978), the field has advanced significantly. Fundamental ideas were presented by the RSA and Goldwasser-Micali algorithms, which made it possible to perform particular algebraic operations on ciphertexts, such as addition and multiplication (Geng et al., 2019; Shafi and Micali, 1984). Later developments that supported several operations, including the BGN cryptosystem in 2005 (Boneh et al., 2005) and Paillier encryption in 1999 (Paillier, 1999), expanded the scope (Kumar et al., 2022; Geng et al., 2019;

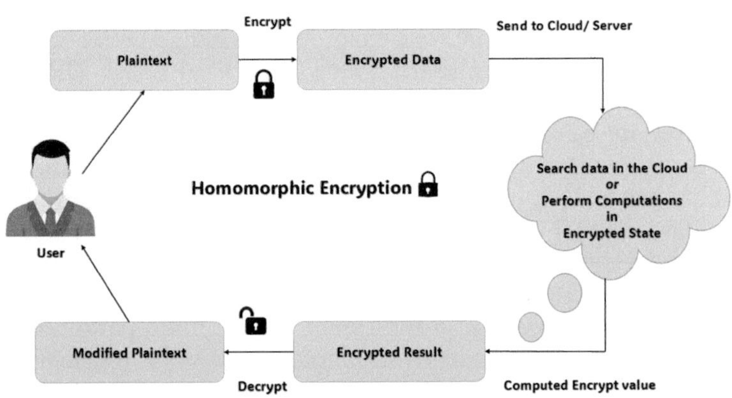

Figure 14.3: Homomorphic encryption.

Boneh et al., 2005). An important turning point was reached in 2009 with Gentry's revolutionary completely HE system, which allowed for infinite operations on ciphertext using methods like bootstrapping and lattice-based constructs (Geng et al., 2019; Shafi and Micali, 1984).

Homomorphic encryption is being employed in contemporary applications to improve cloud computing infrastructures' security and adaptability. Users can make sure that only they have the decryption key by encrypting data before sending it to the cloud. This keeps sensitive data out of the hands of cloud administrators or operators.

This method allows cloud systems to have strong computing capabilities while also improving data security (Sun et al., 2020).

With applications ranging from cloud computing to secure machine learning to encrypted communication, HE has become a key component of privacy-preserving technology. It is an essential tool for protecting sensitive data in increasingly data-driven environments since it can process encrypted data without sacrificing privacy.

3.2 *Zero-Knowledge Proofs for Secure Data Sharing*

Zero-knowledge proofs (ZKPs) are a novel cryptographic technique that allows one party to demonstrate to another the accuracy of information without revealing the underlying data, guaranteeing strong privacy and security in sensitive data transfers (Ramezan and Meamari, 2024; Zhang et al., 2024). For applications where confidentiality is crucial, such as identity verification, safe financial transactions, and handling sensitive data, this feature makes ZKPs important (Ramezan and Meamari, 2024; Zhang et al., 2024). ZKPs have emerged as a key component of blockchain systems by guaranteeing privacy-preserving authentication, which reduces the risks of data leakage during verification procedures while boosting confidence in decentralized environments (Ramezan and Meamari, 2024; Zhang et al., 2024). ZKPs provide an essential security layer in edge computing by enabling safe, real-time data exchange across dispersed networks without affecting user privacy (Feng et al., 2022; Zhou et al., 2024). This functionality is very helpful in traditional centralized systems that would not be able to adequately protect data integrity in latency-sensitive applications (Zhou et al., 2024). Furthermore, ZKP frameworks' versatility has made it possible to integrate them with other cutting-edge technologies like HE and AI, paving the way to secure computations on encrypted data and privacy-preserving analytics (Ramezan and Meamari, 2024; Zhou et al., 2024).

Therefore, ZKPs play a crucial role in multi-party compute environments, enabling several stakeholders to work together safely without disclosing sensitive or proprietary information, thereby complying with strict data privacy laws like General Data Protection

Regulation (GDPR) and Health Insurance Portability and Accountability Act (HIPAA) (Zhang et al., 2024). They are also a crucial part of blockchain-based solutions, such as supply chain management and decentralized banking, because of their capacity to authenticate identities, confirm transactions, and enforce policies while protecting privacy (Ramezan and Meamari, 2024). ZKP protocols are becoming increasingly important in contemporary cryptographic systems due to their ongoing improvement, which is opening up novel possibilities for secure and private solutions in a variety of fields (Feng et al., 2022; Zhou et al., 2024).

When HE and ZKPs are combined, strong, privacy-preserving agricultural ecosystems can be produced. For instance, a farmer could utilize ZKPs to show compliance with sustainability measures while concealing operational facts, like crop yields or input usage, by encrypting the data. This joint strategy opens the door for digital trust in agricultural systems by guaranteeing data protection while upholding accountability. In order to foster innovation in sustainable farming methods, these technologies can also facilitate research partnerships that study encrypted, aggregated data from several farms without compromising the privacy of individual data. Adopting HE and ZKPs in agriculture has many advantages. They increase stakeholder trust, lower the risk of data misuse, and improve data privacy and security. These technologies also facilitate regulatory compliance, encourage teamwork, and make advanced analytics possible, all of which contribute to increased agricultural efficiency and sustainability. HE and ZKPs have the potential to revolutionize the agricultural industry by tackling important issues like data security and transparency. This will encourage more intelligent, secure, and sustainable farming methods.

Figure 14.4 is adapted and modified based on Tyagi and Kathuria (2022). ZKPs allow regulatory-compliant interactions where a party can prove they have valid data (e.g., a patient record or consent) without revealing the actual sensitive content. GDPR and HIPAA are two acts or regulations provided by the government.

(i) *GDPR alignment*: Data minimization, purpose limitation, and integrity are preserved.

(ii) *HIPAA alignment*: Protected health information (PHI) is never directly exposed during verification.

There are mainly two actors in a ZKP:

(i) *Prover*: The one who has private or sensitive data (like a hospital or a company).

(ii) *Verifier*: The one who wants to verify something about that data (like an auditor, regulator, or user) without seeing the actual data.

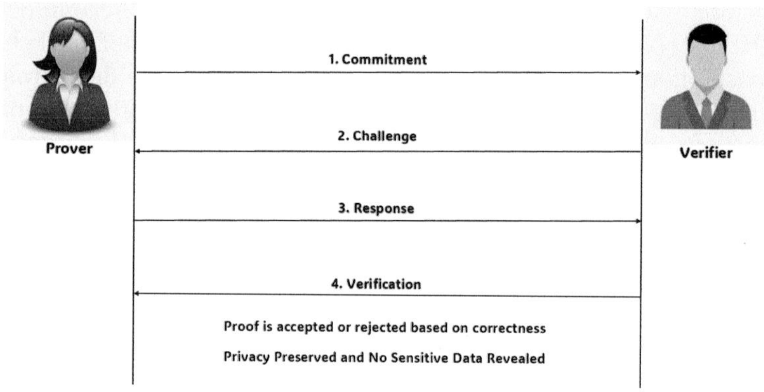

Figure 14.4: Zero-knowledge proof.

The four different phases are:

(i) *Commitment*: The Prover sends encrypted or masked information (proof) related to a secret without revealing it.

(ii) Challenge: The Verifier sends a challenge, usually a random question, related to the commitment.

(iii) Response: The Prover sends a response that only someone with knowledge of the secret could produce.

(iv) Verification: The Verifier checks if the response is valid and consistent with the challenge and commitment without learning the actual secret.

3.3 *Cryptographic Mechanisms in Blockchain Applications*

The strength of blockchain technology lies in the incorporation of state-of-the-art cryptographic techniques, which ensure anonymity, data integrity, and security within decentralized ecosystems. Hash functions such as SHA-256 are integral to blockchain operations, converting input data into outputs of a specified length while ensuring immutability and resistance to tampering (Ma et al., 2020; Desai et al., 2019). Public Key Cryptography (PKC) enables safe communication and identity verification by utilizing paired keys, such as private and public. The public key is used for verifying transactions, while the private key is used for signing transactions (Desai et al., 2019; Bhutta et al., 2021). In addition to PKC, digital signatures, like the Elliptic Curve Digital Signature Algorithm (ECDSA), increase transaction integrity and non-repudiation by safely linking transactions to their originators (Bhutta et al., 2021; Li et al., 2021).

Beyond these fundamentals, consensus processes are supported by cryptographic approaches, with Proof of Stake (PoS) using staking protocols to achieve security and fairness and Proof of Work (PoW) using hash-based puzzles (Zheng et al., 2017; Majeed et al., 2021). ZKPs are crucial for protecting sensitive data in agricultural IoT because they improve privacy by verifying statements without disclosing further information (Mousavi et al., 2021; Mahajan and Junnarkar, 2023). With HE, one can do computations on the encrypted data while still preserving the confidentiality of that data; hence, the agricultural data is transmitted and analysed (Mahajan and Junnarkar, 2023; Christo et al., 2021). Secure access control for sensitive agricultural data is also provided through efficient methods of key management like hierarchical deterministic wallets and multi-signature schemes (Christo et al., 2021; Abduljabbar et al., 2023).

Blockchain-based data transfers anonymize user identities through new privacy-enhancing techniques like cryptographic mixing, ring signatures, and confidential transactions (Abduljabbar et al., 2023). Hybrid cryptographic techniques maximize blockchain performance for safe and scalable data transmission by combining symmetric and asymmetric cryptography (Majeed et al., 2021; Mousavi et al., 2021). To ensure the durability and security of applications for agricultural IoT and beyond, future developments such as lattice-based cryptography and quantum-resistant algorithms seek to strengthen blockchain systems against threats from quantum computing (Mahajan and Junnarkar, 2023; Abduljabbar et al., 2023).

By guaranteeing data truthfulness, transparency, and confidentiality in the management of supply chains and traceability systems, these cryptographic techniques empower stakeholders in the agriculture sector. Hash functions and PKC keep sensitive farm data, including crop yields and soil conditions, away from manipulation and unauthorized access (Ma et al., 2020; Desai et al., 2019). Mechanisms of consensus and privacy tools make the participants feel secure with an immutable record of transactions like the delivery of produces and payment verification (Zheng et al., 2017; Majeed et al., 2021; Abduljabbar et al., 2023). While ZKPs protect private data when collaborating with third parties, HE enables secure data sharing for precision agricultural analytics (Mahajan and Junnarkar, 2023; Christo et al., 2021). Moreover, hybrid cryptography methods and quantum-resistant solutions position agricultural IoT systems for future scalability and resilience, ensuring reliable and efficient sector-wide operations (Majeed et al., 2021; Mahajan and Junnarkar, 2023). Table 14.1 presents the comparison for different cryptographic techniques with respect to their cost, uses, scalability, and level of security concerns.

Table 14.1: Comparison of cryptographic techniques in agricultural IoT.

Cryptographic Technique	Security Level	Computational Cost	Scalability	Uses in Agricultural Applications
Homomorphic Encryption	High	High	Medium	Secure analysis of encrypted crop yield data by cloud servers without decrypting sensitive farmer data
Zero-Knowledge Proofs	High	Medium	High	Proving the authenticity of organic produce certification without revealing farmer identity or full data records
Traditional Cryptography (e.g., AES, RSA)	Medium	Low	High	Encrypting data from soil sensors before uploading it to the cloud storage

4. Blockchain and Cryptography Integration in Agricultural IoT

Cryptography and blockchain in agricultural IoT extend beyond traceability and security. This integration unlocks advanced features including regulatory compliance, decentralized decision-making, and predictive analytics. Blockchain's decentralized and immutable conception protects agricultural data while allowing smart contracts to automate intricate procedures like dynamic pricing, subsidy distribution, and compliance checks (Dey and Shekhawat, 2021; Zhao et al., 2023). This is supported by cryptography with advanced techniques that will allow privacy-preserving data sharing using HE and ZKPs, thus allowing computations and verifications to be done on encrypted data without exposing sensitive information (Mahalingam and Sharma, 2024; Zhaoliang et al., 2021). For instance, crop health predictions can be collaboratively analysed from multiple farms without revealing individual farm data. The blockchain also allows seamless integration with the cloud, so large agricultural datasets can be managed in an efficient and scalable manner that does not incur excessive costs in decentralized storage (Zhu and Li, 2021; Chaganti et al., 2022). This further enables tamper-proof tracking of pesticide use and carbon footprint metrics, which have become increasingly critical concerns for sustainability and environmental impact (Xie et al., 2017; Zhaoliang et al., 2021). These innovations place blockchain and cryptography as foundational technologies in the future of precision agriculture: enabling secure, transparent, and intelligent agricultural ecosystems (Velmurugadass et al., 2021; Zhu and Li, 2021; Dey and Shekhawat, 2021; Mahalingam and Sharma, 2024; Xie et al., 2017; Zhaoliang et al., 2021; Zhao et al., 2023; Chaganti et al., 2022).

4.1 Solutions for Secure Data Storage

Integration of blockchain technology and cryptographic methods brings a revolution to secure cloud storage in agricultural IoT, providing solutions for advanced security to the sensitive data in agriculture. Blockchain decentralizes the storage of data; that is, it distributes data across multiple nodes, thus preventing risks associated with single points of failure and centralized data breaches (Velmurugadass et al., 2021; Mahalingam and Sharma, 2024; Zhao et al., 2023). Cryptographic algorithms like the Elliptic Curve Integrated Encryption Scheme (ECIES) encrypt data before storage so that only the authorized parties have access to the data (Velmurugadass et al., 2021; Xie et al., 2017; Chaganti et al., 2022). Novel implementations include integrating blockchain with Distributed Hash Tables (DHT) or Inter-Planetary File System (IPFS) for scalability and further decentralization in order to produce tamper-proof and loss-resistant systems (Zhaoliang et al., 2021; Zhao et al., 2023).

The immutability of blockchain allows data to never be changed without being agreed upon and, therefore, it provides an audit trail for compliance and traceability (Zhu and Li, 2021; Dey and Shekhawat, 2021; Chaganti et al., 2022). Automated access control of smart contracts allows the stakeholders to manage permissions and thus this facilitates transparency and data privacy (Zhaoliang et al., 2021; Chaganti et al., 2022). This dual-layer security approach improves data integrity, allowing farmers to safely store sensitive information such as crop yields, pesticide use, and financial transactions in compliance with stringent data protection regulations (Zhu and Li, 2021; Mahalingam and Sharma, 2024; Xie et al., 2017).

The integration of cryptography with blockchain's decentralized architecture can help the agricultural sector achieve a secure, scalable, and transparent cloud storage ecosystem, which is critical for modern agricultural IoT applications (Velmurugadass et al., 2021; Zhu and Li, 2021; Dey and Shekhawat, 2021; Mahalingam and Sharma, 2024; Xie et al., 2017; Zhaoliang et al., 2021; Zhao et al., 2023; Chaganti et al., 2022).

4.2 Protocols for Decentralized Data Sharing

Decentralized data sharing protocols are the cornerstones for ensuring safe, transparent, and efficient collaboration among the various stakeholders within the agricultural ecosystem. The protocol employs blockchain technology, which directly allows peer-to-peer data exchange without a central authority, so that all parties have access to the same verified data in real time (Velmurugadass et al., 2021; Zhu and Li, 2021; Zhaoliang et al., 2021). Decentralized protocols remove intermediaries, thereby increasing trust and reducing disputes while maintaining data authenticity and confidentiality through cryptographic techniques (Velmurugadass et al., 2021; Zhaoliang et al., 2021).

One of the advantages of peer-to-peer decentralized data sharing is that smart contracts can automate and govern the terms of the agreement. Self-executing contracts can define and enforce pre-established rules for the conditions of data exchange, and that data can be shared safely only with specific, authorized parties (Velmurugadass et al., 2021; Dey and Shekhawat, 2021; Zhao et al., 2023). For instance, a farmer could share crop real-time data with suppliers by allowing access based on specific conditions like purchase agreements or resource needs allocation through a smart contract (Zhu and Li, 2021; Mahalingam and Sharma, 2024). This not only enhances trust but also innovates and improves efficiency in the agricultural value chain by enabling real-time decision-making and resource optimization (Dey and Shekhawat, 2021; Zhaoliang et al., 2021; Chaganti et al., 2022).

Other protocols, such as the IPFS, improve the sharing of decentralized data by providing for off-chain storage of large datasets in agriculture, with a reference to the data on the blockchain (Xie et al., 2017; Chaganti et al., 2022). The hybrid approach is then guaranteed to be efficient in retrieving and sharing data while keeping the integrity and provenance of the data (Xie et al., 2017). Moreover, the decentralized identity protocols, such as DIDs, are a solid framework for user identity and permission management. These protocols will only allow authorized parties to access or share specific data, thereby improving the privacy and security of agricultural IoT applications (Xie et al., 2017; Chaganti et al., 2022).

Another important characteristic of decentralized data-sharing protocols is that they provide the capability to have safe and efficient devices-to-devices communication in IoT. Their ability to allow direct interactions between devices or with blockchain networks minimizes latencies, reduces response times, and reduces the number of points of failure in communication (Zhao et al., 2023; Chaganti et al., 2022). IoT devices in agricultural environments can send information like weather conditions or soil moisture levels directly to stakeholders or blockchain networks, thus enabling real-time monitoring and decision-making (Zhaoliang et al., 2021; Chaganti et al., 2022). Such mechanisms as verification with cryptographic processes ensure integrity and traceability of data so that the stakeholders can track the history and origin of agricultural products (Xie et al., 2017; Zhao et al., 2023).

This decentralized protocol integration into agricultural IoT environments not only adds security and transparency to the data but also ensures better resource management and sustainability in farming. By using blockchain and advanced cryptography techniques, decentralized data-sharing protocols present a transformative solution to deal with the issues of data management and collaboration in agriculture (Velmurugadass et al., 2021; Zhu and Li, 2021; Dey and Shekhawat, 2021; Mahalingam and Sharma, 2024; Xie et al., 2017; Zhaoliang et al., 2021; Zhao et al., 2023; Chaganti et al., 2022).

4.3 *Automated Transactions Using Smart Contracts*

Smart contracts are self-executing contracts with the terms of the agreement directly embedded into code, operating on blockchain technology (Velmurugadass et al., 2021; Zhu and Li, 2021; Dey and Shekhawat, 2021). They facilitate automated transactions in agricultural IoT ecosystems by enabling trustless, transparent, and efficient processes (Mahalingam and Sharma, 2024; Xie et al., 2017; Zhaoliang et al., 2021). These contracts eliminate the need for intermediaries, reduce fraud risks, and enhance operational efficiency across various agricultural applications (Zhao et al., 2023; Chaganti et al., 2022). For instance, a smart contract can automatically release payment to a farmer once IoT sensors confirm the delivery of crops or agricultural products, accelerating the payment process and reducing costs by removing intermediaries (Velmurugadass et al., 2021; Zhu and Li, 2021; Dey and Shekhawat, 2021). This process enhances trust among stakeholders, as the execution is transparent and verifiable on the blockchain (Xie et al., 2017; Zhaoliang et al., 2021). Smart contracts also enforce compliance with agricultural standards and regulations. For example, a contract can automatically verify that the delivered produce meets quality or pesticide usage standards, as recorded by IoT sensors, before triggering payments or approvals, ensuring adherence to predefined conditions and fostering accountability within the agricultural value chain (Mahalingam and Sharma, 2024; Xie et al., 2017; Zhao et al., 2023).

Additionally, smart contracts enable the automation of insurance claims. When IoT devices record adverse weather conditions or crop damage, the contract can trigger an insurance payout based on predefined thresholds, reducing the time and effort required for claim settlements while minimizing disputes (Zhaoliang et al., 2021). They also facilitate secure and automated data-sharing agreements. For instance, when a sensor detects that a crop has matured, the contract can trigger data access permissions or payments based on agreed conditions, ensuring privacy, reducing manual intervention, and fostering collaboration among stakeholders such as farmers, buyers, and regulators (Velmurugadass et al., 2021; Zhao et al., 2023; Chaganti et al., 2022). The transparency of blockchain-based smart contracts allows all parties to verify the terms and execution of agreements, eliminating disputes and promoting collaboration in agricultural practices (Dey and Shekhawat, 2021; Chaganti et al., 2022).

Smart contracts derive their functionality from real-time data inputs provided by IoT devices. For example, they can be programmed to trigger actions based on metrics such as crop yield thresholds, delivery confirmations, or environmental conditions, ensuring that transactions and processes align with actual conditions on the ground and optimizing efficiency (Mahalingam and Sharma, 2024; Zhao et al., 2023; Chaganti et al., 2022). Their integration offers numerous benefits, including automation that reduces transaction times and operational overhead (Zhu and Li, 2021; Xie et al., 2017), cost savings by eliminating intermediaries (Dey and Shekhawat, 2021; Zhaoliang et al., 2021), transparent execution that fosters trust among stakeholders (Velmurugadass et al., 2021; Chaganti et al., 2022), and automated enforcement of standards to ensure compliance with regulatory requirements (Mahalingam and Sharma, 2024; Zhao et al., 2023). In conclusion, smart contracts are revolutionizing the agricultural sector by automating transactions, enhancing trust, and improving operational efficiency, marking a significant step towards achieving secure, sustainable, and transparent agricultural practices (Zhaoliang et al., 2021; Chaganti et al., 2022).

5. Applications in the Field of Agriculture

Agriculture is also significantly being transformed with digital technologies where blockchain is posing as a capable means to extend security, transparency, and efficiency. The process of the agriculture supply chain dealing with various intermediaries such as producers, distributors, retailers, and regulators entails inefficiencies, fraud, and no real-time traceability (Vijayaragavan et al., 2022). Blockchain, when coupled with cryptographic methods, IoT, AI, and HE, facilitates secure and automatic data management, thus overcoming such challenges (Zhou et al., 2020). The combination of distributed ledgers, smart contracts, and decentralized identity verification is revolutionizing food safety, supply chain logistics, and trust management in agriculture (Lei et al., 2022). Recent advancements in quantum-resistant cryptographic methods, such as lattice-based encryption, further enhance the security of agricultural blockchain networks, ensuring protection against emerging cyber threats (Markovic et al., 2020).

5.1 Food Safety and Provenance Traceability

Food safety and provenance traceability are currently the leading concerns of the global food supply chain, wherein there are risks of contamination, counterfeiting, and regulatory non-compliance (Vijayaragavan et al., 2022). Blockchain, when integrated with IoT sensors and AI, is a secure and intelligent system of traceability that ensures authenticity from farm to table (Malik et al., 2018). IoT sensors in storage and shipping containers constantly read environmental conditions including temperature, moisture, and presence of contaminants (Dedeoglu et al., 2023). These observations are permanently saved in a permissioned blockchain that prevents data modification and allows tracking of data audit (Zhou et al., 2020). AI-based prediction algorithms read blockchain-archived data to identify potential risks, including contamination or spoiling, and send automatic preventive interventions (Lei et al., 2022). ZKP also increases compliance as it enables food suppliers to demonstrate conformity to safety standards without revealing sensitive business data (Iftekhar and Cui, 2021). Furthermore, blockchain-based smart contracts can also apply automatic recall processes upon contamination so that harmful food is quickly taken out of circulation (Malik et al., 2018). This combination of blockchain with AI and cryptographic methods removes inefficiencies and fraudulence in food safety procedures, and the whole supply chain becomes more robust and transparent (Lei et al., 2022). With the increasing threats of quantum computing to traditional cryptographic security, post-quantum cryptography, such as lattice-based encryption, is being explored to further enhance food safety blockchain implementations, ensuring long-term resilience (Markovic et al., 2020).

Figure 14.5 shows the design to ensure secure, transparent, and real-time monitoring of products across the entire supply chain lifecycle. The model comprises six interconnected stages, each contributing to data integrity, stakeholder collaboration, and consumer trust.

(i) *Data Collection via IoT Sensors*: In the first stage, IoT devices and sensors are deployed across various points in the supply chain (e.g., farms, warehouses, transportation vehicles) to capture critical data such as temperature, humidity, location, and timestamps. This ensures automated and accurate real-time data acquisition directly from the source.

(ii) *Data Encryption and Storage on Blockchain*: The collected data is encrypted using cryptographic techniques to ensure confidentiality and tamper-resistance. Once encrypted, it is stored on a blockchain ledger, which guarantees immutability, integrity, and transparency. Each data point is time-stamped and linked with a unique block, enabling secure historical tracking.

(iii) *Cloud Computing for Real-Time Data Access*: While blockchain ensures secure storage, cloud computing facilitates real-time data access and

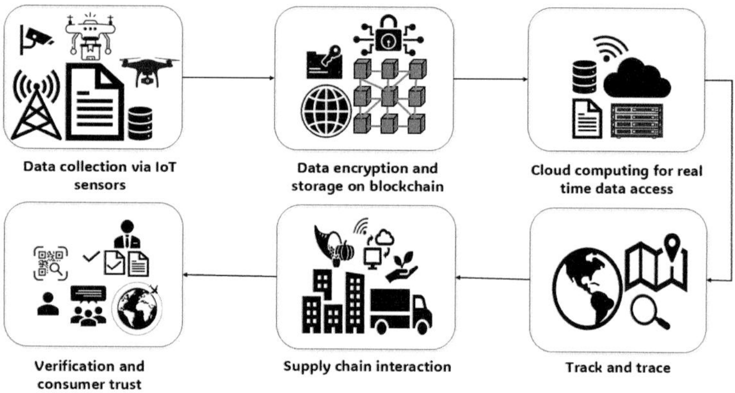

Figure 14.5: Blockchain-enabled traceability model.

processing. Stakeholders across the supply chain (e.g., producers, distributors, retailers) can interact with the data through cloud platforms to monitor status, generate analytics, and make timely decisions.

(iv) *Track and Trace*: With data securely stored and accessible, the system enables end-to-end traceability of products throughout the supply chain. Each item can be tracked from its origin to the final destination, helping identify bottlenecks, reduce delays, and verify product authenticity.

(v) *Supply Chain Interaction*: At this stage, all authorized entities involved in the supply chain can interact with the blockchain network. Smart contracts may automate transactions, while data sharing and validation take place without centralized control, improving coordination, efficiency, and transparency among participants.

(vi) *Verification and Consumer Trust*: Finally, the accumulated data can be used to verify product quality, origin, and handling conditions. This builds consumer trust by providing transparent information, often through QR codes or mobile apps, allowing end-users to verify that the product meets safety and ethical standards.

5.2 Enhancing Supply Chains Post-Harvest

Post-harvest supply chain inefficiencies such as delays, fraud, and the absence of real-time visibility cause massive food wastage and financial losses (Vijayaragavan et al., 2022). Blockchain, in conjunction with AI-based analytics and decentralized automation, streamlines the supply chain by establishing a common, tamper-evident record of transactions (Zhou et al., 2020). Decentralized supply chain platforms developed on

Hyperledger Fabric or Ethereum-based permissioned blockchains allow all parties, such as farmers, logistics companies, and retailers, to have access to authenticated, real-time data, eliminating miscommunication and delays (Dedeoglu et al., 2023). Predictive analytics models powered by AI utilize past blockchain transaction records to predict demand and streamline logistics so that food arrives at its destination before it spoils (Lei et al., 2022). Cross-chain interoperability enables agricultural blockchains to communicate with financial and logistics networks seamlessly, facilitating instant payment for farmers and automated contract enforcement (Iftekhar and Cui, 2021). In addition, lattice-based cryptography guarantees that sensitive information, including pricing negotiations and trade agreements, can be securely computed on encrypted data without revealing proprietary information (Prashar et al., 2020). Quantum-secure blockchain solutions are also being integrated into agricultural logistics to protect against future cyber threats, ensuring long-term sustainability and data integrity in the food supply chain (Markovic et al., 2020). These advances in technology produce an optimized, transparent, and fraud-resistant agricultural supply chain (Malik et al., 2018).

The post-harvest processing flowchart is presented in Figure 14.6, which has been adapted and modified from Butkovsky and Ilina (2023) and Mutungi et al. (2020). The post-harvest process is essential in ensuring food quality, safety, and efficiency in agricultural supply chains.

The flowchart follows a linear sequence from harvesting to distribution:

1. Harvesting → 2. Cleaning → 3. Drying → 4. Storage → 5. Processing → 6. Packaging → 7. Distribution

Each step is dependent on the previous one, ensuring that agricultural products maintain high quality, safety, and efficiency throughout

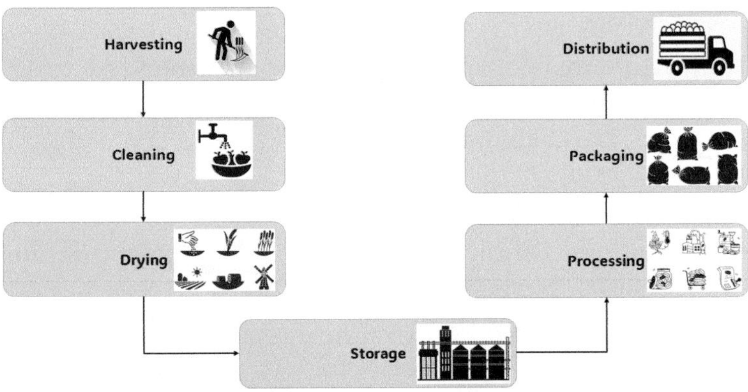

Figure 14.6: Post-harvest flowchart.

the supply chain. Blockchain-enabled traceability systems track and authenticate every step, from farm to table, reducing risks of fraud, foodborne illnesses, and inefficiencies.

(i) *Harvesting*: The process begins with harvesting, where crops are collected at peak ripeness to ensure maximum nutritional value and quality. Proper techniques such as manual picking, mechanized harvesting, or combined methods are used depending on the crop type. Timely harvesting is crucial to prevent overripening, decay, or pest infestation that could affect storage and processing.

(ii) *Cleaning*: Once harvested, crops undergo cleaning to remove dirt, leaves, stones, and other impurities. Cleaning methods include manual sorting, water washing, air blowing, and mechanical cleaning to ensure that only quality produce moves forward. This step helps in preventing contamination and prepares the crops for drying or storage.

(iii) *Drying*: It is a critical step that reduces moisture content to prevent fungal growth, spoilage, and insect infestation. There are two main types of drying:

- Traditional drying methods: Sun drying, natural air drying.
- Artificial drying methods: Mechanical dryers, heated air dryers, solar dryers.

Drying ensures that grains, fruits, and other produce remain in optimal condition for storage and transportation.

(iv) *Storage*: After drying, crops are stored under controlled conditions to maintain quality. The different storage methods include:

- Traditional storage: Clay pots, underground pits, sacks.
- Modern storage: Hermetic bags, metal silos, cold storage warehouses.

Temperature, humidity, and ventilation are monitored using IoT sensors and blockchain-enabled systems to prevent spoilage.

(v) *Processing*: The stored produce is then processed into usable forms. This stage involves:

- Milling: Removing husks, grinding grains into flour.
- Grinding and crushing: Preparing raw materials for further refinement.
- Sorting and grading: Categorizing products based on size, weight, and quality.

Blockchain and cloud computing play a role in ensuring data integrity, quality monitoring, and traceability during processing.

(vi) *Packaging*: Once processed, agricultural products are packaged for transportation and sale. Packaging techniques ensure food safety, extend shelf life, and enhance branding. Smart packaging solutions, such as QR codes and blockchain-based labels, allow consumers to trace the product's journey from farm to market.

(vii) *Distribution*: Finally, packaged products enter the distribution phase, where they are transported to retailers, wholesalers, or directly to consumers. This stage involves logistics optimization, supply chain tracking, and compliance with food safety regulations. Blockchain and cryptographic security solutions ensure that data related to transportation conditions, storage temperatures, and shipment times remain tamper-proof and transparent.

This structured post-harvest process ensures that agricultural products reach consumers in a safe, fresh, and high-quality state, reducing losses and improving trust in the food supply chain.

5.3 *Dealing with Untrusted Parties' Trust*

Agricultural supply chains have various unverified actors such as small-scale farmers, suppliers, intermediaries, and retailers, creating a major task of managing trust (Vijayaragavan et al., 2022). Blockchain, combined with decentralized identity verification and AI-driven fraud prevention, delivers trust and data integrity in agricultural transactions (Dedeoglu et al., 2023). Decentralized Identity (DID) solutions eliminate identity fraud by authenticating stakeholders' credentials through blockchain-based digital signatures (Lei et al., 2022). Self-sovereign identity (SSI) products allow farmers and suppliers to safely verify digitally signed certificates, like organic farming certifications, in tamper-proof form without the need for centralized authorities (Malik et al., 2018). Additionally, blockchain's IPFS provides secure off-chain storage for regulatory documents, safety audits, and transaction histories, reducing storage costs while maintaining accessibility (Iftekhar and Cui, 2021). AI-driven fraud detection models scan blockchain transactions in real time to detect abnormalities such as fake transactions, double entries, or supply chain tampering (Zhou et al., 2020). To further enhance security and resilience, blockchain networks are incorporating quantum-secure cryptographic mechanisms such as hash-based signatures and lattice-based encryption to safeguard trust models against potential quantum attacks (Markovic et al., 2020). Through the integration of blockchain, cryptography security, and AI analytics, the agricultural industry can eliminate fraud, maintain stakeholder accountability, and develop a transparent and effective supply chain system (Prashar et al., 2020).

Integration of blockchain with cryptography security measures, AI, and IoT is transforming agriculture by rendering food safety, supply chain management, and trust of stakeholders safer and more transparent (Vijayaragavan et al., 2022). Smart contract automatization of transactions, logistics optimization with the help of analytics via AI, and privacy-preserving cryptographic techniques protect data transmission (Dedeoglu et al., 2023). As quantum computing advances, the adoption of post-quantum cryptographic techniques such as lattice-based encryption is becoming crucial for ensuring the long-term security of blockchain applications in agriculture (Markovic et al., 2020). These technologies are bringing on a more efficient, sustainable, and fraud-free agricultural system that is revolutionizing the future of food distribution and production (Lei et al., 2022).

6. Technological Progress and Difficulties

The integration of blockchain and cryptography in secure exchange of data in the cloud for agricultural IoT has a number of technological advancements and challenges. As digitalization of agricultural supply chains increases, blockchain offers more data security, traceability, and transparency. Yet, scalability, cost, and security weaknesses are some of the challenges that need to be overcome to facilitate broad adoption. This section discusses the consensus mechanisms, cost factors, and solutions to security issues in blockchain-based cloud data exchange for agricultural IoT applications (Albshaier et al., 2024; Ali and Sofi, 2022).

6.1 Consensus Processes and Scalability of the System

Blockchain technology encounters major scalability issues when incorporated into agricultural IoT systems and safe cloud data exchange due to the computational load of consensus procedures. The computationally demanding nature of traditional PoW makes it inappropriate for large-scale cloud and IoT applications. In order to improve scalability while lowering energy consumption and computational costs, alternative consensus mechanisms like PoS, Delegated Proof-of-Stake (DPoS), Byzantine Fault Tolerance (BFT), and Proof-of-Authority (PoA) have been proposed (Albshaier et al., 2024; Ali and Sofi, 2022). In addition to increasing transaction throughput, hybrid blockchain designs that combine public and private blockchains with specific consensus techniques designed for resource-constrained contexts also preserve decentralization (Ali and Sofi, 2022; Rao et al., 2024).

Additionally, layered blockchain structures like dual-chain models that isolate transaction validation from data storage allow real-time IoT applications to operate well without taxing blockchain nodes (Krishna et al., 2021; Si et al., 2019). Layer-2 and off-chain solutions have been designed to speed up transactions and reduce network congestion. Protocols such as the Lightning Network and sidechains allow transactions to be processed off-chain before being recorded on the main blockchain, thus alleviating bottlenecks in network processing (Rao et al., 2024; Habib et al., 2022). Sharding further improves performance by partitioning the blockchain into smaller segments, reducing the computational load on individual nodes.

In agricultural IoT, consensus techniques are essential for assessing the effectiveness, security, and scalability of blockchain-based systems. PoS lowers energy consumption but may bring centralization issues if stake distribution is unequal, whereas PoW demands a lot of computing power, making it inappropriate for IoT devices with limited resources (Albshaier et al., 2024; Ali and Sofi, 2022). Layer-2 scaling solutions, such as the Lightning Network, state channels, and sidechains, boost transaction processing capacity and decrease network congestion while maintaining security (Rao et al., 2024; Habib et al., 2022).

The smooth transmission of agricultural data, such as weather, soil health, and supply chain logistics, depends on these scalable solutions. Despite these developments, blockchain scalability is still a problem that has to be solved by constant research into techniques like edge computing, sharding, and AI-driven optimization to strike a balance between computational efficiency and decentralization (Ali and Sofi, 2022; Torky and Hassanein, 2020).

6.2 Cost Evaluation

Several cost-related issues affecting feasibility and efficiency arise when blockchain is implemented in secure cloud data exchange. Bitcoin and other PoW-based blockchains demand a lot of processing power, which raises the cost of energy. Additionally, due to their increased operating efficiency and reduced energy requirements, alternative consensus techniques such as PoS and PoA have become more and more popular (Rao et al., 2024; Habib et al., 2022). Small businesses may find public blockchain networks, like Ethereum, unfeasible due to their changing transaction costs, which are dependent on network congestion. To lower these expenses, scalability options like as sharding and Layer-2 protocols have been implemented (Rao et al., 2024; Krishna et al., 2021).

Another major issue is storage costs because on-chain data storage is costly and necessitates more processing power and storage space. Off-chain storage solutions allow critical data to be stored externally while blockchain secures transaction integrity, reducing expenses while maintaining data immutability (Chaganti et al., 2022; Si et al., 2019). Hybrid blockchain architectures—integrating public and private chains—offer cost-effective alternatives, allowing sensitive agricultural data to be stored on private chains while leveraging public chains for verification (Ali and Sofi, 2022; Krishna et al., 2021).

Investments in the development of smart contracts, governance models, and secure server upkeep are required to meet the infrastructure expenses for blockchain adoption in cloud environments. IBM and Microsoft provide scalable, on-demand blockchain infrastructure through Blockchain-as-a-service (BaaS) offerings, which lower the cost burden (Ali and Sofi, 2022; Krishna et al., 2021). Additionally, a hybrid approach combining on-chain verification with off-chain computation optimizes cost efficiency by minimizing the blockchain's computational burden while maintaining high security standards (Chaganti et al., 2022; Si et al., 2019).

Cost optimization strategies, including energy-efficient consensus mechanisms, permissioned blockchain networks, and hybrid on-chain or off-chain storage, further enhance affordability and adoption in agricultural IoT applications (Chaganti et al., 2022; Si et al., 2019).

7. Future Prospects Beyond Agriculture

The interplay of blockchain and cryptography has transformed data security, transparency, and traceability of resources in agricultural IoT, and these technologies are becoming more and more scalable to other vital areas like healthcare, finance, energy, and governance (Rao et al., 2024). This scalability is made possible by the distinctive ability of the technologies to provide tamper resistance, decentralized verification, and privacy-preserving information exchange (Habib et al., 2022).

7.1 Blockchain and Cryptography's Scalability to other Domains

In healthcare, blockchain provides data provenance and Electronic Health Record (EHR) system interoperability through the utilization of permissioned networks such as Hyperledger Fabric in combination with privacy-preserving methods such as HE. Blockchain allows patients control of their medical records, while institutions can share anonymized data in a secure manner for research purposes (Habib et al., 2022).

In finance, decentralized finance (DeFi) platforms use smart contracts to automate lending and asset trading without the need for centralized intermediaries, thus improving transparency and minimizing costs. ZKPs support transactional privacy by allowing verification without revealing sensitive user information (Daraghmi et al., 2024).

Supply chains benefit from real-time tracking and validation of products utilizing blockchain's non-editable ledger, avoiding counterfeiting and allowing trusted audits with cryptographic hash functions and digital signatures. Blockchain further improves traceability in pharmaceuticals, electronics, and luxury goods (Rao et al., 2024).

In the energy industry, decentralized energy markets are made possible by blockchain-based peer-to-peer trading platforms, allowing consumers to securely trade excess renewable energy. Solutions such as Internet of Things Application Tangle enable zero-fee microtransactions and improved scalability for smart grids (Habib et al., 2022).

Governance solutions encompass blockchain-supported digital identities that minimize fraud and enable secure authentication of citizens, and immutable and transparent e-voting systems to improve electoral integrity (Feng et al., 2020). Scalability techniques such as sharding, Directed Acyclic Graphs (DAGs), and Layer-2 protocols are also being investigated for enabling mainstream usage across these fields (Rao et al., 2024).

7.2 *Developments in the Management of Sustainable Resources*

Blockchain plays an essential role in optimizing resources and environmental monitoring through transparent and verifiable trails of data. In water management, blockchain-enabled sensors allow real-time consumption monitoring and leak detection, thereby increasing irrigation efficiency and conservation (Lin et al., 2017).

Blockchain combined with IoT in sustainable forestry and agriculture enables ethical sourcing, tracking deforestation, and compliance with sustainability through smart contracts. Blockchain may be applied to waste management systems to track disposal actions and encourage accountability (Feng et al., 2020).

Blockchain's unalterable records are revolutionizing carbon markets, with smart contracts verifying carbon offsets automatically and offering public access to emissions data. Stakeholder trust is boosted, and credit issuance and trading are simplified (Lin et al., 2017).

In renewable energy systems, blockchain regulates energy flow through smart meters, allowing households to sell excess solar energy directly to others, while cryptographic protocols guarantee tamper-resistant records (Habib et al., 2022). Attempts are also being made to minimize blockchain's computational load so that it can be deployed energy-efficiently for sustainability tracking (Feng et al., 2020).

7.3 *Data Security and Privacy Opportunities*

Homomorphic encryption allows for secure computation on encrypted data in cloud environments, enabling privacy-preserving analytics without exposing underlying information. This is important in industries where sensitive information, such as medical or financial data, needs to be processed without compromise. By providing identification authentication without revealing credentials, ZKPs are revolutionizing user verification and significantly reducing the risk of identity theft and unauthorized access (Rao et al., 2024).

Blockchain networks are being secured against quantum computer threats with quantum-resistant cryptographic methods, such as lattice-based cryptography, that ensure long-term protection against decryption attacks. Decentralized identity systems substitute centralized logins with blockchain-based solutions, providing users with control over their data while authenticity is ensured via verifiable credentials. Blockchain secures IoT networks by recording device interactions on immutable blockchains, enabling anomaly detection, spoofing prevention, and securely enforcing firmware updates (Rao et al., 2024).

For cross-border data exchange, permissioned blockchain platforms offer fine-grained access control, assuring jurisdictional data compliance alongside facilitating efficient global transactions. Despite progress, research is ongoing to enhance scalability, minimize latency, and balance computational efficiency with robust privacy guarantees in blockchain systems (Rao et al., 2024).

The flexibility of blockchain and cryptography continues to redefine different industries, much beyond agriculture, by providing scalable, transparent, and secure models for dealing with digital assets and sensitive data. With technologies such as HE and quantum-resistant algorithms, future systems are likely to support increasingly sophisticated privacy and security needs in a decentralized way (Rao et al., 2024).

8. Conclusion

The intersection of blockchain technology and cryptography in the field of cloud-based agriculture IoT systems has created revolutionary capacities for securing data transfer, improving traceability, and empowering decentralized trust systems. This chapter has offered an in-depth analysis of the ways in which these technologies can be used to meet the intricate needs of agricultural data management ranging from secure integration of sensors and tamper-resistance of crop tracking to facilitating smart contracts in food supply chains and sustainable resource management.

8.1 Summary of Key Insights

As farming increasingly moves towards data-intensive and digitally networked systems, the necessity for secure, reliable, and effective data exchange frameworks becomes critical. The convergence of blockchain technology and cryptography in cloud-based agricultural IoT infrastructures is a compelling solution to this problem. These technologies combine to build tamper-proof data ecosystems, facilitate trust among stakeholders, and support decentralized decision-making while preserving data privacy and sovereignty.

Through this chapter, we discussed how blockchain increases traceability, transparency, and accountability, especially in situations like food supply chain verification, soil tracking, and climate-resilient agriculture. We also examined how innovative cryptographic technologies like HE, ZKPs, and secure multi-party computation (SMPC) facilitate privacy-preserving computations in distributed systems.

These technologies are not just theoretical constructs, they are actively transforming agricultural practices by promoting cooperation without loss of confidentiality, allowing automated contracts with the use of smart contracts, and facilitating compliance with changing regulatory requirements. Importantly, they allow both small-scale farmers and large enterprises to participate in a secure and equitable digital ecosystem.

Furthermore, the chapter emphasized how blockchain and cryptographic solutions are scalable across agricultural subdomains, from livestock management and crop traceability to water resource optimization and smart farming logistics. This scalability shows their timeliness and potency in addressing actual problems with long-lasting, sustainable impact.

8.2 Blockchain and Cryptography's Future in Agriculture

With agriculture coming under increasing pressure to become more efficient, transparent, and sustainable under the dictates of climate change and global demand for food, blockchain and cryptography will have an increasingly important role to play. The future lies in interoperable, decentralized agricultural platforms that can securely integrate sensor data, supply chain events, weather predictions, and market trends using blockchain-backed distributed data models and advanced cryptographic protocols. As climate uncertainty, population growth, and supply chain complexity intensify, agricultural systems must become more resilient, autonomous, and intelligent. Blockchain and cryptography will be at the heart of this transformation.

Future advances in privacy-driven data analytics, tokenized agricultural assets, and blockchain-facilitated IoT marketplaces will transform agricultural data monetization, exchange, and security. For instance, blockchain-based carbon credit platforms have the potential to reward sustainable operations, while federated learning–enabled AI models have the ability to support yield forecasts and pest management without compromising on farmers' sensitive data.

Emerging frameworks like blockchain federated learning can facilitate collaborative, privacy-preserving AI models trained across distributed farm nodes without centralizing data, thereby democratizing precision agriculture. Cross-chain interoperability, decentralized identifiers (DIDs), and verifiable credentials are expected to become fundamental tools for global agricultural networks (e.g., for livestock, crop certification, carbon credits) to seamlessly and securely interact and create a unified data ecosystem that supports both real-time operational decisions and long-term policy planning. By reducing redundancy, fostering confidence, and guaranteeing equitable data governance, this will result in open data ecosystems where farmers, governments, researchers, and agribusinesses may collaborate.

From a cryptographic perspective, attribute-based encryption (ABE), SMPC, and privacy-preserving smart contracts will enhance data access management, limiting access the analysis of sensitive farm data to trusted parties. These technologies will make it possible for farmers, governments, consumers, and agribusinesses to work together seamlessly while having strict data sovereignty and compliance with international data protection laws.

The broader integration of blockchain-enabled cloud computing with IoT, AI, and geospatial technologies will open new frontiers in autonomous farm management—from drone-based crop health monitoring and AI-assisted irrigation to tokenized incentives for sustainable practices and dynamic risk management in agricultural insurance.

As such systems develop, support from policies, standardization, and capacity-building for rural and marginalized groups will be needed. Blockchain and cryptography should not be perceived as luxury technologies but rather as facilitators of inclusion, justice, and transparency.

8.3 Future Scope

The future of agriculture as a digitally safe, transparent, and smart system depends on our capacity to integrate the latest technologies in a responsible and innovative manner. The management of trust, data ownership, and value transfer in the agricultural ecosystem is being revolutionized by blockchain and cryptography, which are new features added to the existing systems.

A rich area for multidisciplinary research is the convergence of blockchain and cryptography with cloud and IoT technologies in agriculture. Opportunities lie in developing lightweight consensus mechanisms for low-power IoT devices, optimizing cryptographic protocols for real-time data environments, and creating interoperable frameworks that bridge diverse agricultural technique platforms. Researchers are encouraged to explore cross-disciplinary approaches, combining cryptographic engineering, distributed ledger design, agronomy, and cloud architecture to create solutions that are scalable, secure, and socio-economically impactful. Practitioners must place ethical deployment, smallholder farmer inclusivity, and sustainability first as they embrace these technologies. Solutions must be not only technologically feasible but also socio-economically feasible, such that farmers are not merely sources of data but direct beneficiaries of digital change.

Finally, secure exchange and processing of agricultural data are no longer luxuries but necessities. Blockchain and cryptography will redefine the digital foundation of agriculture, allowing for a future in which food systems are transparent, resilient, and sustainably managed.

In the journey towards resilient digital agricultural infrastructure, blockchain and cryptography will serve as the backbone, ensuring that trust is verifiable, data is untampered, and innovation is boundless.

References

Abduljabbar, Z.A., Nyangaresi, V.O., Jasim, H.M., Ma, J., Hussain, M.A., Hussien, Z.A. and Aldarwish, A.J. (2023). Elliptic curve cryptography-based scheme for secure signaling and data exchanges in precision agriculture. *Sustainability* 15(13): 10264.

Ahmed, A., Parveen, I., Abdullah, S., Ahmad, I., Alturki, N. and Jamel, L. (2024). Optimized data fusion with scheduled rest periods for enhanced smart agriculture via blockchain integration. *IEEE Access* 12: 15171–15193.

Akella, G.K., Wibowo, S., Grandhi, S. and Mubarak, S. (2023). A systematic review of blockchain technology adoption barriers and enablers for smart and sustainable agriculture. *Big Data and Cognitive Computing* 7(2): 86.

Albshaier, L., Budokhi, A. and Aljughaiman, A. (2024). A review of security issues when integrating IoT with cloud computing and blockchain. *IEEE Access* 12: 109560–109595.

Ali, J. and Sofi, S.A. (2022). Blockchain enabled architecture with selective consensus mechanisms for IoT based Saffron-agri value chain. *Scalable Computing: Practice and Experience* 23(4): 457–472.

Arulananth, T.S., Baskar, M., Anbarasu, V., Thiagarajan, R., Rajendran, T. and Balaji, A. (2021). Multi party secure data access management in cloud using user centric block chain data encryption. *Pattern Recognition Letters* 152: 295–301.

Astill, J., Dara, R.A., Campbell, M., Farber, J.M., Fraser, E.D., Sharif, S. and Yada, R.Y. (2019). Transparency in food supply chains: A review of enabling technology solutions. *Trends in Food Science & Technology* 91: 240–247.

Bairagi, S.I. and Bang, A.O. (2015). Cloud computing: History, architecture, security issues. In *National Conference Convergence*, 28.

Bhutta, M.N.M., Khwaja, A.A., Nadeem, A., Ahmad, H.F., Khan, M.K., Hanif, M.A., Song, H., Alshamari, M. and Cao, Y. (2021). A survey on blockchain technology: Evolution, architecture and security. *IEEE Access* 9: 61048–61073.

Boneh, D., Goh, E.J. and Nissim, K. (2005). Evaluating 2-DNF formulas on ciphertexts. pp. 325–341. *In*: Kilian, J. (ed.). *Theory of Cryptography: Second Theory of Cryptography Conference*, TCC 2005, Cambridge, MA, USA, February 10–12, 2005. Proceedings 2. Springer, Berlin, Heidelberg.

Butkovsky, V.A. and Ilina, O.A. (2023). Grain storage. pp. 199–206. *In*: Peter R. Shewry, Hamit Koksel and John R.n. Taylor (eds.). *ICC Handbook of 21st Century Cereal Science and Technology*. Academic Press.

Chaganti, R., Varadarajan, V., Gorantla, V.S., Gadekallu, T.R. and Ravi, V. (2022). Blockchain-based cloud-enabled security monitoring using internet of things in smart agriculture. *Future Internet* 14(9): 250.

Christo, M.S., Jesi, V.E., Priyadarsini, U., Anbarasu, V., Venugopal, H. and Karuppiah, M. (2021). Ensuring improved security in medical data using ECC and blockchain technology with edge devices. *Security and Communication Networks* 2021(1): 6966206.

Daraghmi, E., Jayousi, S., Daraghmi, Y., Daraghmi, R. and Fouchal, H. (2024). Smart contracts for managing the agricultural supply chain: A practical case study. *IEEE Access* 12: 125462–125479.

Dedeoglu, V., Malik, S., Ramachandran, G., Pal, S. and Jurdak, R. (2023). Blockchain meets edge-AI for food supply chain traceability and provenance. In *Comprehensive Analytical Chemistry* 101: 251–275. Elsevier.

Desai, H., Kantarcioglu, M. and Kagal, L. (2019). A hybrid blockchain architecture for privacy-enabled and accountable auctions. In *2019 IEEE International Conference on Blockchain (Blockchain)*, 34–43. IEEE.

Dey, K. and Shekhawat, U. (2021). Blockchain for sustainable E-agriculture: Literature review, architecture for data management, and implications. *Journal of Cleaner Production* 316: 128254.

Feng, H., Wang, X., Duan, Y., Zhang, J. and Zhang, X. (2020). Applying blockchain technology to improve agri-food traceability: A review of development methods, benefits and challenges. *Journal of Cleaner Production* 260: 121031.

Feng, T., Yang, P., Liu, C., Fang, J. and Ma, R. (2022). Blockchain data privacy protection and sharing scheme based on zero-knowledge proof. *Wireless Communications and Mobile Computing* 2022(1): 1040662.

Ferrag, M.A., Shu, L., Yang, X., Derhab, A. and Maglaras, L. (2020). Security and privacy for green IoT-based agriculture: Review, blockchain solutions, and challenges. *IEEE Access* 8: 32031–32053.

Gad, A.G., Mosa, D.T., Abualigah, L. and Abohany, A.A. (2022). Emerging trends in blockchain technology and applications: A review and outlook. *Journal of King Saud University-Computer and Information Sciences* 34(9): 6719–6742.

Geng, Y. (2019). Homomorphic encryption technology for cloud computing. *Procedia Computer Science* 154: 73–83.

Guo, H. and Yu, X. (2022). A survey on blockchain technology and its security. *Blockchain: Research and Applications* 3(2): 100067.

Habib, G., Sharma, S., Ibrahim, S., Ahmad, I., Qureshi, S. and Ishfaq, M. (2022). Blockchain technology: Benefits, challenges, applications, and integration of blockchain technology with cloud computing. *Future Internet* 14(11): 341.

Hang, L., Ullah, I. and Kim, D.H. (2020). A secure fish farm platform based on blockchain for agriculture data integrity. *Computers and Electronics in Agriculture* 170: 105251.

Iftekhar, A. and Cui, X. (2021). Blockchain-based traceability system that ensures food safety measures to protect consumer safety and COVID-19 free supply chains. *Foods* 10(6): 1289.

Iqbal, R. and Butt, T.A. (2020). Safe farming as a service of blockchain-based supply chain management for improved transparency. *Cluster Computing* 23: 2139–2150.

Jiang, P., Zhang, L., You, S., Van Fan, Y., Tan, R.R., Klemeš, J.J. and You, F. (2023). Blockchain technology applications in waste management: Overview, challenges and opportunities. *Journal of Cleaner Production* 421: 138466.

Kalimuthu, V.K. and PrabuPelavendran, M.J. (2024). Blockchain based secure data sharing in precision agriculture: A comprehensive methodology incorporating deep learning and hybrid encryption model. *Brazilian Archives of Biology and Technology* 67: e24230858.

Krishna, K.M., Borole, Y.D., Rout, S., Negi, P., Deivakani, M. and Dilip, R. (2021). Inclusion of cloud, blockchain and IoT based technologies in agriculture sector. pp. 1–8. *In*: Husni Teja Sukmana and Dewi Khairani (eds.). *2021 9th International Conference on Cyber and IT Service Management (CITSM)*. IEEE.

Kumar, R., Kumar, J., Khan, A.A., Ali, H., Bernard, C.M., Khan, R.U. and Zeng, S. (2022). Blockchain and homomorphic encryption based privacy-preserving model aggregation for medical images. *Computerized Medical Imaging and Graphics* 102: 102139.

Lei, M., Xu, L., Liu, T., Liu, S. and Sun, C. (2022). Integration of privacy protection and blockchain-based food safety traceability: Potential and challenges. *Foods* 11(15): 2262.

Li, W., He, M. and Haiquan, S. (2021). An overview of blockchain technology: Applications, challenges and future trends. pp. 31–39. *In*: Li Wenzheng and Yang Jix (eds.). *2021 IEEE 11th International Conference on Electronics Information and Emergency Communication (ICEIEC)*. IEEE.

Lin, Y.P., Petway, J.R., Anthony, J., Mukhtar, H., Liao, S.W., Chou, C.F. and Ho, Y.F. (2017). Blockchain: The evolutionary next step for ICT E-agriculture. *Environments* 4(3): 50.

Liu, Z., Wang, S. and Liu, Y. (2023). Blockchain-based integrity auditing for shared data in cloud storage with file prediction. *Computer Networks* 236: 110040.

Ma, Y., Sun, Y., Lei, Y., Qin, N. and Lu, J. (2020). A survey of blockchain technology on security, privacy, and trust in crowdsourcing services. *World Wide Web* 23: 393–419.

Mahajan, H.B. and Junnarkar, A.A. (2023). Smart healthcare system using integrated and lightweight ECC with private blockchain for multimedia medical data processing. *Multimedia Tools and Applications* 82(28): 44335–44358.

Mahalingam, N. and Sharma, P. (2024). An intelligent blockchain technology for securing an IoT-based agriculture monitoring system. *Multimedia Tools and Applications* 83(4): 10297–10320.

Majeed, U., Khan, L.U., Yaqoob, I., Kazmi, S.A., Salah, K. and Hong, C.S. (2021). Blockchain for IoT-based smart cities: Recent advances, requirements, and future challenges. *Journal of Network and Computer Applications* 181: 103007.

Malik, S., Kanhere, S.S. and Jurdak, R. (2018). Productchain: Scalable blockchain framework to support provenance in supply chains. In *2018 IEEE 17th International Symposium on Network Computing and Applications (NCA)*, 1–10. IEEE.

Markovic, M., Jacobs, N., Dryja, K., Edwards, P. and Strachan, N.J. (2020). Integrating Internet of Things, provenance, and blockchain to enhance trust in last mile food deliveries. *Frontiers in Sustainable Food Systems* 4: 563424.

Mousavi, S.K., Ghaffari, A., Besharat, S. and Afshari, H. (2021). Security of Internet of Things using RC4 and ECC algorithms (Case study: Smart irrigation systems). *Wireless Personal Communications* 116(3): 1713–1742.

Murthy, C.V.B., Shri, M.L., Kadry, S. and Lim, S. (2020). Blockchain based cloud computing: Architecture and research challenges. *IEEE Access* 8: 205190–205205.

Mutungi, C., Gaspar, A. and Abass, A. (2020). Postharvest Operations and Quality Specifications for Rice: A Trainer's Manual for Smallholder Farmers in Tanzania. IITA, Ibadan, Nigeria.

Nakamoto, S. (2009). Bitcoin: A peer-to-peer electronic cash system. Available at https://bitcoin.org/bitcoin.pdf (Accessed on 26 September 2025).

Nguyen, T.Q., Das, A.K. and Tran, L.T. (2019). NEO smart contract for drought-based insurance. In *2019 IEEE Canadian Conference of Electrical and Computer Engineering (CCECE)*, 1–4. IEEE.

Paillier, P. (1999). Public-key cryptosystems based on composite degree residuosity classes. In *International Conference on the Theory and Applications of Cryptographic Techniques*, 223–238. Springer, Berlin, Heidelberg.

Pincheira, M., Vecchio, M., Giaffreda, R. and Kanhere, S.S. (2021). Cost-effective IoT devices as trustworthy data sources for a blockchain-based water management system in precision agriculture. *Computers and Electronics in Agriculture* 180: 105889.

Prashar, D., Jha, N., Jha, S., Lee, Y. and Joshi, G.P. (2020). Blockchain-based traceability and visibility for agricultural products: A decentralized way of ensuring food safety in India. *Sustainability* 12(8): 3497.

Rahman, W., Hossain, M.M., Hasan, M.M., Iqbal, M.S., Rahman, M.M., Hasan, K.F. and Moni, M.A. (2024). Automated detection of harmful insects in agriculture: A smart framework leveraging IoT, Machine Learning, and blockchain. *IEEE Transactions on Artificial Intelligence* 5(9): 4787–4798.

Rajasekaran, A.S., Azees, M. and Al-Turjman, F. (2022). A comprehensive survey on blockchain technology. *Sustainable Energy Technologies and Assessments* 52: 102039.

Ramezan, G. and Meamari, E. (2024). zk-IoT: Securing the Internet of Things with zero-knowledge proofs on blockchain platforms. *arXiv preprint arXiv:2402.08322*.

Rao, I.S., Kiah, M.M., Hameed, M.M. and Memon, Z.A. (2024). Scalability of blockchain: A comprehensive review and future research direction. *Cluster Computing* 27(5): 5547–5570.

Regueiro, C., Seco, I., De Diego, S., Lage, O. and Etxebarria, L. (2021). Privacy-enhancing distributed protocol for data aggregation based on blockchain and homomorphic encryption. *Information Processing & Management* 58(6): 102745.

Ren, W., Wan, X. and Gan, P. (2021). A double-blockchain solution for agricultural sampled data security in Internet of Things network. *Future Generation Computer Systems* 117: 453–461.

Rivest, R.L., Adleman, L. and Dertouzos, M.L. (1978). On data banks and privacy homomorphisms. *Foundations of Secure Computation* 4(11): 169–180.

Salah, K., Nizamuddin, N., Jayaraman, R. and Omar, M. (2019). Blockchain-based soybean traceability in agricultural supply chain. *IEEE Access* 7: 73295–73305.

Shafi, G. and Micali, S. (1984). Probabilistic encryption. *Journal of Computer and System Sciences* 28(2): 270–299.

Si, H., Sun, C., Li, Y., Qiao, H. and Shi, L. (2019). IoT information sharing security mechanism based on blockchain technology. *Future Generation Computer Systems* 101: 1028–1040.

Sun, W., Fang, H., Zheng, S. and Qian, Q. (2020). Blockchain and homomorphic encryption for digital copyright protection. In *2020 IEEE Intl Conf on Parallel & Distributed Processing with Applications, Big Data & Cloud Computing, Sustainable Computing & Communications, Social Computing & Networking (ISPA/BDCloud/SocialCom/SustainCom)*, 754–761. IEEE.

Takale, D.G., Mahalle, P.N. and Sule, B. (2024). Blockchain-powered direct farm-to-consumer supply chains. *Journal of Computer Based Parallel Programming* 9(1): 34–39.

Torky, M. and Hassanein, A.E. (2020). Integrating blockchain and the Internet of Things in precision agriculture: Analysis, opportunities, and challenges. *Computers and Electronics in Agriculture* 178: 105476.

Trienekens, J.H., Wognum, P.M., Beulens, A.J. and Van Der Vorst, J.G. (2012). Transparency in complex dynamic food supply chains. *Advanced Engineering Informatics* 26(1): 55–65.

Tyagi, S. and Kathuria, M. (2022). Role of zero-knowledge proof in blockchain security. In *2022 International Conference on Machine Learning, Big Data, Cloud and Parallel Computing (COM-IT-CON)*, Volume 1, 738–743. IEEE.

Vangala, A., Das, A.K., Kumar, N. and Alazab, M. (2020). Smart secure sensing for IoT-based agriculture: Blockchain perspective. *IEEE Sensors Journal* 21(16): 17591–17607.

Velmurugadass, P., Dhanasekaran, S., Anand, S.S. and Vasudevan, V. (2021). Enhancing blockchain security in cloud computing with IoT environment using ECIES and cryptography hash algorithm. *Materials Today: Proceedings* 37: 2653–2659.

Vijayaragavan, S., PunarSelvam, E. and Kuppurasu, N. (2022). Decentralized block chain provenance security system using secure sharable advanced encryption standard for distributed agriculture information security. *NeuroQuantology* 20(8): 6738.

Vinueza-Naranjo, P.G., Nascimento-Silva, H.A., Rumipamba-Zambrano, R., Ruiz-Gomes, I., Rivas-Lalaleo, D. and Patil, N.J. (2021). IoT-based smart agriculture and poultry farms for environmental sustainability and development. In *Information and Knowledge in Internet of Things*, 379–406. Springer International Publishing, Cham.

Wognum, P.N., Bremmers, H., Trienekens, J.H., Van Der Vorst, J.G. and Bloemhof, J.M. (2011). Systems for sustainability and transparency of food supply chains–current status and challenges. *Advanced Engineering Informatics* 25(1): 65–76.

Xie, C., Sun, Y. and Luo, H. (2017). Secured data storage scheme based on block chain for agricultural products tracking. pp. 45–50. *In*: Juan E. Guerrero (ed.). *2017 3rd International Conference on Big Data Computing and Communications (BIGCOM)*. IEEE.

Zhang, B., Pan, H., Li, K., Xing, Y., Wang, J., Fan, D. and Zhang, W. (2024). A blockchain and zero knowledge proof based data security transaction method in distributed computing. *Electronics* 13(21): 4260.

Zhao, Y., Li, Q., Yi, W. and Xiong, H. (2023). Agricultural IoT data storage optimization and information security method based on blockchain. *Agriculture* 13(2): 274.

Zhaoliang, L., Huang, W. and Wang, D. (2021). Functional agricultural monitoring data storage based on sustainable block chain technology. *Journal of Cleaner Production* 281: 124078.

Zheng, Z., Xie, S., Dai, H., Chen, X. and Wang, H. (2017). An overview of blockchain technology: Architecture, consensus, and future trends. In *2017 IEEE International Congress on Big Data (BigData Congress)*, 557–564. IEEE.

Zhou, L., Diro, A., Saini, A., Kaisar, S. and Hiep, P.C. (2024). Leveraging zero knowledge proofs for blockchain-based identity sharing: A survey of advancements, challenges and opportunities. *Journal of Information Security and Applications* 80: 103678.

Zhou, X., Zheng, F., Zhou, X., Chan, K.C., Gururajan, R., Wu, Z. and Zhou, E. (2020). From traceability to provenance of agricultural products through blockchain. *Web Intelligence* 18(3): 181–189.

Zhu, L. and Li, F. (2021). Agricultural data sharing and sustainable development of ecosystem based on block chain. *Journal of Cleaner Production* 315: 127869.

Index

About the Editors

Dr. Randhir Kumar received his Ph.D. in the department of Information Technology from NIT Raipur, India. He completed his Postdoctoral from department of Electrical Engineering, IIT Hyderabad. He is currently working as an Associate Professor, Department of Computer Science and Engineering SRM University, Amaravati, Andhra Pradesh, India. He has published his research articles in leading journal and conferences from IEEE, Elsevier, Springer, and John Wiley. His paper has been published in some of the high impact factor journals such as – IEEE Internet of Things, IEEE Transactions on Intelligent Transportation Systems, IEEE Transactions on Network Science and Engineering, IEEE Transactions on Green Communications and Networking, IEEE Transactions on Industrial Informatics, IEEE Intelligent Systems, IEEE Consumer Electronics Magazine, IEEE COMSNETs, IEEE ICC, MobiCom, GlobeCom, Computer Networks, JPDC, and Transactions on Emerging Telecommunications Technologies (ETT Wiley). His paper was recognized as most cited paper of year 2020–2021 in one of the reputed journals, i.e., Transactions on Emerging Telecommunications Technologies. He received best paper presentation award in one of the reputed conferences, i.e., GLOBECOM in the year 2022. He has qualified UGC-NET in the year of 2018. He has been awarded as Best Engineer Trainee by Honeywell Technology, India in the year 2009. Additionally, he has been listed in the Top 2% Global Scientists list published by Stanford University and Elsevier in the year 2023, 2024, and 2025. He is active reviewer of many of the reputed journals like IEEE TDSC, IEEE TGCN, IEEE TNSM, IEEE TII, IEEE Access, Journal of Super Computing, Journal of Ambient Intelligent and Humanized Computing, and International Journal of Information Security and Privacy, IGI global. His research interest includes Cryptographic Techniques, Information Security, Blockchain Technology, Digital Twin and Services, Software Engineering, and Web Mining. He is also a member of IEEE, IAENG.

Prabhat Kumar received his Ph.D. degree in Information Technology, National Institute of Technology Raipur, Raipur, India, under the prestigious fellowship of Ministry of Human Resource and Development (MHRD) funded by the Government of India in 2022. Thereafter, he worked with Indian Institute of Technology Hyderabad, India, as a Post-doctoral Researcher under project "Development of Indian Telecommunication Security Assurance Requirements for IoT devices". He is currently working as Assistant Professor with the Department of Software Engineering, LUT School of Engineering Science, LUT University, Lappeenranta, Finland. He has many research contributions in the area of Machine Learning, Deep Learning, Federated Learning, Big Data Analytics, Cybersecurity, Blockchain, Cloud Computing, Internet of Things, Digital Twin and Software Defined Networking. He has authored or co-authored over 28+ top-tier journal/conference articles, including 13+ IEEE TRANSACTIONS/ Magazine papers. One of his Ph.D. publication was recognized as a top cited article by WILEY in 2020–21. Some of his research findings are published in top cited journals and conferences, such as IEEE TII, IEEE TITS, IEEE TNSE, IEEE TGCN, IEEE IoT-J, IEEE Intelligent Systems, IEEE Consumer Electronics Magazine, IEEE MICRO, JSA (Elsevier), ComCom (Elsevier), Comnet (Elsevier), JPDC (Elsevier), ICDCN, IEEE ICC, ACM MobiCom and IEEE GLOBECOM. He is an Expert Evaluator of top scientific journals and conferences, including IEEE TII, IEEE TITS, IEEE TNSE, IEEE TGCN, IEEE JBHI, IEEE IoTJ, IEEE Network Magazine, IEEE IoT Magazine, IEEE Access, ACM TALLIP, ComCom and IEEE ICC. He is also an IEEE Member.

Dr. Sobin C.C. has vast expertise in studies of "Delay Tolerant Networks (DTNs)", "Wireless Networks", and "Internet of Things (IoT)". Dr. Sobin's M. Tech. and Ph.D. research from premier institutes in India, such as IIT Madras and IIT Roorkee enabled to acquire in-depth knowledge in developing routing protocols for DTNs and designing IoT-based applications. Also, well-versed in building IoT applications over DTN in case of limited Internet connectivity. PI published articles relevant to his area of expertise in leading reputed journals in the specified field (Journal of Network and Computer Applications, Wireless Personal Communications, International Journal of Communication Systems, etc.). He is currently working as Professor, School of Computer Science (SoCS), University of Petroleum and Energy Studies, Dehradun.

For Product Safety Concerns and Information please contact our
EU representative GPSR@taylorandfrancis.com Taylor & Francis
Verlag GmbH, Kaufingerstraße 24, 80331 München, Germany